Beginning XML with C# 7

XML Processing and
Data Access for C# Developers

Second Edition

Bipin Joshi

Apress®

Beginning XML with C# 7: XML Processing and Data Access for C# Developers

Bipin Joshi
301 Pitruchhaya, Thane, India

ISBN-13 (pbk): 978-1-4842-3104-3   ISBN-13 (electronic): 978-1-4842-3105-0
https://doi.org/10.1007/978-1-4842-3105-0

Library of Congress Control Number: 2017961825

Cover image by Freepik (`www.freepik.com`)

Managing Director: Welmoed Spahr
Editorial Director: Todd Green
Acquisitions Editor: Steve Anglin
Development Editor: Matthew Moodie
Technical Reviewer: Michael Thomas
Coordinating Editor: Mark Powers
Copy Editor: Kezia Endsley

Distributed to the book trade worldwide by Springer Science+Business Media New York, 233 Spring Street, 6th Floor, New York, NY 10013. Phone 1-800-SPRINGER, fax (201) 348-4505, e-mail `orders-ny@springer-sbm.com`, or visit `www.springeronline.com`. Apress Media, LLC is a California LLC and the sole member (owner) is Springer Science + Business Media Finance Inc (SSBM Finance Inc). SSBM Finance Inc is a **Delaware** corporation.

For information on translations, please e-mail `rights@apress.com`, or visit `http://www.apress.com/rights-permissions`.

Apress titles may be purchased in bulk for academic, corporate, or promotional use. eBook versions and licenses are also available for most titles. For more information, reference our Print and eBook Bulk Sales web page at `http://www.apress.com/bulk-sales`.

Any source code or other supplementary material referenced by the author in this book is available to readers on GitHub via the book's product page, located at `www.apress.com/9781484231043`. For more detailed information, please visit `http://www.apress.com/source-code`.

Printed on acid-free paper

This work is dedicated to Lord Shiva, who, I believe,
resides in each one of us as pure consciousness.

Contents

About the Author xvii

About the Technical Reviewer xix

Introduction xxi

■Chapter 1: Introducing XML and the .NET Framework 1

What Is XML? 1

Benefits of XML 2

XML-Driven Applications 3

Rules of XML Grammar 5

Markup Is Case Sensitive 6

A Document Must Have One and Only One Root Element 6

A Start Tag Must Have an End Tag 6

Start and End Tags Must Be Properly Nested 7

Attribute Values Must Be Enclosed in Quotes 7

DTD and XML Schema 7

Parsing XML Documents 8

XSLT 9

XPath 10

The .NET Framework 11

.NET Framework and XML 12

Assemblies and Namespaces 13

The Classic XML Parsing Model of the .NET Framework 14

The LINQ-Based Parsing Model of the .NET Framework 14

.NET Configuration Files 15

ADO.NET 17

ASP.NET Web Forms Server Controls 17

XML Serialization 18

Web Services, WCF Services, and Web API 19

XML Documentation 19

XAML Markup 21

SQL Server XML Features 21

Working with Visual Studio 21

Creating Windows Forms Applications 22

Creating Class Libraries 25

Summary 28

■Chapter 2: Manipulating XML Documents Using the Document Object Model 29

Using the DOM Parser 29

Knowing When to Use DOM 31

A Sample XML Document 32

Opening an Existing XML Document for Parsing 33

Navigating Through an XML Document 35

Looking for Specific Elements and Nodes 36

Retrieving Specific Elements Using the GetElementsByTagName() Method 37

Retrieving Specific Elements Using the GetElementById() Method 38

Selecting Specific Nodes Using the SelectNodes() Method 41

Selecting a Single Specific Node Using the SelectSingleNode() Method 43

Modifying XML Documents 44

Navigating Between Various Nodes 45

Modifying Existing Content 46

Deleting Existing Content 47

Adding New Content 48

Using Helper Methods 50

Dealing with Whitespace 50

Dealing with Namespaces...54

Understanding Events of the XmlDocument Class 55

Summary..58

■Chapter 3: Reading and Writing XML Documents.......................................59

What Are XML Readers and Writers?...59

When to Use Readers and Writers...60

Reader Classes..60

The XmlTextReader Class 60

The XmlValidatingReader Class 60

The XmlNodeReader Class 60

Reading XML Documents Using XmlTextReader 61

Opening XML Documents 61

Reading Attributes, Elements, and Values 63

Improving Performance by Using Name Tables 65

Dealing with Namespaces..66

Moving Between Elements...66

The ReadSubTree() Method 66

The ReadToDescendant() Method 67

The ReadToFollowing() Method 67

The ReadToNextSibling() Method...68

The Skip() Method 68

Moving Between Attributes 69

Reading Content..69

The ReadInnerXml() Method 70

The ReadOuterXml() Method..70

The ReadString() Method 70

Writing XML Documents Using XmlTextWriter...71

Exporting Columns As Elements...75

Exporting Columns As Attributes 75

Specifying Character Encoding...75

Formatting the Output 76

Including Namespace Support 78

Dealing with Nontextual Data..81

Serializing Data 82

Deserializing Data...83

Summary..84

■**Chapter 4: Accessing XML Documents Using the XPath Data Model**..................85

Overview of XPath...85

Location Path...86

Axis 86

Node Tests 86

Predicates..87

Putting It All Together..87

XPath Functions...87

The XPath Data Model 89

Creating XPathNavigator..89

Navigating an XML Document Using XPathNavigator..90

Selecting Nodes...92

Navigating Between Attributes 96

Retrieving Inner and Outer XML...97

Getting an XmlReader from XPathNavigator 99

Getting an XmlWriter from XPathNavigator 102

Editing XML Documents with the XPathNavigator Class 104

Summary..109

■**Chapter 5: Validating XML Documents** 111

Providing Structure for XML Documents 111

Document Type Definition (DTD) 112

XML Data Reduced (XDR) Schema...112

XML Schema Definition (XSD) Schema..112

Creating Structure for an XML Document 112

The Structure of Employees.xml...112

Creating the DTD 113

Creating the XML Schema 115

Creating Schemas by Using the Schema Object Model (SOM)......................... 126

The Core SOM Classes...126

Creating an XML Schema Using the SOM...128

Attaching the DTD and XML Schemas to XML Documents............................... 135

Inline DTDs 136

External DTDs 136

Inline XML Schema 137

External XML Schema..137

Adding Frequently Used Schemas to the Schema Cache..138

Using XmlReader to Validate XML Documents 139

Using XmlDocument to Validate XML Documents 142

Using XPathNavigator to Validate XML Documents.. 145

Specifying XML Schema via Code.. 145

Summary.. 147

■Chapter 6: Transforming XML with XSLT 149

Overview of XSLT... 149

Applying Templates Using <xsl:apply-templates> 153

Branching Using <xsl:if>...154

Branching Using <xsl:choose> and <xsl:when> 156

Transforming Elements and Attributes 158

The XslCompiledTransform Class.. 161

Performing Transformations Using XslCompiledTransform 161

Passing Arguments to a Transformation..164

Using Script Blocks in an XSLT Style Sheet...166

Using Extension Objects 170

Compiling XSLT Style Sheets...171

Summary.. 173

■**Chapter 7: XML in ADO.NET** **175**

Overview of ADO.NET Architecture 175

Connected Data Access 175

Disconnected Data Access 176

ADO.NET Data Providers 177

ADO.NET Classes 178

XML and Connected Data Access 180

Using the ExecuteXmlReader() Method 180

XML and Disconnected Data Access 182

Understanding DataSet 183

Understanding DataAdapter 184

Working with DataSet and DataAdapter 186

Saving DataSet Contents As XML 192

Reading XML Data into DataSet 197

Generating Menus Dynamically Based On an XML File 200

Reading Only the Schema Information 202

Creating a Typed DataSet 204

Using Visual Studio to Create a Typed DataSet 205

Using the xsd.exe Tool to Create a Typed DataSet 210

Summary 210

■**Chapter 8: XML Serialization** **211**

Understanding the Flavors of Serialization 211

Classes Involved in the XML Serialization 212

Serializing and Deserializing Objects Using XmlSerializer 212

Handling Events Raised During Deserialization 215

Serializing and Deserializing Complex Types 217

Serialization and Inheritance 221

Customizing the Serialized XML 224

Serializing and Deserializing Objects Using DataContractSerializer 227

    Customizing the Serialized XML 230

Serializing and Deserializing Objects Using SoapFormatter 231

    Customizing SOAP Serialization 234

Summary 237

■ Chapter 9: XML in Web Services 239

What Are Web Services? 239

Creating and Consuming Web Services 240

    Creating a Web Service 241

    Creating a Proxy for a Web Service 254

    Creating a Form That Calls the Web Methods 256

Understanding SOAP 259

    Using SOAP Headers 260

    Customizing the XML Serialization 264

Understanding the WSDL Document 265

    The Messages 266

    The Type Definitions 266

    The Port Types 267

    The Binding 267

    The Service 267

    A Summary of WSDL 267

Summary 267

■ Chapter 10: XML in WCF and Web API 269

Operations Based Services vs. Resource Based Services 270

Understanding WCF Vocabulary 270

Creating and Consuming a WCF Service 271

    Creating the Service 271

    Hosting the Service 276

    Consuming the Service 279

    Testing the Host and Client 282

Hosting a WCF Service in IIS..284

Understanding the Role of XML in WCF Services 287

Using XmlSerializer Instead of DataContractSerializer..288

Understanding REST Services 289

Creating a REST Service Using WCF..290

Creating a Client That Consumes the EmployeeManager REST Service............................294

Creating a REST Service Using Web API 298

Creating a Client That Consumes the EmployeeManager Web API Service 301

Using XmlSerializer Instead of DataContractSerializer..303

Summary 304

■Chapter 11: XML in SQL Server..**305**

Using XML Extensions to the SELECT Statement 305

The FOR XML Clause...305

Using OPENXML..313

Using SQLXML Features 315

The SQLXML Managed Classes 315

The XML Data Type..328

Creating a Table with an XML Column 329

Inserting, Modifying, and Deleting XML Data...329

Methods of the XML Data Type 330

XML Data Modification Language (XML DML)..332

XQuery Support in the XML Data Type..333

Summary 333

■Chapter 12: XML in .NET Framework...**335**

Using XAML to Define the WPF User Interface 335

Displaying XML Data in a WPF Application 340

Using XML in ASP.NET 342

XML and ASP.NET...343

The XML Data Source Control..351

Working with Site Maps 359

Using a SiteMapPath Control 361

Using a SiteMapDataSource Control 362

Using the XML Control 363

Using the .NET Framework Configuration System 365

Structure of the web.config File 367

Web.config Inheritance 367

Using Web.config for Common Configuration Tasks 367

Storing and Retrieving Application Configuration Settings 368

Storing and Retrieving Database Connection Strings 369

Using Forms Authentication 371

Configuring Session State 374

Displaying Custom Error Pages 376

Documenting Code with XML Comments 378

Creating a Class Library 378

Using Sandcastle Help File Builder to Generate Help Files 383

Summary 385

■Chapter 13: Working with LINQ to XML 387

Overview of LINQ 387

Working with LINQ Queries 388

Classic XML Technologies vs. LINQ to XML 393

Working with XML Fragments 393

Visual Construction of XML Trees 394

Ease in Namespace Handling 394

Renaming XML Nodes 394

Static Methods to Load XML 394

Whitespace Handling 394

XML Transformation 394

When to Use LINQ to XML 394

LINQ to XML Class Hierarchy 395

Opening an Existing XML Document for Parsing 395

    Navigating Through an XML Tree 397

Looking for Specific Elements and Attributes 399

    Retrieving Specific Elements Using the Descendants() Method... 399

    Searching on the Basis of Attribute Values... 400

Modifying XML Data 402

    Loading the XML Document.. 403

    Navigating Between Various Nodes.. 403

    Adding New Content.. 404

    Modifying Existing Content... 405

    Deleting Existing Content 405

    Saving the Modified XML Tree to a File.. 406

    Displaying Employee Details 406

    Events of the XElement Class.. 407

Dealing with Whitespace.. 408

Dealing with Namespaces.. 411

    Specifying Namespaces While Constructing Elements 412

Validating XML Documents.. 413

Transforming XML Trees... 415

    Changing the Shape of an XML Tree.. 416

    Projecting a New Type 418

Summary... 419

■Appendix A: Creating a Custom XmlReader and XmlWriter 421

Creating a Custom XmlReader 421

    Inheriting from XmlReader 422

    Creating the TableReader Class 423

    Using the TableReader Class 431

Creating a Custom XmlWriter 433

    Inheriting from XmlWriter 434

    Creating the RssWriter Class 435

    Using the RssWriter Class 441

Summary 442

■Appendix B: Resources 443

W3C Web Site for XML Specifications 443

W3C Web Site for XML Schema Specifications 443

W3C Web Site for XPath-Related Information 443

W3C Web Site for XSL-Related Information 443

W3C Web Site for SOAP Specifications 443

System.Xml Reference 443

.NET/ASP.NET/WCF/Web API 444

Wikipedia—XML Section 444

Author's Web Site on .NET and Web Development 444

XML Notepad—XML Editor 444

Sandcastle Help File Builder 444

SQLXML Programming 444

Index 445

About the Author

Bipin Joshi is a software consultant, trainer, author, and yoga mentor who writes about seemingly unrelated topics: software development and yoga! He conducts online training courses to help developers learn ASP.NET and web technologies better and faster. Currently his focus is ASP.NET, ASP.NET Core, C#, JavaScript frameworks, and design/architectural patterns. More details about his training courses are available at http://www.binaryintellect.com.

Bipin has been programming since 1995 and has worked with the .NET Framework since its inception. He is a published author and has authored or co-authored more than 10 books and numerous articles on .NET technologies. He regularly writes about ASP.NET and other cutting-edge web technologies on his web site at http://www.binaryintellect.net. Bipin is a Microsoft Most Valuable Professional (MVP) and a former Microsoft Certified Trainer (MCT).

Having embraced the yoga way of life, he enjoys the intoxicating presence of God and writes about yoga on his web site at http://www.bipinjoshi.org. Bipin has also penned a few books on yoga and teaches yoga and meditation to selected individuals. He can be reached through his web sites.

About the Technical Reviewer

Michael Thomas has worked in software development for more than 20 years as an individual contributor, team lead, program manager, and vice president of engineering. Michael has more than 10 years of experience working with mobile devices. His current focus is in the medical sector, using mobile devices to accelerate information transfer between patients and health care providers.

Introduction

The Internet has brought a huge difference in the way we develop and use software applications. Applications have become more complex and distributed, connecting heterogeneous systems.

With such a radical change, the role of XML is highly significant. XML has already established itself as a standard way of data encoding and transfer. In spite of the popularity of formats such as JSON (JavaScript Object Notation), XML is still being used in a wide range of applications, including enterprise applications. XML comes with a family of technologies such as XSLT, XPath, and XSD, that provide a fuller support for transforming, querying, and validating the underlying data.

No wonder that Microsoft's .NET Framework provides such a strong support for XML. Data access, raw parsing, serialization, configuration, code documentation, and services are some of the examples where the .NET Framework harnesses the power and flexibility of XML.

The .NET Framework comes with a plethora of classes that allow you to work with XML data. This book demystifies XML and allied technologies. Reading and writing XML data, using DOM, ADO.NET integration with XML, SQL Server XML features, applying XSLT style sheets, SOAP, use of XML in services (ASMX/WCF/Web API), and configuration systems are some of the topics that this book explores in detail. Neat and concise examples scattered throughout the book will help you understand the practical use of the topic under consideration. The book can also act as a handy reference when developers go on the job.

Who Is This Book For?

This book is for developers who are familiar with the .NET Framework and want to dive deep into the XML features of .NET. This book will not teach you XML manipulation using non-Microsoft tools. All the examples in this book are presented in C#, and hence working knowledge of C# is assumed. In some chapters, familiarity with LINQ, ADO.NET, and SQL Server is necessary, although I have provided a brief overview along with the respective topics.

Software Required

In order to work with the examples presented in this book, you need the following software:

- *Visual Studio 2017:* I used the Professional Edition of the product but for most of the examples you can also use the Community Edition.

- *.NET Framework 4.7 and C# 7:* I used .NET Framework 4.7 to build the examples discussed in this book. The examples and code fragments are written using C# 7.

- *SQL Server with Northwind sample database:* In the examples that rely on a database, I used SQL Server 2012 Developer Edition. You may also use some later version of the product if you so wish. Throughout the book we use data from the Northwind sample database. So, you need it ready in the SQL Server. You can download the required scripts from Microsoft's official web site.

- *SQLXML 4.0 SP1:* In the examples that discuss SQLXML programming, you need SQLXML 4.0 SP1 installed on your machine. It can be downloaded from Microsoft's official web site.

- *Sandcastle Help File Builder (SHFB):* In the examples that discuss XML code commenting, you need SHFB to generate the documentation. You can download it from its GitHub page.

- *Browser*: In the examples that require a web browser, I used Firefox. But any other browser should also work.

Structure of This Book

The book is divided into 13 chapters and two appendices.

Chapters 1 to 4 talk about navigating, reading, and writing XML documents by using classes from the System.Xml namespace. In these chapters, you learn to use classes such as XmlDocument, XmlReader, XmlWriter, and XPathNavigator.

Manipulating XML data is just one part of the story. Often you need to validate and transform it so that it becomes acceptable to your system. Chapters 5 and 6 deal with XML document validation and XSLT transformations, respectively.

The .NET Framework technologies themselves use XML in many ways. This is often under the hood, but for any XML developer, knowing where this occurs is essential. To that end, Chapters 7 to 10 cover topics such as ADO.NET integration with XML, XML serialization, and ASMX/WCF/Web API services.

Microsoft has not limited the use of XML only to areas such as ADO.NET, serialization, and services. SQL Server incorporates many XML-related features. These features are discussed in Chapter 11. Although this topic isn't strictly one of the XML features of .NET Framework, many developers will find it useful, because many real-world projects developed using the .NET Framework use SQL Server as a datastore.

Chapter 12 covers many other areas where the .NET Framework uses XML. Some of them include XAML, ASP.NET server controls, XML configuration files, and XML comments.

Language Integrated Query (LINQ) includes what is known as LINQ to XML. It can be used to handle XML data in LINQ-style. Chapter 13 is dedicated to this programming model. Here, you will learn about core LINQ to XML features, including parsing and loading XML trees the LINQ to XML way and validating and projecting XML data.

Finally, the two appendices supplement what you learned throughout the book by providing some more information and resources.

Downloading the Source Code

The complete source code for the book is available for download at the book's companion web site. Visit www.apress.com and go to this book's information page. You can then download the source code from the Source Code/Downloads section.

Contacting the Author

You can reach me via my web site at http://www.binaryintellect.net. You can also follow me on various social networking sites (visit my web site for the links).

CHAPTER 1

■ ■ ■

Introducing XML and the .NET Framework

Over the years XML has emerged as one of the most important standards for data representation and transportation. No wonder that Microsoft has embraced it fully in the .NET Framework. This chapter provides an overview of what XML is and how it is related to the .NET Framework. Many of the topics discussed in this chapter might be already familiar to you. Nevertheless, I will cover them briefly here so as to form a common platform for further chapters. Specifically, this chapter covers the following:

- Features and benefits of XML

- Rules of XML grammar

- Brief introduction to allied technologies such as DTD, XML Schema, parsers, XSLT, and XPath

- Overview of the .NET Framework

- Use of XML in the .NET Framework

- Introduction to Visual Studio

If you find these concepts highly familiar, you may want to skip ahead to Chapter 2.

What Is XML?

XML stands for *Extensible Markup Language* and is a markup language used to describe data. It offers a standardized way to represent textual data. Often the XML data is also referred to as an XML document. The XML data doesn't perform anything on its own; to process that data, you need to use a piece of software called a *parser*. Unlike Hypertext Markup Language (HTML), which focuses on how to present data, XML focuses on how to represent data. XML consists of user-defined tags, which means you are free to define and use your own tags in an XML document.

XML was approved as a recommendation by the World Wide Web Consortium (W3C) in February 1998. Naturally, this very fact contributed a lot to such a wide acceptance and support for XML in the software industry.

Now that you have brief idea about XML, let's see a simple XML document, as illustrated in Listing 1-1.

© Bipin Joshi 2017
B. Joshi, *Beginning XML with C# 7*, https://doi.org/10.1007/978-1-4842-3105-0_1

Listing 1-1. A Simple XML Document

```
<?xml version="1.0" encoding="utf-8" ?>
<customers>
  <customer ID="C001">
    <name>Nancy Davolio</name>
    <email>nancy@localhost</email>
    <comments>
      <![CDATA[Regular customer since 1995]]>
    </comments>
  </customer>
  <customer ID="C002">
    <name>Steven Buchanan</name>
    <email>steven@localhost</email>
    <comments>
      <![CDATA[New customer interested in multiple services]]>
    </comments>
  </customer>
</customers>
```

Many rules govern the creation of such XML documents. But we will save them for later discussion.

Benefits of XML

Why did XML become so popular? Well, this question has many answers, and I will present some of the important ones in this section.

XML Is an Industry Standard

As you learned previously, XML is a W3C recommendation. This means it is an industry standard governed by a vendor-independent body. History shows that vendor-specific proprietary standards don't get massive acceptance in the software industry. This non-acceptance affects overall cross-platform data sharing and integration. Being an industry standard has helped XML gain huge acceptance.

XML Is Self-Describing

XML documents are self-describing. Because of markup tags, they are more readable than, say, comma-separated values (CSV) files.

XML Is Extensible

Markup languages such as HTML have a fixed set of tags and attributes—you cannot add your own tags. XML, on the other hand, allows you to define your own markup tags.

XML Can Be Processed Easily

Traditionally, the CSV format was a common way to represent and transport data. However, to process such data, you need to know the exact location of the commas (,) or any other delimiter used. This makes reading and writing the document difficult. The problem becomes severe when you are dealing with a number of altogether different and unknown CSV files.

As I said earlier, XML documents can be processed by a piece of software called a parser. Because XML documents use markup tags, a parser can read them easily. Parsers are discussed in more detail later in this chapter.

XML Can Be Used to Easily Exchange Data

Integrating cross-platform and cross-vendor applications is always difficult and challenging. Exchanging data in heterogeneous systems is a key problem in such applications. Using XML as a data-exchange format makes your life easy. XML is an industry standard, so it has massive support, and almost all vendors support it in one way or another.

XML Can Be Used to Easily Share Data

The fact that XML is nothing but textual data ensures that it can be shared among heterogeneous systems. For example, how can the data generated by a Windows Forms application running on a Windows machine be accessible in a Java application running on a Unix box? XML is the answer.

XML Can Be Used to Create Specialized Vocabularies

As you already know, XML is an extensible standard. By using XML as a base, you can create your own vocabularies. Wireless Application Protocol (WAP), Wireless Markup Language (WML), and Simple Object Access Protocol (SOAP) are some examples of specialized XML vocabularies.

XML-Driven Applications

Now that you know the features and benefits of XML, let's see what all these benefits mean to modern software systems.

Figure 1-1 shows a traditional web-based application. The application consists of ASP.NET pages hosted on a web server. The client, in the form of a web browser, requests various web pages. On receiving the requests, the web server processes them and sends the response in the form of HTML content. This architecture sounds good at first glance, but suffers from several shortcomings:

- It considers only web browsers as clients.

- The response from the web server is always in HTML. That means a desktop-based application may not render this response at all.

- The data and presentation logic are tightly coupled. If we want to change the presentation of the same data, we need to make considerable changes.

- Tomorrow, if some other application wants to consume the same data, it cannot be shared easily.

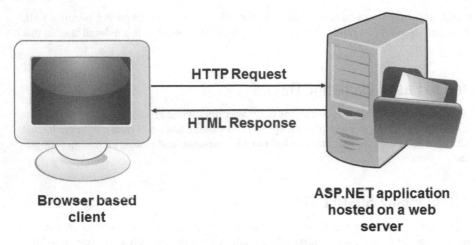

HTTP Request

HTML Response

Browser based client

ASP.NET application hosted on a web server

Figure 1-1. *Classic architecture for developing applications*

Now, let's see how XML can come to the rescue in such situations.

■ **Note**   For the sake of easy understanding the example discussed here is deliberately kept very simple and straightforward. In a more realistic case there could be one or more services involved that return the XML data. The applications then consume those services as and when required. You will learn how XML and services are related in later chapters.

Have a look at Figure 1-2, where there are multiple types of clients. One is a web browser, and the other is a desktop application. Both send requests to the server along with XML data (if any). The server processes the requests and sends back the data in XML format. The web browser applies a style sheet (discussed later) to the XML data to transform it into HTML markup. The desktop application, on the other hand, parses the data by using an XML parser (discussed later) and displays it in a grid. Much more flexible than the previous architecture, isn't it? The advantages of the new architecture are as follows:

- The application has multiple types of clients. It is not tied only to web browsers.

- There is loose coupling between the client and the processing logic.

- New types of clients can be added at any time without changing the processing logic on the server.

- The data and the presentation logic are neatly separated from each other. Web clients have one set of presentation logic, whereas desktop applications have their own presentation logic.

- Data sharing becomes easy, because the outputted data is in XML format.

4

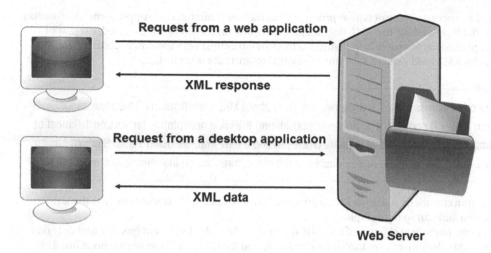

Figure 1-2. *XML-driven architecture*

Rules of XML Grammar

In the "What Is XML?" section, you saw one example of an XML document. However, I didn't talk about any of the rules that you need to follow while creating it. It's time now to discuss those rules of XML grammar. If you have worked with HTML, you will find that the rules of XML grammar are stricter than the HTML ones. However, this strictness is not a bad thing, because these rules help ensure that there are no errors while we parse, render, or exchange data.

Before I present the rules in detail, you need to familiarize yourself with the various parts of an XML document. Observe Figure 1-3 carefully.

```
Customers.xml ⇄ ×
 1   <?xml version="1.0" encoding="utf-8" ?>
 2   <!-- This is list of customers -->
 3 ⊟<customers>
 4 ⊟   <customer ID="C001">
 5       <name>Nancy Davolio</name>
 6       <email>nancy@localhost</email>
 7 ⊟     <comments>
 8         <![CDATA[Regular customer since 1995]]>
 9       </comments>
10     </customer>
11 ⊟   <customer ID="C002">
12       <name>Steven Buchanan</name>
13       <email>steven@localhost</email>
14 ⊟     <comments>
15         <![CDATA[New customer interested in multiple services]]>
16       </comments>
17     </customer>
18   </customers>
```

Figure 1-3. *Parts of a typical XML document*

Line 1 is called a processing instruction. A *processing instruction* is intended to supply some information to the application that is processing the XML document. Processing instructions are enclosed in a pair of `<?` and `?>`. The xml processing instruction in Figure 1-3 has two attributes: version and encoding. The W3C recommendations for XML hold version 1.0, hence the version attribute is set to 1.0.

■ **Note** You may come across XML 1.1 while reading more about XML specifications. There are minor differences between XML 1.0 and XML 1.1. However, considering the wide acceptance for version 1.0 most of the XML documents prefer to mention that version. When you add a new XML file using Visual Studio it has its version attribute set to 1.0. You can find more details about these differences on the official web site of W3C.

Line 2 represents a comment. A *comment* can appear anywhere in an XML document after the xml processing instruction and can span multiple lines.

Line 3 contains the *document element* of the XML document. An XML document has one and only one document element. XML documents are like an inverted tree, and the document element is positioned at the root. Hence, the document element is also called a *root element*. Each element (whether or not it is the document element) consists of a start tag and an end tag. The start tag is `<customers>`, and the end tag is `</customers>`.

It is worthwhile to point out the difference between three terms: element, node, and tag. When you say *element*, you are essentially talking about the start tag and the end tag of that element together. When you say *tag*, you are talking about either the start tag or end tag of the element, depending on the context. When you say *node*, you are referring to an element and all its inner content, including child elements and text.

Inside the `<customers>` element, you have two `<customer>` nodes. The `<customer>` element has one attribute called ID. The attribute value is enclosed in double quotes. The `<customer>` element has three child elements: `<name>`, `<email>`, and `<comments>`. The text values inside elements, such as `<name>` and `<email>`, are often called *text nodes*. Sometimes, the text content that you want to put inside a node may contain special characters such as `<` and `>`. To represent such content, you use a character data (CDATA) section. Whatever you put inside the CDATA section is treated as a literal string. The `<comments>` tag shown in Figure 1-3 illustrates the use of a CDATA section.

Now that you have this background, you're ready to look at the basic rules of XML grammar. Any XML document that conforms to the rules mentioned next is called a *well-formed document*.

Markup Is Case Sensitive

Just like some programming languages, such as C#, XML markup is case sensitive. That means `<customer>`, `<Customer>`, and `<CUSTOMER>` all are treated as different tags.

A Document Must Have One and Only One Root Element

An XML document must have one and only one root element. In the preceding example, the `<customers>` element is the root element. Note that it is mandatory for XML documents to have a root element.

A Start Tag Must Have an End Tag

Every start tag must have a corresponding end tag. In HTML, this rule is not strictly followed—for example, tags such as `<br>` (line break), `<hr>` (horizontal rule), and `<img>` (image) are often used with no end tag at all. In XML, that would not be well formed. The end tag for elements that do not contain any child elements or text can be written by using shorter notation. For example, assuming that the `<customer>` tag doesn't contain any child elements, you could have written it as `<customer ID="C001"/>`.

Start and End Tags Must Be Properly Nested

In HTML, the rule about properly nesting tags is not followed strictly. For example, the following markup shows up in the browser correctly:

```
<B><I>Hello World</B></I>
```

This, however, is illegal in XML, where the nesting of start and end tags must be proper. The correct representation of the preceding markup in XML would be as follows:

```
<B><I>Hello World</I></B>
```

Attribute Values Must Be Enclosed in Quotes

In HTML, you may or may not enclose the attribute values. For example, the following is valid markup in HTML:

```
<IMG SRC=myphoto.jpg>
```

However, this is illegal in XML. All attribute values must be enclosed in quotes. Thus the accepted XML representation of the preceding markup would be as follows:

```
<IMG SRC="myphoto.jpg" />
```

DTD and XML Schema

Creating well-formed XML documents is one part of the story. The other part is whether these documents adhere to an agreed structure, or *Schema*. That is where Document Type Definition (DTD) and XML Schemas come into the picture.

DTDs and XML Schemas allow you to convey the structure of your XML document to others. For example, if I tell you to create an XML file, what structure will you follow? What is the guarantee that the structure that you create is the one that I have in mind? The problem is solved if I give you a DTD or an XML Schema for the document. Then, you have the exact idea as to how the document should look and what its elements, attributes, and nesting are.

The XML documents that conform to some DTD or XML Schema are called *valid documents*. Note that an XML document can be well formed, but it may not be valid if it doesn't have an associated DTD or Schema.

DTDs are an older way to validate XML documents. Nowadays, XML Schema—also called XML Schema Definition or XSD—is more commonly used to validate XML documents because of the advantages it offers. You will learn about the advantages of XSD over DTD in Chapter 5. Throughout our discussion, when I talk about validating XML documents, I will be referring to XML Schemas.

Parsing XML Documents

XML data by itself cannot do anything; you need to process that data to do something meaningful. As I have said, the software that processes XML documents is called a parser (or XML processor). XML parsers allow you read, write, and manipulate XML documents. XML parsers can be classified in three categories depending on how they process XML documents:

- DOM-based parsers (*DOM* stands for *Document Object Model*)

- SAX-based parsers (*SAX* stands for *Simple API for XML*)

- Pull-model parsers

DOM-based parsers are based on the W3C's DOM recommendations and are possibly the most common and popular. They look at your XML document as an inverted tree structure. Thus, our XML document shown in Figure 1-3 will be looked at by a DOM parser as shown in Figure 1-4.

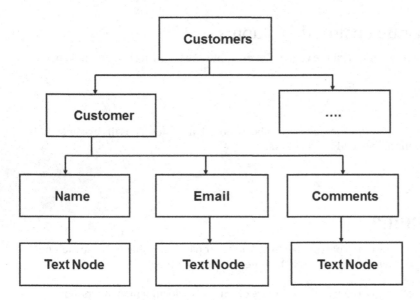

Figure 1-4. *The DOM representation of an XML document*

DOM-based parsers are read-write parsers, which means you can read as well as write to the XML document. They allow random access to any particular node of the XML document, and therefore, they need to load the entire XML document in memory. This also implies that the memory footprint of DOM-based parsers is large. DOM-based parsers are also called *tree-based parsers* for obvious reasons.

SAX-based parsers do not read the entire XML document into memory at once. They essentially scan the document serially from top to bottom. When they encounter various parts of the document, they raise events, and you can handle these events to read the document. SAX parsers are read-only parsers, which means you cannot use them to modify an XML document. They are useful when you want to read huge XML documents and loading such documents into memory is not advisable. These types of parsers are also called *event-based parsers.*

Pull-model parsers iterate through an XML document sequentially. They use the iterator design pattern to create an iterator. The iterator sequentially visits various parts of a document such as elements and attributes. You can inspect the type of the item under consideration to determine whether it's a start tag, end tag, or a text node. You can also read its attributes. Moreover, you can move the iterator to the next item. The .NET Framework's XmlReader falls in this category.

Parsers can also be classified as validating and nonvalidating. *Validating parsers* can validate an XML document against a DTD or XML Schema as they parse the document. On the other hand, *nonvalidating parsers* lack this ability.

■ **Note**   LINQ to XML offers an in-memory way of reading and writing XML documents. You will learn more about LINQ to XML later in this chapter. Chapter 13 covers the LINQ features as applicable to XML data manipulation in fuller details.

XSLT

XML solves the problem of data representation and exchange. However, often we need to convert this XML data into a format understood by the target application. For example, if your target is a web browser, the XML data must be converted to HTML before displaying in the browser.

Another example is that of business-to-business (B2B) applications. Let's say that application A captures order data from the end user and represents it in some XML format. This data then needs to be sent to application B that belongs to some other business. It is quite possible that the XML format as generated by application A is different from that required by application B. In such cases, you need to convert the source XML data to a format acceptable to the target system. In short, in real-world scenarios you need to transform XML data from one form to another.

That is where XSLT comes in handy. *XSLT* stands for *Extensible Style Sheet Language Transformations* and allows you to transform XML documents from one form into another. Figure 1-5 shows how this transformation happens.

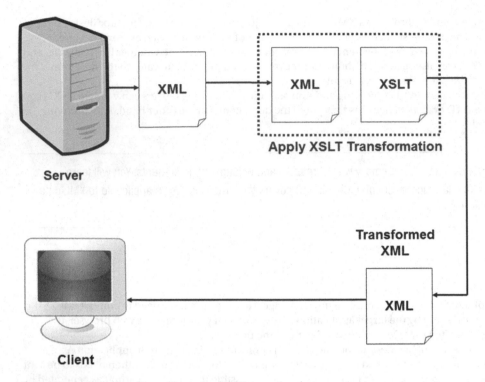

Figure 1-5. *XML transformation using XSLT*

XPath

Searching for and locating certain elements within an XML document is a fairly common task. *XPath* is an expression language that allows you to navigate through elements and attributes in an XML document. XPath consists of various XPath expressions and functions that you can use to look for and select elements and attributes matching certain patterns. XPath is also a W3C recommendation. Figure 1-6 shows an example of how XPath works.

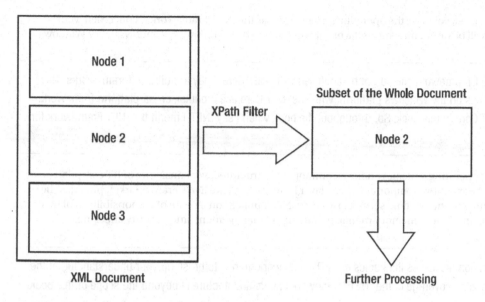

Figure 1-6. *Using XPath to select nodes*

The .NET Framework

Microsoft's *.NET Framework* is a platform for building Windows- and web-based applications, components, and services. Figure 1-7 shows the stack of the .NET Framework.

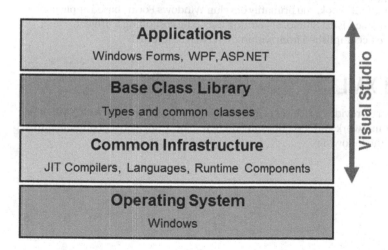

Figure 1-7. *Stack of the .NET Framework*

At the bottom level, you have the operating system. As far as the .NET Framework is concerned, your operating system will be one of the various flavors of Windows such as Windows 7, Windows 8.x, or Windows 10.

■ **Note** The .NET Framework should not be confused with .NET Core. They are different frameworks. The .NET Framework runs on the Windows platform, whereas .NET Core is a modular, cross-platform framework. We don't use .NET Core in this book. So, throughout the book when I say .NET, I mean the .NET Framework for Windows.

On top of the operating system, you have common infrastructure layer consisting of JIT compilers, languages, and other runtime components. This layer is the heart of the .NET Framework. It provides the executing environment and runtime services to all the .NET applications. Some of responsibilities of this layer include JIT compilation, memory management, thread management, and security checking.

■ **Note** This section discusses the basics of .NET Framework merely to brush up your understanding of the subject matter. Detailed coverage of the .NET Framework and its architecture is beyond the scope of this book.

On top of the Common Infrastructure layer, a huge collection of classes called the Base Class Library gets installed. The Base Class Library provides classes to perform almost everything that you need in your application. It includes classes for file input/output (IO), database access, XML manipulation, web programming, socket programming, and many more things. If you are developing a useful application in .NET, chances are that you will use one or another of the classes in the Base Class Library.

The top layer consists of various application models. Some of the choices are Windows Forms, Windows Presentation Foundation, and ASP.NET. In this book, you primarily develop Windows Forms based applications.

To develop these applications, you use Visual Studio. So, writing the code, compiling a project, debugging the code, and such tasks are accomplished from within the Visual Studio IDE.

.NET Framework and XML

The .NET Framework Base Class Library provides a rich set of classes that allows you to work with XML data. The relationship between the .NET Framework and XML doesn't end here. There are a host of other features that use XML. These features include the following:

- XML parsing
- XML transformation
- .NET configuration files
- ADO.NET
- ASP.NET Web Forms server controls
- XML serialization
- Web services, WCF services, and Web API
- XML documentation

- XAML markup
- SQL Server XML features

In this section, you will take a brief look at each of these features.

Assemblies and Namespaces

The XML-related classes from the Base Class Library are physically found in an assembly called System.Xml. dll. This assembly contains several namespaces that encapsulate various XML-related classes. The LINQ to XML classes are physically available in the System.Xml.Linq.dll assembly. In the following sections, you will take a brief look at some of the important namespaces from these assemblies.

System.Xml Namespace

The System.Xml namespace is one of the most important namespaces. It provides classes for reading and writing XML documents. Classes such as XmlDocument represent the .NET Framework's DOM-based parser, whereas classes such as XmlTextReader and XmlTextWriter allow you to quickly read and write XML documents. This namespace also contains classes that represent various parts of an XML document; these classes include XmlNode, XmlElement, XmlAttribute, and XmlText. We will be using many of these classes throughout this book.

System.Xml.Schema Namespace

The System.Xml.Schema namespace contains various classes that allow you to work with Schemas. The entire Schema Object Model (SOM) of .NET is defined by the classes from this namespace. These classes include XmlSchema, XmlSchemaElement, XmlSchemaComplexType, and many others.

System.Xml.XPath Namespace

The System.Xml.XPath namespace provides classes and enumerations for finding and selecting a subset of the XML document. These classes provide a cursor-oriented model for navigating through and editing the selection. The classes include XPathDocument, XPathExpression, XPathNavigator, XPathNodeIterator, and more.

System.Xml.Xsl Namespace

The System.Xml.Xsl namespace provides support for XSLT transformations. By using the classes from this namespace, you can transform XML data from one form to another. The classes provided by this namespace include XslCompiledTransform, XslTransform, XsltSettings, and so on.

System.Xml.Serialization Namespace

The System.Xml.Serialization namespace provides classes and attributes that are used to serialize and deserialize objects to and from XML format. These classes are extensively used in web services infrastructures. The main class provided by this namespace is XmlSerializer. Some commonly used attributes classes such as XmlAttributeAttribute, XmlRootAttribute, XmlTextAttribute, and many others are also provided by this namespace.

System.Xml.Linq Namespace

The System.Xml.Linq namespace contains classes related to the LINQ to XML features. Using these classes, you can manipulate XML documents and fragments efficiently and easily. Some of the important tasks that you can accomplish include loading XML from files or streams, creating XML trees via code, querying XML trees using LINQ operators, modifying XML trees, validating XML trees against Schemas, and transforming XML trees. Some of the frequently used classes from the System.Xml.Linq namespace are XDocument, XElement, XNode, XAttribute, and XText.

The Classic XML Parsing Model of the .NET Framework

The previous sections discussed three types of parsers: DOM- or tree-based parsers, SAX- or event-based parsers, and pull-model parsers. Out of these three models, the .NET Framework supports two.

In the .NET Framework, you can categorize the XML parsers into two flavors:

- Parser based on the DOM

- Parsers based on the pull-model or reader model

The first thing that may strike you is the lack of a SAX-based parser. But don't worry, the reader-based parsers provide similar functionality in a more efficient way.

The DOM-based parser of the .NET Framework is represented chiefly by a class called XmlDocument. By using this parser, you can load, read, and modify XML documents just as you would with any other DOM-based parser.

The reader-based parsers use a cursor-oriented approach to scan the XML document. The main class that is at the heart of these parsers is XmlReader. You also have XmlWriter at your disposal that allows you to write XML documents. These two classes are abstract classes, and other classes (such as XmlTextReader and XmlTextWriter) inherit from them. You can also create your own readers and writers if you so wish.

Thus to summarize, the .NET Framework supports DOM parsing and also provides a reader-model based parsers. I will be discussing these parsers thoroughly in subsequent chapters.

The LINQ-Based Parsing Model of the .NET Framework

Language Integrated Query, or LINQ, is a set of features that allows you to query in-memory collections, databases, and XML documents in a unified fashion. This implies that, irrespective of the underlying data source, your code will query the data in the same way. LINQ comes in three flavors:

- LINQ to objects

- LINQ to ADO.NET

- LINQ to XML

LINQ to objects provides a set of standard query operators for querying in-memory objects. The in-memory objects must implement the IEnumerable<T> interface. The most common objects for querying are generic List and Dictionary objects.

LINQ to ADO.NET provides a set of features for working with data from relational databases. LINQ to ADO.NET comes in three flavors: LINQ to DataSet, which allows you to query ADO.NET DataSet objects, and LINQ to SQL, which allows you to query relational databases such as SQL Server, and LINQ to Entities, which allows you to query Entity Framework entities.

LINQ to XML is a new approach to programming with XML data. It provides the in-memory document modification capabilities of the DOM in addition to supporting LINQ query operators. LINQ to XML operations are more lightweight than traditional DOM operations. Classes such as XDocument, XElement, XNode, XAttribute, and XText provide functionality equivalent to XmlDocument and its family of classes, as you'll see later in this book.

.NET Configuration Files

Almost all real-world applications require configuration, which includes things such as database connection strings, file system paths, security schemes, and other such settings. Prior to the introduction of the .NET Framework, developers often used .ini files or the Windows registry to store such configuration settings. But these approaches have their own flaws: no standardization, more coding time, more effort, and repeated coding for the same task.

Thankfully, the .NET Framework takes a streamlined and standardized approach to configuring applications. It relies on XML-based files for storing configuration information. That means .NET developers need not resort to .ini files or the Windows registry. Some of the advantages of using XML files instead of the classic approaches are as follows:

- Because XML files are more readable, the configuration data can be stored in a neat and structured way.

- To read the configuration information, the .NET Framework provides built-in classes. That means you need not write any custom code to access the configuration data.

- Storing the configuration information in XML files makes it possible to deploy it easily along with the application. In the past, Windows-registry–based configuration posed various deployment issues.

- There are no dangers in manipulating the XML configuration files for your application. In the past, developer's needed to tamper with the Windows registry that is risky and often created unwanted results.

- .NET Framework configuration files are not limited to using the predefined XML tags. You can extend the configuration files to add custom sections.

- Sometimes, the configuration information includes some confidential data. .NET Framework configuration files can be encrypted easily, giving more security to your configuration data. The encryption feature is a built-in part of the framework needing no custom coding from the developer.

The overall configuration files of the .NET Framework are of three types:

- Application configuration files
- Machine configuration files
- Security configuration files

Application configuration files store configuration information applicable to a single application. For Windows Forms and console-based applications, the name of the configuration file takes the following form:

```
<assembly name>.exe.config
```

That means that if you are developing a Windows application called HelloWorld.exe, its configuration filename must be HelloWorld.exe.config. The markup from Listing 1-2 shows sample configuration information for a Windows Forms–based application.

Listing 1-2. XML Markup from an Application Configuration File

```xml
<?xml version="1.0" encoding="utf-8" ?>
<configuration>
  <appSettings>
    <add key="defaultemail"
         value="someone@localhost"/>
  </appSettings>
</configuration>
```

On the other hand, a configuration file for an ASP.NET web application is called `web.config`. The markup in Listing 1-3 shows a sample `web.config` file.

Listing 1-3. XML Markup from a web.config File

```xml
<?xml version="1.0"?>
    <configuration>
        <connectionStrings>
          <add name="connstr"
                     connectionString="Data Source=.\SQLEXPRESS;
                     Integrated Security=True;
                     AttachDbFilename=|DataDirectory|AspNetDb.mdf"
                     providerName="System.Data.SqlClient"/>
        </connectionStrings>
    <system.web>
        <compilation debug="true"/>
        <authentication mode="Forms">
        <forms name="login" loginUrl="login.aspx">
        </forms>
        </authentication>
        <authorization>
            <deny users="?"/>
        </authorization>
        <membership defaultProvider="AspNetSqlProvider">
                <providers>
                        <add
                                name="AspNetSqlProvider"
                                type="System.Web.Security.SqlMembershipProvider"
                                connectionStringName="connstr"
                                passwordFormat="Clear"
                                enablePasswordRetrieval="true"
                                requiresQuestionAndAnswer="true"
                                maxInvalidPasswordAttempts="3">
                        </add>
                </providers>
        </membership>
    </system.web>
</configuration>
```

When you install the .NET Framework on a machine, a file named `machine.config` gets created under the installation folder of the .NET Framework. This file is the master configuration file and contains configuration settings that are applied to all the .NET applications running on that machine. The settings from machine.config can be overridden by using the application configuration file. Because the settings from machine.config are applied to all the .NET applications, it is recommended that you alter this file with caution. Generally, only server administrators and web-hosting providers modify this file.

The .NET Framework offers a secure environment for executing applications. It needs to check whether an assembly is trustworthy before any code in the assembly is invoked. To test the trustworthiness of an assembly, the framework checks the permission granted to it. This is called *Code Access Security*. Permissions granted to an assembly can be configured by using the security configuration files. These files are supposed to be changed using Code Access Security Policy tool (Caspol.exe). It is recommended that you alter these files only if you are aware of the impact they are going to have on security policy.

ADO.NET

For most business applications, data access is where the rubber meets the road. In .NET, *ADO.NET* is the technology for handling data access. Many new applications now use Entity Framework or similar frameworks to add OR/M (Object-Relational Mapping) capabilities to their applications. Entity Framework internally uses ADO.NET to get its job done.

ADO.NET gives a lot of emphasis to disconnected data access, though connected data access is also possible. A class called DataSet forms the cornerstone of the overall disconnected data architecture of ADO.NET. A DataSet class can be easily serialized as an XML document, and hence, it is ideal for data interchange, cross-system communication, and the like. The SqlCommand allows you to read data stored in Microsoft SQL Server and return it as an XML reader (XmlReader). XML-related features of ADO.NET are covered in detail in Chapter 7.

ASP.NET Web Forms Server Controls

You learned that the ASP.NET configuration file (web.config) is an XML file. The use of XML in ASP.NET doesn't end there. ASP.NET Web Forms use a special XML vocabulary to represent its server controls, which are programmable controls that can be accessed from server-side code. Consider the markup shown in bold in Listing 1-4.

Listing 1-4. Server Control Markup

```
<%@ Page Language="C#" %>
<script runat="server">
protected void Button1_Click(object sender, EventArgs e)
{
Label2.Text = TextBox1.Text;
}
</script>

<html xmlns="http://www.w3.org/1999/xhtml" >
<body>
<form id="form1" runat="server">
<asp:Label ID="Label1" runat="server" Text="Enter some text :"></asp:Label>
<asp:TextBox ID="TextBox1" runat="server"></asp:TextBox>
<asp:Button ID="Button1" runat="server" Text="Submit" OnClick="Button1_Click" />
<asp:Label ID="Label2" runat="server"></asp:Label>
</form>
</body>
</html>
```

The preceding fragment shows the markup of a few ASP.NET Web Forms server controls. As you can see, a Label control is represented by the <asp:Label> markup tag. Similarly, a Button control is represented by the <asp:Button> markup tag. This is a special vocabulary of XML and follows all the rules of XML grammar.

XML Serialization

Modern applications seldom run on a single machine. They are distributed and span more than one machine. Figure 1-8 shows a simple distributed application spanning three machines.

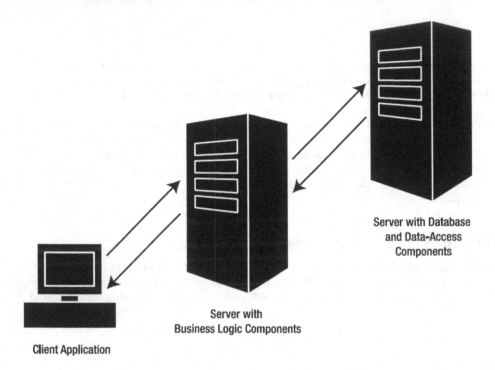

Figure 1-8. *A simple distributed application*

Here, the database and data-access components are located on a separate server. Similarly, business logic components are located on their own server, and the client applications access these components through a network. Imagine that the client wants some data from the database to display to the end user. The data is pulled out from the database from data-access components. But how will it reach the client? That is where serialization comes into the picture.

Serialization is a process by which data is written to some medium. In the preceding example, the medium is a network—but it can be a file or any other stream. The data-access components will serialize the requested data so that it can reach the client application. The client application then deserializes it—that is, it reads from the medium and reconstructs the data in an object or any other data structure. In the case of XML serialization, this data is serialized in the XML format. XML serialization is used extensively by web services, WCF services, and Web API.

The XmlSerializer and DataContractSerializer classes can be used to serialize and deserialize your objects.

Web Services, WCF Services, and Web API

With the evolution of the Internet, distributed applications are spanning different geographical locations. You may have one server residing in the United States with clients talking to it from India. It is quite possible that the clients and server are running two entirely different platforms (Windows and Unix, for example). In such cases, it is necessary that a standard mode of communication be established between the server and clients so that communication can take place over the Internet. That is where web services come into the picture.

Formally speaking, *web services* are a programmable set of APIs that you can call over a network by using industry-standard protocols: HTTP, XML, and an XML-based protocol called SOAP (as noted earlier in this chapter, *SOAP* stands for *Simple Object Access Protocol*). You can think of a web service as a web-callable component.

Because a web service is supposed to serve cross-platform environments, it relies heavily on XML. HTTP, XML, and SOAP form the pillars of web services architecture. Web services are industry standards, and just like XML, they are standardized by the W3C.

Have a look at Figure 1-8 again. Assume that the three machines involved are connected via the Internet and not a LAN. The components will now be replaced with web services, and they will perform the same jobs as the components did previously. In such cases, the client will call a web service residing on the business logic server, which in turn calls a web service residing on the database server. The requested data is sent back to the client in XML format (SOAP). It doesn't matter whether the client is a Windows desktop application, a Java application, or a web application. Powerful, isn't it? You will explore web services in later chapters.

Although web services are powerful, they have limitations of their own. Especially, the bulkiness of the data due to the verbose XML-based protocols make web services heavy. That's why new frameworks were developed to build services. Notably Windows Communication Foundation (WCF) and Web API are quite commonly used these days to build services. WCF is a generic framework for building services, whereas Web API is a framework for building RESTful (Representational State Transfer) services. Both of these frameworks—WCF and Web API—can deal with XML data. You will learn how in later chapters.

XML Documentation

Everybody knows the importance of well-documented code. However, this important task is often not given proper attention. One of the reasons is that comments left by the developer are not properly captured while creating program documentation or help files. C# as well as Visual Basic support a special commenting syntax that is based on XML. These XML comments can be converted into HTML documentation later. Just to give you a feel of how it works, see the C# code shown in Listing 1-5.

Listing 1-5. XML Commenting Syntax

```
/// <summary>
/// This is the starting point.
/// </summary>
/// <param name="args">
/// This parameter receives command line arguments.
/// </param>
static void Main(string[] args)
{
}
```

As you can see, the XML commenting syntax uses three slashes (`///`). The tags such as `<summary>` and `<parameter>` are built-in tags, and I will cover them in detail in subsequent chapters. To generate XML documentation out of this code, you need to view the project properties, as shown in Figure 1-9.

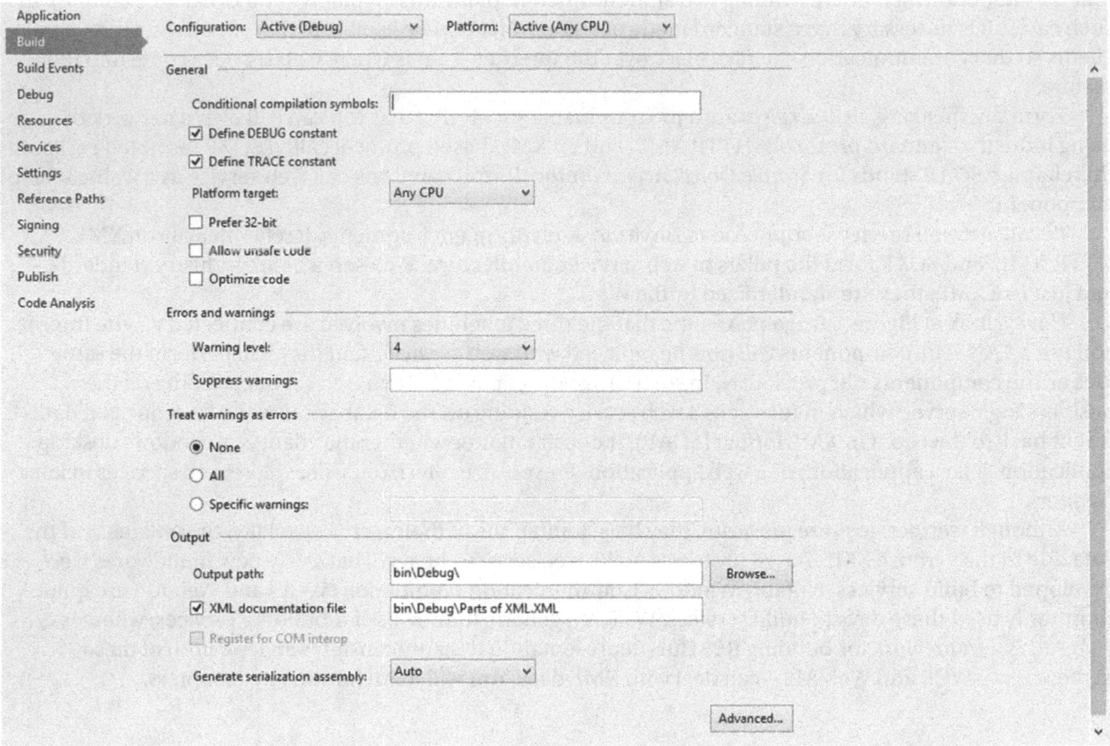

Figure 1-9. *Configuring a project for XML documentation*

Notice the check box titled XML Documentation File. After you select this check box and specify the output path, the compiler generates an XML file, as shown in Listing 1-6.

Listing 1-6. Resultant XML Comments

```xml
<?xml version="1.0"?>
<doc>
    <assembly>
        <name>Parts of XML</name>
    </assembly>
    <members>
        <member name="M:Parts_of_XML.Program.Main(System.String[])">
            <summary>
                This is the starting point.
            </summary>
```

```
        <param name="args">
            This parameter receives command line arguments.
        </param>
      </member>
    </members>
</doc>
```

You can now apply an Extensible Style Sheet Language (XSL) style sheet to the preceding XML file to get HTML documentation out of it. You can also use third-party tools that utilize this XML to generate sophisticated help files.

XAML Markup

XAML (Extensible Application Markup Language) is a special vocabulary of XML used to define a user interface. For example, WPF applications use XAML to define their user interface. The XAML markup typically resides in files with the extension .xaml. The code responsible for the functioning of the application (runtime logic such as event handlers and methods) is housed in a C# class.

The XAML markup is an XML markup and hence follows all the rules of XML grammar. You can create/edit an XAML markup in any XML/text editor but Visual Studio provides a rich editor to work with it.

SQL Server XML Features

SQL Server is one of the most powerful database engines used today. Moreover, it is from the creators of the .NET Framework. Naturally, you can expect good XML support in the product.

SQL Server provides some extensions to the SELECT statement, such as FOR XML, AUTO, EXPLICIT, PATH, and RAW, that return the requested data in XML form. The XML data returned by these queries can be retrieved using the ExecuteXmlReader() method of the SqlCommand object. Further, Microsoft has released a set of managed classes called SQLXML that facilitate reading, processing, and updating data to and from SQL Server databases in XML format. Finally, SQL Server provides the xml data type to store XML data. I cover these features at length in Chapter 11.

Working with Visual Studio

Throughout the remainder of this book, you will be using Visual Studio 2017 for developing various applications. Hence, it is worthwhile to quickly illustrate how Visual Studio can be used to develop Windows and web applications. Note that this section is not intended to give you a detailed understanding of Visual Studio. Detailed coverage of these topics is beyond the scope of this book. I will restrict our discussion to the features that you need later in this book while building various examples.

■ **Note**   Though the examples in this book are developed by using the professional edition of Visual Studio 2017, for most of the examples, you can also use Visual Studio 2017 Community Edition. You can download Visual Studio 2017 Community Edition from https://www.visualstudio.com.

Creating Windows Forms Applications

In this section, you will learn how to create a Windows Forms application using Visual Studio. To begin creating such an application, choose File ➤ New ➤ Project from the menu bar. This opens the New Project dialog box, shown in Figure 1-10.

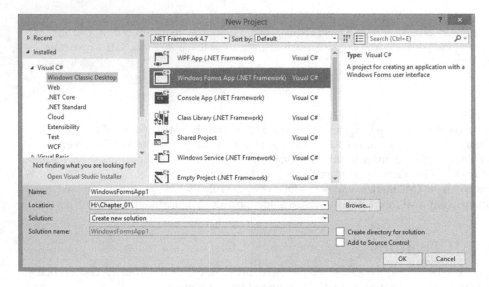

Figure 1-10. *Creating a Windows Forms application in Visual Studio*

■ **Note** The .NET Framework allows you to build Windows desktop applications using Windows Forms and Windows Presentation Foundation. In this book, we use Windows Forms to build most of the examples because it's quite easy to develop applications using Windows Forms. And it doesn't require knowledge of any additional technologies such as WPF and XAML (and also the associated Visual Studio designer). Using Windows Forms will allow us to stay focused on the main theme of this book, which is XML features of the .NET Framework.

Under Installed Templates, select Visual C#. This will display all the project templates applicable to the C#. Now, choose Windows Forms App from the templates. Type **HelloWindowsWorld** for the project name. Also, choose an appropriate location from your disk to store the project files. If you want, you can also specify a solution name for the Visual Studio solution file. Finally, click the OK button to create the project.

Your Visual Studio IDE should resemble Figure 1-11.

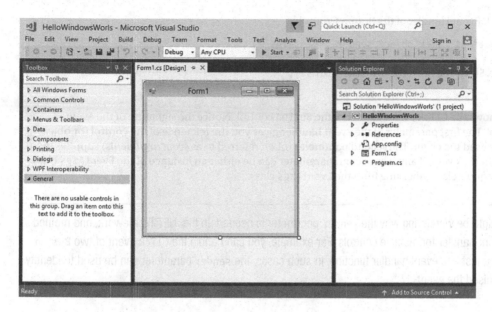

Figure 1-11. *A newly created Windows application in the Visual Studio IDE*

The project contains a single Windows Form. You can drag and drop controls from the toolbox onto the form and handle their events. Just to illustrate how this is done, drag and drop a Button control onto the form. Open the Properties window by using the View menu (or by pressing F4) and set its Text property to Click Me. Your form should now look similar to Figure 1-12.

Figure 1-12. *Windows form with a Button control*

Double-click the Click Me button to go into its Click event handler. Type in the code shown in Listing 1-7.

Listing 1-7. Click Event Handler of the Button Control

```
private void button1_Click(object sender, EventArgs e)
{
    MessageBox.Show("Hello from Windows Forms");
}
```

The code shows the Click event handler of the Button control. Notice the signature of the event handler carefully. The first parameter of the event handler gives you the reference of the control (or object in general) that raised the event. The second parameter (often referred to as *event arguments*) supplies more information about the event, if any. The second parameter can be either an instance of the EventArgs class directly or of any other class inheriting from the EventArgs class.

■ **Note**   You might be wondering why the sender parameter is needed. In the .NET Framework, one method can act as an event handler for multiple controls. For example, you can handle the Click event of two Button controls by writing just one event handler function. In such cases, the sender parameter can be used to identify the control that raised the event.

When you double-click a control, Visual Studio automatically takes you to its default event handler. However, you can wire various events and their handlers manually by using the Properties window. Figure 1-13 shows how this is done.

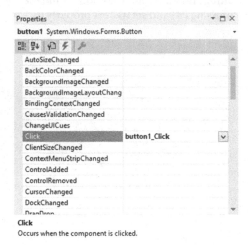

Figure 1-13. *Wiring events and their handlers manually*

Inside the event handler, we used the MessageBox class to display a message box. The Show() method of the MessageBox class has many overloads. We used the one that accepts a message to be displayed to the user.

Now, use the Build menu to compile the application. Compiling the application will create an executable .NET assembly. Though you can run the .exe directly, you may prefer to run the application via the Visual Studio IDE so that you can debug it if required. To run the application, choose Debug ➤ Start Debugging from the menu (or press F5). Figure 1-14 shows a sample run of the application.

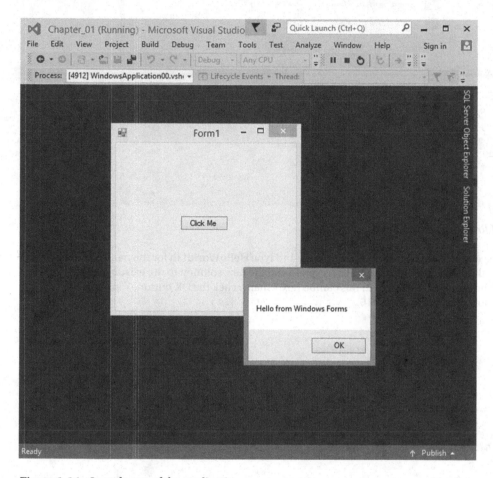

Figure 1-14. *Sample run of the application*

Creating Class Libraries

A project of type Windows Forms Application outputs an .exe assembly. Generally, such applications present some type of user interface to the user. However, at times, you need to code functionality and create a component. Such components reside as dynamic link libraries (.dll files) and generally do not include any presentation logic. To create dynamic link libraries by using Visual Studio, you need to create a project of type Class Library.

To learn how to create and consume class libraries, you will create a Class Library project. The resultant assembly will be consumed by the Windows Forms application that you developed in the preceding section.

Again, choose File ➤ New ➤ Project from the menu to open the New Project dialog, shown in Figure 1-15.

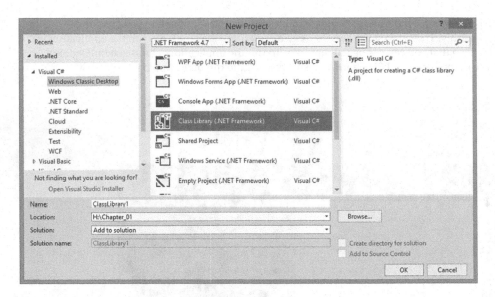

Figure 1-15. *Adding a Class Library project*

This time select the Class Library project template and type **HelloWorldLib** for the name. At the bottom of the dialog box, there is a combo box that allows you to add the new solution to the existing solution. Ensure that you choose Add to Solution in this combo box. Finally, click the OK button. Your Solution Explorer should now resemble Figure 1-16.

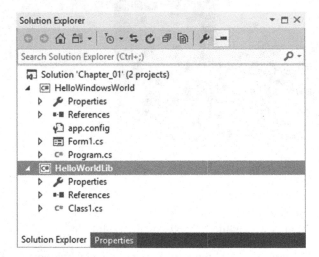

Figure 1-16. *The Visual Studio IDE after adding the class library project*

By default, the class library contains one class. You can, of course, add more classes at a later stage if required. Now, add a method named HelloWorld() in the class library. The method is shown in Listing 1-8.

Listing 1-8. HelloWorld() Method

```
public string HelloWorld()
{
  return "Hello from Windows Forms";
}
```

The method simply returns a string to the caller. Once we compile the class library as outlined before, our class library is ready to be consumed in another application.

Choose Projects ➤ Add Reference (make sure you are in HelloWindowsWorld project) from the menu to open the Add Reference dialog box (see Figure 1-17).

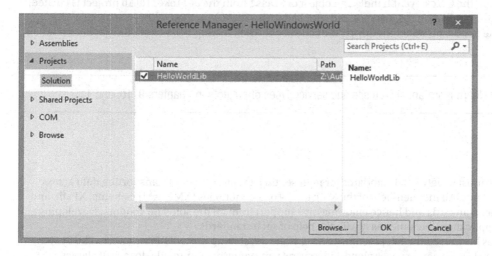

Figure 1-17. *Adding a reference through the Add Reference dialog box*

This dialog box contains several nodes on the left. The Assemblies and COM options are used to add a reference to built-in .NET Framework assemblies and COM components, respectively. The Projects option is used to add a reference to another project from the same solution. The Browse option can be used to add a reference to assemblies located somewhere on your machine. In our example, you need to add a reference to the HelloWorldLib assembly from the Projects option.

Now, change the code of the Windows Forms application as shown in Listing 1-9.

Listing 1-9. Modified Code of the Windows Forms Application

```
using System;
using System.Windows.Forms;
using HelloWorldLib;

namespace HelloWindowsWorld
{
    public partial class Form1 : Form
    {
```

```
    public Form1()
    {
        InitializeComponent();
    }

    private void button1_Click(object sender, EventArgs e)
    {
        Class1 obj = new Class1();
        MessageBox.Show(obj.HelloWorld());
    }
  }
}
```

Notice the code marked in bold. The code imports the HelloWorldLib namespace with the help of a using statement. In the Click event handler, an object of Class1 from the HelloWorldLib project is created. HelloWorld() is then called on the instance and supplied to the Show() method of the MessageBox class.

If you run the application after modifying the code as shown in Listing 1-9, you should get the same result as before.

■ **Note**   You will learn more about web site and service types of projects in Chapters 9, 10, and 12.

Summary

XML is one of the most widely used standards for representing, exchanging, and transporting data across heterogonous systems. All the members of the XML family of technologies (XML, XML Schema, XPath, and XSLT) are industry standards and hence enjoy massive support from all the software vendors. Developing cross-platform applications becomes easy with the help of such standards.

Microsoft has harnessed the full potential of XML while developing the .NET Framework. The System. Xml and System.Xml.Linq namespaces along with several sub-namespaces provide dozens of classes that allow you to read, write, and modify XML documents. The configuration files of .NET Framework applications exclusively use XML markup. Service development frameworks such as web services, WCF, and Web API also use XML. The C# language supports XML commenting, which you can use to generate XML documentation for your applications. The .NET Framework also allows you to leverage XML-related features of SQL Server easily.

CHAPTER 2

■ ■ ■

Manipulating XML Documents Using the Document Object Model

Chapter 1 discussed various flavors of parsers—tree-based parsers, event-based parsers, and pull-model parsers. You also learned that the Document Object Model (DOM) is a set of APIs for manipulating XML documents. To that end, this chapter covers all the essential functionality offered by the .NET Framework's DOM classes. Specifically this chapter covers the following topics:

- System.Xml classes related to DOM

- Knowing when to use DOM

- Reading XML documents using DOM

- Writing XML documents using DOM

- Dealing with whitespace and namespaces

- Handling events of the XmlDocument class

Using the DOM Parser

The System.Xml namespace provides a set of classes that together allow DOM manipulation of an XML document. At the heart of DOM manipulation in .NET Framework is a class called XmlDocument. This class is the DOM parser of the .NET Framework. Just like any other DOM parser, XmlDocument looks at your XML document as a tree. It loads the XML document and builds its tree representation (consisting of elements, attributes, comments, and so on) in memory.

For example, consider Listing 2-1.

Listing 2-1. Parts of a Typical XML Document

```
<?xml version="1.0"?>
<customers>
  <customer ID="C001">
    <name>Nancy Davolio</name>
    <email>nancy@localhost</email>
    <comments>
      <![CDATA[Regular customer since 1995]]>
    </comments>
  </customer>
```

© Bipin Joshi 2017
B. Joshi, *Beginning XML with C# 7*, https://doi.org/10.1007/978-1-4842-3105-0_2

```
<customer ID="C002">
  <name>Steven Buchanan</name>
  <email>steven@localhost</email>
  <comments>
    <![CDATA[New customer interested in multiple services]]>
  </comments>
</customer>
</customers>
```

The preceding XML document consists of the parts listed in Table 2-1.

Table 2-1. *Parts of the XML Document*

Part Name	Type of Part
`<?xml ...?>`	Processing instruction
`customers`	Document element or root node
`customer`	Element
`ID`	Attribute of the `<customer>` element
`name`	Child element of the `<customer>` element
`email`	Child element of the `<customer>` element
`comments`	Child element of the `<customer>` element

In addition to what is shown in the preceding table, the `<name>`, `<email>`, and `<comments>` elements contain text values that are called text nodes.

The preceding document is loaded in memory by the DOM parser as a tree and resembles Figure 2-1.

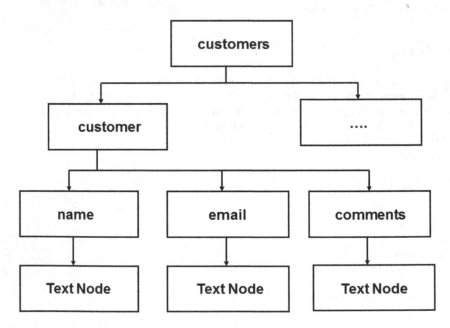

Figure 2-1. *Tree representation of an XML document*

Each part of the preceding diagram is actually a node. In .NET, a node is represented by an abstract class called XmlNode. Even text values and attributes are nodes. They are of course handled differently from the other nodes.

Each of the parts mentioned in Table 2-1 is represented by a class, each of which is described in Table 2-2.

Table 2-2. *XML DOM Classes*

Part of XML Document	Class Representing the Part
Document element	XmlElement
Processing instructions	XmlProcessingInstruction
Element	XmlElement
Attribute	XmlAttribute
Text values	XmlText
Nodes	XmlNode

All of the classes in Table 2-2 inherit directly or indirectly from an abstract base class XmlNode. While using the XmlDocument class, you will often use one or another of the classes from Table 2-2.

Knowing When to Use DOM

Before you go ahead and use DOM for accessing your XML documents, you should understand the areas to which DOM is best suited and areas where its use should be avoided.

The decision of whether to use DOM is governed by the following core factors:

- *Read/write access*: DOM allows you to read and write the XML document. But do you really need to change the underlying document?

- *Memory footprint*: DOM loads the entire document in memory. Naturally the memory footprint of DOM is larger. Are your documents large, say over 100MB?

- *Type of access*: DOM allows you to access any node randomly. This is possible because the entire document tree is available in memory. Do you need such access? Or is sequential access sufficient?

Answers to the preceding questions will help you to decide whether to use DOM. To summarize, DOM is best suited in the following scenarios:

- You want to modify the XML documents, that is, read-only access is not sufficient.

- You want to access various nodes randomly, that is, sequential access is not sufficient.

- You want to process documents that are small in size.

- The memory footprint is not a constraint.

A Sample XML Document

Throughout this chapter, we will be using an XML document that resides on the disk as a file named Employees.xml. The Employees.xml file is shown in Listing 2-2.

Listing 2-2. A Sample XML Document

```xml
<?xml version="1.0" encoding="utf-8" ?>
<!-- This is list of employees -->
<employees>
  <employee employeeid="1">
    <firstname>Nancy</firstname>
    <lastname>Davolio</lastname>
    <homephone>(206) 555-9857</homephone>
    <notes>
      <![CDATA[Education includes a BA in psychology from Colorado State University
      in 1970. She also completed "The Art of the Cold Call." Nancy is a member of
      Toastmasters International.]]>
    </notes>
  </employee>
  <employee employeeid="2">
    <firstname>Andrew</firstname>
    <lastname>Fuller</lastname>
    <homephone>(206) 555-9482</homephone>
    <notes>
      <![CDATA[Andrew received his BTS commercial in 1974 and a Ph.D. in international
      marketing from the University of Dallas in 1981. He is fluent in French and Italian
      and reads German. He joined the company as a sales representative, was promoted to
      sales manager in January 1992 and to vice president of sales in March 1993. Andrew
      is a member of the Sales Management Roundtable, the Seattle Chamber of Commerce, and
      the Pacific Rim Importers Association.]]>
    </notes>
  </employee>
  <employee employeeid="3">
    <firstname>Janet</firstname>
    <lastname>Leverling</lastname>
    <homephone>(206) 555-3412</homephone>
    <notes>
      <![CDATA[Janet has a BS degree in chemistry from Boston College (1984).
      She has also completed a certificate program in food retailing management. Janet was
      hired as a sales associate in 1991 and promoted to sales representative in February
      1992.]]>
    </notes>
  </employee>
</employees>
```

This XML document represents a list of employees. The <employees> element forms the document element and contains three <employee> child elements. The <employee> element has an attribute called employeeid and four sub-elements: <firstname>, <lastname>, <homephone>, and <notes>. The <notes> element contains descriptive data that is stored as CDATA.

■ **Note**   You might have guessed that the Employees.xml file is based on the Employees table of the Northwind database—a sample database for the SQL Server. Of course, we don't need the Northwind database for the examples of this chapter.

To create an XML file, you can enlist the help of the Visual Studio IDE, which enables you to quickly create XML documents by auto-completing end tags, putting attributes in quotes, and showing errors related to the document not being well formed. Because we will be using this file often, I recommend that you create it and keep it in a handy location on your hard disk.

Opening an Existing XML Document for Parsing

To open an existing XML document, you need to use the XmlDocument class. The XmlDocument class allows you to open XML documents in three common ways:

- You can specify the path to, or URL of, the XML file.

- You can use a stream object such as FileStream that contains the XML data.

- You can hold a string in memory that contains the XML data.

To see how each of the preceding approaches can be used, you need to develop a Windows Forms application like the one shown in Figure 2-2.

Figure 2-2. *Opening an XML document*

The application consists of three radio buttons for selecting the place from where the XML document is to be loaded. There is a text box for entering the file path, URL, or XML string. Finally, there is a button titled Open Document that opens the XML file depending on the selection and shows a message box with a success message.

■ **Note** I have not included any input validation or exception handling in the examples so as to keep the examples focused on the XML-related code. The code in this book's download contains the basic validation checks and exception handling wherever necessary.

Listing 2-3 shows the Click event handler of the button.

Listing 2-3. Opening an XML Document

```
private void button1_Click(object sender, EventArgs e)
{
  try
  {
    XmlDocument doc = new XmlDocument();
    if (radioButton1.Checked)
    {
      doc.Load(textBox1.Text);
    }
    if (radioButton2.Checked)
    {
      FileStream stream = new FileStream(textBox1.Text, FileMode.Open);
      doc.Load(stream);
      stream.Close();
    }
    if (radioButton3.Checked)
    {
      doc.LoadXml(textBox1.Text);
    }
    MessageBox.Show("XML Document Opened Successfully!");
  }
  catch(Exception ex)
  {
    MessageBox.Show(ex.Message);
  }
}
```

The code creates an instance of the XmlDocument class. The XmlDocument class has two important methods: Load() and LoadXml(). The former method can take a file system path, URL, or stream object pointing to the XML document that you want to open. The latter method accepts a string containing the XML data to be loaded. Depending on the selection made by the user, either Load() or LoadXml() is called. Note that depending on the selection, your text box should contain a URL, a file system path, or raw XML data.

■ **Note** You must import the System.IO and System.Xml namespaces to successfully compile the code shown in Listing 2-3. This applies to most of the examples illustrated in this chapter.

You can run the application and supply the path of the Employees.xml file that we created earlier.

Navigating Through an XML Document

An XML document consists of one or more nodes, and nodes can be nested inside other nodes. Such nested nodes are called *child nodes*.

The XmlNode class has a collection called ChildNodes that contains a list of child nodes of the node under consideration. Note that most of the other DOM-related classes are inherited directly or indirectly from the XmlNode class, and hence the ChildNodes collection is also available to them. Further, the XmlNode class has properties such as ParentNode, FirstChild, LastChild, NextSibling, and PreviousSibling that allow you to navigate to the corresponding node. Thus the ParentNode property will allow you to access the parent node of the current node, and the NextSibling property will allow you to access the next node at the same level as that of the current node.

To see how these properties can be used, we will develop a Windows Forms application. The application navigates through the Employees.xml file and displays a TreeView control with various nodes nested as per the document structure.

The application is shown in Figure 2-3.

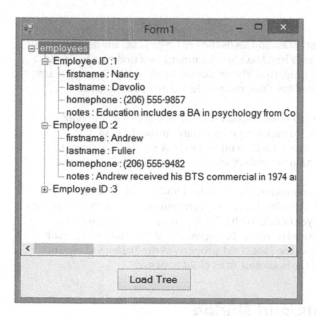

Figure 2-3. *Navigating through an XML document by using DOM*

The application consists of a TreeView control and a button titled Load Tree. After you click the button, the application loads the Employees.xml file by using the XmlDocument class. It then iterates through all the child nodes and reads the values of the attributes and nodes. The XML nodes are then added to the TreeView as TreeNodes.

Listing 2-4 shows the Click event handler of the Load Tree button.

Listing 2-4. Loading the Tree

```
private void button1_Click(object sender, EventArgs e)
{
  XmlDocument doc = new XmlDocument();
  doc.Load($"{Application.StartupPath}\\employees.xml");
```

```
TreeNode root = new TreeNode(doc.DocumentElement.Name);
treeView1.Nodes.Add(root);
foreach (XmlNode node in doc.DocumentElement.ChildNodes)
{
  TreeNode employee = new TreeNode("Employee ID :" +
    node.Attributes["employeeid"].Value);
  root.Nodes.Add(employee);
  if (node.HasChildNodes)
  {
    foreach (XmlNode childnode in node.ChildNodes)
    {
      TreeNode n2 = new TreeNode(childnode.Name + " : "+ childnode.InnerText);
      employee.Nodes.Add(n2);
    }
  }
}
}
```

The code creates an instance of the XmlDocument class and loads the Employees.xml file using its Load() method. Then the code adds the root node of the TreeView. The XML document root node is <employees> and can be accessed by using the DocumentElement property of the XmlDocument class. The DocumentElement property is of type XmlElement. It has a property called Name that returns the name of the element (employees, in our case).

The <employees> node contains three <employee> child nodes, which can be accessed by using the ChildNodes property of the DocumentElement. A foreach loop then iterates through them. With each iteration, a new TreeNode is added to the TreeView with the employee ID as the text. To access the employeeid attribute, we use the Attributes collection of the XmlNode class. You can specify either an attribute's index or name to retrieve its value.

The code then checks whether the <employee> nodes have further child nodes. This is done using a Boolean property of the XmlNode class called HasChildNodes. If this property returns true, another foreach loop iterates through the child nodes of the <employee> node. With each iteration, a new TreeNode is added with text same as the name of the child node and its value. To retrieve the data inside nodes such as <firstname>, <lastname>, and so on, the code uses the InnerText property of the XmlNode class. The InnerText property returns concatenated values of the node and all its child nodes.

Looking for Specific Elements and Nodes

Often we are not interested in the entire XML document loaded in memory but a part of it. This requires us to search for a specific element or node for further processing. There are several methods used to search the XML document:

- Retrieving specific elements using the GetElementsByTagName() method
- Retrieving specific elements using the GetElementById() method
- Selecting specific nodes using the SelectNodes() method
- Selecting a single specific node using the SelectSingleNode() method

Retrieving Specific Elements Using the GetElementsByTagName() Method

The GetElementsByTagName() method of the XmlDocument class accepts the name of the tag (excluding < and >) and returns all the nodes matching that tag name. The matching nodes are returned as an XmlNodeList. The XmlNodeList class represents a collection of XmlNode objects.

To see GetElementsByTagName() in action, we need to develop a Windows Forms application like the one shown in Figure 2-4.

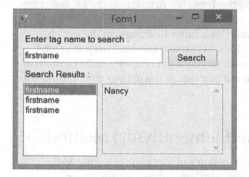

Figure 2-4. *Using the GetElementsByTagName() method*

The application consists of a text box to enter the tag name to look for. After you click the Search button, the matching tags are displayed in the list box. Selecting a tag from the list box displays its contents in a read-only text box.

The code that makes the preceding form work is shown in Listing 2-5.

Listing 2-5. Using the GetElementsByTagName() Method

```
XmlNodeList list = null;

private void button1_Click(object sender, EventArgs e)
{
  XmlDocument doc = new XmlDocument();
  doc.Load($"{Application.StartupPath}\\employees.xml");
  list = doc.GetElementsByTagName(textBox1.Text);
  listBox1.Items.Clear();
  foreach (XmlNode node in list)
  {
    listBox1.Items.Add(node.Name);
  }
}

private void listBox1_SelectedIndexChanged(object sender, EventArgs e)
{
  textBox2.Text = list[listBox1.SelectedIndex].InnerXml;
}
```

The code declares a variable of type XmlNodeList at the form level. This variable needs to be declared at the form level because we need to access it in two event handlers.

In the Click event handler of the Search button, an XmlDocument instance is created. The Employees.xml file is loaded into it by using its Load() method. The code then calls the GetElementsByTagName() method of the XmlDocument object, which accepts the tag name to look for. In our application, the tag is specified in textBox1. As mentioned earlier, the return value of the GetElementsByTagName() method is of type XmlNodeList. The XmlNodeList class stores the collection of XmlNode objects. The code then iterates through the returned XmlNodeList and adds each node name into the list box.

The user can select any of the nodes displayed in the list box. In order to show the contents of the selected node, the code handles the SelectedIndexChanged event of the list box. Inside the SelectedIndexChanged event handler, the selected node is retrieved from the XmlNodeList we stored previously. The contents of the selected node are displayed using the InnerXml property of the XmlNode class, which returns all the XML content that is inside the node under consideration.

To see how the application works, run it from the Visual Studio IDE. Enter **firstname** in the search text box and click the Search button. The list box should display three firstname entries. This is expected because our XML document contains three <employee> nodes, each having a <firstname> child element of its own. Click any of the firstname entries from the list box. The text box beside the list box should show the value of the firstname node.

Retrieving Specific Elements Using the GetElementById() Method

Often, our XML elements have an attribute that is unique for each instance of that element in the XML document. We may want to look for a specific element based on this attribute value. This process is analogous to looking for a record in a database based on its primary key. The difference, however, is that the XmlDocument class does not know automatically that a specific attribute is acting as a primary key for that element. Formally, such an attribute is called the *ID* of that element.

To convey this information, you must use a DTD or Schema. Both of these techniques can mark an attribute as the ID of the element, and the XmlDocument class can then understand them as IDs. After you have a DTD or Schema attached to your XML document, you can call the GetElementById() method of the XmlDocument class. The GetElementById() method accepts the ID of the element to search for and returns that element as an instance of the XmlElement class. You can then access the sub-elements or text inside this element.

To illustrate the use of the GetElementById() method, we will build an application like the one shown in Figure 2-5.

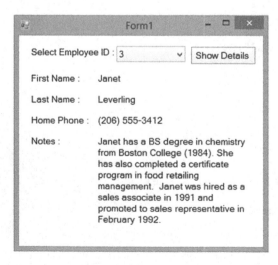

Figure 2-5. *Using the GetElementByID() method*

The application consists of a combo box showing a list of employee IDs. After you select an ID and click the Show Details button, the details such as firstname, lastname, homephone, and notes are displayed.

Before you proceed with the application development, you must modify the Employees.xml file, as shown in Listing 2-6.

Listing 2-6. XML File with DTD

```
<?xml version="1.0" encoding="utf-8" standalone="yes" ?>
<!-- This is list of employees -->
<!DOCTYPE employees [
  <!ELEMENT employees ANY>
  <!ELEMENT employee ANY>
  <!ELEMENT firstname ANY>
  <!ELEMENT lastname ANY>
  <!ELEMENT homephone ANY>
  <!ELEMENT notes ANY>
  <!ATTLIST employee employeeid ID #REQUIRED>
]>

<employees>
  <employee employeeid="1">
    <firstname>Nancy</firstname>
    <lastname>Davolio</lastname>
    <homephone>(206) 555-9857</homephone>
    <notes>
        <![CDATA[Education includes a BA in psychology from Colorado State University
        in 1970. She also completed "The Art of the Cold Call." Nancy is a member of
        Toastmasters International.]]>
    </notes>
  </employee>
  <employee employeeid="2">
    <firstname>Andrew</firstname>
    <lastname>Fuller</lastname>
    <homephone>(206) 555-9482</homephone>
    <notes>
        <![CDATA[Andrew received his BTS commercial in 1974 and a Ph.D.
        in international marketing from the University of Dallas in 1981.
        He is fluent in French and Italian and reads German. He joined the company as a
        sales representative, was promoted to sales manager in January 1992 and to vice
        president of sales in March 1993. Andrew is a member of the Sales Management
        Roundtable, the Seattle Chamber of Commerce, and the Pacific Rim Importers
        Association.]]>
    </notes>
  </employee>
  <employee employeeid="3">
    <firstname>Janet</firstname>
    <lastname>Leverling</lastname>
    <homephone>(206) 555-3412</homephone>
```

```
  <notes>
    <![CDATA[Janet has a BS degree in chemistry from Boston College (1984).
      She has also completed a certificate program in food retailing management. Janet was
      hired as a sales associate in 1991 and promoted to sales representative in February
      1992.]]>
  </notes>
 </employee>
</employees>
```

The document looks almost identical to the original. However, an important piece is added at the top (see the markup shown in bold). We have added a DTD for our document. I will not go into the details of the DTD here, but suffice it to say that the ATTLIST section defines an attribute called employeeid for the <employee> element. More important, the employeeid attribute is marked as the ID and is also a REQUIRED attribute. This is how the XmlDocument class knows which attribute of an element is acting as an ID.

If you look at the source code of the application, you will see a form-level variable of type XmlDocument called doc:

```
XmlDocument doc = new XmlDocument();
```

The Load event handler of the form bears the code shown in Listing 2-7.

Listing 2-7. Populating the Combo Box

```
private void Form1_Load(object sender, EventArgs e)
{
  doc.Load($"{Application.StartupPath}\\employees.xml");
  foreach (XmlNode node in doc.DocumentElement.ChildNodes)
  {
    string employeeid = node.Attributes["employeeid"].Value;
    comboBox1.Items.Add(employeeid);
  }
}
```

The code loads the new Employees.xml file in the XmlDocument instance we created earlier by using its Load() method. A foreach loop then iterates over all the <employee> nodes. With each iteration, the employeeid attribute of the <employee> node is retrieved using the Attributes collection of the XmlNode class. The attribute value is added to the combo box.

When the user selects a particular ID, the details of that employee are displayed. This is accomplished in the Click event handler of the Show Details button. The code inside the Click event handler is shown in Listing 2-8.

Listing 2-8. Calling the GetElementById() Method

```
private void button1_Click(object sender, EventArgs e)
{
  XmlElement ele= doc.GetElementById(comboBox1.SelectedItem.ToString());
  label6.Text = ele.ChildNodes[0].InnerText;
  label7.Text = ele.ChildNodes[1].InnerText;
  label8.Text = ele.ChildNodes[2].InnerText;
  label9.Text = ele.ChildNodes[3].InnerText;
}
```

The code calls the GetElementById() method of the XmlDocument class and passes the employee ID to look for. The GetElementById() method returns the matching element as an object of type XmlElement. Because the XmlElement class inherits from the XmlNode class, the ChildNodes collection is available to the XmlElement class also. To retrieve the values of the <firstname>, <lastname>, <homephone>, and <notes> nodes, the ChildNodes collection is accessed by using the index of the corresponding element. Finally, the InnerText property of each XmlNode gives the text inside the appropriate node.

Selecting Specific Nodes Using the SelectNodes() Method

In complex cases, you may want to search for a node matching a pattern. This is accomplished with the help of XPath. Though XPath is not the subject of this chapter, I give you a glimpse of how it can be used. I explain XPath fully in Chapter 4.

The XmlDocument class has a method called SelectNodes() that accepts the XPath criteria for filtering the available nodes. It returns an XmlNodeList containing the matching nodes.

To see how the SelectNodes() method works, we need to develop a Windows Forms application, as shown in Figure 2-6.

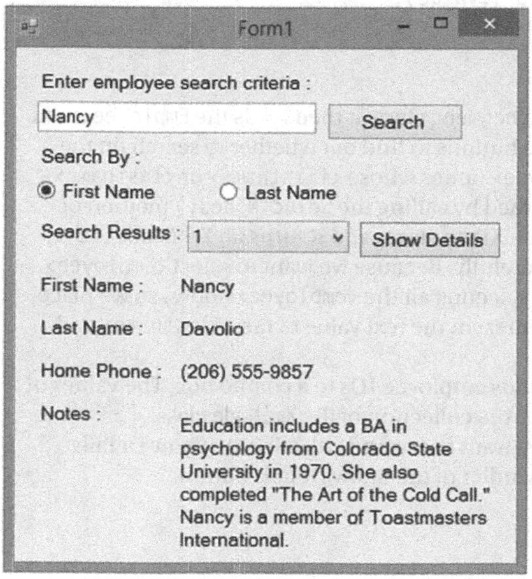

Figure 2-6. *Using the SelectNodes() method*

The application consists of a text box for entering the first name or last name of an employee. The radio buttons allow you to choose whether to look for matching first names or last names. Upon clicking the Search button, the SelectNodes() method is called. The returned <employee> nodes are collected in an XmlNodeList. The combo box displays the list of matching employee IDs. You can select an employee ID and click the Show Details button to display the employee details.

If you look at the source code of the application, you will find a declaration of a variable of type XmlNodeList at the form level:

```
XmlNodeList list = null;
```

We declare the variable at the form level because it is used in multiple event-handler functions.

The Click event handler of the Search button is shown in Listing 2-9.

Listing 2-9. Using the SelectNodes() Method

```
private void button1_Click(object sender, EventArgs e)
{
  XmlDocument doc = new XmlDocument();
  doc.Load($"{Application.StartupPath}\\employees.xml");
  if (radioButton1.Checked)
  {
    list = doc.SelectNodes($"//employee[./firstname/text()='{textBox1.Text}']");
  }
  else
  {
    list = doc.SelectNodes($"//employee[./lastname/text()='{textBox1.Text}']");
  }
  foreach (XmlNode node in list)
  {
    comboBox1.Items.Add(node.Attributes["employeeid"].Value);
  }
}
```

The preceding code first creates an instance of the XmlDocument class. It then loads the Employees.xml file by using the Load() method. Further, it checks the radio buttons to find out whether to search on the basis of first name or last name. We want to search <employee> nodes whose <firstname> or <lastname> matches the value entered in the text box. This is accomplished by calling the SelectNodes() method of the XmlDocument class. The SelectNodes() method takes the XPath string and returns an XmlNodeList containing the matching nodes. Look at the XPath syntax carefully. Because we want to select <employee> nodes, we specify //employee. But we are not interested in selecting all the <employee> nodes, so we place the filtering criterion in a pair of square brackets ([ ]). To represent the text value of the <firstname> and <lastname> nodes, we use the text() XPath function.

The code then iterates through the XmlNodeList and adds employee IDs to a combo box. The values of the employeeid attributes are retrieved by using the Attributes collection of the XmlNode class.

The user will select the employee ID whose details they want to see and will click the Show Details button. Listing 2-10 shows the code from the Click event handler of the Show Details button.

Listing 2-10. Displaying Employee Details

```
private void button2_Click(object sender, EventArgs e)
{
  label8.Text = list[comboBox1.SelectedIndex].ChildNodes[0].InnerText;
  label9.Text = list[comboBox1.SelectedIndex].ChildNodes[1].InnerText;
  label10.Text = list[comboBox1.SelectedIndex].ChildNodes[2].InnerText;
  label11.Text = list[comboBox1.SelectedIndex].ChildNodes[3].InnerText;
}
```

The code simply retrieves the desired XmlNode from the XmlNodeList. The child nodes of the node are accessed by using the ChildNodes collection. The InnerText property of the XmlNode class returns the text from each child node.

Selecting a Single Specific Node Using the SelectSingleNode() Method

The SelectSingleNode() is very similar to the SelectNodes() method that you just learned, with one difference. Instead of returning a list of XmlNode objects in the form of an XmlNodeList, it simply returns the first matching XmlNode.

To test this method, you can modify the previous example, as shown in Listing 2-11.

Listing 2-11. Using the SelectSingleNode() Method

```
XmlNode node = null;

private void button1_Click(object sender, EventArgs e)
{
  XmlDocument doc = new XmlDocument();
  doc.Load($"{Application.StartupPath}\\employees.xml");
  if (radioButton1.Checked)
  {
    node = doc.SelectSingleNode($"//employee[./firstname/text()='{textBox1.Text}']");
  }
  else
  {
    node = doc.SelectSingleNode($"//employee[./lastname/text()='{textBox1.Text}']");
  }
  if (node != null)
  {
    comboBox1.Items.Add(node.Attributes["employeeid"].Value);
  }
}

private void button2_Click(object sender, EventArgs e)
{
  label8.Text = node.ChildNodes[0].InnerText;
  label9.Text = node.ChildNodes[1].InnerText;
  label10.Text = node.ChildNodes[2].InnerText;
  label11.Text = node.ChildNodes[3].InnerText;
}
```

The code now declares a variable of type XmlNode at the form level. The Click event handler of the Search button calls the SelectSingleNode() method, which accepts the same XPath expression as in the previous example. This method returns the first matching node instead of an XmlNodeList, though our search criteria may not necessarily return any matching node. Therefore, the code accesses the XmlNode variable only if it is not null. In the Click event of the Show Details button, the XmlNode variable node is used to retrieve employee details.

Modifying XML Documents

Up until this point, we have seen how to read XML documents; how to navigate through them; and how to search them on the basis of tag names, IDs, and XPath expressions. But what about modifying them? That's the topic of this section.

Often business requirements call for modification of the underlying XML document. This modification can be an addition, a deletion, or a change of nodes or attributes. As you saw previously, DOM is a read-write parser. That means DOM APIs also allow you to modify the document.

To illustrate the use of several System.Xml classes for modifying XML documents, we are going to develop a Windows Forms application like the one shown in Figure 2-7.

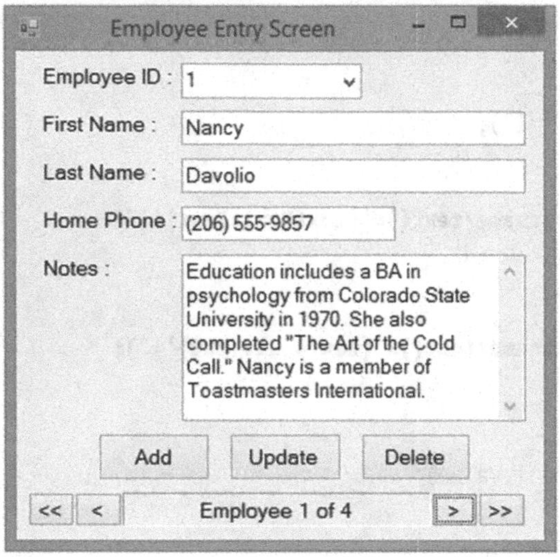

Figure 2-7. *Data entry screen for the Employees.xml file*

The application represents a complete data entry screen for the Employees.xml file. The application allows us to do the following tasks:

- Navigate among the available employees with the help of VCR buttons (the buttons used to navigate to the previous, next, first, and last records are often called *VCR buttons*).

- Add a new employee.

- Modify the details of a particular employee. The employee ID attribute acts like a primary key for our XML document, and hence it cannot be changed.

- Delete an existing employee.

If you look at the source code of the preceding application, you will see two form-level variables, as shown here:

```
XmlDocument doc = new XmlDocument();
int CurrentNodeIndex = 0;
```

The XmlDocument instance is used throughout the application. The integer variable CurrentNodeIndex is used to keep track of the current employee record that is being displayed (it is mainly used by the navigational buttons).

The Load event handler of the form is shown in Listing 2-12.

Listing 2-12. Filling Controls

```
private void Form1_Load(object sender, EventArgs e)
{
  doc.Load($"{Application.StartupPath}\\employees.xml");
  foreach (XmlNode node in doc.DocumentElement.ChildNodes)
  {
    comboBox1.Items.Add(node.Attributes["employeeid"].Value);
  }
  FillControls();
}
```

The preceding code loads the Employees.xml file by using the Load() method. It then iterates through all the <employee> nodes and fills the combo box with employee IDs. The employeeid attribute is retrieved by using the Attributes collection of the XmlNode class. Finally, the code calls a helper method called FillControls(). This method simply displays first name, last name, home phone, and notes from the current <employee> node in various text boxes. We will be looking at the FillControls() method shortly.

Navigating Between Various Nodes

The application allows you to navigate between various <employee> nodes with the help of VCR navigation buttons. Listing 2-13 shows how the navigation buttons work.

Listing 2-13. Working of Navigation Buttons

```
//go to first record
private void button4_Click(object sender, EventArgs e)
{
  CurrentNodeIndex = 0;
  FillControls();
}

//go to previous record
private void button5_Click(object sender, EventArgs e)
{
  CurrentNodeIndex--;
  if (CurrentNodeIndex < 0)
  {
    CurrentNodeIndex = 0;
  }
  FillControls();
}

//go to next record
private void button6_Click(object sender, EventArgs e)
{
```

```
    CurrentNodeIndex++;
    if (CurrentNodeIndex >= doc.DocumentElement.ChildNodes.Count)
    {
      CurrentNodeIndex = doc.DocumentElement.ChildNodes.Count-1;
    }
    FillControls();
}

//go to last record
private void button7_Click(object sender, EventArgs e)
{
    CurrentNodeIndex = doc.DocumentElement.ChildNodes.Count - 1;
    FillControls();
}
```

In the Click event of the First Record (<<) button, the code sets the CurrentNodeIndex variable to 0 and calls the FillControls() method. The FillControls() method then populates various controls based on the value of the CurrentNodeIndex variable.

The Click event handler of the Previous Record (<) button decrements the CurrentNodeIndex variable. If the value becomes less than zero, the event handler sets it to 0. The FillControls() method is then called.

In the Click event handler of the Next Record (>) button, the code increments the CurrentNodeIndex variable. If the value goes beyond the total number of <employee> nodes, the event handler sets a new value of the total number of employee nodes minus one. This is necessary because just like any other collection in .NET, the ChildNodes collection is zero based.

Finally, the Click event handler of the Last Record (>>) button sets the CurrentNodeIndex variable to the total number of employee nodes minus one.

Now that you know how the navigation system of the application works, let's move on to the more interesting part—modifying, deleting, and adding XML content.

Modifying Existing Content

To modify an <employee> node, we first need to retrieve it from the list of <employee> nodes. The ID of the employee will be taken from the combo box. To retrieve the <employee> node, we can use the SelectNodes() or SelectSingleNode() method. In our example, because there can be only one <employee> node matching the given employee ID, SelectSingleNode() is a better choice. After a reference to the <employee> node is retrieved, we can change its child nodes. The complete code implementing this logic is shown in Listing 2-14.

Listing 2-14. Modifying Existing Content

```
private void button2_Click(object sender, EventArgs e)
{
    XmlNode node=doc.SelectSingleNode($"//employee[@employeeid='{comboBox1.Text}']");
    if (node != null)
    {
      node.ChildNodes[0].InnerText = textBox1.Text;
      node.ChildNodes[1].InnerText = textBox2.Text;
      node.ChildNodes[2].InnerText = textBox3.Text;
      XmlCDataSection notes = doc.CreateCDataSection(textBox4.Text);
      node.ChildNodes[3].ReplaceChild(notes, node.ChildNodes[3].ChildNodes[0]);
    }
```

```
doc.Save($"{Application.StartupPath}\\employees.xml");
}
```

First, the code retrieves the <employee> node matching the selected employee ID by using the SelectSingleNode() method. Carefully note the XPath expression that is used. In XPath expressions, attributes are prefixed with the @ symbol. Thus @employeeid refers to the employeeid attribute of the <employee> node. The SelectSingleNode() method returns the selected node in the form of an XmlNode object. Before we proceed and change its contents, we need to ensure that the SelectSingleNode() has returned a node. This is done by checking whether the node returned is null or otherwise.

The XmlNode returned from the SelectSingleNode() method will be an <employee> node. That means it will have four child nodes: <firstname>, <lastname>, <homephone>, and <notes>. The InnerText property of these four child nodes is nothing but the text values of the corresponding node. Inside the if condition, the code sets the InnerText property of all four child nodes to the values from respective text boxes. There is one interesting thing to note here. The <notes> element contains free text that can feature special markup symbols such as <, >, and ". If we simply assign the InnerText property of the <notes> node to the new value, it can create problems when accessing the document later.

Remember that we wrote the contents of the <notes> node as a CDATA section to avoid just such a problem, so we must write the new data as a CDATA section as well. The CDATA section is represented by a class called XmlCDataSection. The CreateCDataSection() method of the XmlDocument class creates a new CDATA section with the supplied text (the entire text supplied is placed within <![CDATA[. . .]]>). To change the content of an existing CDATA section, the code calls the ReplaceChild() method of the XmlNode class. The ReplaceChild() method accepts the new node and the old node as parameters. The old node is then replaced with the new node.

After you make any changes to an XML document, the entire document must be saved to disk in order to persist the changes. This is accomplished using the Save() method of the XmlDocument class. The Save() method accepts the target path where you would like to save the file. In our example, because we want to overwrite the existing Employees.xml file with the modified version, we supply the same path as that of the original file.

Deleting Existing Content

Deleting an <employee> node requires finding it from the list of available employees based on the employee ID and then removing it from the document. The code that implements the delete feature is shown in Listing 2-15.

Listing 2-15. Deleting a Node

```
private void button3_Click(object sender, EventArgs e)
{
    XmlNode node = doc.SelectSingleNode($"//employee[@employeeid='{comboBox1.Text}']");
    if (node != null)
    {
        doc.DocumentElement.RemoveChild(node);
    }
    doc.Save($"{Application.StartupPath}\\employees.xml");
    UpdateLabel();
}
```

The code retrieves the node that we want to delete by using the SelectsSingleNode() method. To delete a node from the ChildNodes collection, the XmlNode class provides a method called RemoveChild(). The RemoveChild() method accepts a reference to the XmlNode that is to be removed from the ChildNodes collection. In our case, we want to remove the entire <employee> node, which is a child node of the <employees> root element. Hence the code calls the RemoveChild() method on the DocumentElement, that is, the root node of the document.

After the node is deleted, the file is saved to disk by using the Save() method of the XmlDocument class. The UpdateLabel() helper method simply updates the current record number displayed on the status label.

Adding New Content

The code that adds a new employee is a bit lengthier than our previous examples. It is more interesting too. You will now learn how to create XML document contents from the ground up. Creating elements, attributes, text nodes, and CDATA sections will all be demystified in this section.

First of all, let's count the elements, attributes, and nodes that we need to create in order to add a new employee to our XML document. Here is a list of nodes that we need to add:

- An <employee> element
- A <firstname> element
- A <lastname> element
- A <homephone> element
- A <notes> element
- An employeeid attribute for the <employee> element
- A text node for the <firstname> value
- A text node for the <lastname> value
- A text node for the <homephone> value
- A CDATA section for the <notes> value

Note one important thing: the text that appears as the value of the <firstname>, <lastname>, <homephone>, and <notes> elements is also treated as a node.

The complete code that implements an employee addition is shown in Listing 2-16.

Listing 2-16. Adding a New Node

```
private void button1_Click(object sender, EventArgs e)
{
  XmlElement employee = doc.CreateElement("employee");
  XmlElement firstname = doc.CreateElement("firstname");
  XmlElement lastname = doc.CreateElement("lastname");
  XmlElement homephone = doc.CreateElement("homephone");
  XmlElement notes = doc.CreateElement("notes");

  XmlAttribute employeeid = doc.CreateAttribute("employeeid");
  employeeid.Value = comboBox1.Text;
```

```
XmlText firstnametext = doc.CreateTextNode(textBox1.Text);
XmlText lastnametext = doc.CreateTextNode(textBox2.Text);
XmlText homephonetext = doc.CreateTextNode(textBox3.Text);
XmlCDataSection notestext = doc.CreateCDataSection(textBox4.Text);

employee.Attributes.Append(employeeid);
employee.AppendChild(firstname);
employee.AppendChild(lastname);
employee.AppendChild(homephone);
employee.AppendChild(notes);

firstname.AppendChild(firstnametext);
lastname.AppendChild(lastnametext);
homephone.AppendChild(homephonetext);
notes.AppendChild(notestext);

doc.DocumentElement.AppendChild(employee);
doc.Save($"{Application.StartupPath}\\employees.xml");

UpdateLabel();
}
```

The code creates five elements by using the CreateElement() method of the XmlDocument class. These five elements are <employee>, <firstname>, <lastname>, <homephone>, and <notes>. The CreateElement() method accepts the tag name of the element and returns an object of type XmlElement. Note that XmlElement inherits from the XmlNode class.

An attribute is represented by the XmlAttribute class and is created using the CreateAttribute() method of the XmlDocument class. The CreateAttribute() method accepts the attribute name as a parameter, in this case employeeid. The value of the attribute can be assigned by setting the Value property of the XmlAttribute class.

The code proceeds to create three text nodes that represent the values of the <firstname>, <lastname>, and <homephone> elements, respectively. Text nodes are represented by a class called XmlText. To create these text nodes, the code uses the CreateTextNode() method of the XmlDocument class. The CreateTextNode() method accepts the value of the text node as a parameter.

As I said earlier, the <notes> element contains character data (CDATA), and a CDATA section is represented by a class called XmlCDataSection. As we did before, we create the CDATA section by using the CreateCDataSection() method of the XmlDocument class.

This completes the element, attribute, and node creation. The code then proceeds to nest various elements as per the required XML structure.

All the attributes of an XmlNode are stored in its Attributes collection. To add the employeeid attribute to the <employee> element, the Append() method of Attributes collection is used. The Append() method accepts an instance of the XmlAttribute class.

The AppendChild() method of the XmlNode class accepts another XmlNode and makes it a child of the node on which AppendChild() has been called. The code calls the AppendChild() method on the <employee> element and adds all the remaining four elements as its children.

Next, the code adds all the text nodes and CDATA section to their respective parents by using the same AppendChild() method.

Finally, the entire <employee> node is appended to the DocumentElement, that is, the <employees> root node. Because we added a new node to the document, the Save() method is needed to save the changed document to disk.

Using Helper Methods

In the preceding code, we frequently used two helper methods: FillControls() and UpdateLabel(). These methods are shown in Listing 2-17.

Listing 2-17. Helper Methods Used in the Application

```
private void FillControls()
{
  XmlNode node = doc.DocumentElement.ChildNodes[CurrentNodeIndex];
  comboBox1.Text = node.Attributes["employeeid"].Value;
  textBox1.Text = node.ChildNodes[0].InnerText;
  textBox2.Text = node.ChildNodes[1].InnerText;
  textBox3.Text = node.ChildNodes[2].InnerText;
  textBox4.Text = node.ChildNodes[3].InnerText;
  UpdateLabel();
}

private void UpdateLabel()
{
  label6.Text = $"Employee {(CurrentNodeIndex + 1)} of {doc.DocumentElement.ChildNodes.
  Count}";
}
```

The FillControls() method retrieves a reference to the <employee> node to be displayed. The index for this node is indicated by the CurrentNodeIndex variable. The employeeid is retrieved from the Attributes collection of the node and displayed in the combo box. Other text boxes are populated with the InnerText of <firstname>, <lastname>, <homephone>, and <notes>, respectively.

The UpdateLabel() method simply sets the Text property of the navigation status label to the current employee index.

Dealing with Whitespace

You have learned how to read and write XML documents by using XmlDocument and associated classes. During various operations, we hardly bothered with whitespace. *Whitespace* includes characters such as space, tab, carriage return, and so on. By default, when you load the document (either via the Load() method or the LoadXml() method) or save the document (by using the Save() method), the XmlDocument class will ignore any whitespace. You can toggle this behavior by using a Boolean property called PreserveWhitespace. Setting this property to true will preserve the whitespace, whereas setting it to false will ignore it.

To see the difference the PreserveWhitespace property makes, let's create a simple application like the one shown in Figure 2-8.

Figure 2-8. *Importance of the PreserveWhiteSpace property*

The application consists of a check box that allows you to toggle whether to preserve the whitespace. When you click the Load Document button, it simply loads the Employees.xml file by using the Load() method and displays the entire content in a message box.

The code inside the Click event handler of the Load Document button is shown in Listing 2-18.

Listing 2-18. Loading a Document

```
private void button1_Click(object sender, EventArgs e)
{
  XmlDocument doc = new XmlDocument();
  doc.PreserveWhitespace = checkBox1.Checked;
  doc.Load($"{Application.StartupPath}\\employees.xml");
  MessageBox.Show(doc.InnerXml);
}
```

The code creates an instance of the XmlDocument class and sets its PreserveWhitespace property to the property selected via the check box. That means if the user selects the check box, true will be assigned; otherwise, false will be assigned. Then the Employees.xml file is loaded by using the Load() method. The complete content of the file is retrieved by using the InnerXml property of the XmlDocument instance and displayed in a message box.

Figure 2-9 shows the message box that is displayed when you deselect the check box. In contrast, Figure 2-10 shows the message box when the check box is selected.

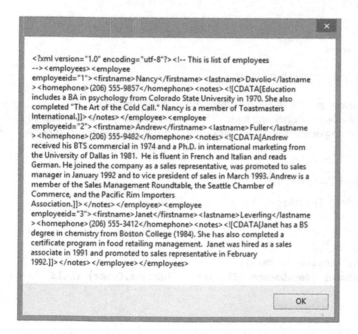

Figure 2-9. Output with the PreserveWhitespace property set to false

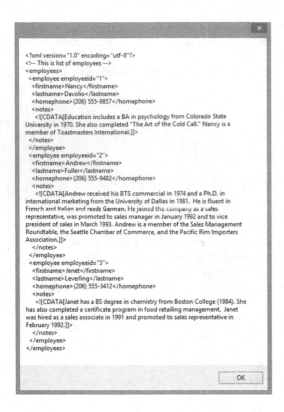

Figure 2-10. *Output with the PreserveWhitespace property set to true*

You can see the difference: the second message box shows that the whitespace is preserved.

Does the PreserveWhitespace property affect your parsing logic? The answer to this question is yes. To illustrate the effect of this property on the parsing of the document, let's modify the preceding application as shown in Listing 2-19.

Listing 2-19. Effect of the PreserveWhitespace Property

```
private void button1_Click(object sender, EventArgs e)
{
  XmlDocument doc = new XmlDocument();
  doc.PreserveWhitespace = checkBox1.Checked;
  doc.Load($"{Application.StartupPath}\\employees.xml");
  MessageBox.Show($"Employee node contains {doc.DocumentElement.ChildNodes.Count} child
  nodes");
}
```

The preceding code is almost identical to the previous example, but this time, the message box shows the total number of child nodes of the document element, that is, the root node <employees>. See Figures 2-11 and 2-12 for the resulting message boxes with the PreserveWhitespace property set to false and true, respectively.

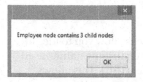

Figure 2-11. *Result when the PreserveWhitespace property is false*

Figure 2-12. *Result when the PreserveWhitespace property is true*

Surprised? We have three <employee> elements in our document. That means the <employees> node has three child nodes. The message box from Figure 2-11 is consistent with this fact. However, when you set the PreserveWhitespace property to true, the message box shows that the <employees> element has seven child nodes. Preserving whitespace added four child nodes to the <employees> element. These extra nodes are of type XmlWhiteSpace. If you are accessing various nodes by their indexes, toggling whitespace can cause your logic to fail. There is one more class related to whitespace: XmlSignificantWhitespace. The XmlSignificantWhitespace class represents whitespace between markup in a mixed content node.

It is important to understand the difference between XmlWhiteSpace and XmlSignificantWhitespace. Consider the markup shown in Listing 2-20.

Listing 2-20. Understanding the Difference Between the XmlWhiteSpace and XmlSignificantWhiteSpace Classes

```xml
<?xml version="1.0" ?>
<root>
  <fullname>Nancy Davolio</fullname>
  <address>
    507 - 20th Ave. E. Apt. 2A
    Seattle,
    WA 98122
    USA
  </address>
</root>
```

In the markup shown in Listing 2-20, there are several areas of whitespace. First, there is whitespace between tags such as <root>, <fullname>, and <address>. Remember that in XML, carriage returns and line feeds are also considered whitespace. The whitespace between various elements is used mainly to improve readability of the document and is represented by the XmlWhiteSpace class. Second, there is whitespace embedded in the content of the <address> node. For example, there is a carriage return and line feed after the text Seattle as well as WA 98122. This type of whitespace is represented by the XmlSignificantWhiteSpace class.

Dealing with Namespaces

The concept of XML namespaces is analogous to .NET namespaces. XML namespaces allow you to identify elements as part of a single group (a namespace) by uniquely qualifying element and attribute names used in an XML document. Each namespace is identified by a Uniform Resource Identifier (URI). This allows developers to combine information from different data structures in a single XML document without causing ambiguity and confusion among element names.

For example, assume that you have two XML fragments, one related to employees and another related to customers. Further assume that both fragments contain a tag called <name>. The problem is that when you mix them together, you have ambiguity for the <name> tag. XML namespaces come in handy in such situations.

To see how .NET Framework provides support for XML namespaces, we will modify Employees.xml, as shown in Listing 2-21.

Listing 2-21. XML Document with Namespaces

```xml
<?xml version="1.0" encoding="utf-8" ?>
<!-- This is list of employees -->
<emp:employees xmlns:emp="http://localhost/employees">
  <emp:employee employeeid="1">
    <emp:firstname>Nancy</emp:firstname>
    <emp:lastname>Davolio</emp:lastname>
    <emp:homephone>(206) 555-9857</emp:homephone>
    <emp:notes>
        <![CDATA[Education includes a BA in psychology from Colorado State University
        in 1970. She also completed "The Art of the Cold Call." Nancy is a member of
        Toastmasters International.]]>
    </emp:notes>
  </emp:employee>
  <emp:employee employeeid="2">
    <emp:firstname>Andrew</emp:firstname>
    <emp:lastname>Fuller</emp:lastname>
    <emp:homephone>(206) 555-9482</emp:homephone>
    <emp:notes>
        <![CDATA[Andrew received his BTS commercial in 1974 and a Ph.D.
        in international marketing from the University of Dallas in 1981. He is fluent
        in French and Italian and reads German. He joined the company as a sales
        representative, was promoted to sales manager in January 1992 and to vice president
        of sales in March 1993. Andrew is a member of the Sales Management Roundtable, the
        Seattle Chamber of Commerce, and the Pacific Rim Importers Association.]]>
    </emp:notes>
  </emp:employee>
  <emp:employee employeeid="3">
    <emp:firstname>Janet</emp:firstname>
    <emp:lastname>Leverling</emp:lastname>
    <emp:homephone>(206) 555-3412</emp:homephone>
    <emp:notes>
        <![CDATA[Janet has a BS degree in chemistry from Boston College (1984). She has also
        completed a certificate program in food retailing management. Janet was hired as a
        sales associate in 1991 and promoted to sales representative in February 1992.]]>
    </emp:notes>
  </emp:employee>
</emp:employees>
```

It's the same document, but we added a namespace to it. Look at the markup shown in bold. In the root element <employees>, we specified an XML namespace called emp with a URI http://localhost/employees. Though it is a common practice to use URLs as namespace URIs, any unique string would work. Note how all the tag names are prefixed with emp. You can access namespace details by using three properties of the XmlNode class: NamespaceURI, Prefix, and LocalName.

To illustrate how these properties are used, we will develop an application like the one shown in Figure 2-13.

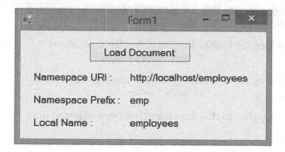

Figure 2-13. *Retrieving namespace details*

The application loads our new version of Employees.xml and extracts the NamespaceURI, Prefix, and LocalName properties of the document element. The namespace details are shown in labels. Listing 2-22 shows the Click event handler of the Load Document button.

Listing 2-22. Retrieving Namespace Details

```
private void button1_Click(object sender, EventArgs e)
{
  XmlDocument doc = new XmlDocument();
  doc.Load($"{Application.StartupPath}\\employees.xml");
  label4.Text = doc.DocumentElement.NamespaceURI;
  label5.Text = doc.DocumentElement.Prefix;
  label6.Text = doc.DocumentElement.LocalName;
}
```

The code loads the Employees.xml file by using the Load() method. It then simply retrieves the value of the NamespaceURI, Prefix, and LocalName properties. One thing to note is that these three properties are read-only properties. If you want to write these details, you must supply them while creating attributes, elements, and nodes from the XmlDocument class. Methods of the XmlDocument class, such as CreateElement() and CreateAttribute(), have appropriate overloads that allow you to specify namespace details.

Understanding Events of the XmlDocument Class

Whenever you modify an XML document, the XmlDocument class raises several events. These events follow a pre-and post-pattern. Pre-events are raised prior to the actual operation, whereas post-events are raised after the operation is over. These events are summarized in Table 2-3.

Table 2-3. *Events of the XmlDocument Class*

Event Name	Description
NodeChanging	This event is raised when the value of a node belonging to this document is about to be changed.
NodeChanged	This event is raised when the value of a node belonging to this document has been changed.
NodeRemoving	This event is raised when a node belonging to this document is about to be removed from the document.
NodeRemoved	This event is raised when a node belonging to this document has been removed from its parent.
NodeInserting	This event is raised when a node belonging to this document is about to be inserted into another node.
NodeInserted	This event is raised when a node belonging to this document has been inserted into another node.

Each of the events specified in the preceding table receives an event argument parameter of type XmlNodeChangedEventArgs. The XmlNodeChangedEventArgs class provides several properties. Some of them are listed in Table 2-4.

Table 2-4. *Properties of the XmlNodeChangedEventArgs Class*

Property	Description
Action	Supplies information about the action that is causing the node to change. This property is an enumeration of type XmlNodeChangedAction. Possible values include Change, Remove, and Insert.
OldParent	Returns the parent XmlNode of the node being changed prior to the operation.
NewParent	Returns the parent XmlNode of the node being changed after the operation.
OldValue	Returns the value of the node prior to the operation.
NewValue	Returns the value of the node after the operation is complete.
Node	Returns an XmlNode object representing the node being affected.

To see some of these events in action, we will modify the same employee data-entry application that we developed previously.

Modify the Form_Load event handler as shown in Listing 2-23.

Listing 2-23. Attaching Event Handlers

```
private void Form1_Load(object sender, EventArgs e)
{
  doc.Load($"{Application.StartupPath}\\employees.xml");

  doc.NodeChanged += new XmlNodeChangedEventHandler(doc_NodeChanged);
  doc.NodeInserted += new XmlNodeChangedEventHandler(doc_NodeInserted);
  doc.NodeRemoved += new XmlNodeChangedEventHandler(doc_NodeRemoved);
```

```
foreach (XmlNode node in doc.DocumentElement.ChildNodes)
{
   comboBox1.Items.Add(node.Attributes["employeeid"].Value);
}
FillControls();
}
```

Note the lines marked in bold. The code attaches event handlers to the NodeChanged, NodeRemoved, and NodeInserted events, respectively. These events are of delegate type XmlNodeChangedEventHandler.

The code in Listing 2-24 shows these event handlers.

Listing 2-24. Handling Events of the XmlDocument Class

```
void doc_NodeRemoved(object sender, XmlNodeChangedEventArgs e)
{
   MessageBox.Show($"Node {e.Node.Name} removed successfully!");
}

void doc_NodeInserted(object sender, XmlNodeChangedEventArgs e)
{
   MessageBox.Show($"Node {e.Node.Name} added successfully!");
}

void doc_NodeChanged(object sender, XmlNodeChangedEventArgs e)
{
   MessageBox.Show($"Node {e.Node.Name} changed successfully!");
}
```

The code in each event handler simply displays the node being affected in a message box. To test these events, you need to run the application and try updating, deleting, and adding new employees. You will find that with every such operation, the NodeChanged, NodeRemoved, and NodeInserted events are raised. Figure 2-14 shows a sample run of the application.

Figure 2-14. *Handling events of the XmlDocument class*

Summary

This chapter presented a detailed examination of the XmlDocument class—the .NET Framework's DOM parser. You worked with several other classes, including XmlNode, XmlElement, XmlAttribute, and XmlText. You learned how to load XML documents, how to navigate through them, how to read the content, and finally how to modify them. You also learned how whitespace and namespaces can be dealt with. Finally, you handled various events of XmlDocument that are raised when you change the document in some way.

You can build on what you have learned so far. For example, you can create your own custom extensions of XmlDocument and other classes by inheriting from them. Though the need to do so is rare, this task can be accomplished by inheriting from these classes and adding extra properties and methods.

CHAPTER 3

■ ■ ■

Reading and Writing XML Documents

Chapter 2 gave you a detailed understanding of the .NET Framework's DOM parser, that is, the XmlDocument class. You also learned when to use DOM parsers. In this chapter, you are going to learn about XML reader and writer classes. The topics discussed include the following:

- Using reader and writer classes

- Knowing when to use these classes instead of DOM

- Reading XML documents by using the XmlTextReader class

- Writing XML documents by using the XmlTextWriter class

- Dealing with non-textual data

What Are XML Readers and Writers?

DOM-based parsers are best suited for modifying XML documents that are small. However, with huge XML documents, DOM access can pose problems in terms of memory footprint and performance. In such cases, an alternative must be adopted so that we can read and write XML documents without these limitations. Traditionally, event-based parsers based on the SAX specifications were used to deal with such scenarios. The .NET answer, however, is a bit different.

The .NET Framework provides a pull-model parser in the form of a class called XmlReader. XmlReader provides read-only access to XML documents in a forward-only fashion. Though SAX and XmlReader sound similar, they behave differently. Any SAX-based parser essentially raises events as various parts of the XML document are encountered. Thus it works on a push model. On the other hand, the XmlReader class allows you to iterate through the document and access the required content rather than raising events. Thus it uses a pull model. As you will see later, this pull model is more flexible from a development point of view. The XmlReader class does not load the entire document in memory, resulting in a small memory footprint. Because it is read-only, it is faster too.

Just as XmlReader allows you to read XML documents, a class called XmlWriter allows you to write XML documents. Like XmlReader, XmlWriter also uses a forward-only model. However, it offers write-only functionality.

The XmlReader and XmlWriter classes are abstract classes. That means you will not be able to instantiate and use them directly in your code. Fortunately, the System.Xml namespace contains two ready-to-use classes that inherit from these base classes. Those classes are XmlTextReader and XmlTextWriter. The former inherits from XmlReader, whereas the latter inherits from XmlWriter.

© Bipin Joshi 2017
B. Joshi, *Beginning XML with C# 7*, https://doi.org/10.1007/978-1-4842-3105-0_3

When to Use Readers and Writers

In the previous section, you learned that DOM parsers are a poor choice when working with huge XML documents. In general, you can say that XmlReader is better suited when

- You need to only read the document.
- The document is huge.
- You need to keep the memory footprint small.
- You want to work with many XML documents that are reasonably large in size.
- You do not want to access various parts of the document randomly.

Similarly, XmlWriter is better suited when

- You want to only write content.
- You want to keep the memory footprint small.
- You are writing huge XML documents and looking for better performance.

Reader Classes

As you've seen, the XmlReader is an abstract class. That means you cannot instantiate it directly in your applications; you must inherit from it to make any use of it. Fortunately, the .NET Framework provides three implementations of the XmlReader class that you can use in your code. These implementations are discussed briefly in this section.

The XmlTextReader Class

The XmlTextReader class can be used to parse XML documents. This class has very fast parsing abilities. It checks that the underlying documents are well formed but does not validate them against a DTD or Schema.

The XmlValidatingReader Class

The XmlValidatingReader class can validate an XML document against a DTD or Schema.

The XmlNodeReader Class

The XmlNodeReader class allows you to read XML data from the DOM tree. The constructor of XmlNodeReader takes a parameter of type XmlNode. This XmlNode can be obtained as a result of an XPath query or directly from a DOM document. In terms of properties and methods, the XmlNodeReader class closely resembles the XmlTextReader class.

Reading XML Documents Using XmlTextReader

In this section, you learn the following:

- How to open XML documents by using the XmlTextReader class

- How to read and access the content

- How to deal with whitespace

- How to work with name tables

- How to deal with namespaces

Let's begin by opening XML documents. Throughout our examples, we will be using the same Employees.xml file that we used earlier in the book.

Opening XML Documents

To illustrate how XML documents can be opened for reading, we will develop a Windows Forms application like the one shown in Figure 3-1.

Figure 3-1. Reading XML documents by using XmlTextReader

The application allows you to choose the location from which the document is to be opened. The possible locations are URL, stream, or string. Depending on the choice, you need to enter the URL, filename, or XML string in the text box and click the Open Document button. Clicking the Open Document button opens the document and displays a success message box.

The XmlReader class can read an XML document from either a URL or a stream. The stream can by any kind of stream, such as a FileStream or MemoryStream. To read a string, first you need to read the string into a MemoryStream and then feed this MemoryStream to the XmlReader class. The code from Listing 3-1 shows these three techniques.

Listing 3-1. Loading an XML Document in XmlTextReader

```
private void button1_Click(object sender, EventArgs e)
{

  XmlTextReader reader;

  if (radioButton1.Checked)
  {
    reader = new XmlTextReader(textBox1.Text);
  }

  if (radioButton2.Checked)
  {
    FileStream stream=File.OpenRead(textBox1.Text);
    reader = new XmlTextReader(stream);
    //some processing code
    stream.Close();
    reader.Close();
  }

  if (radioButton3.Checked)
  {
    MemoryStream ms=new MemoryStream();
    byte[] data=ASCIIEncoding.ASCII.GetBytes(textBox1.Text);
    ms.Write(data,0,data.Length);
    reader = new XmlTextReader(ms);
    //some processing code
    ms.Close();
    reader.Close();
  }

  MessageBox.Show("XML Document Opened Successfully!");
}
```

■ **Note**   Make sure to import the System.Xml and System.IO namespaces before writing the preceding code. The XmlTextReader class resides in the System.Xml namespace, and the MemoryStream class resides in the System.IO namespace.

The code declares a variable of type XmlTextReader. It then checks to see which radio button has been selected. If the user wants to use a URL, a new instance of XmlTextReader is created by passing the URL in the constructor.

If the user decides to read the file from disk, it is first read into a stream. This is done by using the OpenRead() method of the File class. The OpenRead() method opens the specified file in read-only mode. The resulting FileStream is then passed in the constructor of the XmlTextReader class.

The third condition reads the string into MemoryStream. Note the use of the GetBytes() method to convert a string into a byte array. The resulting byte array is written to the MemoryStream object. Finally, this MemoryStream instance is supplied to the constructor of the XmlTextReader class.

A message box simply displays a message confirming that the document was opened successfully.

Reading Attributes, Elements, and Values

In this section, we are going to develop a Windows Forms application that will display a tree of various elements and their values. In the process, you will learn how to read attributes, elements, and text nodes from an XML document by using the XmlTextReader class.

The application is shown in Figure 3-2.

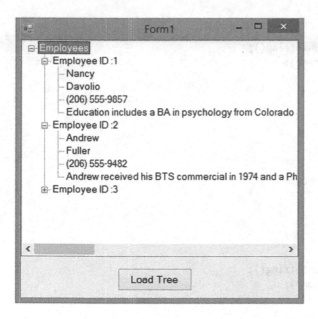

Figure 3-2. *Reading an XML document by using XmlTextReader*

The application consists of a TreeView control and a Button control. Clicking the Load Tree button displays the entire tree of nodes in the tree view as shown.

The core logic goes in the Click event handler of the Load Tree button and is shown in Listing 3-2.

Listing 3-2. Loading the Tree

```
private void button1_Click(object sender, EventArgs e)
{
  XmlTextReader reader =
    new XmlTextReader($"{Application.StartupPath}\\employees.xml");
  reader.WhitespaceHandling = WhitespaceHandling.None;
  TreeNode employeenode=null;
  TreeNode rootnode = null;

  while (reader.Read())
  {
    if (reader.NodeType == XmlNodeType.Element)
    {
      if (reader.Name == "employees")
      {
        rootnode = treeView1.Nodes.Add("Employees");
      }
```

```
      if (reader.Name == "employee")
      {
        string employeeid = reader.GetAttribute("employeeid");
        employeenode = new TreeNode("Employee ID :" + employeeid);
        rootnode.Nodes.Add(employeenode);
      }

      if (reader.Name == "firstname")
      {
        string firstname = reader.ReadElementString();
        TreeNode node = new TreeNode(firstname);
        employeenode.Nodes.Add(node);
      }

      if (reader.Name == "lastname")
      {
        reader.Read();
        string lastname = reader.Value;
        TreeNode node = new TreeNode(lastname);
        employeenode.Nodes.Add(node);
      }

      if (reader.Name == "homephone")
      {
        string homephone = reader.ReadElementString();
        TreeNode node = new TreeNode(homephone);
        cmployeenode.Nodes.Add(node);
      }

      if (reader.Name == "notes")
      {
        string notes = reader.ReadElementString();
        TreeNode node = new TreeNode(notes);
        employeenode.Nodes.Add(node);
      }
    }
    reader.Close();
}
```

The code creates an instance of the XmlTextReader class by passing the path of the XML file. The WhitespaceHandling property of XmlTextReader governs the behavior of the reader while reading whitespace. This property is an enumeration of type WhitespaceHandling and has three possible values: All, None, or Significant. We set WhitespaceHandling to ignore any whitespace. This will simplify our coding.

A while loop repeatedly calls the Read() method of XmlTextReader. The Read() method reads the next node from the file and returns true if the next node can be read successfully; otherwise, it returns false.

Inside the while loop, the code retrieves the type of node by using the NodeType property of the XmlTextReader class. The NodeType property is an enumeration of type XmlNodeType and can have values such as Attribute, CDATA, Comment, Element, EndElement, Text, Whitespace, SignificantWhitespace, and so on. Note that the start and end elements are represented separately. This is because, while scanning the document, the XmlTextReader class reads start elements (for example, <employee>) and end elements (for example, </employee>) separately. In our example, we are interested only in start elements and therefore the if condition checks only for a node type of Element.

The code then checks the name of each element. This is done by checking the Name property of the XmlTextReader class and executing code depending on the element name:

- If the element name is employees, the code adds the root node of the TreeView control.

- If the element name is employee, the code retrieves the employeeid attribute. To retrieve attribute values, XmlTextReader provides a method called GetAttribute(), which accepts the name of the attribute whose value is to be retrieved and returns the value as a string. A tree node is then added for this employee.

- If the element name is firstname, the text value inside it needs to be retrieved. This is done with the help of the ReadElementString() method, which returns the text content within the current element. For us it will return the first name of the employee. Note that you can also use ReadElementContentAsString() method for this purpose.

- The next if condition contains a variation on reading element values. It also illustrates the cursor-oriented model of XmlTextReader. When this if condition is triggered, the XmlTextReader is pointing to the <lastname> element. When we call the Read() method again, the cursor moves to the text node inside the <lastname> element. The Value property of XmlTextReader then returns the value of the text node.

- The values of the homephone and notes elements are read along the same lines.

Finally, the XmlTextReader is closed by using its Close() method.

Improving Performance by Using Name Tables

Whenever XmlTextReader parses any XML file, it creates a list of element names found in that document. This list is called a *name table*. Imagine that you are parsing dozens of separate files that have the same structure as Employees.xml. That means the XmlTextReader class needs to generate the same name table again and again. You can improve the efficiency of this process by supplying a ready-made name table, represented by the XmlNameTable class, for further parsing. The XmlNameTable class is an abstract class, but the .NET Framework provides a class called NameTable that inherits from it. You can therefore use this NameTable class in your code.

The code fragment in Listing 3-3 will use the name tables clear.

Listing 3-3. Using Name Tables

```
NameTable table = new NameTable();
XmlTextReader reader1 =
  new XmlTextReader($"{Application.StartupPath}\\employees1.xml",table);
//read using reader1 here
XmlTextReader reader2 =
  new XmlTextReader($"{Application.StartupPath}\\employees2.xml",table);
XmlTextReader reader3 =
  new XmlTextReader($"{Application.StartupPath}\\employees3.xml",table);
//process further
```

The code creates a new instance of the NameTable class, which will naturally be empty. Then an instance of XmlTextReader is created. This time the constructor takes two parameters: a filename and a NameTable. When you read the XML document for the first time, that is, using reader1, the supplied NameTable instance is populated. That means we have a NameTable ready for use. The same NameTable is supplied as a parameter to reader2 and reader3; they will in turn use this ready-made NameTable, thus improving the efficiency of the code.

Dealing with Namespaces

The XmlTextReader class has the same three XML namespace-related properties as the XmlNode class. The properties are NamespaceURI, Prefix, and LocalName. Their meaning is the same as discussed in Chapter 2.

■ **Note**   In the example you just developed, a concrete implementation of XmlReader in the form of XmlTextReader was used. You can also create a reader using the Create() method of the XmlReader class. You will learn about the Create() method in Chapter 5.

Moving Between Elements

In the previous example, you learned how to navigate through and read an XML document by using XmlTextReader. There are some additional methods of XmlTextReader that allow you to move between elements and read the content. This section presents these methods.

The ReadSubTree() Method

The ReadSubTree() method reads sub-nodes of the current node and returns the sub-tree as another XmlReader instance. This method is useful when you are parsing huge documents but want to work with a small section at a time. Figure 3-3 shows pictorially how this method works.

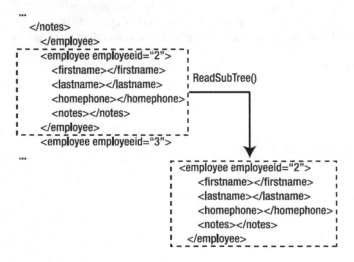

Figure 3-3. *Using the ReadSubTree() method*

From the figure, you can see that if you call ReadSubTree() when your XmlTextReader is on an <employee> node of the document, the ReadSubTree() method returns another XmlReader containing that <employee> node and all its child nodes (that is, the sub-tree of the <employee> node).

The ReadToDescendant() Method

The ReadToDescendant() method advances the XmlTextReader to the next occurrence of the specified child node. This method comes in handy when you want to jump to a specific node rather than sequentially moving there. Figure 3-4 shows how this method works.

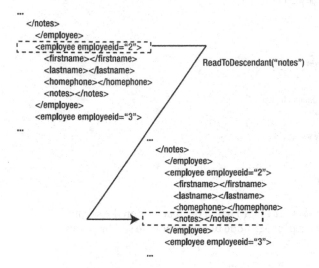

Figure 3-4. *Using the ReadToDescendant() method*

As shown in Figure 3-4, if you call the ReadToDescendant() method when you are on an <employee> node and specify notes as the target element, your reader jumps to the next <notes> element.

The ReadToFollowing() Method

The ReadToFollowing() method is very similar to the ReadToDescendant() method, with one difference. The ReadToDescendant() method can jump to the specified element only if it is a descendant of the current node, whereas the ReadToFollowing() method jumps to the first occurrence of the specified element, be it a descendant or not.

■ **Note**   Notice the difference between the ReadToDescendant() and ReadToFollowing() methods. Assuming that you are on the <employee> node of the second employee and wish to jump to the <notes> node of the same employee, you would use the ReadToDescendant() method. On the other hand, if you are on the <firstname> node of the second employee and wish to jump to the next occurrence of the <firstname> node, you would use the ReadToFollowing() method.

The ReadToNextSibling() Method

The ReadToNextSibling() method moves the reader from the current element to the next element at the same level. Figure 3-5 shows how this method works.

```
...
  </notes>
    </employee>
    <employee employeeid="2">
      <firstname></firstname>
      <lastname></lastname>
      <homephone></homephone>            ReadToNextSibling("employee")
      <notes></notes>
    </employee>
    <employee employeeid="3">                   ...
...                                          </notes>
                                               </employee>
                                               <employee employeeid="3">
                                                 <firstname></firstname>
                                                 <lastname></lastname>
                                                 <homephone></homephone>
                                                 <notes></notes>
                                               </employee>
                                               <employee employeeid="4">
                                             ...
```

Figure 3-5. *Using the ReadToNextSibling() method*

As you can see in Figure 3-5, if you call ReadToNextSibling() when the reader is on the second <employee> node, the reader will jump to the third <employee> node because they are sibling nodes.

The Skip() Method

The Skip() method skips the child elements and jumps directly to the next element. Skip() comes in handy when you want to bypass child nodes depending on a certain condition. Figure 3-6 shows how this method works.

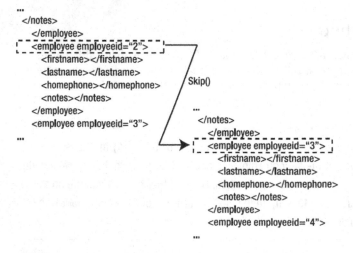

Figure 3-6. *Using the Skip() method*

Note the difference between the ReadToNextSibling() method and the Skip() method. The former advances the reader to the next sibling element, whereas the latter advances the reader to the next possible element (not necessarily a sibling node) after bypassing the child nodes.

Moving Between Attributes

The XmlTextReader class also provides four methods for moving between attributes. These methods, which are useful only for element nodes, are as follows:

- The MoveToAttribute() method accepts the index or name of the attribute to navigate to and moves the reader to the attribute.

- The MoveToFirstAttribute() method takes the reader to the first attribute of the current element.

- The MoveToNextAttribute() method moves the reader to the next attribute of the current element.

- The MoveToElement() method moves the reader back to the element node whose attributes were just read.

Figure 3-7 shows how all these methods work.

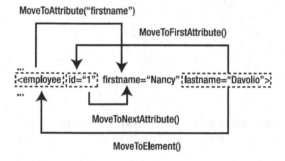

***Figure 3-7.** Moving between attributes*

As you can see in Figure 3-7, if you call MoveToAttribute() by passing firstname as the parameter, the reader moves to the firstname attribute. When you are on the lastname attribute, calling MoveToFirst() will take the reader to the id attribute. Calling MoveToNextAttribute() when the reader is on the id attribute will advance the reader to the firstname attribute. Finally, calling MoveToElement() from any attribute will take the reader back to the <employee> element.

Reading Content

In our previous example, we used the Value property and the ReadElementString() method to read content from an element. In this section, you are going to see a few more ways to read the content.

The ReadInnerXml() Method

The ReadInnerXml() method reads all the XML content inside the current node and returns it as a string. The returned string does not contain the current node markup. For example, if you call ReadInnerXml() when your reader is on the first <employee> element, the method will return the markup as shown in Listing 3-4.

Listing 3-4. Result of the ReadInnerXml() Method

```
<firstname>Nancy</firstname>
<lastname>Davolio</lastname>
<homephone>(206) 555-9857</homephone>
<notes>
<![CDATA[Education includes a BA in psychology from Colorado State University in 1970.
She also completed "The Art of the Cold Call." Nancy is a member of Toastmasters
International.]]>
</notes>
```

The ReadOuterXml() Method

The ReadOuterXml() method is similar to the ReadInnerXml() method, but the difference is that it also includes the markup of the current element. For example, if you call ReadOuterXml() while the reader is on the first <employee> element, ReadOuterXml() will return the markup as shown in Listing 3-5.

Listing 3-5. Result of the ReadOuterXml() Method

```
<employee employeeid="1">
  <firstname>Nancy</firstname>
  <lastname>Davolio</lastname>
  <homephone>(206) 555-9857</homephone>
  <notes>
<![CDATA[Education includes a BA in psychology from Colorado State University in 1970.
She also completed "The Art of the Cold Call." Nancy is a member of Toastmasters
International.]]>
  </notes>
</employee>
```

The ReadString() Method

The ReadString() method reads the contents of an element or a text node as a string. It simply returns all the text from the element until any markup is encountered. For example, look at the XML markup shown here:

```
<node1>
  <node2>
    Hello World <node3>This is some text</node3>
  </node2>
</node1>
```

If you call ReadString() when the reader is on <node2>, ReadString() will return Hello World and not the remaining markup from <node3>.

Writing XML Documents Using XmlTextWriter

In the previous sections, you learned how XmlTextReader can be used to read XML documents in a sequential fashion. Reading XML documents is just half of the story; often you also need to write XML documents.

The counterpart of XmlTextReader is another class called XmlTextWriter. The XmlTextWriter class allows you to quickly serialize XML documents to a file or any stream. The XmlTextWriter class inherits from an abstract class: XmlWriter. In this section, you will learn how this class can be used to write XML documents.

To see the XmlTextWriter class in action, you will build a Windows Forms application like the one shown in Figure 3-8.

Figure 3-8. *Using the XmlTextWriter class*

The application allows you to export data from any table of a SQL Server database into an XML file. As shown in Figure 3-8, the application accepts a database connection string, a table name to export, and the destination XML filename where the data is to be exported. The two radio buttons allow you to select whether all the columns are to be exported as elements or attributes in the resultant document. Clicking the Export Data button exports the data to the specified file.

The code needs to import the following namespaces:

```
using System.Data.SqlClient;
using System.Xml;
```

The System.Data.SqlClient namespace represents the SQL Server Data Provider of the .NET Framework and supplies classes related to data access such as SqlConnection and SqlCommand.

The Click event handler of the Export Data button contains the code shown in Listing 3-6.

Listing 3-6. Exporting Data

```csharp
private void button1_Click(object sender, EventArgs e)
{
    SqlConnection cnn = null;
    SqlCommand cmd = null;
    SqlDataReader reader = null;
    XmlTextWriter writer = null;

    try
    {
        cnn = new SqlConnection(textBox1.Text);
        cmd = new SqlCommand();
        cmd.Connection = cnn;
        cmd.CommandText = $"select * from {textBox2.Text}";
        cnn.Open();
        reader = cmd.ExecuteReader();
        writer = new XmlTextWriter(textBox3.Text, null);
        writer.WriteStartDocument();
        writer.WriteComment($"File exported on {DateTime.Now}");
        writer.WriteStartElement("table");
        while (reader.Read())
        {
            if (radioButton1.Checked)
            {
                writer.WriteStartElement("row");
                for (int i = 0; i < reader.FieldCount; i++)
                {
                    writer.WriteStartElement(reader.GetName(i));
                    writer.WriteString(reader.GetValue(i).ToString());
                    writer.WriteEndElement();
                }
                writer.WriteEndElement();
            }
            else
            {
                writer.WriteStartElement("row");
                for (int i = 0; i < reader.FieldCount; i++)
                {
                    writer.WriteAttributeString(reader.GetName(i),
                    reader.GetValue(i).ToString());
                }
                writer.WriteEndElement();
            }
        }
        writer.WriteEndElement();
    }
    catch (Exception ex)
    {
        MessageBox.Show(ex.Message);
    }
```

```
finally
{
    writer.Close();
    reader.Close();
    cnn.Close();
}
}
```

The code creates an instance of the SqlConnection class by passing a database connection string as the parameter. The SqlConnection class represents a database connection. In order to execute queries against a database, a SqlCommand object is created. The Connection property of SqlCommand represents the SqlConnection object through which the queries are to be executed. The CommandText property indicates the SQL query that is to be executed. In our example, we need to form a SELECT query by concatenating the name of the table as entered by the user (of course, in a real-world application, you should avoid forming queries this way due to security reasons).

The code then opens the connection with the help of the Open() method of SqlConnection. The ExecuteReader() method fires the SELECT statement as indicated by the CommandText property and returns a SqlDataReader object. The SqlDataReader object is like a read-only and forward-only cursor and allows you to iterate through the result set.

The code then proceeds to create an instance of the XmlTextWriter class, which can write directly to a disk file or to any stream. In our example, we write the data directly to the specified disk file. The second parameter of the constructor is the encoding of the data to be written. If this parameter is null, the XmlTextWriter writes the data as UTF-8 (Unicode Transformation Format, 8-bit encoding form) and omits the encoding attribute from the XML processing instruction. After the XmlTextWriter instance is ready, the actual writing process begins.

When the user selects to export all the columns as XML elements, the resultant document will bear the structure shown in Figure 3-9.

Figure 3-9. *Columns exported as elements*

The root element is <table>, which contains one or more <row> elements. Each <row> element further contains child elements, depending on the number of columns in the table. The child elements assume the same name as the database column name.

Similarly, when the user opts to export all the columns as attributes, the resultant document will bear the structure shown in Figure 3-10.

Figure 3-10. *Columns exported as attributes*

The root element is <table> again, which will contain one or more <row> elements. Each <row> element will have one or more attributes representing the column values. The attribute name will be the same as the column name.

All XML documents need to have the XML processing instruction at the top. To include this processing instruction, we call the WriteStartDocument() method. Then the code writes a comment specifying the date and time at which the file is exported. The WriteComment() method accepts the comment string and writes it into the document. The root element <table> is then written to the document by using the WriteStartElement() method, which accepts the name of the element to be written and writes it to the file. Note that you need not specify the < and > characters while specifying the element name. Thus, when you pass table as the parameter to the WriteStartElement() method, it writes <table> into the file.

The code now starts iterating through the available records. The Read() method of the SqlDataReader class advances the record pointer to the next row and reads values from that row. It returns true if the record can be read successfully; otherwise, it returns false.

Exporting Columns As Elements

If the columns are to be exported as elements (that is, the first radio button is selected), the `<row>` element will not have any attributes. A for loop iterates through all the columns of the current row. The `FieldCount` property of the `SqlDataReader` class returns the total number of columns in the result set. With each iteration of the for loop, a new element is created by using the `WriteStartElement()` method. This time the `WriteStartElement()` method accepts the column name returned by the `GetName()` method of the `SqlDataReader` class, which accepts the column index and returns the column name.

To write the actual value of the column, the `WriteString()` method is called. This method accepts the string to be written, which in our example is retrieved by using the `GetValue()` method of `SqlDataReader`. The `GetValue()` method accepts a column index and returns the contents as an object. The code then calls the `ToString()` method on the returned object to get its string representation.

After the element value is written, the code calls the `WriteEndElement()` method of `XmlTextWriter` to write the innermost end element to the file. The `WriteEndElement()` method correctly writes the end element depending on the nesting of the document.

When you run the application and export your table, your output should resemble Figure 3-9.

Exporting Columns As Attributes

If the column values are to be written as attributes instead of elements, a similar process is followed. This time, however, the code uses the `WriteAttributeString()` method of `XmlTextWriter` to write the attributes. The `WriteAttributeString()` method accepts two parameters: the name of the attribute and the value of the attribute.

After writing all the end elements, the code closes the `XmlTextWriter` by calling its `Close()` method. Similarly, `SqlDataReader` and `SqlConnection` are also closed.

When you run the application and export your table, your output should resemble Figure 3-10.

Specifying Character Encoding

In the previous example, we constructed the `XmlTextWriter` class by providing a filename and the character encoding. In this case, the encoding parameter was null, but there a few more encoding options in the .NET Framework. They are available as properties of the `Encoding` class, which resides in the `System.Text` namespace. Some of the common encodings are shown in Table 3-1.

Table 3-1. *Properties of the Encoding Class*

Property	Class Name	Description
Encoding.ASCII	ASCIIEncoding	Represents ASCII encoding. This encoding encodes Unicode characters as single 7-bit ASCII characters.
Encoding.Unicode	UnicodeEncoding	Represents Unicode encoding. This scheme encodes Unicode characters as 2 bytes (UTF-16).
Encoding.UTF7	UTF7Encoding	Represents UTF-7 encoding. The characters are stored in 7-bit format.
Encoding.UTF8	UTF8Encoding	Represents UTF-8 encoding. The characters are stored in 8-bit format. This is the default scheme.

Formatting the Output

If you open the XML document that we created in our previous example in Notepad, it will look like Figure 3-11.

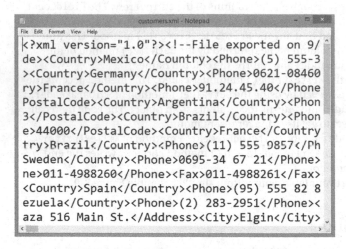

Figure 3-11. *XML document without any formatting*

What's the problem? Well, there is no problem as far as the document being well formed. It does follow all the rules of XML grammar. However, the document lacks proper formatting. Such documents are difficult for the human eye to read. Fortunately, the XmlTextWriter class provides several formatting options that help you create well-formatted documents.

To see how these formatting options work, you need to modify the previous application so it looks like the one shown in Figure 3-12.

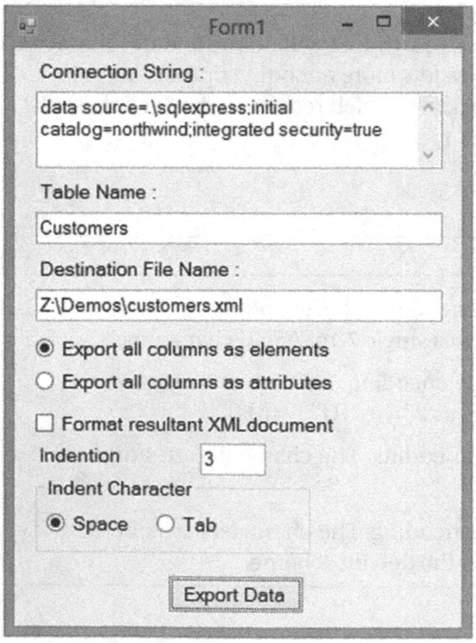

Figure 3-12. *Formatting the XML document*

The application has a check box that toggles whether the document will be formatted. You can specify the indention as well as the indent character (space or tab).

The code in the Click event handler of the Export Data button needs to be modified as shown in Listing 3-7.

Listing 3-7. Formatting XML Document While Writing

```
private void button1_Click(object sender, EventArgs e)
{
  SqlConnection cnn = new SqlConnection(textBox1.Text);
  SqlCommand cmd = new SqlCommand();
  cmd.Connection = cnn;
  cmd.CommandText = $"SELECT * FROM {textBox2.Text}";
  cnn.Open();
  SqlDataReader reader = cmd.ExecuteReader();
  XmlTextWriter writer = new XmlTextWriter(textBox3.Text, null);

  if(checkBox1.Checked)
  {
    writer.Formatting = Formatting.Indented;
    writer.Indentation = int.Parse(textBox4.Text);
    writer.IndentChar = (radioButton3.Checked ? ' ' : '\t');
  }

  writer.WriteStartDocument();
  writer.WriteComment($"File exported on {DateTime.Now}");
  writer.WriteStartElement("table");

  while (reader.Read())
  {
    if (radioButton1.Checked)
    {
      writer.WriteStartElement("row");
      for (int i = 0; i < reader.FieldCount; i++)
      {
        writer.WriteStartElement(reader.GetName(i));
        writer.WriteString(reader.GetValue(i).ToString());
        writer.WriteEndElement();
      }
      writer.WriteEndElement();
    }
    else
    {
      writer.WriteStartElement("row");
      for (int i = 0; i < reader.FieldCount; i++)
      {
        writer.WriteAttributeString(reader.GetName(i),
                                    reader.GetValue(i).ToString());
      }
      writer.WriteEndElement();
    }
  }
}
```

```
    writer.WriteEndElement();
    writer.Close();
    reader.Close();
    cnn.Close();
}
```

Note the code marked in bold. The `Formatting` property of `XmlTextWriter` governs whether the document will be formatted. The `Formatting` property is an enumeration of type `Formatting` and contains two possible values: None and `Indented`. The `Indentation` property of `XmlTextWriter` specifies the number of indent characters to be written in the document. This property is useful only if `Formatting` is set to `Indented`. The `IndentChar` property holds the character to be used for indentation. Though you can specify any valid character for `IndentChar`, space and tab are commonly used.

If you export the `Customers` table after making the preceding modifications, the resultant document should resemble Figure 3-13.

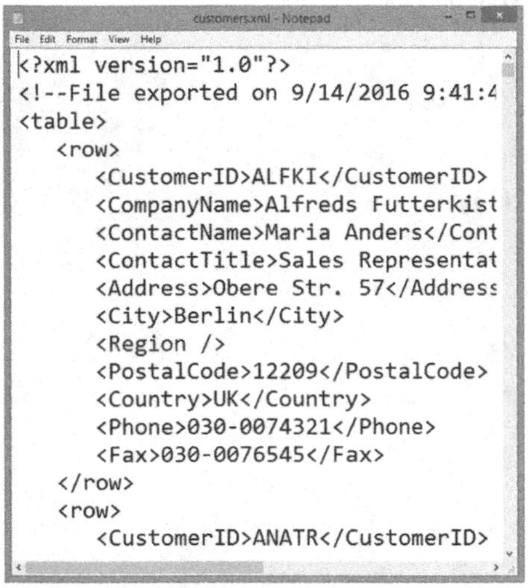


```
<?xml version="1.0"?>
<!--File exported on 9/14/2016 9:41:4
<table>
    <row>
        <CustomerID>ALFKI</CustomerID>
        <CompanyName>Alfreds Futterkist
        <ContactName>Maria Anders</Cont
        <ContactTitle>Sales Representat
        <Address>Obere Str. 57</Address
        <City>Berlin</City>
        <Region />
        <PostalCode>12209</PostalCode>
        <Country>UK</Country>
        <Phone>030-0074321</Phone>
        <Fax>030-0076545</Fax>
    </row>
    <row>
        <CustomerID>ANATR</CustomerID>
```

Figure 3-13. *Well-formatted XML document*

Much better than the previous one, isn't it?

Though not covered by our application, you can also set the `QuoteChar` property to decide which character to use for enclosing attribute values. The default value for `QuoteChar` is the double-quote character.

Including Namespace Support

Recall from Chapter 2 and the earlier discussion in this chapter that XML namespaces provide a method for uniquely qualifying element and attribute names used in an XML document by associating them with a namespace. When you create XML documents by using `XmlTextWriter`, you may need to include namespace support for the resultant document. That is what you are going to see in this section.

Various methods of `XmlTextWriter`, such as `WriteStartElement()`, provide overloads that can be used to specify namespace and prefix information. To see how these overloads can be used, you need to modify the previous application so it looks like the one shown in Figure 3-14.

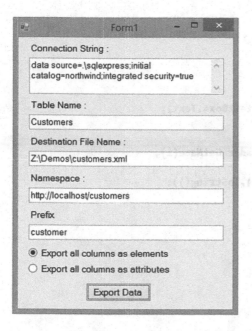

Figure 3-14. *Namespace support in XmlTextWriter*

As you can see in Figure 3-14, there are text boxes for accepting the namespace URI and prefix from the user. The modified code that adds namespace support is shown in Listing 3-8.

Listing 3-8. Namespace Support in XmlTextWriter

```
private void button1_Click(object sender, EventArgs e)
{
  SqlConnection cnn = new SqlConnection(textBox1.Text);
  SqlCommand cmd = new SqlCommand();
  cmd.Connection = cnn;
  cmd.CommandText = $"SELECT * FROM {textBox2.Text}";
  cnn.Open();
  SqlDataReader reader = cmd.ExecuteReader();
  XmlTextWriter writer = new XmlTextWriter(textBox3.Text, null);
  writer.WriteStartDocument();
  writer.WriteComment($"File exported on {DateTime.Now}");
  writer.WriteStartElement(textBox5.Text, "table", textBox4.Text);

  while (reader.Read())
  {
    if (radioButton1.Checked)
    {
      writer.WriteStartElement(textBox5.Text, "row", textBox4.Text);
      for (int i = 0; i < reader.FieldCount; i++)
      {
        writer.WriteStartElement(textBox5.Text, reader.GetName(i),
                                 textBox4.Text);
        writer.WriteString(reader.GetValue(i).ToString());
```

```
      writer.WriteEndElement();
    }
    writer.WriteEndElement();
  }
  else
  {
    writer.WriteStartElement(textBox5.Text, "row", textBox4.Text);
    for (int i = 0; i < reader.FieldCount; i++)
    {
      writer.WriteAttributeString(textBox5.Text, reader.GetName(i),
                                  textBox4.Text,
                                  reader.GetValue(i).ToString());
    }
    writer.WriteEndElement();
  }
}
writer.WriteEndElement();
writer.Close();
reader.Close();
cnn.Close();
}
```

Notice the lines marked in bold. The WriteStartElement() and WriteAttributeString() methods have an overload that accepts a prefix and namespace URI. If you create XML documents by using these overloads, your document should resemble Figure 3-15.

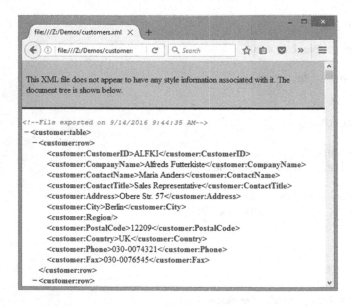

Figure 3-15. *XML document with namespaces and prefix added*

Notice how the namespace has been added to the <table> element:

```
<customer:table xmlns:customer="http://localhost/customers">
```

Also notice how each element now bears the prefix.

Dealing with Nontextual Data

Up until now, we have been using XmlReader and XmlWriter to read textual data. However, at times you may need to deal with nontextual data as well. For example, you may want to serialize image files or binary files as XML data in order to pass it over the Internet in a firewall-friendly way. Thankfully, both XmlTextReader and XmlTextWriter provide ways to handle such situations.

To help you understand how XmlTextReader and XmlTextWriter can be used to work with nontextual data, we will develop an application like the one shown in Figure 3-16.

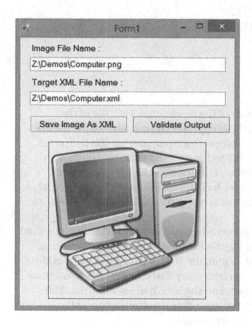

Figure 3-16. *Dealing with nontextual data*

The application allows you to read any image file and serialize it as an XML document. You can specify the source image filename and the destination XML filename in the text boxes. After you save the image as an XML document, you can validate whether the serialized image is correct by loading it in a picture box.

Serializing Data

Listing 3-9 shows the Click event handler of the Save Image as XML button.

Listing 3-9. Writing Base64 Data

```
private void button1_Click(object sender, EventArgs e)
{
  XmlTextWriter writer = new XmlTextWriter(textBox2.Text, null);
  FileStream fs = File.OpenRead(textBox1.Text);
  byte[] data = new byte[fs.Length];
  fs.Position = 0;
  fs.Read(data, 0, data.Length);
  fs.Close();
  writer.WriteStartDocument();
  writer.WriteStartElement("imagefile");
  writer.WriteAttributeString("filename", textBox1.Text);
  writer.WriteAttributeString("size", data.Length.ToString());
  writer.WriteBase64(data,0,data.Length);
  writer.WriteEndElement();
  writer.Close();
}
```

The code creates an XmlTextWriter object by passing the path of the destination XML file to the constructor. Then a FileStream is created for reading data from the image file. The contents of the file are read by using the Read() method of the FileStream class, which accepts three parameters: the byte array to read the data into, the start index in the byte array from where the writing should start, and the length of data to read. The XmlTextWriter then starts writing the document. It first writes the XML processing instruction and the <imagefile> element. The <imagefile> element has two attributes: filename and size. The filename attribute stores the complete path of the image file that is being serialized as XML. The size attribute contains the size of the source image file.

Image files contain nontextual data. You have a couple of options when you want to serialize nontextual data into XML files. You can use either hexadecimal encoding or Base64 encoding for the serialization. In our example, we use Base64 encoding. To write data into Base64 format, the XmlTextWriter class provides a method called WriteBase64(), which accepts three parameters: a byte array that contains the nontextual data, the index of the byte array from which the writing should start, and the length of data to write. The WriteBase64() method writes the supplied byte array as a Base64 string inside the destination XML element. Figure 3-17 shows how the XML file looks after serializing an image file.

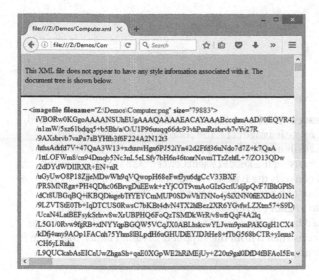

Figure 3-17. Image file serialized in Base64 format

Now that you know how to write nontextual data by using XmlTextWriter, you're ready to see how to use XmlTextReader to read the document back.

Deserializing Data

The Click event handler of the Validate Document button contains the code shown in Listing 3-10.

Listing 3-10. Reading Base64 Data

```
private void button2_Click(object sender, EventArgs e)
{
  XmlTextReader reader = new XmlTextReader(textBox2.Text);
  reader.WhitespaceHandling = WhitespaceHandling.None;

  while (reader.Read())
  {
    if (reader.NodeType == XmlNodeType.Element)
    {
      if (reader.Name == "imagefile")
      {
        int length = int.Parse(reader.GetAttribute("size"));
        string filename = reader.GetAttribute("filename");
        byte[] imagedata = new byte[length];
        int i = reader.ReadElementContentAsBase64(imagedata, 0, length);
        MemoryStream ms = new MemoryStream();
        ms.Write(imagedata, 0, imagedata.Length);
        Image image = Image.FromStream(ms);
```

```
        pictureBox1.Image = image;
        ms.Close();
      }
    }
  }
}
```

The code creates an instance of the XmlTextReader class by passing the XML document we just created. It then starts reading the document. If the element name is imagefile, the code reads the two attributes filename and size. Based on the value of the size attribute, a byte array is created with that much capacity. The contents of the <imagefile> element are read by using the ReadElementContentAsBase64() method.

The ReadElementContentAsBase64() method converts the Base64 encoded string into a byte array. The method returns an integer indicating the number of bytes written to the array. The byte array filled by the ReadElementContentAsBase64() is written to a MemoryStream object; the MemoryStream is then converted into an Image object. This is accomplished by using the FromStream() static method of the Image class, which returns an instance of the Image class constructed from the supplied stream. Finally, the Image instance is assigned to the Image property of the picture box control.

Summary

This chapter covered two important classes: XmlTextReader and XmlTextWriter. They are implementations of the abstract base classes XmlReader and XmlWriter, respectively. The XmlTextReader class represents a read-only parser that can parse XML documents very quickly. Because it does not load the entire XML document in memory, its memory footprint is small. It provides a cursor-oriented model to read the XML documents. The XmlTextWriter class allows you to quickly create XML documents and serialize nontextual data in Base64 or hexadecimal format.

You can also create your own custom readers and writers by inheriting from the XmlReader and XmlWriter abstract classes.

CHAPTER 4

Accessing XML Documents Using the XPath Data Model

In Chapters 2 and 3, you learned how to read and write XML documents by using the XmlDocument, XmlReader, and XmlWriter classes. These classes allow you to access the underlying documents, but by themselves they hardly provide a way to query and retrieve the data. That is why we need something that allows us to navigate, query, and retrieve data from XML documents easily and efficiently. The XPath standard is designed to do just that.

The .NET Framework namespace System.Xml.XPath provides a complete set of classes that allow you to query and retrieve data from an XML document by using the XPath data model. Recollect that in Chapter 2 we used the SelectNodes() and SelectSingleNode() methods that use XPath expressions. In this chapter, I discuss XPath at length. Specifically, you will learn about the following:

- The location path, axis, and node tests

- The XPath built-in functions

- How to use the XPathNavigator class along with XPath

- How to read and write XML data by using the XPathNavigator class

Overview of XPath

XPath provides a way to query and select a part of an XML document. To work with XPath expressions, you must understand some of the basic terminology. Specifically, you must be comfortable with the following terms:

- Location path

- Axis

- Node tests

- Predicates

© Bipin Joshi 2017
B. Joshi, *Beginning XML with C# 7*, https://doi.org/10.1007/978-1-4842-3105-0_4

Location Path

We are all familiar with the Windows file system. In the file system, each file has a path and we denote that path by using a specific notation. Similarly, various parts of an XML document, such as elements and attributes, also have a location. The location is indicated by a specific XPath syntax called the *location path*, which allows you to select a set of nodes from an XML document. A location path consists of an axis, a node test, and predicates.

Axis

When dealing with file system paths, we normally start with the drive letter. Thus the drive letter forms the basis for locating the file. A similar role is played by the axis for XML documents. The *axis* partitions the XML document based on the current node, so by using an axis you specify the starting point to apply node tests and predicates. The available axes are listed in Table 4-1.

Table 4-1. *XPath Axes*

Axis	Description
Self	Represents the current node (often the context node)
Child	Represents the children of the context node
Parent	Represents the parent of the context node
Attribute	Represent attributes of the context node
Descendant	Represents all the child nodes of the context node
Ancestor	Represents parent, grandparent, and so on until the document root
Following	Represents all the nodes that come after the context node
Following-sibling	Represents the sibling nodes following the context node
Preceding	Represents all the nodes that come before the context node
Preceding-sibling	Represents the preceding sibling of the context node

Node Tests

Node tests allow you to test elements and node types for a certain condition and return the selected elements or nodes. You can use the asterisk (*) character to indicate all the nodes. Some of the commonly used node tests are as follows:

- Testing elements with the same name as the supplied element name
- Testing all the nodes of a specific axis
- Testing all the text elements of a specific axis
- Testing all the comments of a specific axis
- Testing all the processing instructions of a specific axis

Predicates

Predicates are Boolean expressions that are used to further filter the nodes selected by the axis and node test. The XPath specifications provide a good number of functions that you can use to form predicates. The return values of these functions can be compared or checked with the help of familiar operators, such as =, !=, <, >, <=, >=, and so on.

Putting It All Together

Now that you know the meaning of the XPath terms, let's see what a location path looks like. The general syntax of a location path is given here:

```
Axis::node-test[predicate]
```

The axis is separated from the rest of the path by the :: operator. The node test typically contains a series of nodes, that is, a path. Finally, the predicate is specified in a set of square brackets. Here is an example of a location path:

```
following::employee[@employeeid='2']
```

The preceding location path points to the employee node following the current node whose employeeid attribute is 2.

Here are the XPath expressions that we used in Chapter 2:

```
//employee[./firstname/text()='some_text']
//employee[@employeeid='1']
```

In both cases, the axis is the root node as indicated by //. The node test consists of a single node (employee). The predicate for the first expression tests whether the text value of the firstname node of the current employee node matches some specific text. The predicate for the second expression checks whether the employeeid attribute (the attribute axis can be abbreviated as @) of the current employee node is 1.

XPath Functions

The XPath specification provides several built-in functions. These functions can be grouped in the following way:

- Functions that work on a set of nodes
- Functions that return a Boolean value
- Functions that work on strings
- Functions that work on numbers

These functions are listed in Tables 4-2 through 4-5.

Table 4-2. *Functions That Work on a Set of Nodes*

Function Name	Description
last()	Returns the number of nodes in the current node set
position()	Returns the index of the context node in the current node set
count()	Returns the total number of nodes in the given node set
id()	Returns a node set containing nodes with an ID attribute matching the specified value
name()	Returns the fully qualified name of the specified node
text()	Returns the text of the specified node
local-name()	Returns the local name of the node
namespace-uri()	Returns the namespace of the node

Table 4-3. *Functions That Return Boolean Values*

Function Name	Description
not()	Returns true if the supplied value is false; otherwise, returns false
true()	Returns true
false()	Returns false

Table 4-4. *Functions That Work on Strings*

Function Name	Description
concat()	Returns a concatenated string
starts-with()	Returns true if the string starts with the specified letters
contains()	Returns true if the string contains the specified string
substring()	Returns part of the specified string
string-length()	Returns the number of characters in the string
translate()	Replaces characters from a string with the specified characters

Table 4-5. *Functions That Work on Numbers*

Function Name	Description
number()	Converts the specified string to its equivalent number
sum()	Returns the sum of numbers
floor()	Returns a number rounded down to the next integer
ceiling()	Returns a number rounded up to the next integer
round()	Returns a number rounded to the nearest integer

Now that you have a good understanding of XPath, location paths, and XPath functions, let's delve further into the .NET Framework's XPath data model.

The XPath Data Model

The XPath data model of the .NET Framework relies on a class called XPathNavigator residing in the System.Xml.XPath namespace. The XPathNavigator class is an abstract class and provides a cursor-based navigation model for the underlying XML data. It also allows you to edit XML documents. You can obtain an XPathNavigator instance from any class that implements the IXPathNavigable interface. The classes that already implement this interface are XmlDocument and XPathDocument.

You have already worked with the XmlDocument class and hence it needs no explanation. The XPathDocument class, which resides in the System.Xml.XPath namespace, provides a read-only representation of an XML document using the XPath data model. It loads the document in memory and naturally provides fast access to various parts of the document.

The XPathNavigator instance returned from XmlDocument is editable, whereas that returned by XPathDocument is read-only.

Creating XPathNavigator

You can obtain an instance of XPathNavigator from either XmlDocument or XPathDocument. Both of these classes implement the IXPathNavigable interface and provide a method called CreateNavigator() that creates and returns an object of type XPathNavigator.

To see how these classes can be used, you need to develop a Windows Forms application like the one shown in Figure 4-1.

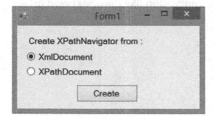

Figure 4-1. *Creating XPathNavigator*

The application consists of two radio buttons that allow you to select whether to use XmlDocument or XPathDocument to create your XPathNavigator. When you click the Create button, the XPathNavigator instance is created depending on the selected radio button. Note that you need to import the System.Xml and System.Xml.XPath namespaces before you write any code. Listing 4-1 shows the code from the Click event handler of the Create button.

Listing 4-1. Creating XPathNavigator

```
private void button1_Click(object sender, EventArgs e)
{
  XPathNavigator navigator = null;
  if (radioButton1.Checked)
  {
    XmlDocument doc = new XmlDocument();
```

```
    doc.Load($"{Application.StartupPath}\\employees.xml");
    navigator = doc.CreateNavigator();
}
else
{
    XPathDocument doc =
        new XPathDocument($"{Application.StartupPath}\\employees.xml");
    navigator = doc.CreateNavigator();
}
MessageBox.Show("Navigator created successfully!");
}
```

The code begins by declaring a variable of type XPathNavigator at the top of the event handler. It then checks which radio button is selected. If the XPathNavigator is to be created from XmlDocument, it creates an instance of the XmlDocument class. It then loads the Employees.xml file with the help of the Load() method of XmlDocument. The CreateNavigator() method of XmlDocument is then called to create and return an instance of the XPathNavigator class.

If the navigator is to be created from XPathDocument, the code creates an instance of the XPathDocument class. There are several overloads on the constructor of this class; our code uses the one that accepts the path to the XML file. The CreateNavigator() method of XPathDocument creates and returns an instance of XPathNavigator. Finally, a message box is displayed just to report the success of the operation.

Navigating an XML Document Using XPathNavigator

In the previous section, you learned to create XPathNavigator from XmlDocument and XPathDocument. In this section, you will see how to use XPathNavigator and access various elements and attributes.

To work through this section, you need to create a Windows Forms application like the one shown in Figure 4-2.

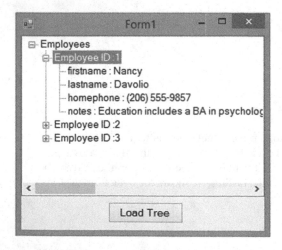

Figure 4-2. *Navigating through XPathNavigator*

The application consists of a TreeView and a button. After you click the Load Tree button, the TreeView is populated with employee information from the Employees.xml file. The Click event handler of the Load Tree button contains the code shown in Listing 4-2.

Listing 4-2. Navigating by Using XPathNavigator

```
private void button1_Click(object sender, EventArgs e)
{
  XPathDocument doc =
    new XPathDocument($"{Application.StartupPath}\\employees.xml");
  XPathNavigator navigator = doc.CreateNavigator();
  navigator.MoveToRoot();
  navigator.MoveToFirstChild();

  TreeNode root = treeView1.Nodes.Add("Employees");

  while (navigator.MoveToNext())
  {
    if (navigator.HasChildren)
    {
      navigator.MoveToFirstChild();
      do
      {
        string id = navigator.GetAttribute("employeeid", "");
        TreeNode empnode = new TreeNode($"Employee ID :{id}");
        root.Nodes.Add(empnode);
        navigator.MoveToFirstChild();

        do
        {
          string name = navigator.Name;
          TreeNode node = new TreeNode($"{name} : {navigator.Value}");
          empnode.Nodes.Add(node);
        } while (navigator.MoveToNext());

        navigator.MoveToParent();
      } while (navigator.MoveToNext());
    }
  }
}
```

The code begins by creating an instance of the XPathDocument class by passing the path of the XML file to its constructor. It then creates an XPathNavigator by calling the CreateNavigator() method of the XPathDocument class. We need to iterate through the document from the root and hence we call the MoveToRoot() method of XPathNavigator. This method moves the cursor of the XPathNavigator to the root of the document. Note that here the root of the document is the node that contains the entire tree of nodes. Because we want to start the iteration from the <employees> node, we call the MoveToFirstChild() method. Calling this method will place the navigator cursor at the <employees> node. A root node of the TreeView is then added.

Next there are three loops. The outermost loop iterates through all the child nodes of the root node. In our case, this loop will be executed just once, because there is only one <employees> node. The second loop iterates through all the <employee> nodes, whereas the innermost loop iterates through the child nodes of the <employee> node, that is, the <firstname>, <lastname>, <homephone>, and <notes> nodes.

The outermost loop uses the MoveToNext() method of the XPathNavigator class to advance the cursor onto the next node. It then decides whether there are any <employee> nodes using the HasChildren property. The HasChildren property returns true if there are child nodes to the current node; otherwise, it returns false. If there are <employee> nodes, the cursor is moved to the first <employee> node by calling the MoveToFirstChild() method, which moves the navigator cursor to the first child node.

Now the code starts iterating through all the <employee> nodes. With each iteration, the value of the employee attribute is retrieved by using the GetAttribute() method. This method accepts two parameters: the name of the attribute to retrieve and the attribute namespace. Because our document does not contain any namespaces, an empty string is passed as the second parameter. A TreeView node is added for that employee ID. The cursor is then moved to the first child node of the <employee> node by using the MoveToFirstChild() method we discussed earlier. After this call, the cursor will be on the <firstname> node.

Now the innermost loop starts. With each iteration, the name of the node is retrieved by using the Name property, and the value of the node is retrieved by using the Value property. The same process is carried out for all the child nodes, that is, <firstname>, <lastname>, <homephone>, and <notes>.

After the innermost loop is finished, the navigator cursor is moved back to the parent <employee> node. This is done with the help of the MoveToParent() method, which moves the cursor pointer to the parent node of the current node. The same process is repeated for the remaining <employee> nodes.

Selecting Nodes

This chapter began with a brief overview of XPath and its vocabulary, including terms such as *axis*, *node test*, *predicate*, and *function*. You might be wondering where they come into the picture. It's time now to see those features in action.

To test various XPath expressions, we will create a simple application that looks like the one shown in Figure 4-3.

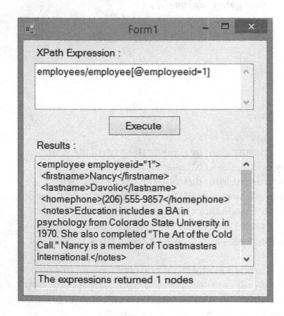

Figure 4-3. *Executing XPath expressions*

The application consists of a text box positioned at the top to enter XPath expressions. After you click the Execute button, the given expression is executed and its results are displayed in another text box at the bottom. The label at the bottom displays the total number of rows returned by the expression. Listing 4-3 shows the Click event handler of the Execute button.

Listing 4-3. Using the Select() Method

```
private void button1_Click(object sender, EventArgs e)
{
  XPathDocument doc =
    new XPathDocument($"{Application.StartupPath}\\employees.xml");
  XPathNavigator navigator = doc.CreateNavigator();
  XPathNodeIterator iterator = navigator.Select(textBox1.Text);
  try
  {
    label3.Text = $"The expressions returned {iterator.Count} nodes";
    if (iterator.Count > 0)
    {
      while (iterator.MoveNext())
      {
        textBox2.Text = iterator.Current.OuterXml;
      }
    }
    else
    {
      textBox2.Text = "No results";
    }
  }
  catch (Exception ex)
  {
    MessageBox.Show(ex.Message);
  }
}
```

The code creates an instance of XPathDocument by passing the path of the Employees.xml file. Then an XPathNavigator is obtained by using the CreateNavigator() method of XPathDocument. The code then calls the Select() method of XPathNavigator, which accepts an XPath expression and returns an instance of XPathNodeIterator.

The XPathNodeIterator class allows you to iterate through the returned nodes and has a number of properties and methods to assist you. To start with, the Count property tells you how many nodes were selected by the Select() method. After you are satisfied that there were some results, you can iterate through the selected nodes by using the MoveNext() method. On each node, you then use the Current property to get a reference to the XPathNavigator positioned at the current node. You can then call any of the methods and properties of XPathNavigator.

In our example, we simply display the OuterXml property of the underlying XPathNavigator in a text box. Though not used in our example, the CurrentPosition property of XPathNodeIterator returns the current index of the node being accessed.

Now let's try some XPath expressions by using our application. Some XPath expressions relevant to our XML document (Employees.xml) are given in Table 4-6.

Table 4-6. *Examples of XPath Expressions*

Purpose	Expression
To select an employee whose employee ID is 1	`employees/employee[@employeeid=1]`
To select the employee whose first name is Andrew	`employees/employee[firstname/text()='Andrew']`
To select the last employee from the document	`employees/employee[last()]`
To select the employee whose index is 2	`employees/employee[position()=2]`
To select an employee whose name contains *Nancy*	`employees/employee[contains(firstname, 'Nancy')]`
To select the name of the first employee	`employees/employee/firstname[text()]`

Selecting Single Nodes

The `Select()` method returns all the nodes that are obtained after evaluating the XPath expression. There is a method called `SelectSingleNode()` that executes the supplied XPath expression and returns an `XPathNavigator` object (and not an `XPathNodeIterator`) that contains the first matching node for the specified expression. You can then use the `XPathNavigator` object to navigate through the nodes. `SelectSingleNode()` comes in handy when you know that your XPath expression is going to return just one node. For example, in our document we can use `SelectSingleNode()` to extract an employee matching a specific employee ID.

To illustrate the use of `SelectSingleNode()`, you need to develop an application like the one shown in Figure 4-4.

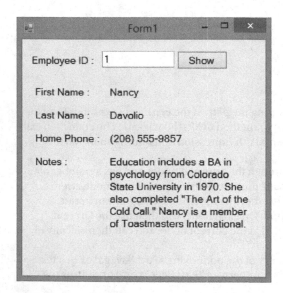

Figure 4-4. *Using the SelectSingleNode() method*

The application contains a text box to accept an employee ID and nine labels. Clicking the Show button displays details of an employee, and because the employee ID is unique in Employees.xml, we can safely use SelectSingleNode() here. Listing 4-4 shows the relevant code.

Listing 4-4. Calling the SelectSingleNode() Method

```
private void button1_Click(object sender, EventArgs e)
{
  XPathDocument doc =
    new XPathDocument($"{Application.StartupPath}\\employees.xml");
  XPathNavigator navigator = doc.CreateNavigator();
  XPathNavigator result =
    navigator.SelectSingleNode($"employees/employee
    [@employeeid={textBox1.Text}]");
  result.MoveToFirstChild();
  do
  {
    switch (result.Name)
    {
      case "firstname":
        label6.Text=result.Value;
        break;
      case "lastname":
        label7.Text=result.Value;
        break;
      case "homephone":
        label8.Text=result.Value;
        break;
      case "notes":
        label9.Text=result.Value;
        break;
    }
  }
  while (result.MoveToNext());
}
```

The code obtains an XPathNavigator object from an XPathDocument class. To retrieve the <employee> node with the specified employee ID, we use SelectSingleNode(), by supplying the appropriate XPath expression. It in turn returns XPathNavigator object containing the returned node.

The code then iterates through all the child nodes (<firstname>, <lastname>, <homephone>, and <notes>) of the returned <employee> node. With each iteration, the corresponding values are extracted by using the Value property of XPathNavigator.

Selecting Children, Ancestors, and Descendants

In addition to Select() and SelectSingleNode(), you can also use three specialized methods:

- The SelectChildren() method accepts the name of the child node and returns an XPathNodeIterator containing all the child nodes of the current node matching the supplied name.

- The SelectAncestors() method accepts the name of the ancestor nodes to select and returns an XPathNodeIterator containing all the ancestor nodes of the current node.

95

- The SelectDescendants() method accepts a node name and returns an
  XPathNodeIterator containing all the descendant nodes of the current node
  matching the supplied name.

These methods are optimized for performance and hence are faster than the equivalent XPath expressions.

Compiling XPath Expressions

If you are using the same XPath expression again and again, you can improve the performance of your code by using the Compile() method of the XPathNavigator class. This method accepts an XPath expression as a string, compiles it, and returns an instance of the XPathExpression class. This instance can then be supplied to the Select() and SelectSingleNode() methods.

To see the Compile() method in action, you need to modify the example that we developed for selecting nodes (see the "Selecting Nodes" section). The modified code is given in Listing 4-5.

Listing 4-5. Using XPathExpression and the Compile() Method

```
private void button1_Click(object sender, EventArgs e)
{
  XPathDocument doc =
    new XPathDocument($"{Application.StartupPath}\\employees.xml");
  XPathNavigator navigator = doc.CreateNavigator();
  XPathExpression expression = navigator.Compile(textBox1.Text);
  XPathNodeIterator iterator = navigator.Select(expression);
  try
  {
    ...
```

Note the lines marked in bold. The code creates an instance of the XPathExpression class by calling the Compile() method of XPathNavigator. This XPathExpression instance is then passed to the Select() method. The rest of the code of the application remains unchanged. You can pass the same XPathExpression instance to any number of Select() or SelectSingleNode() calls.

Navigating Between Attributes

Previously we accessed the attribute value by using the GetAttribute() method of the XPathNavigator class. However, there is an alternate technique that allows you to move through the available attributes by using three methods of XPathNavigator: MoveToAttribute(), MoveToFirstAttribute(), and MoveToNextAttribute(). These methods allow you to move to a specific attribute, the first attribute, and the next attribute, respectively.

The previous example can be modified as shown in Listing 4-6.

Listing 4-6. Accessing Attributes by Using the MoveTo . . . Methods

```
navigator.MoveToAttribute("employeeid", "");
string id = navigator.Value;
navigator.MoveToParent();
```

As you can see, the code now calls the MoveToAttribute() method instead of GetAttribute(). The MoveToAttribute() method takes the same two parameters as GetAttribute(), that is, the name of the attribute and the attribute namespace. To access the attribute's value this time, we use the Value property of XPathNavigator. Because the cursor has been moved to the employeeid attribute, the Value property returns its value. Before continuing, the cursor is positioned back to the <employee> node by calling the MoveToParent() method.

Retrieving Inner and Outer XML

In the previous sections, we used the Value property of XPathNavigator to access the text of various attributes and nodes. There are two more properties—InnerXml and OuterXml—that return the contents of the XPathNavigator as a string. The InnerXml property returns the complete markup of all the child nodes (excluding any markup of the current node), whereas the OuterXml property returns the complete markup of the node and all the child nodes.

To see how these properties are used, you need to develop an application like the one shown in Figure 4-5.

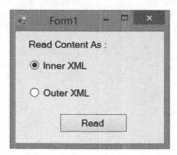

Figure 4-5. *Inner and outer XML*

The application contains two radio buttons to indicate inner or outer XML options. The Read button reads the Employees.xml file and displays the content as per the selection made. Listing 4-7 shows the Click event handler of the Read button containing the relevant code.

Listing 4-7. Using InnerXml and OuterXml Properties

```
private void button1_Click(object sender, EventArgs e)
{
  XPathDocument doc=new XPathDocument($"{Application.StartupPath}\\employees.xml");
  XPathNavigator navigator = doc.CreateNavigator();
  navigator.MoveToRoot();
  navigator.MoveToFirstChild();

  while (navigator.MoveToNext())
  {
    if (radioButton1.Checked)
    {
      MessageBox.Show(navigator.InnerXml);
    }
```

```
    else
    {
      MessageBox.Show(navigator.OuterXml);
    }
  }
}
```

The code creates an instance of XPathDocument as before. The XPathNavigator is then obtained by using the CreateNavigator() method of the XPathDocument class. As you learned in the previous examples, the cursor is positioned at the <employees> node. Finally, the entire content of the <employees> node is retrieved by using the InnerXml and OuterXml properties of the XPathNavigator class. The resultant message boxes for InnerXml and OuterXml are shown in Figures 4-6 and 4-7.

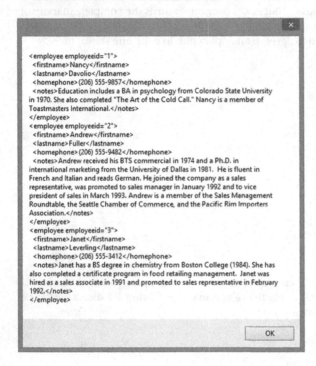

Figure 4-6. *Output of the InnerXml property*

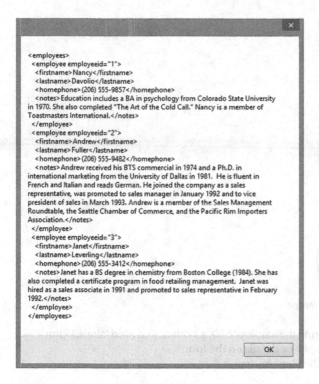

```
<employees>
  <employee employeeid="1">
    <firstname>Nancy</firstname>
    <lastname>Davolio</lastname>
    <homephone>(206) 555-9857</homephone>
    <notes>Education includes a BA in psychology from Colorado State University
in 1970. She also completed "The Art of the Cold Call." Nancy is a member of
Toastmasters International.</notes>
  </employee>
  <employee employeeid="2">
    <firstname>Andrew</firstname>
    <lastname>Fuller</lastname>
    <homephone>(206) 555-9482</homephone>
    <notes>Andrew received his BTS commercial in 1974 and a Ph.D. in
international marketing from the University of Dallas in 1981.  He is fluent in
French and Italian and reads German. He joined the company as a sales
representative, was promoted to sales manager in January 1992 and to vice
president of sales in March 1993. Andrew is a member of the Sales Management
Roundtable, the Seattle Chamber of Commerce, and the Pacific Rim Importers
Association.</notes>
  </employee>
  <employee employeeid="3">
    <firstname>Janet</firstname>
    <lastname>Leverling</lastname>
    <homephone>(206) 555-3412</homephone>
    <notes>Janet has a BS degree in chemistry from Boston College (1984). She has
also completed a certificate program in food retailing management.  Janet was
hired as a sales associate in 1991 and promoted to sales representative in February
1992.</notes>
  </employee>
</employees>
```

OK

Figure 4-7. *Output of the OuterXml property*

Note how OuterXml returns markup of the <employees> node, whereas InnerXml doesn't.

Getting an XmlReader from XPathNavigator

Though XPathNavigator allows you to read the XML document, at times you may want to pass a set of nodes from XPathNavigator to an XmlReader. The XmlReader can then read the returned nodes further. This is accomplished by using the ReadSubTree() method of XPathNavigator.

To demonstrate how an XmlReader can be obtained from an XPathNavigator, you need to build a Windows Forms application like the one shown in Figure 4-8.

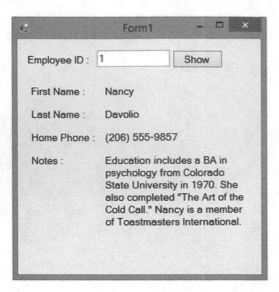

Figure 4-8. *Obtaining XmlReader from XPathNavigator*

The application consists of a text box for entering the employee ID, a button, and nine labels. Upon clicking the Show button, the form displays the employee details on the form.

Listing 4-8 shows the Click event handler of the Show button.

Listing 4-8. Calling the ReadSubtree() Method

```
private void button1_Click(object sender, EventArgs e)
{
  XPathDocument doc=new XPathDocument($"{Application.StartupPath}\\employees.xml");
  XPathNavigator navigator = doc.CreateNavigator();
  navigator.MoveToRoot();
  navigator.MoveToFirstChild();

  while (navigator.MoveToNext())
  {
    navigator.MoveToFirstChild();

    do
    {
      string id = navigator.GetAttribute("employeeid", "");
      if (id == textBox1.Text)
      {
        XmlReader reader=navigator.ReadSubtree();
        DisplayDetails(reader);
      }
    }
    while (navigator.MoveToNext());
  }
}
```

The code begins by creating an instance of XPathDocument. An XPathNavigator is then obtained by calling CreateNavigator(). Then the code iterates through the document. The navigation logic should be familiar to you because we used it in previous examples. With each iteration, the employeeid attribute is checked against the value supplied from the text box. If they match, the ReadSubtree() method of XPathNavigator is called. In this case, this returns an instance of XmlReader that contains one <employee> node and all its child nodes. The returned XmlReader is passed to a helper function called DisplayDetails(), shown in Listing 4-9.

Listing 4-9. DisplayDetails() Helper Function

```
private void DisplayDetails(XmlReader reader)
{
  while (reader.Read())
  {
    if (reader.NodeType == XmlNodeType.Element)
    {
      switch (reader.Name)
      {
        case "firstname":
          label6.Text = reader.ReadString();
          break;
        case "lastname":
          label7.Text = reader.ReadString();
          break;
        case "homephone":
          label8.Text = reader.ReadString();
          break;
        case "notes":
          label9.Text = reader.ReadString();
          break;
      }
    }
  }
  reader.Close();
}
```

The DisplayDetails() function iterates through the supplied XmlReader object, calling its Read() method. With each iteration, the values of the <firstname>, <lastname>, <homephone>, and <notes> nodes are retrieved by using the ReadString() method of the XmlReader class and assigned to the labels. Finally, the reader is closed by calling its Close() method.

■ **Note** The position of XPathNavigator remains unaffected even after calling the ReadSubtree() method.

Getting an XmlWriter from XPathNavigator

Just as you can create an XmlReader from XPathNavigator, you can also create an XmlWriter from it. This is useful in situations where you want to write selected nodes from XPathNavigator to a file or stream. XPathNavigator provides a method called WriteSubtree() that accepts an XmlWriter and writes the current node to it.

To illustrate the use of this technique, you need to develop an application like the one shown in Figure 4-9.

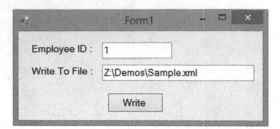

Figure 4-9. *Obtaining an XmlWriter from XPathNavigator*

The application consists of two text boxes: one to accept the employee ID to be extracted, and the other to specify a file path where the extracted employee details are stored.

Listing 4-10 shows the Click event handler of the Write button.

Listing 4-10. Calling the WriteSubtree() Method

```
private void button1_Click(object sender, EventArgs e)
{
  XPathDocument doc =
    new XPathDocument($"{Application.StartupPath}\\employees.xml");
  XPathNavigator navigator = doc.CreateNavigator();
  navigator.MoveToRoot();
  navigator.MoveToFirstChild();

  while (navigator.MoveToNext())
  {
    navigator.MoveToFirstChild();

    do
    {
      string id = navigator.GetAttribute("employeeid", "");
      if (id == textBox1.Text)
      {
        XmlTextWriter writer = new XmlTextWriter(textBox2.Text, null);
        navigator.WriteSubtree(writer);
        writer.Close();
```

```
        if (MessageBox.Show("Do you want to see the file?",
                            "Question",
                            MessageBoxButtons.YesNo) == DialogResult.Yes)
        {
          System.Diagnostics.Process.Start(textBox2.Text);
        }
      }
    }
  while (navigator.MoveToNext());
  }
}
```

The code creates an instance of XPathDocument and XPathNavigator as before. It then starts navigating the document and finds the matching <employee> node. After the matching employee is found, the code creates an instance of XmlTextWriter (recollect that XmlTextWriter inherits from the XmlWriter abstract class), supplying the file path entered in the text box to the constructor. Though our example writes the data to a disk file, any writable stream can be used.

To write the matching employee to XmlTextWriter, the code calls the WriteSubtree() method of XPathNavigator. The WriteSubtree() method accepts any class derived from the XmlWriter base class and writes the contents of the current node to it. In our example, it will be the <employee> node and its child nodes. After the writing is over, the XmlTextWriter is closed by calling its Close() method. The code then asks the user whether to open the resultant file, as shown in Figure 4-10.

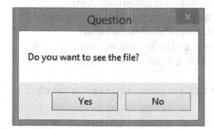

Figure 4-10. *Prompting the user to open the resultant file*

If the user clicks Yes, the resultant XML file is opened in the browser. Note the use of the Process class from the System.Diagnostics namespace. The Start() method of this class accepts a filename and opens it in its associated application. Figure 4-11 shows a sample output document with the <employee> subtree extracted.

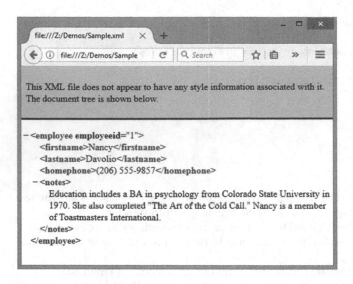

Figure 4-11. *Resultant XML document*

Editing XML Documents with the XPathNavigator Class

Up until now, we have used XPathNavigator to navigate and read values from the underlying XML document. However, it is possible to modify the underlying document also, though the XPathNavigator must be obtained from the XmlDocument class to do so. XPathNavigator instances obtained from XPathDocument are read-only and hence cannot be used for editing. You can check whether an instance of XPathNavigator is editable by using its CanEdit property, which returns true if the instance is editable, and false otherwise.

To see how an XML document can be modified with the help of XPathNavigator, you need to develop an application like the one shown in Figure 4-12.

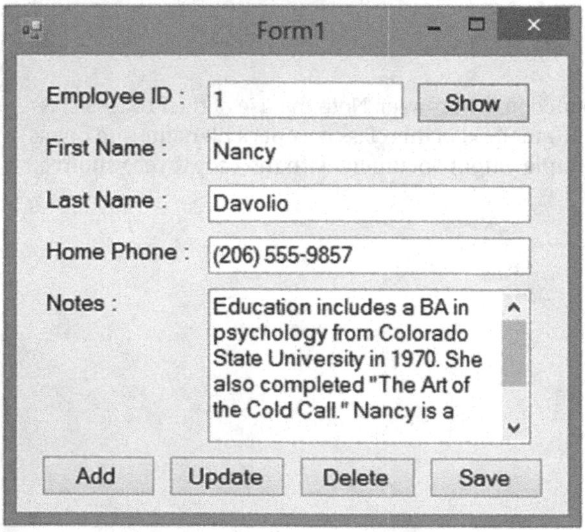

Figure 4-12. *Modifying an XML document by using XPathNavigator*

The application consists of text boxes to supply values for employee ID, first name, last name, home phone, and notes. There are four buttons for adding a new employee, modifying an existing employee, deleting an existing employee, and saving the changed document, respectively. When you enter an employee ID and click the Show button, the details of that employee are displayed in the remaining text boxes. You can change the details as per your requirements and click the Add, Update, or Delete buttons to add, update, or delete an employee, respectively. To save the modified document, you need to click the Save button.

In the source code of the application, you will find two form variables declared, as shown Listing 4-11.

Listing 4-11. Declaring XmlDocument and XPathNavigator

```
XmlDocument doc = new XmlDocument();
XPathNavigator navigator = null;
```

The Employees.xml file is loaded into this XmlDocument, and an XPathNavigator is obtained from it. This code goes in the Load event of the form and is shown in Listing 4-12.

Listing 4-12. Creating XPathNavigator

```
private void Form1_Load(object sender, EventArgs e)
{
  doc.Load($"{Application.StartupPath}\\employees.xml");
  navigator = doc.CreateNavigator();
}
```

When the user enters an employee ID and clicks the Show button, the details of that employee need to be displayed in the remaining text boxes. The Click event handler of the Show button does this job, as shown in Listing 4-13.

Listing 4-13. Retrieving Details of an Employee

```
private void button1_Click(object sender, EventArgs e)
{
  navigator.MoveToRoot();
  navigator.MoveToFirstChild();

  while (navigator.MoveToNext())
  {
    navigator.MoveToFirstChild();

    do
    {
      string id = navigator.GetAttribute("employeeid", "");
      if (id == textBox1.Text)
      {
        navigator.MoveToFirstChild();
        do
        {
          switch (navigator.Name)
          {
            case "firstname":
              textBox2.Text = navigator.Value;
              break;
```

```
          case "lastname":
            textBox3.Text = navigator.Value;
            break;
          case "homephone":
            textBox4.Text = navigator.Value;
            break;
          case "notes":
            textBox5.Text = navigator.Value;
            break;
        }
      }
      while (navigator.MoveToNext());
      navigator.MoveToParent();
    }
  }
  while (navigator.MoveToNext());
  }
}
```

The code should be familiar to you, because we used something similar in previous examples. The code loops through all the `<employee>` nodes and finds the one that matches the supplied employee ID. The values of various child nodes such as `<firstname>`, `<lastname>`, `<homephone>`, and `<notes>` are displayed in the respective text boxes by using the `Value` property of `XPathNavigator`.

Adding Nodes

To add new nodes to the document, the `XPathNavigator` class provides a method called `AppendChild()`. The `AppendChild()` method returns an instance of `XmlWriter`, and by using this `XmlWriter` you can write additional nodes to the document. The newly written nodes are added as child nodes of the current node. Listing 4-14 shows how this is accomplished.

Listing 4-14. Appending New Nodes

```
private void button2_Click(object sender, EventArgs e)
{
  navigator.MoveToRoot();
  navigator.MoveToFirstChild();

  while (navigator.MoveToNext())
  {
    XmlWriter writer = navigator.AppendChild();
    writer.WriteStartElement("employee");
    writer.WriteAttributeString("employeeid", textBox1.Text);
    writer.WriteElementString("firstname", textBox2.Text);
    writer.WriteElementString("lastname", textBox3.Text);
    writer.WriteElementString("homephone", textBox4.Text);
    writer.WriteElementString("notes", textBox5.Text);
    writer.WriteEndElement();
    writer.Close();
  }
}
```

The code first navigates to the `<employees>` node. This is where we want to add a new `<employee>` child node. Then it calls the `AppendChild()` method of the `XPathNavigator`. The returned `XmlWriter` is used to add a new `<employee>` node with an `employeeid` attribute.

The child nodes of the `<employee>` node (`<firstname>`, `<lastname>`, `<homephone>`, and `<notes>`) are also added. The methods such as `WriteStartElement()` and `WriteEndElement()` should already be familiar to you from Chapter 3.

■ **Note**   There are a few other overloads of the `AppendChild()` method. For example, one overload accepts the complete XML markup fragment for the new node and appends it to the current node. However, the one that we used is more flexible.

Modifying Nodes

To modify contents of any of the nodes, the `XPathNavigator` class provides a method called `SetValue()`, which accepts the new value and assigns it to the current node. Listing 4-15 shows how this method can be used.

Listing 4-15. Modifying Content

```
private void button3_Click(object sender, EventArgs e)
{
  navigator.MoveToRoot();
  navigator.MoveToFirstChild();

  while (navigator.MoveToNext())
  {
    navigator.MoveToFirstChild();

    do
    {
      string id = navigator.GetAttribute("employeeid", "");
      if (id == textBox1.Text)
      {
        navigator.MoveToFirstChild();

        do
        {
          switch (navigator.Name)
          {
            case "firstname":
              navigator.SetValue(textBox2.Text);
              break;
            case "lastname":
              navigator.SetValue(textBox3.Text);
              break;
            case "homephone":
              navigator.SetValue(textBox4.Text);
              break;
```

```
            case "notes":
              navigator.SetValue(textBox5.Text);
              break;
          }
        }
        while (navigator.MoveToNext());

        navigator.MoveToParent();
      }
    }
    while (navigator.MoveToNext());
  }
}
```

As before, the code finds out the <employee> node that is to be updated. The switch statement checks the Name property of XPathNavigator for the required node names (firstname, lastname, homephone, and notes). Inside each case, the SetValue() method is called on the navigator by passing the new value from the appropriate text box.

Deleting Nodes

Deleting a node is fairly simple. The DeleteSelf() method of XPathNavigator deletes the current node. After the node is successfully deleted, the cursor is moved to the parent node of the deleted node. Listing 4-16 shows the usage of DeleteSelf().

Listing 4-16. Deleting a Node

```
private void button4_Click(object sender, EventArgs e)
{
  navigator.MoveToRoot();
  navigator.MoveToFirstChild();

  while (navigator.MoveToNext())
  {
    navigator.MoveToFirstChild();

    do
    {
      string id = navigator.GetAttribute("employeeid", "");
      if (id == textBox1.Text)
      {
        navigator.DeleteSelf();
      }
    }
    while (navigator.MoveToNext());
  }
}
```

As in the previous case, the code looks for a specific <employee> node. After it finds the node, it calls the DeleteSelf() method on the navigator.

Saving Changes

It is important to remember that while making any modifications via XPathNavigator, the changes are not saved automatically to disk. The changes affect only the DOM tree loaded in memory, so you need to save the underlying document by calling the Save() method of the XmlDocument class. This is illustrated in Listing 4-17.

Listing 4-17. Saving the Document

```
private void button5_Click(object sender, EventArgs e)
{
   doc.Save($"{Application.StartupPath}\\employees.xml");
}
```

Summary

In this chapter, you learned what XPath is and how to use XPath expressions in the .NET Framework. We covered in detail the XPathNavigator class, which provides a cursor-like model for the XPath data model of the .NET Framework. The XPathNavigator class can be constructed from either of the XPathDocument or XmlDocument classes. The XPathNavigator returned from XPathDocument is read-only, whereas that returned from XmlDocument is editable. You also learned how to select nodes from the XML document by using XPath expressions in string form as well as in compiled form.

CHAPTER 5

■ ■ ■

Validating XML Documents

In Chapters 2, 3, and 4, you learned how to read and write XML documents, though we always assumed that the XML structure (tag names, attribute names, nesting, and so on) contained in the source XML document was correct. However, in many real-world cases this assumption may not be true. For example, a purchase order application might be accepting orders from various customers in XML format. What is the guarantee that each submitted order adheres to the agreed-on XML structure? What if somebody deviates from the agreed-on structure? This is where XML Schema comes into the picture.

XML Schema describes the structure of an XML document; to use an analogy, they serve the same purpose as database schemas. For example, schema of a database table tells you what columns it has, what are their data types, whether they can contain NULL, and so on. XML Schema does something similar for XML documents. With the help of a schema, you can do the following important things:

- You can define metadata—elements, attributes, types and so on—for XML documents.

- You can create XML documents based on the schema.

- You can validate XML documents against the schema.

In this chapter, you learn about the following:

- Various ways to define the structure of an XML document

- What XML Schema is

- How to create XML Schema

- How to validate XML documents against a schema

- How to create schemas programmatically by using the Schema Object Model (SOM)

Providing Structure for XML Documents

As mentioned previously, XML Schema defines the structure of an XML document. In other words, it provides a template, consisting of metadata, for creating and validating XML documents. However, a schema is not the only way to provide structure for an XML document. The .NET Framework supports three ways of defining XML structure:

- Document Type Definition (DTD)

- XML Data Reduced (XDR) Schema

- XML Schema Definition (XSD) Schema

© Bipin Joshi 2017
B. Joshi, *Beginning XML with C# 7*, https://doi.org/10.1007/978-1-4842-3105-0_5

Document Type Definition (DTD)

DTDs are an older way of representing XML structure, but they are still in use. They are a W3C standard, and older applications depend on them for validation. A DTD defines the overall structure of an XML document in terms of acceptable tag names, acceptable attribute names, and so on. An XML document author uses the DTD while creating a document. The same DTD can be used while validating the document also. You should avoid using DTDs in modern applications since they suffer from many disadvantages:

- They use non-XML syntax.
- They are difficult to create as well as to understand.
- You need to specifically learn the DTD syntax.
- They are not extensible.
- They do not support data types.
- They do not support namespaces.

XML Data Reduced (XDR) Schema

While the XSD Schema proposal (discussed next) was under consideration, Microsoft went ahead and created its implementation, called the XML Data Reduced, or XDR, schema specification. However, the XDR Schema specification and the XSD Schema specification are not the same. For the sake of backward compatibility, Microsoft retained support for XDR Schemas in the .NET Framework. If you are creating a new schema for your XML documents, you should use the XSD Schema specification instead of XDR.

XML Schema Definition (XSD) Schema

XSD schema specification or XML Schema is the result of efforts to provide standardization for defining XML structures. The XSD specification is a W3C recommendation. One of the key benefits of XSD is that it supports data types. XSD is an XML document itself and overcomes most of the limitations of DTD. If you are building new schemas for your XML documents, you should create them by using XSD instead of the DTD or XDR standards. XSD has largely superseded DTD and other ways of defining XML document metadata.

Creating Structure for an XML Document

Now that you know the possible ways to define XML structure, let's put each of the ways to use. In this section, you will create a formal structure for the same Employees.xml document by using the DTD and XSD standards. Because XDR is now considered an outdated standard, I will not cover XDR here.

The Structure of Employees.xml

You already know how the Employees.xml file looks. Our aim is to define the structure of the document by using the DTD and XSD standards so that you can validate the document later. The structure of Employees.xml is as follows:

- The root element must be <employees>.
- The root element can contain zero or more <employee> elements.
- The <employee> element must have an attribute called employeeid.

- The <employee> element must contain <firstname>, <lastname>, <homephone>, and <notes> sub-elements.

- The <firstname>, <lastname>, and <homephone> elements contain plain-text values.

- The <notes> element contains character data (CDATA).

- The <firstname>, <lastname>, <homephone>, and <notes> sub-elements must appear in the same order.

Keeping the preceding requirements in mind, let's create the DTD first, followed by the XSD.

Creating the DTD

In this section, you learn how to create a DTD for representing the structure of the Employees.xml file. Listing 5-1 shows the complete DTD for the document.

Listing 5-1. DTD for Employees.xml

```
<!ELEMENT employees (employee*)>
<!ELEMENT employee (firstname,lastname,homephone,notes)>
<!ELEMENT firstname (#PCDATA)>
<!ELEMENT lastname (#PCDATA)>
<!ELEMENT homephone (#PCDATA)>
<!ELEMENT notes (#PCDATA)>
<!ATTLIST employee employeeid CDATA #REQUIRED>
```

The DTD defines the root element of the XML document to be <employees>. This is done by using the <!ELEMENT> declaration, which specifies the name of the element (employees in our case) and content that can go inside it. In our case, the <employees> element can take zero or more <employee> elements and not any other element or text. This constraint is enforced by placing the acceptable element names (employee in our case) in the brackets. The asterisk (*) indicates that zero or more <employee> elements can be placed inside an <employees> element. Similar to *, you can also use the plus sign (+) and question mark (?). The + operator indicates that you can have one or more occurrences of the element, whereas ? indicates that the element is optional.

Next we define the <employee> element by using the same <!ELEMENT> declaration. Because the <employee> element must contain <firstname>, <lastname>, <homephone>, and <notes> sub-elements, they are specified as a comma-separated list. A comma-separated list of elements must appear in the order specified. If you want to allow the elements to appear in any order, you can use the pipe (|) character instead of the comma.

The document then defines each of the sub-elements of the <employee> element. To indicate that the elements contain plain character data and no other sub-elements, we use #PCDATA, which stands for *plain character data*. Thus, the DTD enforces that the <firstname>, <lastname>, <homephone>, and <notes> elements can contain only plain character data and no markup or sub-elements. If our elements contained character data and sub-elements, we could have used ANY instead of #PCDATA. Along the same lines, if our elements are empty (that is, they contain neither character data nor sub-elements), we could have used EMPTY.

Finally, the DTD defines the employeeid attribute for the <employee> element by using the <!ATTLIST> declaration. The <!ATTLIST> declaration takes the element whose attributes are being defined, followed by a list of attributes. The CDATA in the markup indicates that the attribute value contains character data. You can mark the attribute as a unique identifier by specifying its type as ID. The #REQUIRED in the declaration indicates that this attribute is mandatory and must be provided in the document.

■ **Note**   Recollect that in Chapter 2 we used the `GetElementById()` method of the `XmlDocument` class. This method requires that the element to search should have an attribute of type `ID`.

To create the DTD, you can use the Visual Studio IDE. Add a new text file, but name it `Employees.dtd`. Type in the entire markup shown in Listing 5-1 and save the file. Open `Employees.xml` in the Visual Studio IDE and add a `DOCTYPE` declaration to it at the top, as shown in Listing 5-2.

Listing 5-2. Attaching the DTD to an XML Document

```
<?xml version="1.0" encoding="utf-8" ?>
<!DOCTYPE employees SYSTEM "employees.dtd">
<cmployccs>
  <employee employeeid="1">
    <firstname>Nancy</firstname>
    ...
```

As you can see, at the top of the XML file, we have put the `<!DOCTYPE>` declaration. The `<!DOCTYPE>` declaration is used to attach a DTD to an XML file. The `<!DOCTYPE>` declaration is immediately followed by `<employees>`—the root element of the document. The `SYSTEM` identifier specifies the URI of the DTD file that is providing structure to this XML document. In our case, it is `employees.dtd` (it is assumed that the XML document and the DTD are in the same folder).

■ **Note**   Just like the `SYSTEM` identifier, there is `PUBLIC` identifier that is used to specify a well-known public schema that can be used by many applications. The `SYSTEM` identifier, on the other hand, is used to specify a schema that is specific to an application (for example, `employees.dtd` in our case).

You might be wondering why we created the DTD in Visual Studio. Apart from providing IntelliSense, it is not helping much, is it? But wait a moment before you conclude anything, because it has something more to offer. Now add a new XML file in your project, and then add to it the `<!DOCTYPE>` declaration shown in Listing 5-2. When you start creating the document, you will observe that the IDE shows various elements and attributes in IntelliSense. Figure 5-1 shows how this IntelliSense looks.

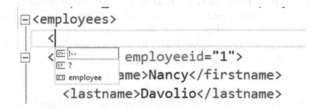

Figure 5-1. *Visual Studio IntelliSense for DTDs*

The IDE also validates your document as you type. It displays error messages if you enter markup or attributes that violate the DTD rules.

Creating the XML Schema

In this section, you learn how to create XSD Schemas in three ways:

- Creating the XML Schema by using the Visual Studio IDE

- Creating the XML Schema from an existing XML document using the Visual Studio IDE

- Creating the XML Schema by using the xsd.exe command-line tool (often called the XML Schema Definition tool)

An XML Schema is typically stored in a file with the extension .xsd. A schema consists of various parts, some of which are listed in Table 5-1.

Table 5-1. Parts of an XSD Schema

Part Name	Description
Element	Represents a single element.
Attribute	Represents a single attribute of an element.
Attribute group	Represents a group of attributes that can be used further in a complex type.
Simple type	A simple type consists of only text values and no sub-elements—for example, string, numbers, date, and so on. Elements as well as attributes can be of the simple type.
Complex type	A complex type consists of one or more simple types. Only elements can be of the complex type.

One of the key advantages of XSD schemas over DTDs is that they support data types. These data types map with the .NET Framework's data types; thus, XSD data types can be represented by their equivalent data types in the .NET Framework. Table 5-2 lists some of the common XSD data types and their .NET counterparts.

Table 5-2. XSD Data Types

XSD Data Type	.NET Data Type	Description
Boolean	System.Boolean	Represents Boolean values (true or false)
Byte	System.SByte	Represents an 8-bit signed integer (byte)
dateTime	System.DateTime	Represents the date and time
decimal	System.Decimal	Represents a decimal number
Double	System.Double	Represents a double precision number
Float	System.Single	Represents a single precision floating number
Int	System.Int32	Represents a 4-byte signed integer
Long	System.Int64	Represents an 8-byte signed integer
String	System.String	Represents string data

Now that you have a brief idea about XSD schemas, their parts, and data types, we will proceed to create XSD schemas by using the various ways described.

115

XSD for Employees.xml

To create any XML Schema, you first need to think about the simple types, complex types, elements, and attributes that go into it. Let's do this exercise for the `Employees.xml` file.

We will create three simple types for `Employees.xml`:

- NameSimpleType: This simple type represents names used in our XML document (first name and last name). It puts restrictions on the names: the minimum length must be three, and the maximum length must be less than 255.

- PhoneSimpleType: This simple type represents phone numbers (the `<homephone>` element of our XML document). It restricts the phone numbers to no more than 20 characters.

- NotesSimpleType: This simple type represents notes (the `<notes>` element of our document). It restricts the notes entered to no longer than 500 characters in length.

These three simple types will make a complex type called `EmployeeType`. The `EmployeeType` complex type consists of the following:

- An element called `<firstname>`, which is of simple type `NameSimpleType`

- An element called `<lastname>`, which is of simple type `NameSimpleType`

- An element called `<homephone>`, which is of simple type `PhoneSimpleType`

- An element called `<notes>`, which is of simple type `NotesSimpleType`

- A required attribute called `employeeid`, which is of type `int`

Finally, we will have an element called `<employees>` that will contain zero or more sub-elements named `<employee>`. The `<employee>` sub-elements will be of complex type `EmployeeType`.

Creating the XSD in Visual Studio Designer

Creating an XML Schema in Visual Studio is easy, because the IDE provides visual tools to create, edit, and explore an XML Schema. To create a new XML Schema, you need to add one to your project by using the Add New Item dialog box. Name the new schema file `Employees.xsd`. Figure 5-2 shows the Add New Item dialog box with the relevant selection.

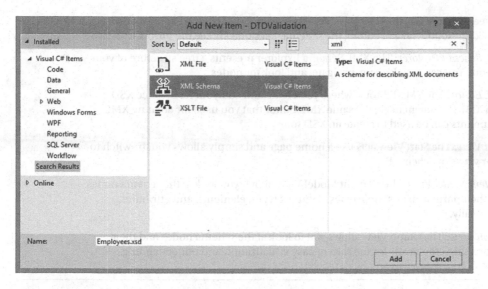

Figure 5-2. *Adding a new XML Schema to your project*

After you have added an XML Schema, you will be presented with the XML Schema Designer or XSD Designer. The XSD Designer is shown in Figure 5-3.

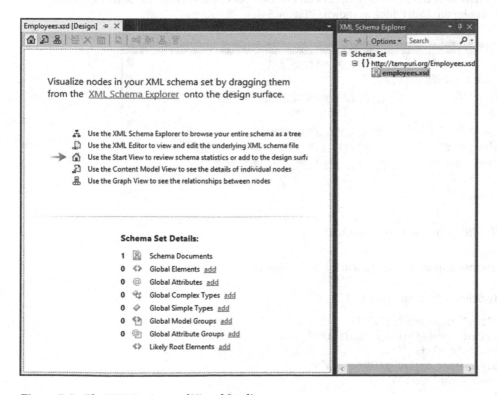

Figure 5-3. *The XSD Designer of Visual Studio*

As you can see in Figure 5-3, the XSD Designer consists of XML Schema Explorer and a few views. It also links to the XML Editor for the sake of editing the schema. Let's quickly see the purpose of each:

- *XML Schema Explorer:* The XML Schema Explorer presents a tree structure of your schema. You can then browse, navigate, and look for nodes.

- *XML Editor:* The XML Editor is where you create and edit your XSD. Since XSD is an XML document itself, the same XML Editor that you used for creating XML documents can be used to create an XSD too.

- *Start View:* The Start View acts like a home page and simply allows you to switch to other views or Schema Explorer.

- *Content Model View:* The Content Model View allows you look at the schema nodes and their parts such as simple types, complex types, elements, and attributes, graphically.

- *Graph View:* The Graph View allows you to look at the schema nodes and their relationship graphically for the sake of easy visualization and understanding.

■ **Note**   Detailed coverage of the XSD Designer is beyond the scope of this book. MSDN documentation contains detailed explanation of each of the parts mentioned here. For our purposes, the XML Editor is sufficient.

Now that you have added Employees.xsd, click on the XML Editor option from the Start View of the XSD Designer. This will open the XML Editor, as shown in Figure 5-4.

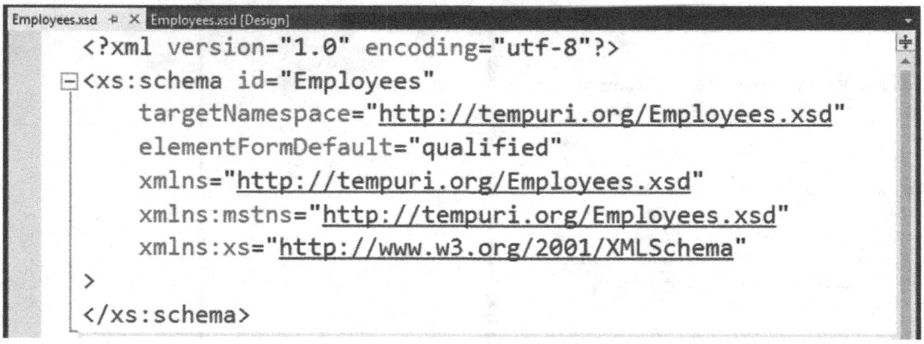

```
Employees.xsd  ⊕ ×  Employees.xsd [Design]
      <?xml version="1.0" encoding="utf-8"?>
    ⊟<xs:schema id="Employees"
          targetNamespace="http://tempuri.org/Employees.xsd"
          elementFormDefault="qualified"
          xmlns="http://tempuri.org/Employees.xsd"
          xmlns:mstns="http://tempuri.org/Employees.xsd"
          xmlns:xs="http://www.w3.org/2001/XMLSchema"
    >
    </xs:schema>
```

Figure 5-4. *XML Editor ready for creating an XSD*

Now, write the markup from Listing 5-3 in the XML Editor.

Listing 5-3. XML Schema for Employees.xml

```
<?xml version="1.0" encoding="utf-8"?>
<xs:schema attributeFormDefault="unqualified"
elementFormDefault="qualified"
xmlns:xs="http://www.w3.org/2001/XMLSchema">
  <xs:element name="employees">
  <xs:complexType>
```

```
    <xs:sequence>
      <xs:element name="employee" type="EmployeeType" minOccurs="0"
                  maxOccurs="unbounded" />
    </xs:sequence>
  </xs:complexType>
</xs:element>
<xs:complexType name="EmployeeType">
  <xs:all>
    <xs:element name="firstname" type="NameSimpleType" />
    <xs:element name="notes" type="NotesSimpleType" />
    <xs:element name="lastname" type="NameSimpleType" />
    <xs:element name="homephone" type="PhoneSimpleType" />
  </xs:all>
  <xs:attribute name="employeeid" type="xs:int" use="required" />
</xs:complexType>
<xs:simpleType name="NameSimpleType">
  <xs:restriction base="xs:string">
    <xs:minLength value="3" />
    <xs:maxLength value="255" />
  </xs:restriction>
</xs:simpleType>
<xs:simpleType name="PhoneSimpleType">
  <xs:restriction base="xs:string">
    <xs:maxLength value="20" />
  </xs:restriction>
</xs:simpleType>
<xs:simpleType name="NotesSimpleType">
  <xs:restriction base="xs:string">
    <xs:maxLength value="500" />
  </xs:restriction>
</xs:simpleType>
</xs:schema>
```

The schema declaration starts with the <schema> tag. The XML namespace http://www.w3.org/2001/ XMLSchema is required and indicates that this is an XML Schema. The xmlns attribute specifies that the namespace prefix for all the tags of this schema will be xs.

Then the schema declares the <employees> element by using the <element> tag. The <employees> element contains sub-elements named <employee>, which are of the complex type EmployeeType. The complex type is indicated by the <complexType> element. There can be zero or more occurrences of <employee> sub-elements as defined by the minOccurs and maxOccurs attributes, respectively. Note the use of the unbounded keyword to indicate that any number of the element can exist.

Next the schema defines a complex type called EmployeeType by using the <complexType> element. The name attribute of <complexType> indicates the name of the complex type being defined. The EmployeeType complex type consists of four sub-elements and one attribute. The elements are declared by using the <element> tag and its two attributes, name and type. The name attribute specifies the name of the element, whereas the type attribute indicates the data type of the element.

The attributes are declared by using the `<attribute>` tag. The `name` attribute of the `<attribute>` element specifies the name of the attribute, and the `type` attribute indicates the data type of the attribute. In our case, the `employeeid` attribute is of type `int` and is required, as indicated by the `use` attribute.

Then the schema defines the `NameSimpleType` simple type by using the `<simpleType>` element. Because we want the data type of `NameSimpleType` to be `string`, we indicated this in the `<restriction>` element. The minimum and maximum length of the element is decided by the `minLength` and `maxLength` attributes, respectively. In our case, the names must be more than 3 characters in length and should not exceed 255 characters.

The `PhoneSimpleType` simple type is defined next. It is a string not exceeding 20 characters. Finally, the `NotesSimpleType` simple type is defined. It is also a string, but it must not exceed 500 characters.

That's it! After you type in the preceding markup in the XML Editor, save the `Employees.xsd` file.

Before we move any further, let's quickly see how the nodes of `Employees.xsd` look in the XML Schema Explorer, Content Model View, and Graph View.

Click on the XML Schema Explorer link from the Start View so as to open the XML Schema Explorer (see Figure 5-5).

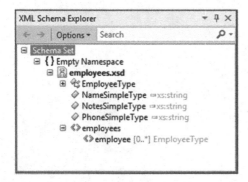

Figure 5-5. *Employees.xsd in XML Schema Explorer*

Notice how the `EmployeeType` complex type and `NameSimpleType`, `NotesSimpleType` and `PhoneSimpleType` simple types are shown. Also shown are the `employees` root element and zero or more occurrences of `employee` element.

If you click on the Content Model View and then drag-and-drop the `employees.xsd` node from the XML Schema Explorer, you will see something similar to Figure 5-6.

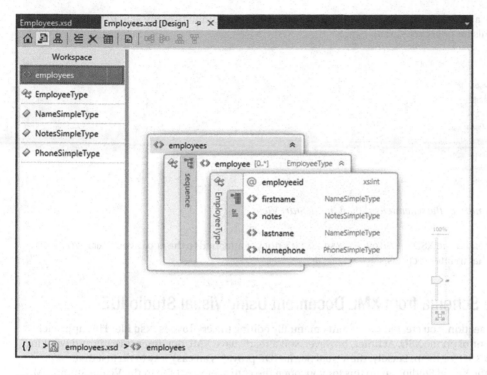

Figure 5-6. *Viewing employees element in the Content Model View*

Notice how the employees element, employee element, and other sub-elements are shown graphically. Of course, if you want to edit something you need to switch to the XML Editor again and make the desired change.

Figure 5-7 shows the various types and elements in the Graph View.

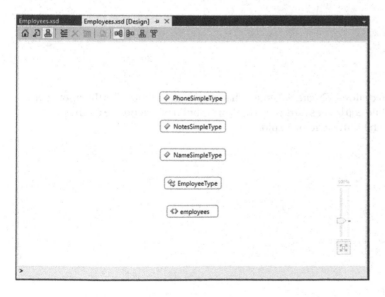

Figure 5-7. *Various types and elements in the Graph View*

Finally, have a look at the bottom part of the Start View. It lists a summary of the schema. Figure 5-8 shows these details for employees.xsd.

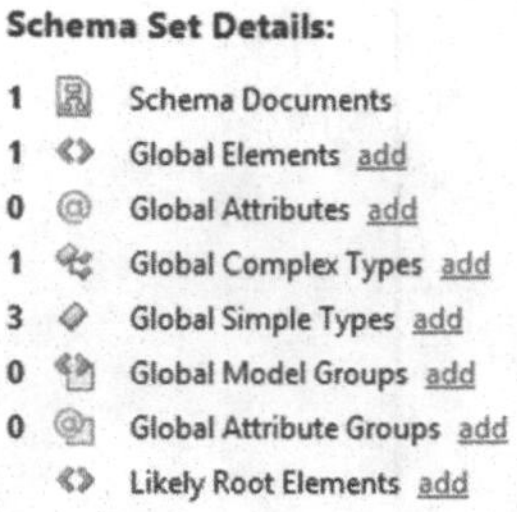

Schema Set Details:

1	🗎	Schema Documents
1	<>	Global Elements _add_
0	@	Global Attributes _add_
1	⬚	Global Complex Types _add_
3	◇	Global Simple Types _add_
0	⬚	Global Model Groups _add_
0	@	Global Attribute Groups _add_
	<>	Likely Root Elements _add_

Figure 5-8. *Summary of the schema as shown in the Start View*

So far you created the XSD—employees.xsd. But it's not yet attached to the employees.xml. You will learn how to do that in later sections.

Creating the Schema from XML Document Using Visual Studio IDE

In the preceding section, you created the schema manually editing the employees.xsd file. This approach gives you total control on the XSD. At times, however, you already have XML documents ready and want to quickly create an XSD for them. Luckily, the Visual Studio IDE provides an easy way to do just that.

To see how the Visual Studio can do this for you, open the employees.xml file in the Visual Studio XML Editor. You will notice that the menu bar now has an extra menu—XML. Figure 5-9 shows this menu.

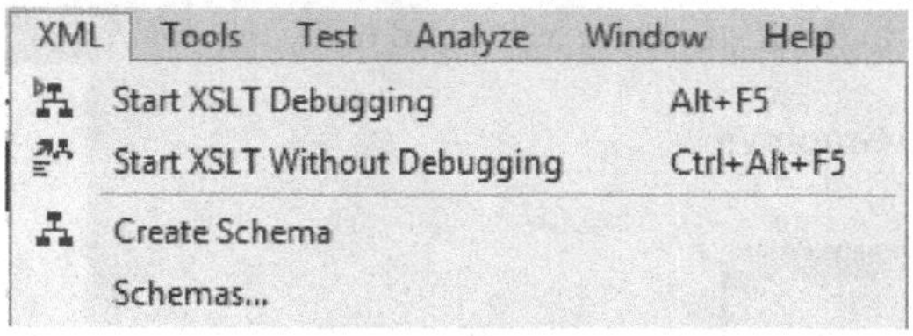

XML	Tools	Test	Analyze	Window	Help
🔧	Start XSLT Debugging		Alt+F5		
᠍	Start XSLT Without Debugging		Ctrl+Alt+F5		
🔧	Create Schema				
	Schemas...				

Figure 5-9. *XML menu of Visual Studio*

Notice that the XML menu has an option—Create Schema—that creates the schema for the open XML document. If you select this option while employees.xml is open, Visual Studio will generate a schema for you. Figure 5-10 shows the schema in the XML Schema Explorer.

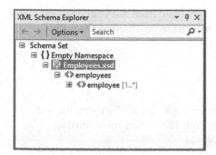

Figure 5-10. XML Schema Explorer showing the newly generated schema

If you observe the complete markup of the schema, it will resemble Listing 5-4.

Listing 5-4. Markup of the Newly Generated Schema

```
<?xml version="1.0" encoding="utf-8"?>
<xs:schema attributeFormDefault="unqualified"
elementFormDefault="qualified"
xmlns:xs="http://www.w3.org/2001/XMLSchema">
  <xs:element name="employees">
    <xs:complexType>
      <xs:sequence>
        <xs:element maxOccurs="unbounded" name="employee">
          <xs:complexType>
            <xs:sequence>
              <xs:element name="firstname" type="xs:string" />
              <xs:element name="lastname" type="xs:string" />
              <xs:element name="homephone" type="xs:string" />
              <xs:element name="notes" type="xs:string" />
            </xs:sequence>
            <xs:attribute name="employeeid" type="xs:unsignedByte" use="required" />
          </xs:complexType>
        </xs:element>
      </xs:sequence>
    </xs:complexType>
  </xs:element>
</xs:schema>
```

You will notice that the schema shown in Listing 5-4 takes care of the basic metadata such as element names, attributes, and their types. If you need customization, you will need to modify the XSD as per your needs.

Creating the Schema by Using the XML Schema Definition Tool

In the preceding section, you used the XML Schema Designer to create a schema. You also created a schema from an existing XML document. There is yet another way to create a schema—using the XML Schema Definition tool. The XML Schema Definition tool (xsd.exe) allows you to create XSD schemas from the following:

- An existing XML document

- An existing XDR Schema

- Types defined in an assembly (.exe or .dll)

The XML Schema Definition tool is provided as `xsd.exe` and can be invoked from the Visual Studio command prompt. In the following sections, you learn how to use this tool to create schemas from XML documents and assemblies.

Creating the Schema from an XML Document

Let's assume that you have the `Employees.xml` file with you and want to create XSD for it by using the `xsd.exe` command-line tool. To do so, open the Visual Studio command prompt. Then enter the following command at the command prompt:

```
xsd.exe "C:\Test\Employees.xml" /outputdir:"C:\Test"
```

The first parameter is the path and filename of the XML file for which the schema is to be generated. It is assumed that the `Employees.xml` file exists in the `C:\Test` folder. The `/outputdir` switch specifies the folder where the resultant XSD file should be created.

After you invoke the command, you will find an `.xsd` file in the specified folder. By default, the name of the schema file is the same as the XML filename. Listing 5-5 shows the schema generated by the tool.

Listing 5-5. Schema Generated by the xsd.exe Tool

```xml
<?xml version="1.0" encoding="utf-8"?>
<xs:schema id="employees" xmlns="" xmlns:xs="http://www.w3.org/2001/XMLSchema" ➡
xmlns:msdata="urn:schemas-microsoft-com:xml-msdata">
  <xs:element name="employees" msdata:IsDataSet="true" ➡
msdata:UseCurrentLocale="true">
    <xs:complexType>
      <xs:choice minOccurs="0" maxOccurs="unbounded">
        <xs:element name="employee">
          <xs:complexType>
            <xs:sequence>
              <xs:element name="firstname" type="xs:string" minOccurs="0" ➡
msdata:Ordinal="0" />
              <xs:element name="lastname" type="xs:string" minOccurs="0" ➡
msdata:Ordinal="1" />
              <xs:element name="homephone" type="xs:string" minOccurs="0" ➡
msdata:Ordinal="2" />
              <xs:element name="notes" type="xs:string" minOccurs="0" ➡
msdata:Ordinal="3" />
            </xs:sequence>
            <xs:attribute name="employeeid" type="xs:string" />
          </xs:complexType>
        </xs:element>
      </xs:choice>
    </xs:complexType>
  </xs:element>
</xs:schema>
```

As you can see, the resultant schema defines a root element called `<employees>`. The `<employees>` element can have zero or more occurrences of the `<employee>` element. The `<employee>` element is defined as a complex type and contains four sub-elements: `<firstname>`, `<lastname>`, `<homephone>`, and `<notes>`. The schema also states that the elements must occur in the same sequence (as indicated by the `<sequence>` tag). The `employeeid` attribute is also defined. You can customize the generated schema to suit your needs.

■ **Note**   You can also invoke the xsd.exe tool at a standard command prompt. However, you need to specify the complete path of the xsd.exe tool while invoking it. Alternatively, you can navigate to the installation folder of .NET where the tool is located and then invoke it. You can even add it to the PATH variable.

Creating the Schema from an Assembly

You might be wondering why you'd need to create a schema from an assembly. This facility, however, comes in handy during XML serialization, during which you often serialize your classes on the wire in XML format. Thus the XSD schema extracted from the assembly represents the metadata of this serialized XML.

■ **Note**   You will learn more about XML serialization in Chapter 8.

To see how the xsd.exe tool can generate a schema from an assembly, we will create a class library project. The class library will have a single class called Employee. The source code of the Employee class is shown in Listing 5-6.

Listing 5-6. The Employee Class

```
namespace ClassLibrary1
{
    public class Employee
    {
      public int EmployeeID { get; set; }
      public string FirstName { get; set; }
      public string LastName { get; set; }
      public string HomePhone { get; set; }
      public string Notes { get; set; }
}
```

The Employee class is quite straightforward and contains five public properties—EmployeeID, FirstName, LastName, HomePhone, and Notes.

After you create the class, make sure to compile it so that its assembly is outputted—ClassLibrary1. dll. Now invoke the xsd.exe tool as shown here:

```
xsd.exe "C:\ ClassLibrary1\bin\Debug\classlibrary1.dll"
/outputdir:"C:\ClassLibrary1"
```

The first parameter to xsd.exe specifies the path and filename of the assembly, whereas the /outputdir switch specifies the target folder where the XSD should be created. Listing 5-7 shows the XSD based on our Employee class.

Listing 5-7. Schema Generated for the Employee Class

```
<?xml version="1.0" encoding="utf-8"?>
<xs:schema elementFormDefault="qualified" ➥
xmlns:xs="http://www.w3.org/2001/XMLSchema">
  <xs:element name="Employee" nillable="true" type="Employee" />
```

```
  <xs:complexType name="Employee">
    <xs:sequence>
      <xs:element minOccurs="1" maxOccurs="1" name="EmployeeID" type="xs:int" />
      <xs:element minOccurs="0" maxOccurs="1" name="FirstName" type="xs:string" />
      <xs:element minOccurs="0" maxOccurs="1" name="LastName" type="xs:string" />
      <xs:element minOccurs="0" maxOccurs="1" name="HomePhone" type="xs:string" />
      <xs:element minOccurs="0" maxOccurs="1" name="Notes" type="xs:string" />
    </xs:sequence>
  </xs:complexType>
</xs:schema>
```

As you can see in Listing 5-7, the schema defines an element named <Employee> that is of complex type Employee. The complex type Employee contains five sub-elements: <EmployeeID>, <FirstName>, <LastName>, <HomePhone>, and <Notes>. As you must have guessed, the names of these elements are extracted from the names of the class properties. These elements must occur in sequence, as indicated by the <sequence> tag. As in the previous case, you can customize this schema to suit your needs.

■ **Note** When you use the preceding command, the tool generates a schema for all the classes in the assembly. You can specify only certain classes by using the /type switch. The xsd.exe tool can also create classes from a schema. This can be helpful for deserializing the XML data in a .NET application.

Creating Schemas by Using the Schema Object Model (SOM)

Up until now, we created schemas by using a variety of techniques, all of which were design-time techniques. That means we ourselves created the schemas by using a text editor, Visual Studio, or the xsd. exe tool. However, there is more to the show than this. The .NET Framework also allows you to create schemas programmatically.

You can load existing schemas or create a new one from the ground up. You can then manipulate the schema by adding or removing various parts such as elements, attributes, simple types, and complex types. After you manipulate the schema as per your requirements, you can then compile it. Compiling a schema ensures that there are no errors in the schema structure.

To perform schema manipulation, the .NET Framework provides a set of classes called the Schema Object Model, or SOM for short. The SOM classes reside in the System.Xml.Schema namespace. The SOM is for schemas what DOM is for XML documents: the SOM classes represent various parts of a schema. For example, to represent a simple type, the SOM provides a class called XmlSchemaSimpleType, and to represent an element, the SOM provides a class called XmlSchemaElement. There are many other classes that represent attributes, facets, groups, complex types, and so on.

In the following section, you learn about some of the core SOM classes. Note that the SOM is very extensive and I do not discuss every available class here.

The Core SOM Classes

Figure 5-11 shows the object hierarchy of the core SOM classes. As you can see, all the SOM classes inherit from an abstract base class called XmlSchemaObject. This class provides common base functionality to all the child classes.

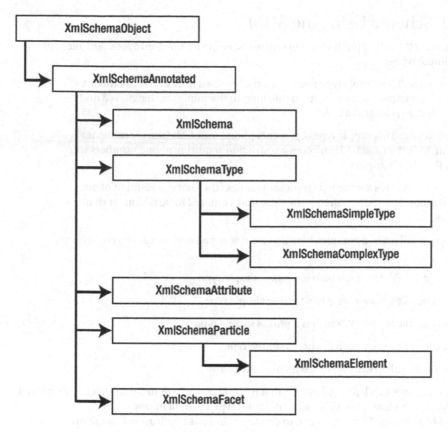

Figure 5-11. *The SOM object hierarchy*

The XmlSchemaAnnotated class represents a base class for any element that can contain annotation elements. Classes such as XmlSchema, XmlSchemaType, XmlSchemaAttribute, XmlSchemaParticle, and XmlSchemaFacet inherit from the XmlSchemaAnnotated class.

■ **Note**   You can use annotation elements to provide information about the XML Schema. Annotations can appear anywhere in a schema to explain any element, attribute, or type definition.

The XmlSchema class represents an in-memory representation of an XML Schema. This class allows you to read, write, and compile XML Schemas.

The XmlSchemaType represents a type in an XML Schema and acts as a base class for all simple and complex types. The XmlSchemaSimpleType and XmlSchemaComplexType classes inherit from this class and allow you to define new simple and complex types, respectively.

The XmlSchemaAttribute represents an attribute of an element. Finally, the XmlSchemaParticle class provides base functionality to all particle types such as XmlSchemaElement.

Creating an XML Schema Using the SOM

Now that you know what the SOM is, let's put it to use to create a schema for our Employees.xml file. The schema will have three simple types:

- *Simple type for* name: This simple type represents names used in our XML document (first name and last name). It restricts the name length; the minimum length is 3 and the maximum length is less than 255.

- *Simple type for* phone: This simple type represents phone numbers (the <homephone> element of our XML document). It enforces a restriction requiring phone numbers to be no longer than 20 characters.

- *Simple type for* notes: This simple type represents notes (the <notes> element of our document). It enforces a restriction requiring the notes entered to be no longer than 500 characters.

These three simple types will make a complex type that represents an employee. The complex type consists of the following:

- An element called <firstname>, which is a name simple type

- An element called <lastname>, which is a name simple type

- An element called <homephone>, which is a phone simple type

- An element called <notes>, which is a notes simple type

- A required attribute called employeeid, which is of type int

Finally, we will have an element called <employees> that will contain zero or more sub-elements named <employee>. The <employee> sub-elements will be of the complex type I just mentioned.

To create the schema by using the SOM, you need to create a Windows application like the one shown in Figure 5-12.

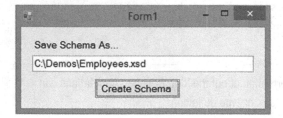

Figure 5-12. *Application for creating a schema by using the SOM*

The application consists of a text box wherein you can specify the full path and name of the destination schema file. Clicking the Create Schema button generates, compiles, and saves the schema to the specified location.

The Click event handler of the Create Schema button is shown in Listing 5-8.

Listing 5-8. Creating a Schema by Using the SOM

```csharp
private void button1_Click(object sender, EventArgs e)
{
  XmlSchema schema = new XmlSchema();

  //define NameSimpleType
  XmlSchemaSimpleType nametype = new XmlSchemaSimpleType();
  XmlSchemaSimpleTypeRestriction nameRes = new XmlSchemaSimpleTypeRestriction();
  nameRes.BaseTypeName =
    new XmlQualifiedName("string", "http://www.w3.org/2001/XMLSchema");
  XmlSchemaMinLengthFacet nameFacet1 = new XmlSchemaMinLengthFacet();
  nameFacet1.Value = "3";
  XmlSchemaMaxLengthFacet nameFacet2 = new XmlSchemaMaxLengthFacet();
  nameFacet2.Value = "255";
  nameRes.Facets.Add(nameFacet1);
  nameRes.Facets.Add(nameFacet2);
  nametype.Content = nameRes;

  //define PhoneSimpleType
  XmlSchemaSimpleType phonetype = new XmlSchemaSimpleType();
  XmlSchemaSimpleTypeRestriction phoneRes = new XmlSchemaSimpleTypeRestriction();
  phoneRes.BaseTypeName =
    new XmlQualifiedName("string", "http://www.w3.org/2001/XMLSchema");
  XmlSchemaMaxLengthFacet phoneFacet1 = new XmlSchemaMaxLengthFacet();
  phoneFacet1.Value = "20";
  phoneRes.Facets.Add(phoneFacet1);
  phonetype.Content = phoneRes;

  //define NotesSimpleType
  XmlSchemaSimpleType notestype = new XmlSchemaSimpleType();
  XmlSchemaSimpleTypeRestriction notesRes = new XmlSchemaSimpleTypeRestriction();
  notesRes.BaseTypeName =
    new XmlQualifiedName("string", "http://www.w3.org/2001/XMLSchema");
  XmlSchemaMaxLengthFacet notesFacet1 = new XmlSchemaMaxLengthFacet();
  notesFacet1.Value = "500";
  notesRes.Facets.Add(notesFacet1);
  notestype.Content = notesRes;

  //define EmployeeType complex type
  XmlSchemaComplexType employeetype = new XmlSchemaComplexType();
  XmlSchemaSequence sequence = new XmlSchemaSequence();
  XmlSchemaElement firstname = new XmlSchemaElement();
  firstname.Name = "firstname";
  firstname.SchemaType = nametype;
  XmlSchemaElement lastname = new XmlSchemaElement();
  lastname.Name = "lastname";
  lastname.SchemaType = nametype;
  XmlSchemaElement homephone = new XmlSchemaElement();
  homephone.Name = "homephone";
  homephone.SchemaType = phonetype;
```

```
XmlSchemaElement notes = new XmlSchemaElement();
notes.Name = "notes";
notes.SchemaType = notestype;

sequence.Items.Add(firstname);
sequence.Items.Add(lastname);
sequence.Items.Add(homephone);
sequence.Items.Add(notes);
employeetype.Particle = sequence;

//define employeeid attribute
XmlSchemaAttribute employeeid = new XmlSchemaAttribute();
employeeid.Name = "employeeid";
employeeid.SchemaTypeName =
  new XmlQualifiedName("int", "http://www.w3.org/2001/XMLSchema");
employeeid.Use = XmlSchemaUse.Required;
employeetype.Attributes.Add(employeeid);

//define top complex type
XmlSchemaComplexType complextype = new XmlSchemaComplexType();
XmlSchemaSequence sq = new XmlSchemaSequence();
XmlSchemaElement employee = new XmlSchemaElement();
employee.Name = "employee";
employee.SchemaType = employeetype;
employee.MinOccurs = 0;
employee.MaxOccursString = "unbounded";
sq.Items.Add(employee);
complextype.Particle = sq;

//define <employees> element
XmlSchemaElement employees = new XmlSchemaElement();
employees.Name = "employees";
employees.SchemaType = complextype;

schema.Items.Add(employees);
//compile the schema
XmlSchemaSet set = new XmlSchemaSet();
set.Add(schema);
set.Compile();
//save the schema
XmlTextWriter writer = new XmlTextWriter(textBox1.Text,null);
schema.Write(writer);
writer.Close();
MessageBox.Show("Schema Created Successfully!");
}
```

The code is a bit lengthy and hence we will dissect it in pieces.

Creating the Schema

An in-memory schema is represented by the XmlSchema class. The code declares an instance of XmlSchema at the top:

```
XmlSchema schema = new XmlSchema();
```

Creating a Simple Type for Names

The schema needs to define a simple type for names. This is defined next:

```
XmlSchemaSimpleType nametype = new XmlSchemaSimpleType();
XmlSchemaSimpleTypeRestriction nameRes = new XmlSchemaSimpleTypeRestriction();
nameRes.BaseTypeName =
  new XmlQualifiedName("string", "http://www.w3.org/2001/XMLSchema");
XmlSchemaMinLengthFacet nameFacet1 = new XmlSchemaMinLengthFacet();
nameFacet1.Value = "3";
XmlSchemaMaxLengthFacet nameFacet2 = new XmlSchemaMaxLengthFacet();
nameFacet2.Value = "255";
nameRes.Facets.Add(nameFacet1);
nameRes.Facets.Add(nameFacet2);
nametype.Content = nameRes;
```

A simple type is represented by the XmlSchemaSimpleType class. The simple type for names has certain restrictions:

- The data type must be a string.

- The minimum length must be 3.

- The length must not exceed 255.

To represent these restrictions, an instance of the XmlSchemaSimpleTypeRestriction class is created. The XmlSchemaSimpleTypeRestriction class's BaseTypeName property, which is of type XmlQualifiedName, specifies the base data type used by this restriction. The XmlQualifiedName class can be used to represent built-in XSD data types such as string and int. In our example, we need string and hence we pass it as the first parameter of the constructor. The second parameter indicates the namespace to which the data type belongs. The minimum and maximum length restrictions can be enforced by facet classes.

The two facet classes we need are XmlSchemaMinLengthFacet and XmlSchemaMaxLengthFacet. These facet classes inherit from the XmlSchemaFacet base class and represent the minimum length and maximum length of the simple type, respectively, indicated by the Value property of each class. The facets are then added to the XmlSchemaSimpleTypeRestriction instance by using its Add() method. Finally, the Content property of the XmlSchemaSimpleType object is set to the restriction we created.

Creating a Simple Type for Phone Numbers

Creating a simple type for phone numbers follows the same procedure as discussed earlier. However, the restriction requirements are slightly different. The relevant code is shown here:

```
XmlSchemaSimpleType phonetype = new XmlSchemaSimpleType();
XmlSchemaSimpleTypeRestriction phoneRes = new XmlSchemaSimpleTypeRestriction();
phoneRes.BaseTypeName =
```

```
  new XmlQualifiedName("string", "http://www.w3.org/2001/XMLSchema");
XmlSchemaMaxLengthFacet phoneFacet1 = new XmlSchemaMaxLengthFacet();
phoneFacet1.Value = "20";
phoneRes.Facets.Add(phoneFacet1);
phonetype.Content = phoneRes;
```

As before, instances of XmlSchemaSimpleType and XmlSchemaSimpleTypeRestriction are created. This time we need only one facet for specifying the maximum length of the phone number. Thus the code declares an instance of XmlSchemaMaxLengthFacet class and sets its Value property to 20. As before, the facet is added to the restriction, and the Content property of the XmlSchemaSimpleType instance is set to the phone number restriction.

Creating a Simple Type for Notes

Creating a simple type for notes is the same as I discussed earlier. The only change is in the maximum length value. The relevant code is shown here:

```
XmlSchemaMaxLengthFacet notesFacet1 = new XmlSchemaMaxLengthFacet();
notesFacet1.Value = "500";
```

Creating a Complex Type That Represents an Employee

A complex type is represented by the XmlSchemaComplexType class. In our example, the four sub-elements (<firstname>, <lastname>, <homephone>, and <notes>) must appear in the same sequence, which is defined by the XmlSchemaSequence class. The code that defines the complex type is shown here:

```
XmlSchemaComplexType employeetype = new XmlSchemaComplexType();
XmlSchemaSequence sequence = new XmlSchemaSequence();
XmlSchemaElement firstname = new XmlSchemaElement();
firstname.Name = "firstname";
firstname.SchemaType = nametype;
XmlSchemaElement lastname = new XmlSchemaElement();
lastname.Name = "lastname";
lastname.SchemaType = nametype;
XmlSchemaElement homephone = new XmlSchemaElement();
homephone.Name = "homephone";
homephone.SchemaType = phonetype;
XmlSchemaElement notes = new XmlSchemaElement();
notes.Name = "notes";
notes.SchemaType = notestype;

sequence.Items.Add(firstname);
sequence.Items.Add(lastname);
sequence.Items.Add(homephone);
sequence.Items.Add(notes);
employeetype.Particle = sequence;

//define employeeid attribute
XmlSchemaAttribute employeeid = new XmlSchemaAttribute();
employeeid.Name = "employeeid";
```

```
employeeid.SchemaTypeName =
  new XmlQualifiedName("int", "http://www.w3.org/2001/XMLSchema");
employeeid.Use = XmlSchemaUse.Required;
employeetype.Attributes.Add(employeeid);
```

This section of the code starts by declaring instances of the XmlSchemaComplexType and XmlSchemaSequence classes. Next we need four elements. Each is defined by an XmlSchemaElement class and should assume one of the simple types defined earlier. The Name property of the XmlSchemaElement class specifies the name of the element; the SchemaType property specifies the data type of the element and can be set to a simple type or a complex type. After all four elements are defined, they are added to the XmlSchemaSequence object by using its Add() method.

After the sequence instance is ready, you need to set the Particle property of the XmlSchemaComplexType object to it. The Particle property specifies the compositor type of the complex type, and an attribute of a complex type is represented by the XmlSchemaAttribute class. The Name property of XmlSchemaAttribute specifies the name of the attribute. The data type of the attribute is specified by using the SchemaTypeName property, which is of type XmlQualifiedName. In our case, the employeeid attribute is an integer and hence the XmlQualifiedName uses int as the data type. The Use property of the XmlSchemaAttribute class indicates how the attribute is used in the XML document. This property is an enumeration of type XmlSchemaUse. In our case, the employeeid attribute is mandatory and hence we set the Use property to Required.

Creating a Top-Level Complex Type

The root element of our XML document needs to have zero or more instances of the <employee> element, which is of the complex type we defined in the previous section. To represent the <employee> element, we define it as another complex type, as shown here:

```
XmlSchemaComplexType complextype = new XmlSchemaComplexType();
XmlSchemaSequence sq = new XmlSchemaSequence();
XmlSchemaElement employee = new XmlSchemaElement();
employee.Name = "employee";
employee.SchemaType = employeetype;
employee.MinOccurs = 0;
employee.MaxOccursString = "unbounded";
sq.Items.Add(employee);
complextype.Particle = sq;
```

The code creates an instance of the XmlSchemaComplexType and XmlSchemaSequence classes as before. This time it creates a single XmlSchemaElement to represent an <employee> element. This element is of type employeetype (the complex type we defined in the previous section).

The MinOccurs property of the XmlSchemaElement class indicates the minimum number of times the element must appear in the document. Along the same lines, the MaxOccursString property indicates the maximum permissible instances of the element. Note that this property accepts numbers as a string. If there is no restriction on the number, you can set it to unbounded. After the element is created, it is added to the sequence, and the sequence is assigned to the Particle property of the XmlSchemaComplexType class.

Creating the Root Element

The schema needs to have the <employees> root element that can contain one or more <employee> elements. The root element is defined as follows:

```
//define <employees> element
XmlSchemaElement employees = new XmlSchemaElement();
employees.Name = "employees";
employees.SchemaType = complextype;
```

As before, an instance of XmlSchemaElement is created. Its Name property is set to employees, and its SchemaType property is set to the top-level complex type we created in the previous section.

Compiling the Schema

Now we have completed all the simple types, complex types, and attributes. We can now add the root element to the schema. This is done by using the Add() method of the Items collection of the XmlSchema class:

```
schema.Items.Add(employees);
```

After the schema is ready, you can compile it. Compiling the schema ensures that the schema is syntactically correct and well formed. The XmlSchemaSet class represents a set of schemas and allows you to compile them. The relevant code is given here:

```
//compile the schema
try
{
  XmlSchemaSet set = new XmlSchemaSet();
  set.Add(schema);
  set.Compile();
}
catch (Exception ex)
{
  MessageBox.Show("Schema compilation failed");
  return;
}
```

The Add() method of the XmlSchemaSet class accepts the XmlSchema objects that are to be added to the schema set. The Compile() method of the XmlSchemaSet class compiles all the schemas in the given set.

Saving the Schema

Now that we have created and compiled the schema, it is ready to be written to disk:

```
XmlTextWriter writer = new XmlTextWriter(textBox1.Text,null);
schema.Write(writer);
writer.Close();
```

The Write() method of the XmlSchema class writes the schema to a stream and has many overloads. We used one that accepts an XmlWriter pointing to the desired file. After the writing operation is over, the XmlWriter is closed.

That's it! You just created a complete schema using the SOM. You can run the application and see how the schema is generated. Figure 5-13 shows the resultant schema.

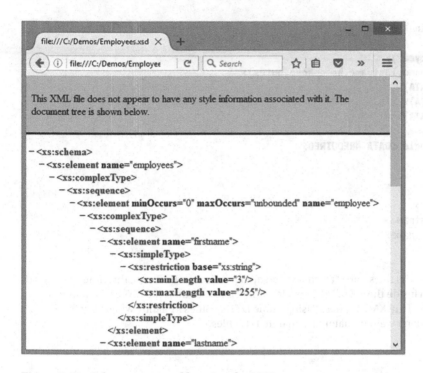

Figure 5-13. *Schema generated by using the SOM*

Attaching the DTD and XML Schemas to XML Documents

Up until this point, you have learned what the DTD and XML Schemas are. You've also learned how to create the DTD and XML Schema. Now it's time to learn how to validate an XML document against the DTD and XML Schema.

Before you can validate an XML document, you must attach a DTD or XML Schema to it. The DTD or XML Schema can be attached via two techniques:

- *Inline DTD or XML schema*: In this technique, the DTD or schema is specified at the top of the XML document.

- *External DTD or XML schema*: In this technique, the DTD or schema resides in its own file—that is, it is external to the XML document. The DTD or schema is then attached to the XML document.

Inline DTDs

To specify a DTD in inline fashion, you need to add a `<!DOCTYPE>` declaration at the top of the XML document. Listing 5-9 shows how this is done for `Employees.xml`.

Listing 5-9. Inline DTD

```
<?xml version="1.0" encoding="utf-8" ?>
<!DOCTYPE employees [
<!ELEMENT employees (employee*)>
<!ELEMENT employee (firstname,lastname,homephone,notes)>
<!ELEMENT firstname (#PCDATA)>
<!ELEMENT lastname (#PCDATA)>
<!ELEMENT homephone (#PCDATA)>
<!ELEMENT notes (#PCDATA)>
<!ATTLIST employee employeeid CDATA #REQUIRED>
]>

<employees>
  <employee employeeid="1">
    <firstname>Nancy</firstname>
    <lastname>Davolio</lastname>
...
```

Notice the markup in bold: it is the same DTD that we created previously. However, this time it is placed inline with the XML document inside the `<!DOCTYPE>` declaration. Note that the `<!DOCTYPE>` declaration must precede the root element of the XML markup. Using inline DTDs comes in handy when your XML documents are small and you don't want to maintain separate DTD files.

External DTDs

External DTDs are stored in separate files, usually with the `.dtd` extension. The DTD is then linked to the XML document using a `<!DOCTYPE>` declaration. Listing 5-10 shows how this is done.

Listing 5-10. External DTD

```
<?xml version="1.0" encoding="utf-8" ?>
<!DOCTYPE employees SYSTEM "employees.dtd">
<employees>
  <employee employeeid="1">
    <firstname>Nancy</firstname>
    <lastname>Davolio</lastname>
...
```

When attaching an external DTD, the `<!DOCTYPE>` declaration is immediately followed by the name of the root element of the XML document (employees in our case). The SYSTEM declaration is followed by the URL of the DTD file. In the preceding example, it is assumed that the DTD resides in a file named `employees.dtd`.

Inline XML Schema

A schema can be specified inline by embedding it within the XML markup itself. As shown in Listing 5-11, the complete schema (starting from `<xs:schema>` to `<xs:/schema>`) is placed immediately inside the root element `<employees>`. The schema must be placed here because an XML document cannot have two root elements.

Listing 5-11. Inline XML Schema

```
<?xml version="1.0" encoding="utf-8" ?>
<employees>
  <xs:schema attributeFormDefault="unqualified" elementFormDefault="qualified"
            xmlns:xs="http://www.w3.org/2001/XMLSchema">
    <xs:element name="employees">
      <xs:complexType>
...
```

Though the XML Editor of Visual Studio supports inline schemas, as a programming recommendation, you should avoid using them. W3C recommendations allow inline schemas, but this support is not a mandatory feature. That means all vendors may not provide support for inline schemas. Further, because they are included within the XML document, they consume more network bandwidth as they are transferred across the wire every time.

External XML Schema

External schemas reside in a physical file, usually with the `.xsd` extension. To attach an external schema to an XML document, you need to modify the root element of the XML document, as shown in Listing 5-12.

Listing 5-12. External XML Schema

```
<?xml version="1.0" encoding="utf-8" ?>
<employees xmlns:xsi="http://www.w3.org/2001/XMLSchema-instance"
           xsi:noNamespaceSchemaLocation="employees.xsd">
  <employee employeeid="1">
    <firstname>Nancy</firstname>
    <lastname>Davolio</lastname>
...
```

As you can see, the `<employees>` root element now has an `xmlns:xsi` attribute that specifies the W3C namespace for XML documents, which are referred to as *XML schema instances*. The `xsi:noNamespaceSchemaLocation` attribute specifies the URL of the schema file (`employees.xsd` in our case).

In the preceding example, our XML document doesn't use a namespace. If it did, we would have to make two changes to our schema and XML documents:

- Add the `targetNamespace` attribute to the schema declaration.

- Use the `xsi:schemaLocation` attribute instead of the `xsi:noNamespaceSchemaLocation` attribute.

Listing 5-13 shows the modified schema, and Listing 5-14 shows the modified XML document.

Listing 5-13. Schema with Target Namespace

```
<xs:schema
  attributeFormDefault="qualified"
  elementFormDefault="qualified"
  xmlns:xs="http://www.w3.org/2001/XMLSchema"
  targetNamespace="myns"
  xmlns="myns">
...
```

As you can see, the schema now has a `targetNamespace` attribute that specifies the target namespace as myns. The XML document must use this namespace, as illustrated in Listing 5-14.

Listing 5-14. XML Document with Namespace

```
<myns:employees
  xmlns:myns="myns"
  xmlns:xsi="http://www.w3.org/2001/XMLSchema-instance"
  xsi:schemaLocation="myns employeesns.xsd">
<myns:employee myns:employeeid="1">
<myns:firstname>Nancy</myns:firstname>
...
```

Note the markup in bold. The root element now declares a namespace called myns, and instead of `xsi:noNamespaceSchemaLocation` it now uses an `xsi:schemaLocation` attribute. Observe carefully how the attribute value is specified: it must contain the namespace name, a space, and then the URL of the XSD file.

Adding Frequently Used Schemas to the Schema Cache

If you find yourself using the same schema files again and again, you may consider adding your schema to the schema cache. Once you store a schema in the schema cache, you can access it readily in the XML Editor of Visual Studio. The schema cache can be seen from the XML ➤ Schemas menu option of Visual Studio. Note that the XML menu option is visible only when you open an XML file in the Visual Studio Editor. Figure 5-14 shows the schemas available by default.

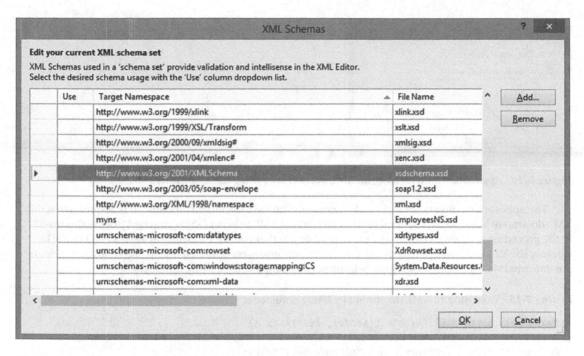

Figure 5-14. *Schema set of Visual Studio*

You can add or remove schemas from the cache by clicking the Add or Remove buttons, respectively. Once you've added a particular schema, you can use it while writing an XML document by selecting the Use This Schema option of the Schema Set dialog (see Figure 5-15).

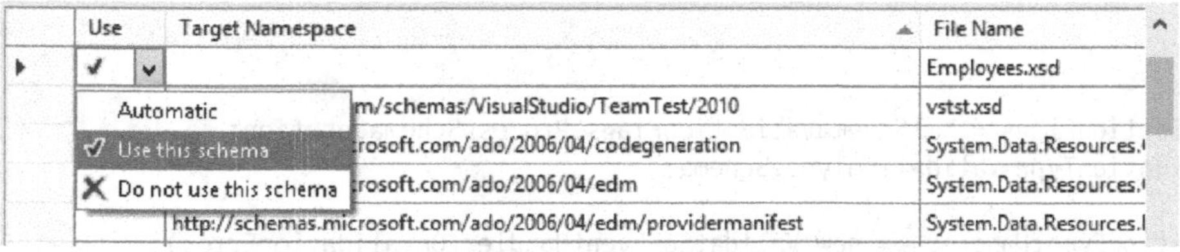

Figure 5-15. *Using a schema from the schema set*

Using XmlReader to Validate XML Documents

The XmlReader class provides you with a way to validate XML documents by using its Create() method, which accepts the URL of the XML document and an instance of the XmlReaderSettings class. The XmlReaderSettings class configures the XmlReader class and can be used to indicate your intention of validating XML documents. You can also wire up an event handler to receive notification about validation errors. The XmlReader instance returned by the Create() method can be used to read the XML document in the same way as you learned in Chapter 3.

To illustrate how to use XmlReader to validate XML documents, you will develop an application like the one shown in Figure 5-16.

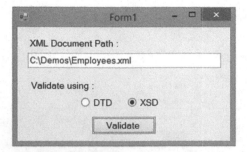

Figure 5-16. *Application for validating an XML document by using the XmlReader class*

The application consists of a text box for accepting the XML document filename. It is assumed that this XML document has either an external DTD or an external XML Schema (XSD) attached to it (as discussed in the preceding sections). The radio buttons indicate whether you are validating against a DTD or XSD. Clicking the Validate button validates the document. Any errors encountered during the validation process are indicated via a message box. Listing 5-15 shows the complete code of the application.

Listing 5-15. Validating an XML Document by Using XmlReader

```csharp
private void button1_Click(object sender, EventArgs e)
{
  XmlReaderSettings settings = new XmlReaderSettings();
  settings.XmlResolver = new XmlUrlResolver();

  if (radioButton1.Checked)
  {
    settings.DtdProcessing = DtdProcessing.Parse;
    settings.ValidationType = ValidationType.DTD;
  }
  else
  {
    settings.ValidationFlags = XmlSchemaValidationFlags.ProcessSchemaLocation;
    settings.ValidationType=ValidationType.Schema;
  }
  settings.ValidationEventHandler += new ValidationEventHandler(OnValidationError);
  XmlReader reader = XmlReader.Create(textBox1.Text, settings);

  while (reader.Read())
  {
    //you can put code here
    //that reads and processes
    //the document
  }

  reader.Close();
  MessageBox.Show("Validation over");
}
```

The code begins by creating an `XmlReaderSettings` object. The `XmlResolver` property of the `XmlReaderSettings` is set to a new `XmlUrlResolver` object so that external DTD or XSD can be located during validation.

If the XML document is to be validated against a DTD (as indicated by the radio buttons), the `DtdProcessing` property of the `XmlReaderSettings` class is set to `DtdProcessing.Parse`. The `DtdProcessing` property decides whether validation against a DTD is allowed. By default, this property is `Prohibit`.

If the document is to be validated against an XML Schema (XSD), the `ValidationFlags` property is set to `ProcessSchemaLocation` (`XmlSchemaValidationFlags` enumeration) so that `XmlResolver` and `XmlReaderSettings` can process the schema locations.

The `ValidationType` property indicates whether `XmlReader` should perform validation and whether to use a DTD or a schema. The `ValidationType` property is an enumeration of type `ValidationType` and has five possible values, as listed in Table 5-3.

Table 5-3. *Possible Values of ValidationType*

Value	Description
None	No validation will be performed. This is the default.
Auto	Automatically decides whether to validate against a DTD or schema by observing the XML document.
DTD	Validation will be performed against a DTD.
Schema	Validation will be performed against an XML Schema (XSD).
XDR	Validation will be performed against an XDR schema.

To trap the validation errors, the `XmlReaderSettings` class raises a `ValidationEventHandler` event. This event is raised only when the `ValidationType` property is other than `None`. The signature of the event-handler function (`OnValidationError()` in our example) must match the one shown here:

```
void OnValidationError(object sender, ValidationEventArgs e)
{
  MessageBox.Show(e.Message);
}
```

The event handler receives a `ValidationEventArgs` object as an event argument, which allows you to examine the underlying exception. You can get the descriptive error message by using the `Message` property as we do in our example. In this case, we simply display a message box with the validation error message.

The code from Listing 5-15 then creates an instance of the `XmlReader` class by calling its `Create()` static method. The URL or path of the XML document and the instance of `XmlReaderSettings` are the arguments. A `while` loop then reads the XML document. If any validation error is detected during this reading operation, the `ValidationEventHandler` event is raised. We could have placed code to read the element and attribute values inside the `while` loop if required (refer to Chapter 3 for information about reading XML documents by using the `XmlReader` class). Finally, the reader is closed.

To test the preceding code, you need to run the application and supply the full path and filenames of an XML document and select from the DTD or XSD radio buttons. You can use the same `Employees.xml` file that we have used throughout this chapter. We also created a DTD and an XML Schema for `Employees.xml` previously. After you click the Validate button, the `XmlReader` will attempt to validate the XML document and notify you of any validation errors. Figure 5-17 shows a message box generated after deliberately removing the required attribute—`employeeid`.

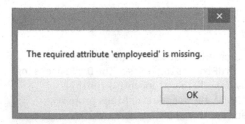

Figure 5-17. *Detecting a validation error*

Using XmlDocument to Validate XML Documents

You are not limited to the XmlReader approach to validate your XML documents; you can also use XmlDocument to validate them. This is useful when you are modifying documents and want to ensure that the new data is consistent with the underlying schema or DTD. The XmlDocument class allows you to validate XML documents in two ways:

- You can validate the document while it is being loaded by the XmlDocument class.

- You can validate the document explicitly when you perform any modification on it such as adding or removing nodes.

In the following example, you will learn how both of the preceding approaches can be used. We will modify the same example that we developed in the "Modifying XML Documents" section of Chapter 2. Figure 5-18 shows the user interface of the application.

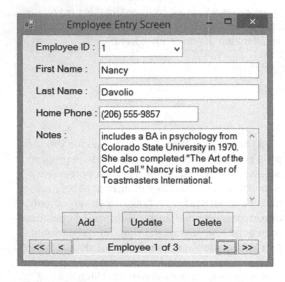

Figure 5-18. *Application for validating XML documents by using XmlDocument*

Because we have already dissected the complete code in Chapter 2, I do not discuss it again here. I discuss only the modifications that are necessary to validate XML documents.

Previously in this section, it was mentioned that XmlDocument allows you to validate XML documents when they are being loaded. This is accomplished by passing a validating reader to the Load() method of the XmlDocument class. Listing 5-16 shows the modified version of the Form_Load event handler.

Listing 5-16. Validating an XML Document When It Is Being Loaded

```
private void Form1_Load(object sender, EventArgs e)
{
  XmlReaderSettings settings = new XmlReaderSettings();
  settings.XmlResolver = new XmlUrlResolver();
  settings.ValidationFlags = XmlSchemaValidationFlags.ProcessSchemaLocation;
  settings.ValidationType = ValidationType.Schema;

  settings.ValidationEventHandler += new
          ValidationEventHandler(OnValidationError);
  XmlReader reader =
    XmlReader.Create($"{Application.StartupPath}\\employees.xml", settings);
  doc.Load(reader);
  reader.Close();

  foreach (XmlNode node in doc.DocumentElement.ChildNodes)
  {
    comboBox1.Items.Add(node.Attributes["employeeid"].Value);
  }
  FillControls();
}
```

Notice the code marked in bold. This code should be familiar to you, because we discussed it in the earlier sections of this chapter. It essentially creates an XmlReaderSettings object and configures it to validate Employees.xml against Employees.xsd. The ValidationEventHandler event is handled by the OnValidationError() method. The XmlReaderSettings object is then passed to the Create() method of the XmlReader class to get an XmlReader object.

The Load() method of XmlDocument accepts the newly created XmlReader object as a parameter, internally iterates through the XmlReader, and then validation takes place. If there are any validation errors, the OnValidationError() method gets called.

Now comes the tricky part. The XmlDocument class allows you to modify the document. Thus a document can be valid when loaded but can become invalid after modification. For example, as per our schema, the telephone number cannot be greater than 20 characters. The user of the form can, however, ignore this restriction, and the loaded document can now have invalid data. This makes it necessary to revalidate the changes made to the document. Fortunately, the XmlDocument class provides a method called Validate() that does the job. Listing 5-17 shows the use of Validate() during the update operation.

Listing 5-17. Validating a Node Explicitly

```
private void button2_Click(object sender, EventArgs e)
{
  XmlNode node =
    doc.SelectSingleNode($"//employee[@employeeid='
{comboBox1.SelectedItem}']");
  if (node != null)
  {
    node.ChildNodes[0].InnerText = textBox1.Text;
```

```
    node.ChildNodes[1].InnerText = textBox2.Text;
    node.ChildNodes[2].InnerText = textBox3.Text;
    XmlCDataSection notes = doc.CreateCDataSection(textBox4.Text);
    node.ChildNodes[3].ReplaceChild(notes, node.ChildNodes[3].ChildNodes[0]);
}

doc.Validate(OnValidationError,node);

if (!isError)
{
    doc.Save($"{Application.StartupPath}\\employees.xml");
}
}
```

Note the code marked in bold. The Validate() method of XmlDocument can validate the entire document or just a node against a previously specified schema or DTD. The Validate() method accepts two parameters: the name of a function that matches the ValidationEventHandler delegate signature and the XmlNode to validate. There is one more overload of Validate() that takes just a function matching the ValidationEventHandler delegate signature and validates the entire document. The OnValidationError function is shown in Listing 5-18.

Listing 5-18. The OnValidationError Function

```
void OnValidationError(object sender, ValidationEventArgs e)
{
    MessageBox.Show(e.Message);
    isError = true;
}
```

The function simply shows the error message in a message box and sets a class-level Boolean variable—isError—to true. This variable is checked to decide whether to save the document. To test the application, modify the phone number of any employee to more than 20 characters and click the Update button. You should see a message box similar to the one shown in Figure 5-19.

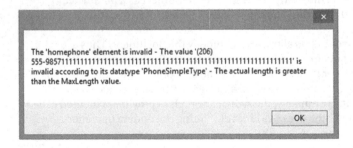

Figure 5-19. *Validation error during saving changes*

Using XPathNavigator to Validate XML Documents

You might be using XPathNavigator to read XML documents and may want to perform validation on those documents. Recollect from Chapter 4 that XPathNavigator can be obtained by using the XmlDocument or XPathDocument classes. The XPathNavigator obtained by using XmlDocument is editable, whereas that obtained by using XPathDocument is read-only. The XPathNavigator class by itself does not allow you to validate data, but you can use the underlying XmlDocument or XPathDocument classes to perform the validation.

We already saw the validation performed by using XmlDocument, but just like XmlDocument, the XPathDocument class allows you to validate XML documents against a schema or DTD during loading. In this case, the constructor of XPathDocument can accept a validating XmlReader to perform the validation. Because the XPathNavigator obtained by using XPathDocument is read-only, there is no way to revalidate the XML document after it has been loaded. Listing 5-19 shows how the XPathNavigator obtained by using XPathDocument can perform the validation.

Listing 5-19. Validating by Using XPathNavigator

```
XmlReaderSettings settings = new XmlReaderSettings();
settings.XmlResolver = new XmlUrlResolver();
settings.ValidationFlags = XmlSchemaValidationFlags.ProcessSchemaLocation;
settings.ValidationType = ValidationType.Schema;
settings.ValidationEventHandler += new ValidationEventHandler(OnValidationError);
XmlReader reader = XmlReader.Create(@"C:\Demos\employees.xml", settings);
XPathDocument doc = new XPathDocument(reader);
XPathNavigator navigator = doc.CreateNavigator();
```

The code creates an XmlReaderSettings object as before. The Create() method of XmlReader accepts this XmlReaderSettings object and returns an XmlReader instance. The XmlReader instance is then supplied to the constructor of the XPathDocument class. The CreateNavigator() method of XPathDocument finally creates the XPathNavigator that can be used to navigate through the XML document.

Specifying XML Schema via Code

In the preceding examples, the Employees.xml file had an associated DTD or XML Schema. Imagine a situation where you have an XML file that doesn't have any schema associated with it, but you want to validate that XML file using some schema.

Suppose you have an application that allows you to export data in XML format. The exported XML file doesn't have any associated schema (inline or external schema file) because it's simply the outcome of the application's export functionality.

Further suppose that a need arises to import these previously exported files into some other application. As a safety measure, you want to ensure that the files being imported adhere to certain schema. But since the exported XML files don't have any schema associated with them, you can't validate them unless you open each file and add schema information into it as discussed earlier.

Luckily, there is a programmatic way to accomplish this task. You can validate such XML files (not having any schema associated with them) by specifying a schema via code. So, rather than the XML file mentioning the schema information, you specify the schema programmatically. To accomplish this task you need to add a schema in the Schemas collection of the XmlReaderSettings. The Schemas collection is an XmlSchemaSet object that represents a cache of XSD schemas. You can add a schema to it using its Add() method.

To understand how this can be done you will develop a Windows Forms application, as shown in Figure 5-20.

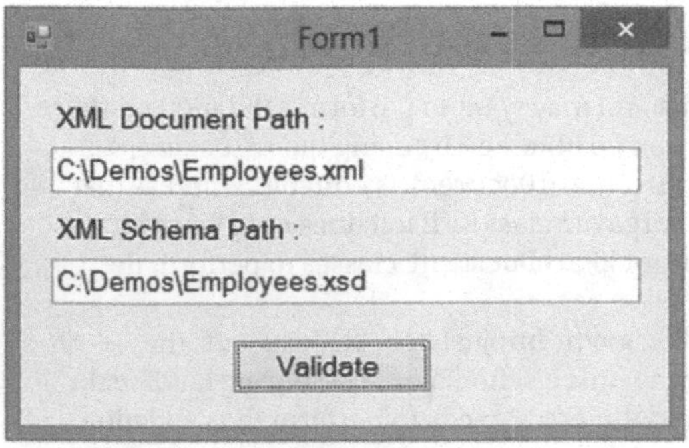

Figure 5-20. Application that attaches a schema via code

The application consists of two text boxes and a button. The first text box is used to specify the path of the XML document, whereas the second text box is used to specify the path of XML Schema (XSD) file. Clicking on the Validate button validates the XML file against the specified XML Schema. Validation errors (if any) are shown using a message box as before.

Listing 5-20 shows the Click event handler of the Validate button.

Listing 5-20. Adding a Schema in XmlSchemaSet

```
private void button1_Click(object sender, EventArgs e)
{
    XmlReaderSettings settings = new XmlReaderSettings();
    settings.ValidationType=ValidationType.Schema;
    settings.Schemas.Add("", textBox2.Text);
    settings.ValidationEventHandler += new ValidationEventHandler(OnValidationError);

    XmlReader reader=XmlReader.Create(textBox1.Text, settings);
    while (reader.Read())
    {
        //you can put code here
        //that reads and processes
        //the document
    }
    reader.Close();
    MessageBox.Show("Validation over");
}
```

Notice the code marked in bold letters. The validationType is set to Schema. This technique of validating XML documents works only for XML Schemas. Further, the code adds an XML Schema to the Schemas collection of the XmlReaderSettings. This way the XML Schema specified in textBox2 is made available to validate the XML document specified in textBox1.

The remainder of the code should be familiar to you, as it has been discussed along with the earlier examples. ");

In order to test this application, remove the schema information from the Employees.xml file and then run the application. Specify the path of the Employees.xml file and the path of Employees.xsd schema file in the respective text boxes. Clicking on the Validate button will validate the XML document. Figure 5-21 shows a sample error message when the employeeid attribute was deliberately removed from the first <employee> element.

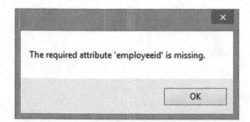

Figure 5-21. *Document validated against schema added programmatically*

Summary

This chapter introduced you to DTDs and schemas. You learned how to create a DTD and an XML Schema. You also learned to use Visual Studio tools for creating schemas. The .NET Framework's Schema Object Model (SOM) is an extensive collection of objects that allows you to create schemas programmatically. You learned some of the important and commonly used classes from the SOM hierarchy.

Creating a schema or DTD is just half of the story. The other half involves actually validating your XML documents against the specified schema or DTD. To validate an XML document against a schema or DTD, you can use several approaches—that is, with the XmlReader, XmlDocument, and XPathNavigator classes. All the approaches essentially rely on two classes: XmlReaderSettings and XmlReader. The former class configures the XmlReader to perform validation. It also attaches an event handler for handling validation events. The latter class actually reads the document and notifies you of validation errors.

CHAPTER 6

■■■

Transforming XML with XSLT

In the previous chapters, we dealt with XML documents and their manipulation. Our interaction with XML documents was limited to reading, writing, querying, and validating them with the help of .NET Framework classes. No doubt these operations are widely needed in real-world XML applications. However, often you also need to transform XML data from one representation to another. For example, you may need to convert XML data into HTML so that it can be displayed in the browser. So, how do we accomplish such a transformation? This is where Extensible Style Sheet Language Transformations (XSLT) comes into the picture.

This chapter covers details of XSLT processing using the .NET Framework classes. Specifically, you will learn the following:

- What XSLT is

- The `XslCompiledTransform` class that is the .NET Framework's XSLT processor

- How to transform XML documents by using `XslCompiledTransform`

- How to use XSLT extension objects

- How to pass parameters to XSLT style sheets

- How to emit script in XSLT style sheets

Overview of XSLT

XML markup often needs to be transformed before it can be put to any use. To cater to this requirement, the W3C introduced Extensible Style Sheet Language (XSL)—a standard for representing style sheets for XML documents. XSL was intended to act along the same lines as Cascading Style Sheets (CSS), which are used to style HTML pages. However, over a period of time, the W3C realized the complexity involved in transforming XML documents, and the overall XSL standards were separated into XSLT, XPath, and XSL-FO. Out of these three main subdivisions, XSLT is intended for transforming XML documents.

■ **Note**   The XPath standard allows you to query and navigate XML documents; Chapter 4 covered XPath. XSL Formatting Objects (XSL-FO) is intended to format XML documents and is beyond the scope of this book.

XSLT consists of elements and functions that together allow you to transform XML documents. To understand how XSLT elements and functions are used, you will see a simple example.

Suppose that you have an XML document as shown in Listing 6-1. As you can see, it is the same `Employees.xml` file that we have been using for all of our examples.

© Bipin Joshi 2017
B. Joshi, *Beginning XML with C# 7*, https://doi.org/10.1007/978-1-4842-3105-0_6

Listing 6-1. Sample XML Document (Employees.xml)

```xml
<?xml version="1.0" encoding="utf-8" ?>
<!-- This is list of employees -->
<employees>
  <employee employeeid="1">
    <firstname>Nancy</firstname>
    <lastname>Davolio</lastname>
    <homephone>(206) 555-9857</homephone>
    <notes>
<![CDATA[Education includes a BA in psychology from Colorado State University in 1970.
She also completed "The Art of the Cold Call." Nancy is a member of Toastmasters
International.]]>
    </notes>
  </employee>
  <employee employeeid="2">
    <firstname>Andrew</firstname>
    <lastname>Fuller</lastname>
    <homephone>(206) 555-9482</homephone>
    <notes>
<![CDATA[Andrew received his BTS commercial in 1974 and a Ph.D. in international marketing
from the University of Dallas in 1981. He is fluent in French and Italian and reads
German. He joined the company as a sales representative, was promoted  to sales manager
in January 1992 and to vice president of sales in March 1993. Andrew is a member of the
Sales Management Roundtable, the Seattle Chamber of Commerce, and the Pacific Rim Importers
Association.]]>
    </notes>
  </employee>
  <employee employeeid="3">
    <firstname>Janet</firstname>
    <lastname>Leverling</lastname>
    <homephone>(206) 555-3412</homephone>
    <notes>
<![CDATA[Janet has a BS degree in chemistry from Boston College (1984).
She has also completed a certificate program in food retailing management.
Janet was hired as a sales associate in 1991 and promoted to sales representative in
February 1992.]]>
    </notes>
  </employee>
</employees>
```

Now further assume that you want to display this XML file in a web browser, as shown in Figure 6-1.

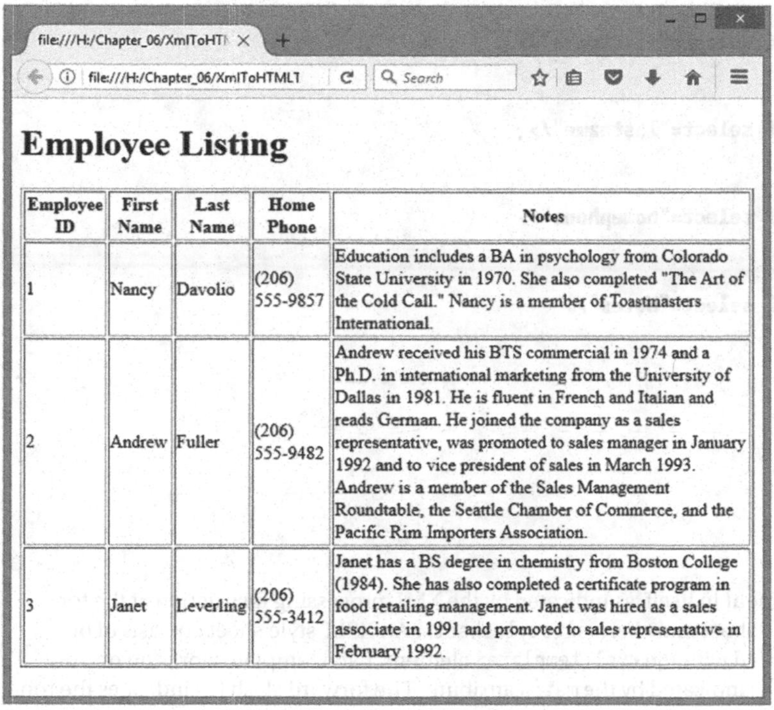

Figure 6-1. *XML document converted to an HTML table*

This means you want to convert XML markup into HTML markup. This transformation is achieved by XSLT. Let's see how.

Listing 6-2 shows Employees.xslt—an XSLT style sheet that will be applied to Employees.xml.

Listing 6-2. XSLT for Transforming Employees.xml into an HTML Table

```
<?xml version="1.0" encoding="UTF-8" ?>
<xsl:stylesheet version="1.0" xmlns:xsl="http://www.w3.org/1999/XSL/Transform">
  <xsl:template match="/">
    <html>
      <body>
        <h1>Employee Listing</h1>
        <table border="1">
          <tr>
            <th>Employee ID</th>
            <th>First Name</th>
            <th>Last Name</th>
            <th>Home Phone</th>
            <th>Notes</th>
          </tr>
          <xsl:for-each select="employees/employee">
            <tr>
              <td>
                <xsl:value-of select="@employeeid"/>
              </td>
```

```
      <td>
        <xsl:value-of select="firstname"/>
      </td>
      <td>
        <xsl:value-of select="lastname"/>
      </td>
      <td>
        <xsl:value-of select="homephone"/>
      </td>
      <td>
        <xsl:value-of select="notes"/>
      </td>
    </tr>
   </xsl:for-each>
  </table>
 </body>
</html>
 </xsl:template>
</xsl:stylesheet>
```

An XSLT file is an XML document in itself, as indicated by the XML processing instruction at the top. The root element of any XSLT style sheet must be <xsl:stylesheet>. An XSLT style sheet consists of one or more templates, which are marked with the <xsl:template> element. Each template works on one or more elements from the XML file as indicated by the match attribute. The forward slash (/) indicates the root element. The match attribute can take any valid XPath expression.

Inside the outermost <xsl:template> element, the markup outputs an HTML table with four columns: Employee ID, First Name, Last Name, and Notes. We want to pick up every <employee> element from the document and extract its attribute and subelement values. The <xsl:for-each> element works like a for each loop in any programming language and selects a node set based on the criteria specified in the select attribute. In our example, because we want to work with <employee> elements, the select attribute is set to employees/employee. The select attribute of <xsl:for-each> can take any valid XPath expression.

Inside the <xsl:for-each> construct, the values of attributes and elements are retrieved by using the <xsl:value-of> element. The select attribute of <xsl:value-of> must be any valid XPath expression that returns the value to be outputted. Note the use of @employeeid to retrieve the value of the employeeid attribute. Thus the employeeid attribute and the values of the four sub-elements (<firstname>, <lastname>, <homephone>, and <notes>) are outputted in the cells of the HTML table.

The same process is repeated for all the employees in the Employees.xml file.

Now that you are familiar with the XSLT style sheet, it's time to attach the style sheet to the XML document. To do so, you must add the markup shown in Listing 6-3 to the Employees.xml file.

Listing 6-3. Attaching an XSLT Style Sheet to an XML Document

```
<?xml version="1.0" encoding="utf-8" ?>
<?xml-stylesheet type="text/xsl" href="Employees.xslt"?>
<!-- This is list of employees -->
<employees>
  <employee employeeid="1">
    <firstname>Nancy</firstname>
...
```

Notice the use of the `<?xml-stylesheet?>` processing instruction. This processing instruction indicates that the type of style sheet being applied is XSL, and it is located at the URL specified by the `href` attribute. After you attach the style sheet to the XML document, you can view the XML file in the browser, and you should see output similar to Figure 6-1.

In the following sections, you will learn a few more constructs of XSLT.

Applying Templates Using <xsl:apply-templates>

The `<xsl:apply-templates>` element applies templates to the elements specified by its `select` attribute. To illustrate the use of `<xsl:apply-templates>`, we will create an XSLT style sheet that renders the XML markup from `Employees.xml`, as shown in Figure 6-2.

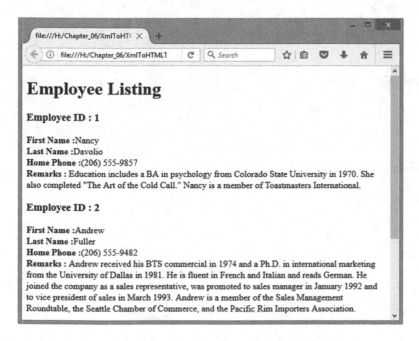

Figure 6-2. *Rendering Employees.xml by applying templates*

The corresponding style sheet is shown in Listing 6-4.

Listing 6-4. Using <xsl:apply-templates>

```
<?xml version="1.0" encoding="UTF-8" ?>
<xsl:stylesheet version="1.0" xmlns:xsl="http://www.w3.org/1999/XSL/Transform">
  <xsl:template match="/">
    <html>
      <body>
        <h1>Employee Listing</h1>
        <xsl:apply-templates/>
      </body>
    </html>
  </xsl:template>
```

```
<xsl:template match="employee">
  <div>
    <h3>Employee ID :
    <xsl:value-of select="@employeeid"/>
    </h3>
    <xsl:apply-templates select="firstname"/>
    <xsl:apply-templates select="lastname"/>
    <xsl:apply-templates select="homephone"/>
    <xsl:apply-templates select="notes"/>
  </div>
</xsl:template>

<xsl:template match="firstname">
  <b>First Name :</b><xsl:value-of select="."/>
  <br />
</xsl:template>

<xsl:template match="lastname">
  <b>Last Name :</b>
  <xsl:value-of select="."/>
  <br />
</xsl:template>

<xsl:template match="homephone">
  <b>Home Phone :</b>
  <xsl:value-of select="."/>
  <br />
</xsl:template>

<xsl:template match="notes">
  <b>Remarks :</b>
  <xsl:value-of select="."/>
  <br />
</xsl:template>

</xsl:stylesheet>
```

This time the topmost `<xsl:template>` element includes an `<xsl:apply-templates>` element. If the `<xsl:apply-templates>` element is used without the `select` attribute, `<xsl:apply-templates>` applies matching templates to all sub-elements. Then, the XSLT declares five templates for the `<employee>`, `<firstname>`, `<lastname>`, `<homephone>`, and `<notes>` elements, respectively.

The template for the `<employee>` element actually decides the order in which the remaining templates will be applied. This is done by specifying the `select` attribute in the `<xsl:apply-templates>` element. The `select` attribute can contain any valid XPath expression.

Branching Using <xsl:if>

The XSLT standard provides the `<xsl:if>` element that is equivalent to the `if` statement provided by many programming languages. Suppose that you want to display details only where the first name is *Nancy*. You can achieve this by using `<xsl:if>`, as shown in Listing 6-5.

Listing 6-5. Using <xsl:if>

```
<?xml version="1.0" encoding="UTF-8" ?>
<xsl:stylesheet version="1.0" xmlns:xsl="http://www.w3.org/1999/XSL/Transform">
  <xsl:template match="/">
    <html>
      <body>
        <h1>Employee Listing</h1>
        <table border="1">
          <tr>
            <th>Employee ID</th>
            <th>First Name</th>
            <th>Last Name</th>
            <th>Home Phone</th>
            <th>Notes</th>
          </tr>
          <xsl:for-each select="employees/employee">>
          <xsl:if test="firstname[text()='Nancy']">
            <tr>
              <td>
                <xsl:value-of select="@employeeid"/>
              </td>
              <td>
                <xsl:value-of select="firstname"/>
              </td>
              <td>
                <xsl:value-of select="lastname"/>
              </td>
              <td>
                <xsl:value-of select="homephone"/>
              </td>
              <td>
                <xsl:value-of select="notes"/>
              </td>
            </tr>
          </xsl:if>
          </xsl:for-each>
        </table>
      </body>
    </html>
  </xsl:template>
</xsl:stylesheet>>
```

This is the same style sheet that we used in our first example, but this time, it includes the <xsl:if>
construct. The test attribute of <xsl:if> tests for a specific condition. The condition in our example checks
whether the value of the <firstname> element (text()) is Nancy. If it is Nancy, the details are outputted
in the resultant HTML table. Figure 6-3 shows a sample view of the Employees.xml file after applying the
preceding style sheet.

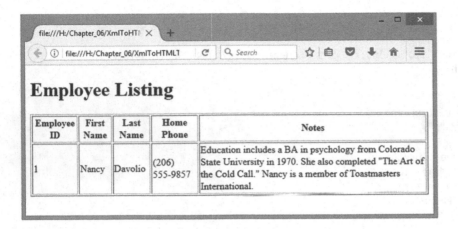

Figure 6-3. *Output after using <xsl:if>*

Branching Using <xsl:choose> and <xsl:when>

The `<xsl:choose>` and `<xsl:when>` elements are equivalent to the `switch` statement used by programming languages. Using our example file, suppose that you want to display an additional column called Qualification in the resultant HTML table. You want to search the notes about an employee for certain qualifications and accordingly want to display them in this additional column. Listing 6-6 shows the style sheet that accomplishes this task.

Listing 6-6. Using <xsl:choose> and <xsl:when>

```
<?xml version="1.0" encoding="UTF-8" ?>
<xsl:stylesheet version="1.0" xmlns:xsl="http://www.w3.org/1999/XSL/Transform">
  <xsl:template match="/">
    <html>
      <body>
        <h1>Employee Listing</h1>
        <table border="1">
          <tr>
            <th>Employee ID</th>
            <th>First Name</th>
            <th>Last Name</th>
            <th>Home Phone</th>
            <th>Notes</th>
            <th>Qualification</th>
          </tr>
          <xsl:for-each select="employees/employee">
            <tr>
              <td>
                <xsl:value-of select="@employeeid"/>
              </td>
              <td>
                <xsl:value-of select="firstname"/>
              </td>
```

```
      <td>
        <xsl:value-of select="lastname"/>
      </td>
      <td>
        <xsl:value-of select="homephone"/>
      </td>
      <td>
        <xsl:value-of select="notes"/>
      </td>
      <td>
      <xsl:choose>
        <xsl:when test="notes[contains(.,'BA')]">
          BA (Arts)
        </xsl:when>
        <xsl:when test="notes[contains(.,'BS')]">
          BS (Science)
        </xsl:when>
        <xsl:when test="notes[contains(.,'BTS')]">
          BTS (Other)
        </xsl:when>
        <xsl:otherwise>
          Unknown
        </xsl:otherwise>
      </xsl:choose>
      </td>
    </tr>
  </xsl:for-each>
  </table>
  </body>
  </html>
  </xsl:template>
</xsl:stylesheet>
```

Notice the markup in bold. The `<xsl:choose>` element starts the `switch` statement. Each individual `<xsl:when>` element tests a specific condition. In our example, we check whether the `<notes>` element contains BA, BS, or BTS, and accordingly emit the qualification of the employee. If the test fails, the markup from `<xsl:otherwise>` is emitted. Figure 6-4 shows the table with the Qualification column added.

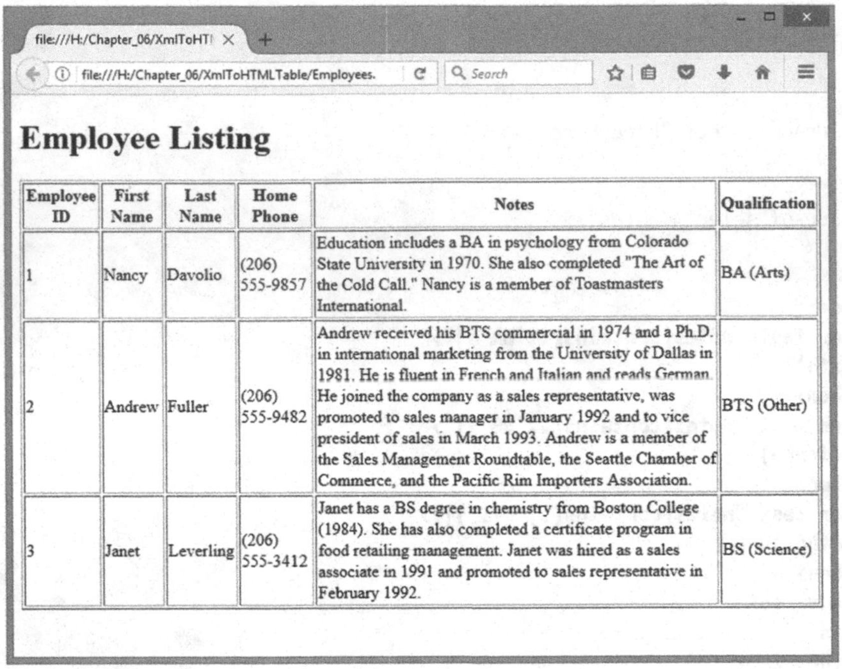

Figure 6-4. Qualification column added by using <xsl:choose> and <xsl:when>

Transforming Elements and Attributes

Up until now, we have transformed XML data into HTML. However, often you may need to transform XML data into another XML representation. For example, a B2B application might be receiving orders electronically in XML format. While receiving such orders, you must ensure that the source XML markup and expected XML markup match. If they do not match, you can apply XSLT transformations to generate the desired markup.

To illustrate how XSLT transformations can convert one XML representation into another, we will transform Employees.xml into another XML representation, as shown in Listing 6-7.

Listing 6-7. Required XML Markup from Employees.xml

```
<?xml version="1.0" encoding="utf-8"?>
<EMPLOYEES>
  <E1 EMPCODE="1">
    <FNAME>Nancy</FNAME>
    <LNAME>Davolio</LNAME>
    <PHONE>(206) 555-9857</PHONE>
    <REMARKS>
      Education includes a BA in psychology from Colorado State University in 1970. She also
      completed "The Art of the Cold Call." Nancy is a member of
Toastmasters International.
    </REMARKS>
  </E1>
  <E2 EMPCODE="2">
    <FNAME>Andrew</FNAME>
```

158

```
<LNAME>Fuller</LNAME>
<PHONE>(206) 555-9482</PHONE>
<REMARKS>
    Andrew received his BTS commercial in 1974 and a Ph.D. in international
marketing from the University of Dallas in 1981. He is fluent in French and
Italian and reads German. He joined the company as a sales representative,
was promoted to sales manager in January 1992 and to vice president of sales
 in March 1993. Andrew is a member of the Sales Management Roundtable,
the Seattle Chamber of Commerce, and the Pacific Rim Importers Association.
    </REMARKS>
  </E2>
  <E3 EMPCODE="3">
    <FNAME>Janet</FNAME>
    <LNAME>Leverling</LNAME>
    <PHONE>(206) 555-3412</PHONE>
    <REMARKS>
    Janet has a BS degree in chemistry from Boston College (1984).
She has also completed a certificate program in food retailing management.
Janet was hired as a sales associate in 1991 and promoted to sales representative in
February 1992.
    </REMARKS>
  </E3>
</EMPLOYEES>
```

Notice the several changes made to the XML markup:

- The root node is now `<EMPLOYEES>` and not `<employees>`.

- Each `<employee>` element is replaced with an element of the form E`<employeeid>`—
  that is, `<E1>`, `<E2>`, and `<E3>`. That means the element name consists of a constant
  part (E) followed by the employee ID.

- The employeeid attribute has now become the `EMPCODE` attribute.

- The `<firstname>`, `<lastname>`, `<homephone>`, and `<notes>` elements have now
  become `<FNAME>`, `<LNAME>`, `<PHONE>`, and `<REMARKS>`, respectively.

The XSLT style sheet that brings about this transformation is shown in Listing 6-8.

Listing 6-8. Transforming Employees.xml

```
<?xml version="1.0" encoding="UTF-8" ?>
<xsl:stylesheet version="1.0" xmlns:xsl="http://www.w3.org/1999/XSL/Transform">
  <xsl:template match="/">
    <EMPLOYEES>
      <xsl:apply-templates/>
    </EMPLOYEES>
  </xsl:template>

  <xsl:template match="employee">
    <xsl:element name="E{@employeeid}">
      <xsl:attribute name="EMPCODE">
        <xsl:value-of select="@employeeid"/>
      </xsl:attribute>
```

```
        <xsl:apply-templates select="firstname"/>
        <xsl:apply-templates select="lastname"/>
        <xsl:apply-templates select="homephone"/>
        <xsl:apply-templates select="notes"/>
    </xsl:element>
  </xsl:template>

  <xsl:template match="firstname">
    <FNAME>
      <xsl:value-of select="."/>
    </FNAME>
  </xsl:template>

  <xsl:template match="lastname">
    <LNAME>
      <xsl:value-of select="."/>
    </LNAME>
  </xsl:template>

  <xsl:template match="homephone">
    <PHONE>
      <xsl:value-of select="."/>
    </PHONE>
  </xsl:template>
  <xsl:template match="notes">
    <REMARKS>
      <xsl:value-of select="."/>
    </REMARKS>
  </xsl:template>
</xsl:stylesheet>
```

Notice the code marked in bold. The topmost <xsl:template> element now contains the <EMPLOYEES> element. The template that matches the <employee> element does an interesting job: the <xsl:element> element is used to define new elements in the resultant output. You might be wondering why we need this element; after all, you can directly specify new element names (as we do for <FNAME>, <LNAME>, <PHONE>, and <REMARKS> later on). Note that we need to create an element name that is E followed by the employee ID. Something like this can be accomplished only by using the <xsl:element> element. Observe carefully how the element name has been formed by specifying the dynamic part (employee ID) in curly brackets. Next, the <xsl:attribute> element defines the EMPCODE attribute. The templates for <firstname>, <lastname>, <homephone>, and <notes> are then applied. In each of these templates, the new markup tag is emitted along with the value of the element.

If you open this file in a web browser, you may not see the desired markup because the output is not HTML this time. The Visual Studio IDE provides an easy way to see the resultant output. Open the XML document (Employees.xml) in the IDE and apply the latest style sheet to it by using the xml-stylesheet processing instruction. Then choose XML ➤ Start XSLT Debugging from the menu. Visual Studio will apply the style sheet to the XML document and display the resultant output.

The XslCompiledTransform Class

Up until now, we have attached XSLT style sheets to XML documents at design time. However, in many real-world cases, you may need to apply them programmatically. For example, you might be generating the XML data at runtime and want to transform it by using XSLT. The XslCompiledTransform class is intended for just such a situation. The XslCompiledTransform class resides in the System.Xml.Xsl namespace and represents the .NET Framework's XSLT processor. It compiles the XSLT style sheets and performs XSLT transformations.

The XslCompiledTransform class can accept XML data to transform it in several forms. Similarly, the output generated by XslCompiledTransform can be in various forms. To be specific, the source of transformation can be as follows:

- An object that implements IXPathNavigator (for example, XmlNode or XPathDocument)

- An XmlReader

- A URL or path of the XML file

The output of the transformation can be in the form of the following:

- An XmlWriter class

- A physical disk file

- A stream (for example, MemoryStream or FileStream)

- An object of a class inheriting from the TextWriter abstract class (for example, StringWriter or StreamWriter)

Performing Transformations Using XslCompiledTransform

In this section, you will learn to use the XslCompiledTransform class. You will develop an application like the one shown in Figure 6-5.

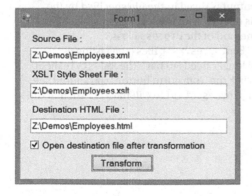

Figure 6-5. *Application to apply XSLT transformations*

As shown in Figure 6-5, the application consists of three text boxes to accept the source XML filename, the XSLT style sheet filename, and the destination HTML filename, respectively. Clicking the Transform button performs the transformation, and the output of the transformation is stored in a file specified by the Destination File text box. You can also open the destination file after a successful transformation by selecting the check box. Listing 6-9 shows the Click event handler of the Transform button.

Listing 6-9. Using the XslCompiledTransform Class

```
private void button1_Click(object sender, EventArgs e)
{
    if(Path.GetExtension(textBox3.Text)!=".htm" &&
        Path.GetExtension(textBox3.Text)!=".html")
    {
        MessageBox.Show("File extension must be .htm or .html");
        return;
    }
    XslCompiledTransform xslt = new XslCompiledTransform();
    xslt.Load(textBox2.Text);
    xslt.Transform(textBox1.Text, textBox3.Text);
    if (checkBox1.Checked)
    {
        System.Diagnostics.Process.Start(textBox3.Text);
    }
}
```

Make sure to import the System.Xml.Xsl namespace because the XslCompiledTransform class resides in it. Notice the code marked in bold. To start with, the code creates an instance of the XslCompiledTransform class. The Load() method of XslCompiledTransform accepts the path of the XSLT style sheet to be applied and loads it for transformation. However, it is the Transform() method that actually performs the transformation by applying the style sheet loaded by using the Load() method. There are several overloads of the Transform() method; the one that we have used accepts two string parameters. The first parameter is the path of the source XML document, and the second parameter is the path of the destination document. After the transformation, the resultant output is saved in the file specified by the second parameter of the Transform() method. Finally, the file is opened with the associated application (typically a web browser for HTML files) by using the Start() method of the Process class.

To test the application, you can use the Employees.xml and Employees.xslt files (see Listing 6-2) that we used earlier in this chapter. Note that Employees.xml no longer needs to have the xml-stylesheet processing instruction. When you supply all the filenames and click the Transform button, you should see the Employees.html file generated in the specified folder. The Employees.html file will have HTML markup shown in Listing 6-10.

Listing 6-10. Output After Applying the Style Sheet

```
<html>
  <body>
    <h1>Employee Listing</h1>
    <table border="1">
      <tr>
        <th>Employee ID</th>
        <th>First Name</th>
        <th>Last Name</th>
```

```
        <th>Home Phone</th>
        <th>Notes</th>
      </tr>
      <tr>
        <td>1</td>
        <td>Nancy</td>
        <td>Davolio</td>
        <td>(206) 555-9857</td>
        <td>
          Education includes a BA in psychology from Colorado State University in 1970.
          She also completed "The Art of the Cold Call." Nancy is a member of Toastmasters
          International.
        </td>
      </tr>
      <tr>
        <td>2</td>
        <td>Andrew</td>
        <td>Fuller</td>
        <td>(206) 555-9482</td>
        <td>
          Andrew received his BTS commercial in 1974 and a Ph.D. in international marketing
          from the University of Dallas in 1981. He is fluent in French and Italian and
          reads German. He joined the company as a sales representative, was promoted to
          sales manager in January 1992 and to vice president of sales in March 1993. Andrew
          is a member of the Sales Management Roundtable, the Seattle Chamber of Commerce,
          and the Pacific Rim Importers Association.
        </td>
      </tr>
      <tr>
        <td>3</td>
        <td>Janet</td>
        <td>Leverling</td>
        <td>(206) 555-3412</td>
        <td>
          Janet has a BS degree in chemistry from Boston College (1984). She has also
          completed a certificate program in food retailing management. Janet was hired as a
          sales associate in 1991 and promoted to sales representative in February 1992.
        </td>
      </tr>
    </table>
  </body>
</html>
```

As you can see, the source XML markup is transformed into HTML markup as specified in the style sheet.

■ **Note** In our example, we converted XML markup into HTML markup. However, you can easily use the `XslCompiledTransform` class to transform source XML into another XML representation.

Passing Arguments to a Transformation

In Listing 6-5, you created a style sheet that transforms details of a single employee, Nancy, by using the `<xsl:if>` element. The problem with our XSLT is that we hard-coded the name *Nancy* in the style sheet. In real-world cases, this name will probably come from a user interface element. Thus, it becomes necessary that the employee's first name be accepted as a parameter in the XSLT rather than a fixed value.

Fortunately, XSLT allows you to declare parameters in your style sheet. These parameters can then be supplied at runtime from your application. A collection of these parameters is represented by the `XsltArgumentList` class, and you can add individual parameters to this collection. To illustrate the use of `XsltArgumentList`, we will develop an application like the one shown in Figure 6-6.

Figure 6-6. *Application for passing parameters to the XSLT style sheet*

The application consists of a single text box for accepting the first name of the employee. Clicking the Transform button applies the style sheet and stores the resultant output in an HTML file. Our XML file remains the same (`Employees.xml`). However, you need to modify the style sheet from Listing 6-5 as shown in Listing 6-11.

Listing 6-11. XSLT Style Sheet with Parameter

```
<?xml version="1.0" encoding="UTF-8" ?>
<xsl:stylesheet version="1.0" xmlns:xsl="http://www.w3.org/1999/XSL/Transform">
  <xsl:param name="firstname"/>
  <xsl:template match="/">
    <html>
      <body>
        <h1>Employee Listing</h1>
        <table border="1">
          <tr>
            <th>Employee ID</th>
            <th>First Name</th>
            <th>Last Name</th>
            <th>Home Phone</th>
            <th>Notes</th>
          </tr>
          <xsl:for-each select="employees/employee">
            <xsl:if test="firstname[text()=$firstname]">
            <tr>
              <td>
                <xsl:value-of select="@employeeid"/>
              </td>
```

```
        <td>
          <xsl:value-of select="firstname"/>
        </td>
        <td>
          <xsl:value-of select="lastname"/>
        </td>
        <td>
          <xsl:value-of select="homephone"/>
        </td>
        <td>
          <xsl:value-of select="notes"/>
        </td>
      </tr>
      </xsl:if>
    </xsl:for-each>
   </table>
  </body>
 </html>
 </xsl:template>
</xsl:stylesheet>
```

Notice the style sheet markup displayed in bold. At the top of the style sheet, we have declared a parameter by using the `<xsl:param>` element. The name attribute of the `<xsl:param>` element indicates the name of the parameter (`firstname` in our example). To use this parameter further in the XSLT, you prefix it with the dollar symbol ($). Notice the `firstname` parameter of the `<xsl:if>` element. Listing 6-12 shows the code that passes this parameter value at the time of actual transformation.

Listing 6-12. Using the XsltArgumentList Class to Pass XSLT Parameters

```
private void button1_Click(object sender, EventArgs e)
{
  string sourcefile = $"{Application.StartupPath}\\employees.xml";
  string xsltfile = $"{Application.StartupPath}\\employees.xslt";
  string destinationfile = $"{Application.StartupPath}\\employees.html";

  FileStream stream = new FileStream(destinationfile, FileMode.Create);

  XslCompiledTransform xslt = new XslCompiledTransform();
  xslt.Load(xsltfile);
  XsltArgumentList arguments = new XsltArgumentList();
  arguments.AddParam("firstname", "", textBox1.Text);
  xslt.Transform(sourcefile, arguments, stream);
  stream.Close();
  if (checkBox1.Checked)
  {
    System.Diagnostics.Process.Start(destinationfile);
  }
}
```

The code declares three string variables to store the paths of the source XML file, the XSLT style sheet file, and the destination HTML file, respectively. Then the code creates a `FileStream` object for writing to the destination HTML file. This `FileStream` object will be passed to the `Transform()` method later.

165

A new instance of the `XslCompiledTransform` class is then created, and the `Load()` method loads the XSLT style sheet. Then comes the important part. The code creates an instance of the `XsltArgumentList` class and adds a parameter to it by using its `AddParam()` method, which takes three parameters: the name of the parameter, the namespace if any, and the parameter value. Then, the `Transform()` method of `XslCompiledTransform` is called by passing the `XsltArgumentList` object that we just created. This time, we pass the source filename, the parameter list, and a stream to which the resultant output will be written. In our case, this stream points to the `Employees.html` file. After the transformation is over, the stream is closed, and the newly generated HTML file is shown to the user.

If you run the application and supply `Nancy` as the parameter value, the resultant HTML file will look like Listing 6-13.

Listing 6-13. Output After Passing the Parameter

```
<html>
  <body>
    <h1>Employee Listing</h1>
    <table border="1">
      <tr>
        <th>Employee ID</th>
        <th>First Name</th>
        <th>Last Name</th>
        <th>Home Phone</th>
        <th>Notes</th>
      </tr>
      <tr>
        <td>1</td>
        <td>Nancy</td>
        <td>Davolio</td>
        <td>(206) 555-9857</td>
        <td>
          Education includes a BA in psychology from Colorado State University in 1970.
          She also completed "The Art of the Cold Call." Nancy is a member of Toastmasters
          International.
        </td>
      </tr>
    </table>
  </body>
</html>
```

As you can see, only one record is transformed, indicating that the output was indeed filtered based on the parameter value.

Using Script Blocks in an XSLT Style Sheet

Though XSLT offers a few programming constructions and built-in functions, it is not a full-fledged programming language in itself. Sometimes, you may need to perform an operation that is beyond the capabilities of XSLT. For example, you may want to connect with a SQL Server database and fetch some data that is used further by the style sheet, or you may need to perform disk IO. To cater to such needs, `XslCompiledTransform` allows you to embed scripts within your XSLT style sheets. After the style sheet is loaded, the embedded code is compiled into Microsoft Intermediate Language (MSIL) and executed at runtime.

Our Employees.xml file stores a subset of information from the Employees table of the Northwind database; it represents only four fields of the actual table: firstname, lastname, homephone, and notes. Let's assume that for some reason you also need the extract the date of birth of each employee at runtime. That means we need to write some ADO.NET code to retrieve the BirthDate column value from the database table. We will do this by embedding a script block in the style sheet. Listing 6-14 shows the complete style sheet.

Listing 6-14. Embedded Script Blocks in the XSLT Style Sheet

```
<?xml version="1.0" encoding="UTF-8" ?>
<xsl:stylesheet version="1.0" xmlns:xsl="http://www.w3.org/1999/XSL/Transform"
xmlns:msxsl="urn:schemas-microsoft-com:xslt"
xmlns:myscripts="urn:myscripts">
<msxsl:script language="C#" implements-prefix="myscripts">
  <msxsl:assembly name="System.Data" />
  <msxsl:using namespace="System.Data" />
  <msxsl:using namespace="System.Data.SqlClient" />
  <![CDATA[
  public string GetBirthDate(int employeeid)
  {
    SqlConnection cnn = new SqlConnection(@"data source=.\sqlexpress;initial ➥
catalog=northwind;integrated security=true");
    SqlCommand cmd = new SqlCommand();
    cmd.Connection = cnn;
    cmd.CommandText = "SELECT birthdate FROM employees WHERE employeeid=@id";
    SqlParameter pDOB = new SqlParameter("@id",employeeid);
    cmd.Parameters.Add(pDOB);
    cnn.Open();
    object obj = cmd.ExecuteScalar();
    cnn.Close();
    DateTime dob = DateTime.Parse(obj.ToString());
    return dob.ToString("MM/dd/yyyy");
  }
  ]]>
</msxsl:script>

<xsl:template match="/">
    <html>
      <body>
        <h1>Employee Listing</h1>
        <table border="1">
          <tr>
            <th>Employee ID</th>
            <th>First Name</th>
            <th>Last Name</th>
            <th>Home Phone</th>
            <th>Birth Date</th>
            <th>Notes</th>
          </tr>
          <xsl:for-each select="employees/employee">
            <tr>
```

```
          <td>
            <xsl:value-of select="@employeeid"/>
          </td>
          <td>
            <xsl:value-of select="firstname"/>
          </td>
          <td>
            <xsl:value-of select="lastname"/>
          </td>
          <td>
            <xsl:value-of select="homephone"/>
          </td>
          <td>
            <xsl:value-of select="myscripts:GetBirthDate(@employeeid)"/>
          </td>
          <td>
            <xsl:value-of select="notes"/>
          </td>
        </tr>
      </xsl:for-each>
    </table>
  </body>
</html>
</xsl:template>
</xsl:stylesheet>
```

Notice the markup in bold. The <xsl:stylesheet> element now has two more attributes. The xmlns:msxsl attribute defines the msxml prefix for the urn:schemas-microsoft-com:xslt namespace. Similarly, the xmlns:myscripts attribute defines a myscripts prefix.

The <msxml:script> block defines one or more functions that are used in the style sheet. The language attribute of the script block indicates the coding language (C# in our example). Your code may need to add a reference to external assemblies, which is done by using the <msxsl:assembly> element. The name attribute of this tag specifies the name of the assembly, excluding the extension. Similarly, the <msxml:using> tag specifies the namespaces to be imported.

The actual function is placed in a CDATA section. In our example, we defined a function called GetBirthDate() that accepts the ID of the employee whose date of birth is to be retrieved and returns the birth date in MM/dd/yyyy format. The code of the function connects to the Northwind database, fires a SELECT query against the employees table, and retrieves the birth date.

■ **Note** Make sure to change the database connection string to suit your development environment.

The GetBirthDate() function is called later in the style sheet by using the namespaceprefix: function_name(parameter list) syntax. The GetBirthDate() function expects the employee ID, which is passed by using the employeeid attribute (@employeeid) as a parameter.

To test our new style sheet, we will develop an application like the one shown in Figure 6-7.

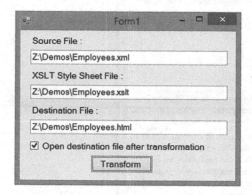

Figure 6-7. *Application for testing our embedded function*

The application user interface is the same as I discussed earlier (see Figure 6-5). However, the code inside the Transform button is slightly different. Listing 6-15 highlights these differences.

Listing 6-15. Enabling Scripting

```
private void button1_Click(object sender, EventArgs e)
{
  XsltSettings settings = new XsltSettings();
  settings.EnableScript = true;
  XslCompiledTransform xslt = new XslCompiledTransform();
  xslt.Load(textBox2.Text,settings,null);
  xslt.Transform(textBox1.Text, textBox3.Text);
  if (checkBox1.Checked)
  {
    System.Diagnostics.Process.Start(textBox3.Text);
  }
}
```

The XsltSettings class specifies the features to support during the transformation. The EnableScript property indicates whether to enable embedded script blocks. The Load() method of the XslCompiledTransform class accepts the XsltSettings object as one of its parameters. If you run the application and specify the three paths, you will get output as shown in Figure 6-8.

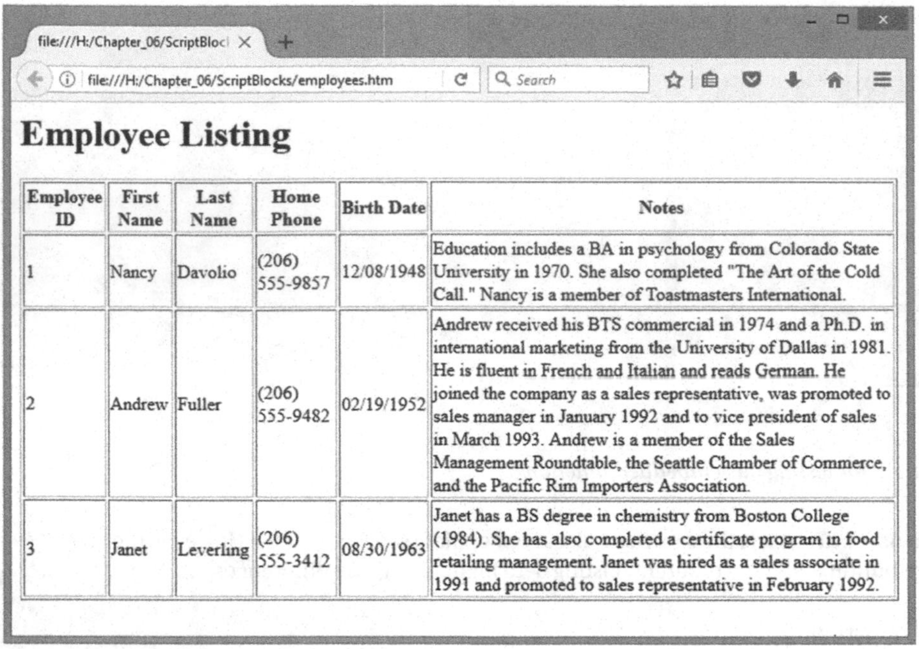

Employee Listing

Employee ID	First Name	Last Name	Home Phone	Birth Date	Notes
1	Nancy	Davolio	(206) 555-9857	12/08/1948	Education includes a BA in psychology from Colorado State University in 1970. She also completed "The Art of the Cold Call." Nancy is a member of Toastmasters International.
2	Andrew	Fuller	(206) 555-9482	02/19/1952	Andrew received his BTS commercial in 1974 and a Ph.D. in international marketing from the University of Dallas in 1981. He is fluent in French and Italian and reads German. He joined the company as a sales representative, was promoted to sales manager in January 1992 and to vice president of sales in March 1993. Andrew is a member of the Sales Management Roundtable, the Seattle Chamber of Commerce, and the Pacific Rim Importers Association.
3	Janet	Leverling	(206) 555-3412	08/30/1963	Janet has a BS degree in chemistry from Boston College (1984). She has also completed a certificate program in food retailing management. Janet was hired as a sales associate in 1991 and promoted to sales representative in February 1992.

Figure 6-8. *Output with the Birth Date column added*

Using Extension Objects

Embedding scripts in the style sheet does indeed provide a handy way to perform operations that are beyond the capabilities of XSLT. However, it doesn't provide a good mechanism for reusing your code. What if you want to use the same function elsewhere in the application or in other style sheets? This is where extension objects come into the picture. Simply put, extension objects are objects external to the style sheet that provide some functionality to the style sheet. Extension objects promote greater code reuse and are more flexible and maintainable than embedded script blocks.

To illustrate the use of extension objects, we will modify our previous example. First, we will put the `GetBirthDate()` function in a separate class called `Employee` rather than embedding it in the style sheet. The newly created `Employee` class should look similar to Listing 6-16.

Listing 6-16. Placing the GetBirthDate() Function in a Class

```
class Employee
{
  public string GetBirthDate(int employeeid)
  {
    SqlConnection cnn = new SqlConnection(@"data source=.\sqlexpress;initial ➥
catalog=northwind;integrated security=true");
    SqlCommand cmd = new SqlCommand();
    cmd.Connection = cnn;
    cmd.CommandText = "SELECT birthdate FROM employees WHERE employeeid=@id";
    SqlParameter pDOB = new SqlParameter("@id", employeeid);
    cmd.Parameters.Add(pDOB);
    cnn.Open();
```

```
    object obj = cmd.ExecuteScalar();
    cnn.Close();
    DateTime dob = DateTime.Parse(obj.ToString());
    return dob.ToString("MM/dd/yyyy");
  }
}
```

The function by itself is the same one that we used before, but it has been encapsulated in the Employee class. Next, you need to modify the Click event handler of the Transform button to resemble Listing 6-17.

Listing 6-17. Using Extension Objects

```
private void button1_Click(object sender, EventArgs e)
{
  XsltSettings settings = new XsltSettings();
  settings.EnableScript = true;
  XslCompiledTransform xslt = new XslCompiledTransform();
  xslt.Load(textBox2.Text,settings,null);

  XsltArgumentList arguments = new XsltArgumentList();
  Employee employee = new Employee();
  arguments.AddExtensionObject("urn:myscripts", employee);

  FileStream stream = new FileStream(textBox3.Text, FileMode.Create);
  xslt.Transform(textBox1.Text, arguments,stream);
  stream.Close();
  if (checkBox1.Checked)
  {
    System.Diagnostics.Process.Start(textBox3.Text);
  }
}
```

Notice the code marked in bold. After loading the style sheet using the Load() method as before, it creates an instance of the XsltArgumentList class, which we used when passing parameters to the style sheet. This time, however, the code uses the AddExtensionObject() method of the XsltArgumentList class. This method accepts the namespace URI and an instance of the extension object. In our case, the Employee class instance acts as an extension object. While calling the Transform() method of XslCompiledTransform, the XsltArgumentList object is passed to it. If you run the application now, you should get a result identical to the previous example.

Compiling XSLT Style Sheets

In all the preceding examples, we used XSLT files directly for the purpose of transformation. If you are dealing with many style sheets, you need to keep track of each and every style sheet name during coding. You also need to deploy all the style sheets along with other project files.

Luckily, the .NET Framework comes with a command-line XSLT compiler, xsltc.exe, that can compile one or more XSLT style sheets into an assembly. You can then load the required style sheet into the XslCompiledTransform instance and apply it to your XML documents.

To illustrate the use of the XSLT compiler, let's compile the `Employees.xslt` that we developed earlier in this chapter. Open a Visual Studio command prompt and issue the following command:

```
xsltc /class:MyStyles.Employees Employees.xslt /out:EmployeeStyles.dll
```

The `/class` switch is used to specify the fully qualified name of the resultant class (`MyStyles.Employees` in our example). The name of the XSLT style sheet follows the class name. If you want to compile multiple style sheets, you can specify multiple pairs of class names and style sheet names. The `/out` switch specifies the name of the output assembly. You can add a reference to this assembly in your project.

To consume the assembly that was just created, we will modify the example shown in Figure 6-5. The modified application is shown in Figure 6-9.

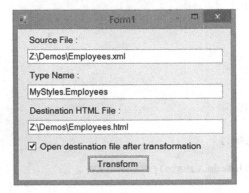

Figure 6-9. *Application for testing compiled style sheets*

The application now accepts the fully qualified type name of the class that represents the XSLT style sheet instead of the XSLT style sheet file path. The code inside the `Click` event of the Transform button now changes as shown in Listing 6-18.

Listing 6-18. Loading the Compiled Style Sheet Using the XslCompiledTransform Class

```
private void button1_Click(object sender, EventArgs e)
{
  if(Path.GetExtension(textBox3.Text) != ".htm" &&
     Path.GetExtension(textBox3.Text) != ".html")
  {
    MessageBox.Show("File extension must be .htm or .html");
    return;
  }
  XslCompiledTransform xslt = new XslCompiledTransform();
  Assembly a = Assembly.Load("EmployeeStyles");
  Type t = a.GetType(textBox2.Text);
  xslt.Load(t);
  xslt.Transform(textBox1.Text, textBox3.Text);
  if (checkBox1.Checked)
  {
    System.Diagnostics.Process.Start(textBox3.Text);
  }
}
```

Notice the code marked in bold. The code uses the Load() method of the Assembly class (System. Reflection namespace) to load the EmployeeStyles assembly we created earlier. Remember that you still need a reference to the EmployeeStyles assembly in your project. The code then gets a Type instance of the compiled style sheet class. It then passes this Type instance to the Load() method of the XslCompiledTransform class.

Summary

This chapter gave you a detailed understanding of XSLT processing in the .NET Framework. By using XSLT style sheets, XML data can be transformed from one form to another. The XslCompiledTransform class represents the .NET Framework's XSLT processor. It allows you to load the style sheets and apply them to source XML. You can also pass parameters while transformation is being carried out, by using the XsltArgumentList class. The XslCompiledTransform class also allows you to embed script blocks. A better way to use your code is to create extension objects, which are more flexible and maintainable than embedded script blocks.

CHAPTER 7

■■ ■

XML in ADO.NET

ADO.NET is a technology for accessing and manipulating databases. XML has been integrated in several ways in ADO.NET. In this chapter, you are going to see how ADO.NET has harnessed the power of XML in data representation. Specifically, this chapter covers the following:

- An overview of XML integration in ADO.NET

- Working with SqlDataReader and XML

- DataSet architecture and disconnected data access

- XML integration in DataSet

- Creating a typed DataSet

Overview of ADO.NET Architecture

ADO.NET provides two ways of working with your data:

- Connected data access

- Disconnected data access

Connected Data Access

In *connected data access*, you establish a connection with the database. Then, as long as you are working with the data, you maintain this live connection. The following are the steps that you typically take when using connected data access:

1. Establish a connection with the database.

2. Open a cursor through the established connection.

3. Iterate through the cursor and work with the data (perform read, modify, and delete operations or even calculations).

4. Update the database, if there are any changes.

5. Close the cursor and the database connection.

© Bipin Joshi 2017

B. Joshi, *Beginning XML with C# 7*, https://doi.org/10.1007/978-1-4842-3105-0_7

The advantage of this model is that you can see changes in the database in real time. However, this approach is not recommended for scalable applications because it can hamper the overall performance and scalability of the system. Also, even though ADO.NET provides cursor-oriented connected data access, it is strictly read-only and forward-only. This incurs fewer overheads and improves performance as compared to updatable cursors.

You will typically use connected data access in the following situations:

- You are developing applications that are online all the time. For example, in a ticket reservation application, it is necessary that you work with the latest data from the database. In such cases, connected data access becomes necessary.

- You want to avoid the overhead of using offline data. When you use queries directly against a database, naturally they bypass any of the intermediate layers that are involved in disconnected data-access techniques. For example, suppose that you want to display a simple employee listing to the end user. This task does not involve any processing as such. Using connected data access in such cases will of course give the best performance.

- You need a cursor model for some reason.

The `Connection`, `Command`, and `DataReader` classes are used for such connected data access. You learn about these classes in later sections.

Disconnected Data Access

Many modern systems need to be distributed and scalable. Consider an example of a distributed application that performs some database-intensive tasks. A typical programming approach is to open a live connection with the database and maintain it as long as the database-related tasks are in progress. This is fine if the number of users is small, but as the user base grows, the available database connections become precious. In such heavily loaded systems, a live connection approach is not recommended. The alternative is to have offline or disconnected access to the data. *Disconnected data access* involves the following steps:

1. Establish a connection with the database.

2. Fetch the data that you require and store it in some offline medium.

3. Close the database connection.

4. Work with the fetched data (perform read, modify, and delete operations or even calculations).

5. Again, open a database connection if you want to update the changes made to the data back to the database.

6. Update the database, if there are any changes.

7. Close the database connection.

As you can see, the database connection is opened only when required. You will typically use disconnected data access in the following situations:

- Your application data can be updated in batches.

- Your application does not need up-to-the minute data from the database.

- You want to pass data across multiple layers of your system.

- You want to pass data from your application to another application.

- Your application data is generated programmatically and is not coming from any data source.

This disconnected data access is provided by a DataAdapter and a DataSet class. You learn more about these classes in upcoming sections.

ADO.NET Data Providers

To communicate with the data source, you need some kind of layer that will facilitate this communication for you. In the early days, Open Database Connectivity (ODBC) drivers provided such a layer. With the introduction of Object Linking and Embedding Database (OLEDB), OLEDB providers did the same job. With ADO.NET, it is data providers that do it for you by providing managed access to the underlying data source. The data source can be a relational database management system (RDBMS) such as SQL Server or it can be some non-relational entity such as XML documents.

Four chief data providers are available out of the box with ADO.NET:

- SQL Server data provider

- OLEDB data provider

- ODBC data provider

- Oracle data provider

You can also build your own data provider if necessary.

Each ADO.NET data provider consists of a set of classes that are similar in structure (this is achieved through certain common base classes and interfaces) but implement provider specific functionality. This makes the overall object model look almost the same, irrespective of the data provider used. The following sections give you a brief introduction to the various data providers available.

SQL Server Data Provider

The SQL Server data provider is specifically designed for Microsoft SQL Server. It is optimized for SQL Server and uses SQL Server's native data format—tabular data stream (TDS) for communication. As this data provider talks with SQL Server via its native format, there are none of the overheads associated with the OLEDB layer.

OLEDB Data Provider

As the name suggests, the OLEDB data provider is used to communicate with any OLEDB-compliant databases such as SQL Server and Oracle. The OLEDB data provider is actually a wrapper over the corresponding OLEDB service provider and thus introduces a small performance overhead. If your database is OLEDB compliant but does not have its own ADO.NET data provider, this is the data provider for you.

ODBC Data Provider

If you are working with an RDBMS that does not have an ADO.NET data provider or an OLEDB provider (say, dBase), this is the data provider available to you.

Oracle Data Provider

The .NET Framework also includes a data provider developed specifically for Oracle databases.

The Assemblies and Namespaces Involved

Now that you have a brief idea about ADO.NET data providers, let's see the related namespaces. We will focus our attention on only the SQL Server data provider and the OLEDB data provider because they are very commonly used in many business applications. All the data-access classes of these two providers reside in the assembly `System.Data.dll`. There are five major namespaces pertaining to the preceding data providers:

- The `System.Data` namespace provides classes and interfaces that are common to all data providers. For example, the `DataSet` class is the same irrespective of whether it is populated with data from SQL Server or another OLEDB database. This namespace also contains interfaces that are implemented by all the data providers.

- The `System.Data.Common` namespace contains classes shared by all the .NET data providers.

- The `System.Data.OleDb` namespace contains all the classes pertaining to the OLEDB data provider. For example, there are classes such as `OleDbConnection`, `OleDbCommand`, and `OleDbParameter`.

- The `System.Data.SqlClient` namespace contains all the classes related to the SQL Server data provider. For example, there are classes such as `SqlConnection`, `SqlCommand`, and `SqlParameter`. As you will see, the `OleDb` and `SqlClient` namespaces contain closely matching classes.

- The `System.Data.SqlTypes` namespace provides classes that represent native data types within SQL Server. For example, the `SqlInt32` class represents the SQL Server integer data type. These classes help in preventing loss of precision while converting decimal or numeric data types. They also help in optimizing type conversion between .NET data types and SQL Server data types.

ADO.NET Classes

Now it's time to become familiar with the common classes that play a vital role in database access. This section gives you a basic introduction to the classes so that you can perform common data-access tasks. Note that in the following section when I specify `Connection`, it is shorthand for the `SqlConnection` and `OleDbConnection` classes. The same convention applies to other classes as well.

Connection (SqlConnection and OleDbConnection)

As the name suggests, the `Connection` classes represent a connection with a database. In order to perform any database operation, you need an open connection with that database. To establish a connection with, say, a SQL Server database, you will need to specify the connection string and then call the `Open()` method of the `SqlConnection` object. Note that after you finish working with the `Connection` object, you should explicitly close it by using the `Close()` method. Otherwise, the object will maintain a live connection with the database.

Command (SqlCommand and OleDbCommand)

ADO.NET Command objects are used to execute SQL queries and stored procedures. You specify the SQL query or stored procedure name by using the CommandText property. You can also specify the type of command (SQL statement or stored procedure) by using the CommandType property. If your query has some parameters, you can add them to the Parameters collection. Before executing the command, you should set its Connection property to an open connection object. Command objects can return only read-only and forward-only result sets in the form of a DataReader.

Parameter (SqlParameter and OleDbParameter)

Often your queries and stored procedures are parameterized. Using parameters allows you to pass external values to your queries and also avoids the risk of SQL injection attack. Parameters are also better in terms of performance because they avoid frequent parsing of queries. The Parameter class represents a parameter of your query or stored procedure.

DataReader (SqlDataReader and OleDbDataReader)

As I mentioned, the Command object can return only read-only and forward-only cursors. The cursor is represented by an object called the DataReader, which is a firehose cursor that provides an optimized way to loop through your results.

■ **Note** Read-only and forward-only cursors are often called *firehose cursors*. They are one of the most efficient ways of transferring data from the server to the client.

To loop through the results, you can use its Read() method that advances the record pointer to the next row.

Note that DataReader does not have MoveXxxx()-style methods that some older data access models used to have. This helps to avoid the common programming mistake of forgetting to call MoveNext() in Do...While loops. Also, note that for DataReader, only one row remains in memory at a time, so DataReader can improve the performance and memory footprint of your application significantly as compared to traditional dynamic cursors.

DataAdapter (SqlDataAdapter and OleDbDataAdapter)

In the section about disconnected data access, you learned that ADO.NET offers a way to work with disconnected data via the DataSet class. The DataSet needs to be populated from the data residing in the data source. Similarly, after you are finished with the data modifications, the data needs to be updated in the underlying data source, and the DataAdapter class is designed just for that. Note that the DataSet class is the same for any kind of data provider (SQL Server or OLEDB), but DataAdapter has separate implementations (SqlDataAdapter and OleDbDataAdapter). This is because, unlike DataSet, which is totally unaware of the underlying data source, DataAdapter needs to communicate with the underlying data source.

DataSet

The DataSet object is at the heart of ADO.NET disconnected architecture. DataSet is somewhat analogous to the Recordset object of ADO, but, unlike Recordset, DataSet always works in a disconnected fashion. Also, DataSet can have more than one set of data.

A DataSet is represented as an XML document over the network, which makes it a great choice for passing data from one component layer to another. It can also be used to integrate heterogeneous systems.

A DataSet can be considered an in-memory representation of a database. Just as a database consists of one or more tables, a DataSet consists of one or more DataTable objects. Each DataTable is a set of DataRow objects. Just like a database, DataTable objects can have relations and constraints. Also, they need not always be populated from the database but can be created and populated programmatically also.

XML and Connected Data Access

In the preceding sections, you saw that the SqlCommand object is used to execute SQL commands and stored procedures against a database. To execute SELECT queries and retrieve the results as XML data, you need to use the ExecuteXmlReader() method of the SqlCommand object. This method executes the SELECT query or stored procedure and returns the results in the form of an XmlReader object. You can then navigate through and access values from the XmlReader, as you learned in Chapter 3.

Using the ExecuteXmlReader() Method

When you use the ExecuteXmlReader() method of SqlCommand, the SELECT query must have the FOR XML clause specified in it. You will learn about the FOR XML clause in detail in Chapter 11. For now it is sufficient to know that this clause ensures that an XML representation of the result set is returned and it must be present.

To see how ExecuteXmlReader() works, you will develop an application like the one shown in Figure 7-1.

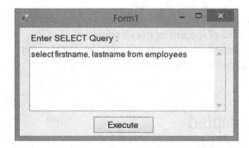

Figure 7-1. *Application for retrieving SQL Server data in XML format*

As you can see, the application consists of a text box for entering SELECT queries. The Execute button allows you to execute the query. The XML results returned from the query are displayed in a browser window.

Before you write the code for the Click event handler of the Execute button, make sure to include the namespaces as shown in Listing 7-1.

Listing 7-1. Importing Relevant Namespaces

```
using System.Data;
using System.Data.SqlClient;
using System.Xml;
using System.IO;
using System.Diagnostics;
```

The Click event handler of the Execute button contains the code shown in Listing 7-2.

Listing 7-2. Using the ExecuteXmlReader() Method

```
private void button1_Click(object sender, EventArgs e)
{
  SqlConnection cnn = new SqlConnection(@"data source=.\sqlexpress;initial ➥
catalog=northwind;integrated security=true");

  SqlCommand cmd = new SqlCommand();
  cmd.Connection = cnn;
  cmd.CommandType = CommandType.Text;
  cmd.CommandText = $"{textBox1.Text} FOR XML AUTO";
  cnn.Open();
  XmlReader reader=cmd.ExecuteXmlReader();
  StreamWriter writer= File.CreateText($"{Application.StartupPath}\\temp.xml");
  writer.Write("<root>");

  while (reader.Read())
  {
    writer.Write(reader.ReadOuterXml());
  }

  writer.Write("</root>");
  writer.Close();
  reader.Close();
  cnn.Close();
  Process.Start($"{Application.StartupPath}\\temp.xml");
}
```

The code creates an instance of the SqlConnection class by passing the database connection string in the constructor.

■ **Note**   Throughout this chapter, it is assumed that you have SQL Server (the Express edition is sufficient) installed on your machine. It is also assumed that you have the Northwind sample database of SQL Server. You can download the necessary scripts from Microsoft's web site. Also, make sure to change the database connection string according to your setup.

Then the code creates a `SqlCommand` object and sets three important properties: `Connection`, `CommandType`, and `CommandText`. The `Connection` property specifies the `SqlConnection` instance that is to be used for firing queries. The `CommandType` property is an enumeration of type `CommandType` and indicates the type of command being executed. In our example, it is a plain SQL statement and hence set to `CommandType.Text`. The `CommandText` property specifies the SQL query or name of the stored procedure to be executed. In our example, the query is being supplied via the text box. While assigning the `CommandText` property, the `FOR XML AUTO` clause is appended to the original query. This clause indicates that the results are returned as a sequence of elements, where the element name is the same as the table name, attribute names are the same as column names, and attribute values are the same as column values. The connection is then established by using the `Open()` method of the `SqlConnection` class.

The query is executed against the database by using the `ExecuteXmlReader()` method, which, as you know, returns an instance of `XmlReader` that points to the result set. In our example, the code creates a physical disk file named `temp.xml`, iterates through the `XmlReader` by using its `Read()` method, and writes the XML data to the file. Notice the use of the `ReadOuterXml()` method to retrieve the XML data. Also, note that the XML data returned by `ExecuteXmlReader()` is in the form of elements and doesn't have a root node as such, so the code adds a `<root>` element to enclose all the returned data.

After the writing of XML data is done, the `StreamWriter`, `XmlReader`, and `SqlConnection` are closed by using the `Close()` method of the respective classes. The `Process` class (residing in the `System.Diagnostics` namespace) opens the `temp.xml` file in a new browser window.

If you run the application and supply a `SELECT` query, you should see the output shown in Figure 7-2.

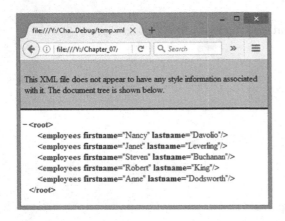

Figure 7-2. *XML data returned by the ExecuteXmlReader() method*

Figure 7-2 shows the output for the following query:

```
SELECT firstname, lastname FROM employees
```

As you can see, the element name is the same as the table name, and columns appear as attributes.

XML and Disconnected Data Access

In the preceding section, you learned the connected way of working by using ADO.NET and `XmlReader`. However, for building scalable applications, connected data access poses problems of its own. In such circumstances, disconnected data access is strongly preferred. In fact, disconnected data access is one of the most important features of ADO.NET.

Two classes—DataSet and SqlDataAdapter—together provide a way to work with database data in disconnected mode. The DataSet object is a totally disconnected one and can even be created manually. The SqlDataAdapter class fills the DataSet with data from a database and later propagates the changes made to the DataSet back to the database. In the next sections, you learn the architecture of DataSet and DataAdapter, and how to work with them.

Understanding DataSet

DataSet is an object for storing results of your queries offline for further processing and can be viewed as an in-memory representation of a database. DataSet consists of one or more DataTable objects, which in turn consist of a collection of DataRow objects. Figure 7-3 gives you a complete picture of the internals of DataSet.

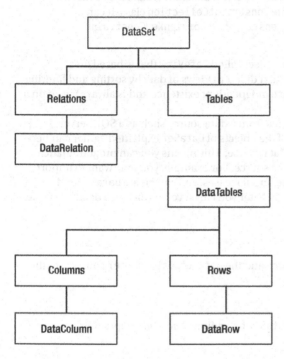

Figure 7-3. *DataSet architecture*

As you can see, DataSet has two primary collections:

- The Tables collection is exposed by the Tables property and consists of a DataTableCollection object that can have zero or more DataTable objects. Each DataTable represents a set of data from the underlying data source.

- The Relations collection is exposed as the Relations property and consists of a DataRelationCollection object. The DataRelationCollection object in turn contains zero or more DataRelation objects. Each DataRelation object represents the parent-child relationship between two DataTable objects.

As stated earlier, DataTable is a set of data and consists of rows and columns. The DataTable class has the following three important collections:

- The Columns collection is exposed as the Columns property and is an instance of the DataColumnCollection class. It contains zero or more DataColumn objects. Each DataColumn object represents a column or field of the DataTable, just like a database column. These columns define the structure of a DataTable.

- The Rows collection is exposed as the Rows property and is an instance of the DataRowCollection class. It contains zero or more DataRow objects. Each DataRow is similar to a database record and contains the actual data of the DataTable.

- Just like a database table, a DataTable can also have constraints, such as unique key constraints and foreign key constraints. The Constraints collection is exposed as the Constraints property and is an instance of the ConstraintCollection class. It can contain zero or more instances of the UniqueConstraint or ForeignKeyConstraint classes.

In addition to the preceding classes, there is a special object called DataView that is based on a DataTable. As the name suggests, DataView is used to present different views of data by sorting and filtering data from the DataTable. Note that DataView does not have independent existence and is always based on a DataTable.

Generally, you will populate your DataSet with the data from a data source such as a SQL Server database. However, DataSet is fully disconnected. Most of the objects of DataSet explained earlier can be created independently without any interaction with any data source. This means you can programmatically create your DataSet without even connecting with any data source. For example, you may want to import a comma-separated list of string data into a database table. In such cases, you can create DataSet and DataTable objects programmatically and populate the data. Later you can save this data to a database table.

Understanding DataAdapter

DataAdapter is a bridge between the underlying data source and the DataSet. DataAdapter comes into the picture when you want to perform any of the following:

- Populate the DataSet from database data

- Update the data source after modifying the DataSet by adding, deleting, or updating DataRow objects

Before seeing an example of how to populate a DataSet and update the data source, you need to understand the architecture of DataAdapter. Take a look at Figure 7-4.

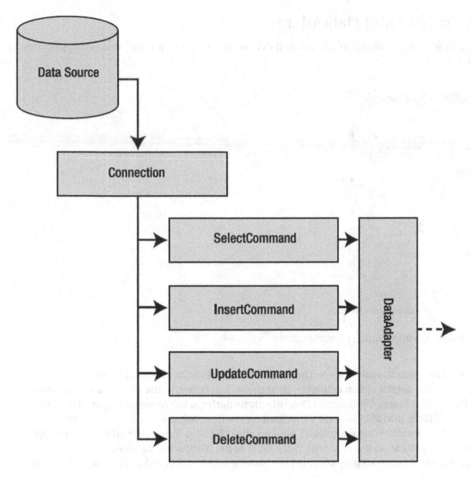

Figure 7-4. DataAdapter architecture

As shown in Figure 7-4, DataAdapter uses four Command objects for executing SELECT, INSERT, UPDATE, and DELETE queries. Each command is represented by the SelectCommand, InsertCommand, UpdateCommand, and DeleteCommand properties of the DataAdapter, respectively. Note that these Command objects are the same as you saw in connected data access. However, each one is assigned a specific task of selecting, inserting, updating, and deleting records from the data source. As with standard Command objects, the CommandText property of these command objects can be any valid SQL query or stored procedure.

DataAdapter provides the Fill() method that uses the Command object specified by the SelectCommand property and populates the DataSet. If you change the DataSet populated by the preceding method and want to propagate the changes back to the underlying data source, you need to set other properties (InsertCommand, UpdateCommand, and so forth) to valid Command instances. DataAdapter provides another method called Update() that uses the Command objects specified by the InsertCommand, UpdateCommand, and DeleteCommand properties and takes the changes from a DataSet back to the underlying data source.

Working with DataSet and DataAdapter

To understand how DataSet and DataAdapter can be used to manipulate data, you will create an application like the one shown in Figure 7-5.

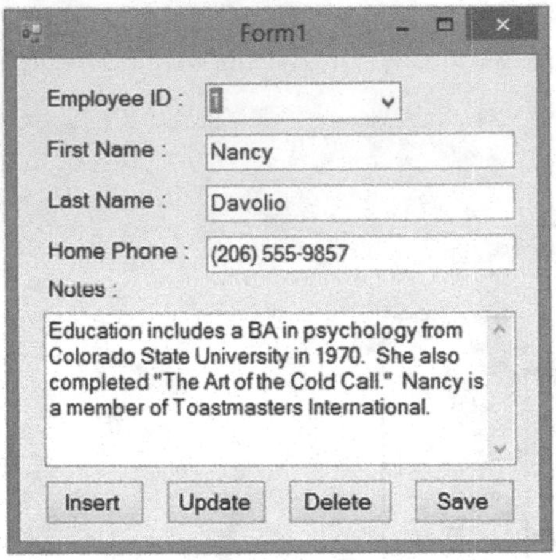

Figure 7-5. *Application to illustrate DataSet functionality*

The application is a typical data-entry screen. The combo box shows a list of all employee IDs. After you select an employee ID, the details of that employee (first name, last name, home phone, and notes) are displayed in the text boxes. The Insert, Update, and Delete buttons perform the respective operations. All the operations—INSERT, UPDATE, and DELETE—are performed on the DataSet and not against the actual database table. After all the operations are completed, you can click the Save button to make all the changes in the actual database. The application uses the Employees table of the Northwind database.

Now let's dissect the application step by step and see how DataSet and DataAdapter have been put to use.

Filling a DataSet

If you see the source code of the preceding application, you will find a few variables declared at the form level. The declaration is shown in Listing 7-3.

Listing 7-3. Form-Level Variables

```
string strConn = @"data source=.\sqlexpress;initial catalog=northwind; ➥
integrated security=true";
DataSet ds = new DataSet();
SqlDataAdapter da = new SqlDataAdapter();
SqlConnection cnn;
```

The strConn string variable stores the database connection string, which uses a local installation of SQL Server Express as indicated by the data source attribute. Then variables of type DataSet, SqlDataAdapter, and SqlConnection are declared. You must ensure that you have imported the System.Data and System.Data.SqlClient namespaces before you declare these variables.

The Form_Load event handler of the form contains the code shown in Listing 7-4.

Listing 7-4. Filling a DataSet

```
private void Form1_Load(object sender, EventArgs e)
{
  cnn = new SqlConnection(strConn);
  SqlCommand cmdEmployees = new SqlCommand();
  cmdEmployees.CommandText = "SELECT * FROM employees";
  cmdEmployees.Connection = cnn;
  da.SelectCommand = cmdEmployees;
  da.Fill(ds, "Employees");
  FillEmployees();
}
```

The code creates a `SqlCommand` object and sets its `CommandText` property to fetch all the records from the `Employees` table. The `Connection` property is set to the `SqlConnection` object created earlier. The `SqlCommand` object just created is assigned to the `SelectCommand` property of the `SqlDataAdapter` instance. The `SelectCommand` property determines the records to be populated in the `DataSet` later.

Next, the `Fill()` method of the `SqlDataAdapter` is called. It takes two parameters: the `DataSet` to be filled and the name of the resultant `DataTable`. Notice that the code neither opens the connection nor closes it. This is so because the `SqlDataAdapter` class does that internally for us. Finally, a helper method, `FillEmployees()`, is called and fills the combo box with the list of employee IDs. The `FillEmployees()` method is discussed later.

■ **Note**   The `SqlDataAdapter` class closes the connection automatically for us only if opened by `SqlDataAdapter` itself. If the connection is opened prior to calling the `Fill()` method, `SqlDataAdapter` will not close it automatically.

Accessing Data from DataSet

When you select an employee ID from the combo box, the employee details should be displayed in the other text boxes. The relevant code is written in the `SelectedIndexChanged` event of the combo box and is shown in Listing 7-5.

Listing 7-5. Accessing Data from a DataSet

```
private void comboBox1_SelectedIndexChanged(object sender, EventArgs e)
{
  string id = comboBox1.SelectedItem.ToString();
  DataRow[] rows = ds.Tables["Employees"].Select($"EmployeeID={id}");
  textBox1.Text = rows[0]["firstname"].ToString();
  textBox2.Text = rows[0]["lastname"].ToString();
  textBox3.Text = rows[0]["homephone"].ToString();
  textBox4.Text = rows[0]["notes"].ToString();
}
```

The code first stores the selected employee ID in a string variable. To find the corresponding employee record from the `DataSet`, we use the `Select()` method of `DataTable`, which accepts the selection criteria and returns an array of `DataRow` objects matching those criteria. In our example, we need to select the employee whose `EmployeeID` column value matches the one selected in the combo box. `EmployeeID` is the primary key column for the `Employees` table and hence we know that it will return only one `DataRow`. The `DataRow` can be accessed by using typical array notation. Notice how the column names are used to access the individual column values. Instead of column names, you could have used column indexes. The various column values are displayed in the respective text boxes.

Adding New Rows

After you enter details of a new employee to be added and click the Insert button, a new row is added to the underlying DataTable. The code that makes it possible is shown in Listing 7-6.

Listing 7-6. Adding a New DataRow

```
private void button2_Click(object sender, EventArgs e)
{
  DataRow row = ds.Tables["Employees"].NewRow();
  row["employeeid"] = comboBox1.Text;
  row["firstname"] = textBox1.Text;
  row["lastname"] = textBox2.Text;
  row["homephone"] = textBox3.Text;
  row["notes"] = textBox4.Text;
  ds.Tables["Employees"].Rows.Add(row);
  FillEmployees();
}
```

The code creates a new DataRow by calling the NewRow() method on the Employees DataTable. The NewRow() method creates a new stand-alone row in memory, matching the schema of the underlying DataTable. Then various column values of the DataRow are assigned. The newly created row is not yet part of the DataTable, so to add it to the DataTable, the Add() method of the Rows collection is called. Finally, the combo box is repopulated so as to display the newly added employee ID.

Updating an Existing Row

To update an existing row, you must find it first and then update the column values. To find a specific row, you can use the same Select() method that we used earlier. This is shown in Listing 7-7.

Listing 7-7. Updating a DataRow

```
private void button1_Click(object sender, EventArgs e)
{
  if (comboBox1.SelectedItem == null)
  {
    MessageBox.Show("Please select Employee ID!");
    return;
  }
  string id = comboBox1.SelectedItem.ToString();
  DataRow[] rows = ds.Tables["Employees"].Select($"EmployeeID={id}");
  rows[0].BeginEdit();
  rows[0]["firstname"] = textBox1.Text;
  rows[0]["lastname"] = textBox2.Text;
  rows[0]["homephone"] = textBox3.Text;
  rows[0]["notes"] = textBox4.Text;
  rows[0].EndEdit();
}
```

188

The code selects the employee record that is to be updated by using the Select() method of the DataTable. The BeginEdit() method of the DataRow class takes the row in edit mode. The column values are then assigned. Finally, the EndEdit() method of the DataRow class is called. This saves the changes to the underlying DataTable.

Deleting a Row

To delete a row, you must locate it first and then call the Delete() method on it. This is illustrated in Listing 7-8.

Listing 7-8. Deleting a DataRow

```
private void button3_Click(object sender, EventArgs e)
{
  if (comboBox1.SelectedItem == null)
  {
    MessageBox.Show("Please select Employee ID!");
    return;
  }
  string id = comboBox1.SelectedItem.ToString();
  DataRow[] rows = ds.Tables["Employees"].Select($"EmployeeID={id}");
  rows[0].Delete();
  FillEmployees();
}
```

The code retrieves the row to be deleted by using the Select() method of the DataTable class. The Delete() method of the DataRow class marks the underlying row for deletion. Finally, the combo box is repopulated so that the deleted employee ID doesn't show up.

Using DataRow States

In the preceding sections, you inserted, updated, and deleted DataRow objects from a DataTable. Whenever you perform any of these operations (insert, update, or delete) on a DataRow, its RowState property is affected automatically. The RowState property is an enumeration of type DataRowState and indicates the state of the DataRow. Table 7-1 shows various possible values of the DataRowState enumeration.

Table 7-1. *DataRowState Enumeration*

RowState Setting	Description
Unchanged	The row is unchanged since it was placed in the DataSet.
Added	The row is newly added to the DataTable.
Modified	The row is changed.
Deleted	The row is deleted from the DataTable.
Detached	The row is created but not yet attached to the DataTable.

The RowState property is used by the helper function FillEmployees(), as shown in Listing 7-9.

Listing 7-9. Using the RowState Property

```
private void FillEmployees()
{
  comboBox1.Items.Clear();
  foreach (DataRow row in ds.Tables["Employees"].Rows)
  {
    if (row.RowState != DataRowState.Deleted)
    {
      comboBox1.Items.Add(row["EmployeeID"].ToString());
    }
  }
}
```

The FillEmployees() method simply iterates through each DataRow from the Employees DataTable and adds the EmployeeID to the combo box. Notice the code marked in bold. Before adding any value in the combo box, the code checks whether the RowState of the row is Deleted. Only those rows whose RowState is not Deleted are added to the combo box.

Saving the Changes to the Database

Up until now, all the changes that we made are saved in the DataSet only; they are yet to be committed back to the database. You can test this by making some changes to the records and then closing the application without clicking the Save button. You will observe that the changes are lost. The Click event handler of the Save button contains code that propagates changes from the DataSet back to the database. Listing 7-10 shows this code.

Listing 7-10. Saving the DataSet Changes to the Database

```
private void button4_Click(object sender, EventArgs e)
{
  SqlCommand cmdInsert = new SqlCommand();
  SqlCommand cmdUpdate = new SqlCommand();
  SqlCommand cmdDelete = new SqlCommand();
  cmdInsert.Connection = cnn;
  cmdUpdate.Connection = cnn;
  cmdDelete.Connection = cnn;
  cmdInsert.CommandText =
    "INSERT INTO employees(firstname,lastname,homephone,notes)
    VALUES(@fname,@lname,@phone,@notes)";
  cmdUpdate.CommandText =
    "UPDATE employees SET firstname=@fname,lastname=@lname,homephone=@phone
    WHERE employeeid=@empid";
  cmdDelete.CommandText = "DELETE FROM employees WHERE employeeid=@empid";

  SqlParameter[] pInsert = new SqlParameter[4];
  pInsert[0] = new SqlParameter("@fname", SqlDbType.VarChar);
  pInsert[0].SourceColumn = "firstname";
  pInsert[1] = new SqlParameter("@lname", SqlDbType.VarChar);
```

```
  pInsert[1].SourceColumn = "lastname";
  pInsert[2] = new SqlParameter("@phone", SqlDbType.VarChar);
  pInsert[2].SourceColumn = "homephone";
  pInsert[3] = new SqlParameter("@notes", SqlDbType.VarChar);
  pInsert[3].SourceColumn = "notes";
  foreach (SqlParameter p in pInsert)
  {
    cmdInsert.Parameters.Add(p);
  }
  SqlParameter[] pUpdate = new SqlParameter[5];
  pUpdate[0] = new SqlParameter("@fname", SqlDbType.VarChar);
  pUpdate[0].SourceColumn = "firstname";
  pUpdate[1] = new SqlParameter("@lname", SqlDbType.VarChar);
  pUpdate[1].SourceColumn = "lastname";
  pUpdate[2] = new SqlParameter("@phone", SqlDbType.VarChar);
  pUpdate[2].SourceColumn = "homephone";
  pUpdate[3] = new SqlParameter("@notes", SqlDbType.VarChar);
  pUpdate[3].SourceColumn = "notes";
  pUpdate[4] = new SqlParameter("@empid", SqlDbType.VarChar);
  pUpdate[4].SourceColumn = "employeeid";
  foreach (SqlParameter p in pUpdate)
  {
    cmdUpdate.Parameters.Add(p);
  }

  SqlParameter[] pDelete = new SqlParameter[1];
  pDelete[0] = new SqlParameter("@empid", SqlDbType.VarChar);
  pDelete[0].SourceColumn = "employeeid";
  foreach (SqlParameter p in pDelete)
  {
    cmdDelete.Parameters.Add(p);
  }

  da.InsertCommand = cmdInsert;
  da.UpdateCommand = cmdUpdate;
  da.DeleteCommand = cmdDelete;
  da.Update(ds,"Employees");
  ds.AcceptChanges();
}
```

The code creates three SqlCommand objects for INSERT, UPDATE, and DELETE operations, respectively. The Connection property of these SqlCommand objects is set to the same SqlConnection object that we declared at the top initially. The CommandText property of each SqlCommand is set to the corresponding SQL statement. Note the use of the @ character to represent parameters. For each of these parameter placeholders, a SqlParameter object needs to be created. This is done by declaring three arrays of the SqlParameter objects: pInsert, pUpdate, and pDelete.

Then each array element is instantiated as a SqlParameter object by passing the parameter name and parameter data type in the constructor of the SqlParameter class. The SourceColumn property of SqlParameter specifies the name of the DataColumn that will be supplying the value for the parameter. All the parameters from the corresponding arrays are added to the Parameters collection of the respective SqlCommand object. These three SqlCommand objects are assigned to the InsertCommand, UpdateCommand, and DeleteCommand properties of the SqlDataAdapter instance that we declared at the top.

The Update() method of the SqlDataAdapter class is then called and takes all the changes—inserts, updates, and deletes—from the DataSet back to the database. The Update() method takes two parameters: the DataSet to be updated, and the name of the DataTable from the DataSet that is to be updated. After the changes are saved to the underlying database, the RowState properties of all the DataRow objects must become Unchanged. This is done by calling the AcceptChanges() method of the DataSet class.

That's it! You can now run the application and test it for the expected functionality.

Saving DataSet Contents As XML

One of the powerful features of the DataSet class is that you can serialize it in XML format, which means that relational data can be saved in XML format. This feature comes in handy while working in offline mode and while transporting data to heterogeneous systems.

The WriteXml() method of the DataSet class writes the contents of the DataSet to a stream or physical file in XML format. Optionally, you can also add schema information. To illustrate the use of WriteXml(), you need to create an application like the one shown in Figure 7-6.

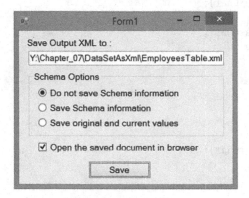

Figure 7-6. *Application that writes DataSet contents as an XML file*

The application consists of a text box for specifying the path of the output XML file. The first two radio buttons specify whether schema information is to be included. The last radio button specifies whether you want to write the original as well as current values to the file. If you select this radio button, the DiffGrams of the original and current values are written in the file.

■ **Note**   *DiffGram* is a special XML format that stores original as well as current row values. SQL Server 2000 introduced capabilities to update the database via UpdateGrams. DiffGram is a subset of UpdateGram.

If selected, the check box opens the saved XML file in a browser. The Save button actually writes the DataSet to the specified file. The Click event handler of the Save button contains the code shown in Listing 7-11.

Listing 7-11. Using the WriteXml() Method

```
private void button1_Click(object sender, EventArgs e)
{
  DataSet ds = new DataSet();
  SqlDataAdapter da =
    new SqlDataAdapter("SELECT employeeid,firstname,lastname,homephone,notes
                        FROM employees",
                       @"data source=.\sqlexpress;initial catalog=northwind;
                         integrated security=true");
  da.Fill(ds, "employees");
  if (radioButton1.Checked)
  {
    ds.WriteXml(textBox1.Text, XmlWriteMode.IgnoreSchema);
  }
  if (radioButton2.Checked)
  {
    ds.WriteXml(textBox1.Text, XmlWriteMode.WriteSchema);
  }
  if (radioButton3.Checked)
  {
    foreach (DataRow row in ds.Tables[0].Rows)
    {
      row.SetModified();
    }
    ds.WriteXml(textBox1.Text, XmlWriteMode.DiffGram);
  }
  if (checkBox1.Checked)
  {
    Process.Start(textBox1.Text);
  }
}
```

The code creates a new DataSet and a SqlDataAdapter. One of the overloads of the SqlDataAdapter constructors accepts the SELECT query and database connection string, and it is this overload that we use. The DataSet is then filled by using the Fill() method of the DataAdapter. The name of the DataTable is specified as employees.

Then a series of if conditions checks the status of the radio buttons. In each of the if conditions, the WriteXml() method of the DataSet class is called, which writes the contents of the DataSet to the specified stream or disk file. Notice that although each of the if conditions calls WriteXml(), the second parameter—XmlWriteMode—is different in each case.

The XmlWriteMode enumeration governs two things. First, it specifies whether schema information is to be written along with the XML contents. Second, it decides whether the output XML data will contain just the current values or both the original and current values. As you saw in the preceding example, the latter format is called DiffGram. The three possible values of the XmlWriteMode enumeration are shown in Table 7-2.

Table 7-2. *XmlWriteMode Values*

Value	Description
IgnoreSchema	Writes the contents of the DataSet as XML data. No XSD Schema information is written.
WriteSchema	Writes the contents of the DataSet as XML data. Also, writes XSD Schema information along with the data.
DiffGram	Writes the contents of the DataSet as DiffGram XML markup. The DiffGram stores the current as well as original column values.

Notice the if condition for radioButton3. Because we have not made any changes to the DataSet as such, the code deliberately marks each row as modified. This is done by using the SetModified() method of the DataRow class. This way, we will be able to see how the DiffGram format stores old and new values.

Finally, the saved XML file is opened in a browser by using the Start() method of the Process class. Figure 7-7 shows a sample run of the application without saving any schema information. Similarly, Figures 7-8 and 7-9 show the output XML file with schema information and DiffGram, respectively.

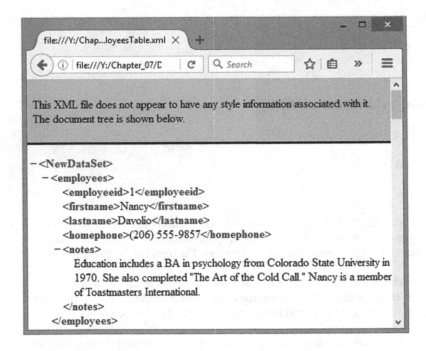

Figure 7-7. *Writing DataSet as XML without schema information*

Figure 7-8. *Writing DataSet as XML with schema information*

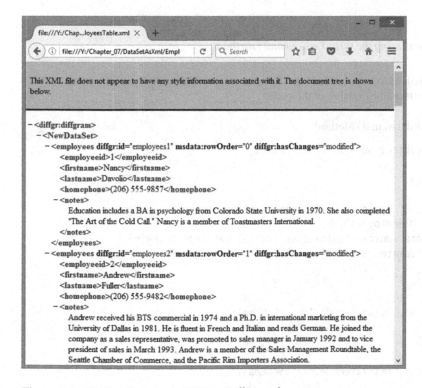

Figure 7-9. *Writing DataSet as XML in DiffGram format*

Notice how the schema information is emitted in Figure 7-8. Also, examine Figure 7-9 carefully. This XML output is in DiffGram format. See how the <diffgr:before> section stores the original values of the DataRows, whereas the current values are displayed at the top.

Saving Only the Schema

The WriteXml() method writes data and optionally XSD Schema information. What if you need to extract only the schema information and not the data itself? The WriteXmlSchema() method does that job by writing only the schema of the DataSet and not the data. To illustrate the use of WriteXmlSchema(), you can modify the preceding application to include an additional radio button. The new interface of the application is shown in Figure 7-10.

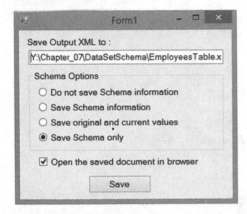

Figure 7-10. *Application for illustrating the WriteXmlSchema() method*

If you select the newly added radio button titled Save Schema only, only the schema of the DataSet will be saved. Listing 7-12 shows the modified version of the code.

Listing 7-12. Using the WriteXmlSchema() Method

```
private void button1_Click(object sender, EventArgs e)
{
  DataSet ds = new DataSet();
  SqlDataAdapter da =
    new SqlDataAdapter("SELECT employeeid,firstname,lastname,homephone,notes
                        FROM employees",
                       @"data source=.\sqlexpress;initial catalog=northwind;
                        integrated security=true");
  da.Fill(ds, "employees");
  if (radioButton1.Checked)
  {
    ds.WriteXml(textBox1.Text, XmlWriteMode.IgnoreSchema);
  }
  if (radioButton2.Checked)
  {
    ds.WriteXml(textBox1.Text, XmlWriteMode.WriteSchema);
  }
```

```
if (radioButton3.Checked)
{
  foreach (DataRow row in ds.Tables[0].Rows)
  {
    row.SetModified();
  }
  ds.WriteXml(textBox1.Text, XmlWriteMode.DiffGram);
}
if (radioButton4.Checked)
{
  ds.WriteXmlSchema(textBox1.Text);
}
if (checkBox1.Checked)
{
  Process.Start(textBox1.Text);
}
}
```

Notice the code marked in bold. The code calls the WriteXmlSchema() method by passing the file in which the schema information will be stored. You will observe that the schema obtained by this method is the same as that obtained by the WriteXml() method with XmlWriteMode.WriteSchema. However, no data is written to the file.

Extracting DataSet Contents As an XML String

The WriteXml()and WriteXmlSchema() methods write XML data and schema to a stream or file, respectively. Sometimes you may want to get the XML data and schema as a string rather than writing to a file. This is accomplished with two methods:

- The GetXml() method returns just the contents of the DataSet in XML format as a string. No schema information is returned.

- Similarly, the GetXmlSchema() method returns the XML Schema of the DataSet as a string. Because these methods return strings, they incur more overhead than WriteXml() and WriteXmlSchema().

Reading XML Data into DataSet

In the preceding sections, you learned to serialize DataSet contents as XML data. There might be cases when you would like to do the opposite—that is, you may need to read XML data into a DataSet and process it further. The ReadXml() method of the DataSet class is the counterpart of the WriteXml() method that we discussed already and allows you to read XML data into a DataSet.

■ **Note**   In the following examples, you will frequently need XML files containing a schema and data. It is recommended that you run the preceding example (Figure 7-10) and save the resultant XML files on your disk for later use.

To illustrate the use of ReadXml(), you need to develop an application like the one shown in Figure 7-11.

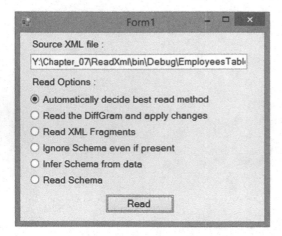

Figure 7-11. *Application that reads XML data into a DataSet*

The application consists of a text box for accepting the source XML file path. There is an array of radio buttons that govern how the XML document will be read by the DataSet. The Read button triggers the read operation. Listing 7-13 shows the complete code that reads the XML data into a DataSet.

Listing 7-13. Using the ReadXml() Method

```csharp
private void button1_Click(object sender, EventArgs e)
{
  DataSet ds = new DataSet();
  XmlReadMode mode=XmlReadMode.Auto;
  if (radioButton1.Checked)
  {
    mode = XmlReadMode.Auto;
  }
  if (radioButton2.Checked)
  {
    mode = XmlReadMode.DiffGram;
  }
  if (radioButton3.Checked)
  {
    mode = XmlReadMode.Fragment;
  }
  if (radioButton4.Checked)
  {
    mode = XmlReadMode.IgnoreSchema;
  }
  if (radioButton5.Checked)
  {
    mode = XmlReadMode.InferSchema;
  }
  if (radioButton6.Checked)
  {
    mode = XmlReadMode.ReadSchema;
  }
```

```
    ds.ReadXml(textBox1.Text, mode);
    MessageBox.Show("XML file read successfully!");
}
```

The code creates a new DataSet object. It then declares a variable of enumeration type XmlReadMode. This enumeration plays an important role in deciding how the XML data will be loaded into the DataSet. You can see all the possible values of the XmlReadMode enumeration in Table 7-3. Then a series of if conditions checks the status of the various radio buttons and sets the value of the XmlReadMode variable. Finally, the ReadXml() method of the DataSet class is called.

Table 7-3. XmlReadMode Values

Value	Description
Auto	Uses the most appropriate read mode from the remaining values (the default)
DiffGram	Loads a DiffGram and applies the changes
Fragment	Loads XML fragments such as the ones created when using the FOR XML clause
IgnoreSchema	Ignores the inline schema present in the source XML document
InferSchema	Infers the schema from the data present and loads the data into the DataSet
ReadSchema	Reads the inline schema present in the XML document

The ReadXml() method has several overloads. The one that we use accepts the name of the XML file to read and the XmlReadMode value. After ReadXml() has finished, the DataSet has populated DataTable objects depending on the source XML document. For example, if you use the EmployeesTable.xml file that we created previously, your DataSet will contain one DataTable called employees.

The XmlReadMode options need more explanation because there are a number of possibilities during the read operation. These options are discussed next.

Using the Automatic Read Operation

The Auto option of the XmlReadMode enumeration uses the most appropriate mechanism while loading the XML data. If the data is a DiffGram, it sets XmlReadMode to DiffGram. If the DataSet already has a schema or the XML document contains an inline schema, it sets XmlReadMode to ReadSchema. Finally, if the DataSet does not already have a schema and the XML document does not contain an inline schema, it sets XmlReadMode to InferSchema.

Reading DiffGrams

The DiffGram option of the XmlReadMode enumeration is exclusively used with DiffGrams. Generally, these DiffGrams will be generated by using the WriteXml() method of DataSet. The schema of the DataSet and the DiffGram must match in order to successfully read the data. Because the DiffGram stores the original and current values of DataRows, the changes are applied after the DiffGram is loaded in the DataSet.

Reading XML Fragments

In the earlier sections of this chapter, you learned that SQL Server provides an extension to the normal SELECT statement in the form of the FOR XML clause. You also saw how the FOR XML clause returns XML data in the form of fragments. If you want to load these XML fragments into a DataSet, you must set XmlReadMode to Fragment.

Ignoring Schema Information

The XML document that you want to load into a DataSet might contain schema information embedded in it. If you want to ignore this schema, you must use the IgnoreSchema option of the XmlReadMode enumeration. If the DataSet already has a schema and the XML data being loaded doesn't match this schema, the data is discarded.

Inferring Schema Information

The InferSchema option of XmlReadMode ignores schema information from the source XML data if present and loads the data into a DataSet. If the DataSet already has its schema, that is extended to accommodate the new data. However, if there is any mismatch between the existing schema and the newly inferred schema, an exception is raised.

Reading Schema Information

The ReadSchema option of XmlReadMode reads the inline schema from the source XML document and loads the schema as well as the data into the DataSet. If the DataSet already contains a schema, it is extended as per the new schema. However, any mismatch between the existing schema and the new schema causes an exception to be thrown.

Generating Menus Dynamically Based On an XML File

The ReadXml() method performs many operations behind the scenes to make our task easier. To get a taste of what it does, you will develop a Windows application that dynamically adds menu items. The application will resemble the one shown in Figure 7-12.

Figure 7-12. *Form showing dynamically loaded menu items*

The form consists of a single MenuStrip control. The menu items are stored in an XML file, as shown in Listing 7-14. Save this file as menus.xml in your application's Bin\Debug folder.

Listing 7-14. XML File Representing the Menu Structure

```xml
<?xml version="1.0" encoding="utf-8" ?>
<menus>
  <topmenu text="File">
    <submenu>New</submenu>
    <submenu>Open</submenu>
    <submenu>Close</submenu>
  </topmenu>
  <topmenu text="Edit">
    <submenu>Cut</submenu>
    <submenu>Copy</submenu>
    <submenu>Paste</submenu>
  </topmenu>
  <topmenu text="Help">
    <submenu>Help</submenu>
    <submenu>Search</submenu>
    <submenu>About</submenu>
  </topmenu>
</menus>
```

The root element of the XML file is <menus>. Inside there can be zero or more <topmenu> items, which represent the top-level menu items. The text attribute of <topmenu> indicates the text of that menu. The <topmenu> element can contain zero or more <submenu> elements, which indicate submenus of the top-level menus. The text of the submenus is specified in the <submenu> element's value.

Let's see how this file can be loaded in a DataSet and how the data can be accessed. Listing 7-15 shows the Load event handler of the form with the required code.

Listing 7-15. Adding Menu Items Dynamically

```csharp
private void Form1_Load(object sender, EventArgs e)
{
  DataSet ds = new DataSet();
  ds.ReadXml($"{Application.StartupPath}\\menus.xml");

  foreach (DataRow topmenu in ds.Tables[0].Rows)
  {
    ToolStripMenuItem item = new ToolStripMenuItem(topmenu["text"].ToString());
    menuStrip1.Items.Add(item);
    DataRow[] submenus= topmenu.GetChildRows(ds.Relations[0]);
    foreach (DataRow submenu in submenus)
    {
      item.DropDownItems.Add(submenu[0].ToString());
    }
  }
}
```

The code creates a new DataSet and reads the menus.xml file that we created earlier. While reading this file, the DataSet does some interesting things:

1. It observes the nesting of the XML data in the file and creates two DataTable objects. The first DataTable stores all the top menus, and the second DataTable stores all the submenus.

2. It creates DataRow objects in the top-menu DataTable and adds a DataColumn to them. The value contained in these columns is the value of the text attribute of the <topmenu> element.

3. It does a similar thing for the submenus DataTable, but loads the element values of the <submenu> items in the column.

4. It sets a DataRelation between the two tables by automatically adding an integer column to both of these DataTable objects.

The code then iterates through all the rows from the first DataTable (the DataTable storing the top menus) and adds ToolStripMenuItem objects to the MenuStrip. The GetChildRows() method is called on each DataRow of the topmenu DataTable. This method accepts a DataRelation object and returns all the DataRow objects from the child table matching that relationship. In our case, the submenu DataTable is the child DataTable. The return value of GetChildRows() is an array of DataRow objects. The second foreach loop iterates through all the elements of this array and adds subitems to the DropDownItems collection of the ToolStripMenuItem class.

If you run the application, you should see something similar to Figure 7-12.

Reading Only the Schema Information

The ReadXml() method allows you to read data and optionally schema information. However, at times you may need to extract just the schema information from the XML file and not the data. The DataSet class provides two methods that allow you to extract schema information from the source XML. They are ReadXmlSchema() and InferXmlSchema().

ReadXmlSchema() accepts the XML with an inline schema and reads just the schema part of it. The schema is then loaded into the DataSet. What if your XML document doesn't contain an inline schema? That is where the InferXmlSchema() method comes into the picture. The InferXmlSchema() method observes the XML markup supplied and then creates a matching schema automatically. The schema is then loaded into the DataSet.

To illustrate both of these methods, you need to develop an application like the one shown in Figure 7-13.

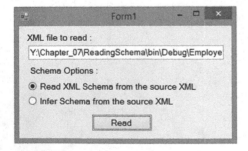

Figure 7-13. *Application that reads schema*

The application consists of a text box for specifying the source XML file. The two radio buttons enable you to decide whether ReadXmlSchema() or InferXmlSchema() is to be called. The code for the Read button reads the schema into a DataSet and displays it in a message box. The code that reads the schema is shown in Listing 7-16.

Listing 7-16. Using the ReadXmlSchema() and InferXmlSchema() Methods

```
private void button1_Click(object sender, EventArgs e)
{
  DataSet ds = new DataSet();
  if (radioButton1.Checked)
  {
    ds.ReadXmlSchema(textBox1.Text);
  }
  if (radioButton2.Checked)
  {
    ds.InferXmlSchema(textBox1.Text,null);
  }
  MessageBox.Show(ds.GetXmlSchema());
}
```

The code creates a new DataSet object. Depending on the radio button selected, the code calls either ReadXmlSchema() or InferXmlSchema(). ReadXmlSchema() accepts the source XML document as a parameter and loads the inline schema from the document into the DataSet. No data is loaded.

The InferXmlSchema() method accepts the source XML document and an array of namespaces (null in our example) and infers the schema from the data. Again, no data is loaded. The loaded schema is shown in a message box by calling the GetXmlSchema() method of the DataSet. Figure 7-14 shows the schema loaded by using ReadXmlSchema(),whereas Figure 7-15 shows the schema loaded by using InferXmlSchema().

Figure 7-14. *Schema extracted by using the ReadXmlSchema() method*

```
<?xml version="1.0" encoding="utf-16"?>
<xs:schema id="NewDataSet" xmlns=""
xmlns:xs="http://www.w3.org/2001/XMLSchema"
xmlns:msdata="urn:schemas-microsoft-com:xml-msdata">
  <xs:element name="NewDataSet" msdata:IsDataSet="true"
msdata:UseCurrentLocale="true">
    <xs:complexType>
      <xs:choice minOccurs="0" maxOccurs="unbounded">
        <xs:element name="employees">
          <xs:complexType>
            <xs:sequence>
              <xs:element name="employeeid" type="xs:string" minOccurs="0" />
              <xs:element name="firstname" type="xs:string" minOccurs="0" />
              <xs:element name="lastname" type="xs:string" minOccurs="0" />
              <xs:element name="homephone" type="xs:string" minOccurs="0" />
              <xs:element name="notes" type="xs:string" minOccurs="0" />
            </xs:sequence>
          </xs:complexType>
        </xs:element>
      </xs:choice>
    </xs:complexType>
  </xs:element>
</xs:schema>
```

Figure 7-15. *Schema extracted by using the InferXmlSchema() method*

As you can see, the schema loaded by both methods is identical in our example.

Creating a Typed DataSet

While discussing DataSet and DataAdapter, we developed an application that allowed us to perform inserts, updates, and deletes on a DataSet and then save those changes back to the database (see Figure 7-6). In that application, we frequently used collections such as Tables and Rows. We also needed to remember column names while accessing their values from a DataRow. Don't you think it is a bit tedious to access data in this fashion? To make things clearer, look at Listings 7-17 and 7-18.

Listing 7-17. Inserting a DataRow by Using an Untyped DataSet

```
private void button2_Click(object sender, EventArgs e)
{
  DataRow row = ds.Tables["Employees"].NewRow();
  row["employeeid"] = comboBox1.Text;
  row["firstname"] = textBox1.Text;
  row["lastname"] = textBox2.Text;
  row["homephone"] = textBox3.Text;
  row["notes"] = textBox4.Text;
  ds.Tables["Employees"].Rows.Add(row);
  FillEmployees();
}
```

Listing 7-18. Inserting a DataRow by Using a Typed DataSet

```
private void button2_Click(object sender, EventArgs e)
{
  EmployeesDataSet.EmployeesRow row = ds.Employees.NewEmployeesRow();
  row.EmployeeID = int.Parse(comboBox1.Text);
  row.FirstName = textBox1.Text;
  row.LastName = textBox2.Text;
  row.HomePhone = textBox3.Text;
  row.Notes = textBox4.Text;
  ds.Employees.AddEmployeesRow(row);
  FillEmployees();
}
```

Both of these listings represent code that inserts a new DataRow into a DataTable. Compare the listings carefully. In Listing 7-17, we access the Employees DataTable and its columns by specifying them in double quotes. That means you need to remember these names when you are coding. However, Listing 7-18 looks different. You will notice that it uses the Employees property to create a new row. Further, it uses column names such as FirstName and LastName as if they are properties. Obviously, the second version is far easier to code and is much neater, which demonstrates what typed DataSets are about.

A typed DataSet is a class that internally derives from DataSet as a base class. It extends this base class further and adds certain properties and methods that make the developer's life easy. When using a typed DataSet, you can access DataTable and DataColumn objects by using their strongly typed names instead of the collection syntax. A typed DataSet has an XSD Schema attached to it that defines the DataTable and DataColumn objects of the DataSet.

Using Visual Studio to Create a Typed DataSet

Now that you know what a typed DataSet is, let's create one for our Employees table. To do so, you first need to add a typed DataSet to your project. Figure 7-16 shows the Add New Item dialog box of Visual Studio, through which you can add a new typed DataSet.

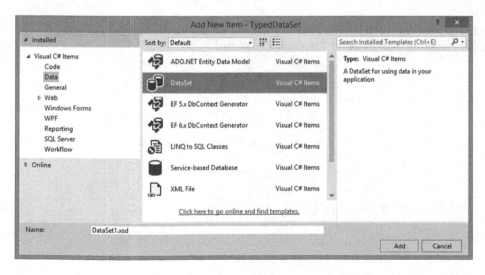

Figure 7-16. Adding a new typed DataSet to your project

After you are on the `DataSet` designer, you can see the `DataSet` toolbox, shown in Figure 7-17.

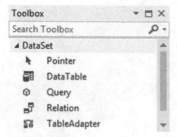

Figure 7-17. *The DataSet toolbox*

As you can see, the toolbox has items such as `DataTable` and `Relation` that you can drag and drop on the `DataSet` designer. For our example, you need to drag and drop a `DataTable` on the `DataSet` designer and set its `Name` property to `Employees`. To add columns to the `DataTable`, you can right-click it and add the required number of columns (see Figure 7-18).

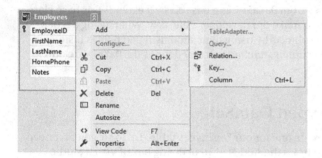

Figure 7-18. *Adding columns to a DataTable*

The name and data type of each column can then be set via the properties window. For example, Figure 7-19 shows the Properties window for the EmployeeID column.

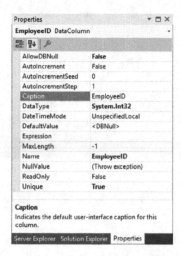

Figure 7-19. *Setting properties of the EmployeeID column*

After designing the Employees DataTable, it should look like Figure 7-20.

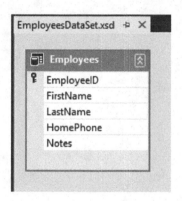

Figure 7-20. *The Employees DataTable in the DataSet designer*

As you are designing the DataSet in the designer, Visual Studio creates a class that inherits from the DataSet class and adds certain properties and methods to it. It also creates certain support files, as you can see in the Solution Explorer (see Figure 7-21).

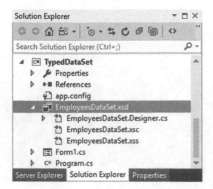

Figure 7-21. *EmployeesDataSet and its associated files*

Next, you need to design the main form of your application, as shown in Figure 7-22.

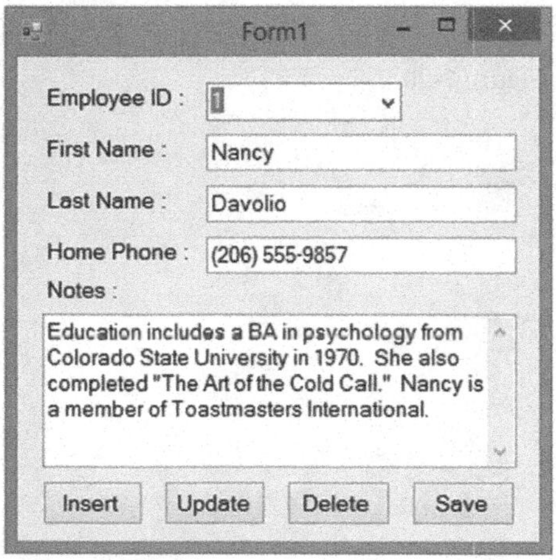

Figure 7-22. *Application that consumes a typed DataSet*

The application behaves exactly the same as the one shown in Figure 7-6 earlier, but this time it uses our typed DataSet. Listing 7-19 shows the variable declarations at the form level.

Listing 7-19. Declaring a Typed DataSet Variable

```
private string strConn = @"data source=.\sqlexpress;
initial catalog=northwind;integrated security=true";
EmployeesDataSet ds = new EmployeesDataSet();
SqlDataAdapter da = new SqlDataAdapter();
SqlConnection cnn;
```

Notice the line marked in bold. The code declares a variable of our typed DataSet, which bears the same name as the DataSet XSD Schema file. This typed DataSet is filled in the Load event of the form. The code in the Load event remains the same as before, but for the sake of completeness, it's shown in Listing 7-20.

Listing 7-20. Filling a Typed DataSet

```
private void Form1_Load(object sender, EventArgs e)
{
  cnn = new SqlConnection(strConn);
  SqlCommand cmdEmployees = new SqlCommand();
  cmdEmployees.CommandText = "SELECT * FROM employees";
  cmdEmployees.Connection = cnn;
  da.SelectCommand = cmdEmployees;
  da.Fill(ds, "Employees");
  FillEmployees();
}
```

The code uses a SqlDataAdapter and calls its Fill() method to populate the typed DataSet. One thing to note here is that the name of the DataTable specified in the Fill() method must match the name of the DataTable that you created in the typed DataSet. Listing 7-21 shows the modified version of the code responsible for inserting, updating, and deleting DataRow objects.

Listing 7-21. Inserting, Updating, and Deleting Data from a Typed DataSet

```
private void button2_Click(object sender, EventArgs e)
{
  EmployeesDataSet.EmployeesRow row = ds.Employees.NewEmployeesRow();
  row.EmployeeID = int.Parse(comboBox1.Text);
  row.FirstName = textBox1.Text;
  row.LastName = textBox2.Text;
  row.HomePhone = textBox3.Text;
  row.Notes = textBox4.Text;
  ds.Employees.AddEmployeesRow(row);
  FillEmployees();
}
private void button1_Click(object sender, EventArgs e)
{
  string id = comboBox1.SelectedItem.ToString();
  EmployeesDataSet.EmployeesRow[] rows =
    (EmployeesDataSet.EmployeesRow[])ds.Employees.Select($"EmployeeID={id}");
  rows[0].BeginEdit();
  rows[0].FirstName = textBox1.Text;
  rows[0].LastName = textBox2.Text;
  rows[0].HomePhone = textBox3.Text;
  rows[0].Notes = textBox4.Text;
  rows[0].EndEdit();
}

  private void button3_Click(object sender, EventArgs e)
  {
    string id = comboBox1.SelectedItem.ToString();
    EmployeesDataSet.EmployeesRow[] rows =
      (EmployeesDataSet.EmployeesRow[])ds.Employees.Select($"EmployeeID={id}");
    rows[0].Delete();
    FillEmployees();
  }
```

Notice the changes made to the original code. In the `Click` event handler of the Insert button, the new `DataRow` is created by calling `NewEmployeesRow()`. The typed `DataSet` automatically show the available `DataTable` objects as properties, and each `DataTable` provides the `NewEmployeesRow()` method to create a new row. The newly created row is of type `EmployeesRow`, which is a class generated by Visual Studio in the `EmployeesDataSet` class. `EmployeesRow` exposes each column of the row as a property, and these properties can then be assigned new values. The newly created row is then added to the `Employees` `DataTable` by using its `AddEmployeesRow()` method. There are similar modifications in the `Click` event handlers of the Update and Delete buttons.

Using the xsd.exe Tool to Create a Typed DataSet

Though Visual Studio provides a visual way to create typed `DataSet`s, the .NET Framework also provides a command line tool called `xsd.exe` that can generate typed `DataSet`s for you. The tool accepts an XML Schema for a `DataSet` and outputs the typed `DataSet` class. Though we will not discuss the `xsd.exe` tool at great length, here is a sample use of it:

```
xsd.exe EmployeesDataSet.xsd /dataset /language:CS /namespace:MyTypedDataSets
```

The command accepts the name of an XML Schema file (`EmployeesDataSet.xsd` in this case). The `/dataset` switch indicates that the tool should generate a typed `DataSet` based on this XML Schema. The `/language` switch specifies the language to be used for the typed `DataSet` class. In our example, we specify the language as C# (`CS`). Finally, the `/namespace` switch specifies the namespace in which the typed `DataSet` class will be placed.

The output of the preceding command will be a class file named `EmployeesDataSet.cs`. You can compile this class file separately into an assembly or add it to your existing project along with other classes.

Summary

ADO.NET is a very important part of the overall .NET Framework. Modern data-driven applications tend to work with relational as well as hierarchical datastores. The ADO.NET object model, though primarily inclined toward RDBMSs, has tight integration with XML.

This chapter gave you a thorough look at the XML features of ADO.NET. You learned how to work with XML data in connected and disconnected mode. The `DataSet` class is the cornerstone of the ADO.NET disconnected model and allows you to read and write XML data, and to work with schemas. Further, typed `DataSet`s make your development easy by providing typed `DataTable` and `DataColumn` names.

CHAPTER 8

■ ■ ■

XML Serialization

Your .NET applications consist of one or more classes. The objects of these classes are used to store state information. As long as your objects are available in the memory of your application, this state information is readily available. But what if you want to persist object state across application shutdowns? At first you may think of saving object state in a relational database. However, databases generally store information in relational format, whereas objects often have a hierarchical structure. Moreover, you would need to create many tables in the database on your own. Storing object data in a database comes with its own overheads. Wouldn't it be nice if the entire object state could be stored to a medium and retrieved later? That is what serialization offers.

Serialization is a process by which object state is persisted to a medium. The medium can be a physical disk file, memory, or even a network stream. The serialized objects can be retrieved later in your application by a process called *deserialization*. The .NET Framework provides extensive support for serialization and uses serialization in many places. Web services, WCF services, and Web API are a few places where serialization is heavily used. In this chapter, you learn about the following topics:

- Understanding the flavors of serialization

- Using the XmlSerializer class to serialize object state in XML format

- Using the DataContractSerializer class to serialize object state in XML format

- Using the SoapFormatter class to serialize object state in SOAP format

- Customizing the serialization process with the help of certain attributes

Understanding the Flavors of Serialization

Serialization can be classified based on the format of serialization or on the depth of serialization. The three commonly used formats in which you can serialize data in the .NET Framework are as follows:

- *Binary*: This format is generally better in terms of performance than the others. However, in terms of extensibility and cross-application integration, the other formats are better.

- *XML*: Objects serialized in this way are stored as plain XML. If you are talking with multiple heterogeneous systems, this format will prove useful. For example, your .NET applications may serialize objects as XML documents, and a Java application may read these serialized objects by using its standard XML parser and work with the data further.

- *Simple Object Access Protocol (SOAP)*: Objects serialized in this way store information as per the SOAP standards. SOAP is the core pillar for web services. SOAP protocol is based on XML.

© Bipin Joshi 2017
B. Joshi, *Beginning XML with C# 7*, https://doi.org/10.1007/978-1-4842-3105-0_8

Serialization using binary format is beyond the scope of this book. This chapter discusses serialization using XML and SOAP formats.

■ **Note** In modern web applications, JSON is increasingly becoming popular as a format for transferring data. Applications using JSON need a mechanism to serialize and deserialize objects in JSON format. Although WCF and Web API can deal with JSON data, we won't discuss that in this book.

The other way to classify serialization is based on the depth of serialization. The two flavors based on the depth of serialization are as follows:

- *Deep serialization*: This serializes all the public, protected, and private members of your class.

- *Shallow serialization*: This serializes only the public members of your class.

In the .NET Framework, the depth of serialization depends on the serializer class you use for the sake of serializing and deserializing objects.

Classes Involved in the XML Serialization

There are three core classes that are used to perform serialization in XML and SOAP formats:

- The XmlSerializer class serializes objects in XML format. It resides in the System. Xml.Serialization namespace. The System.Xml.Serialization namespace physically resides in the System.Xml.dll assembly. Serialization done using XmlScrializer is shallow in nature.

- The DataContractSerializer class serializes objects in XML format. It was added as a part of Windows Communication Foundation (WCF) and resides in the System.Runtime.Serialization namespace. Serialization done using DataContractSerializer is deep in nature.

- The SoapFormatter class serializes objects in SOAP format. It resides in the System. Runtime.Serialization.Formatters.Soap namespace. The System.Runtime. Serialization.Formatters.Soap namespace physically resides in the System. Runtime.Serialization.Formatters.Soap.dll assembly. Serialization done using SoapFormatter is deep in nature.

Serializing and Deserializing Objects Using XmlSerializer

Now that you have a basic understanding of what serialization is, let's delve straight into XML serialization. You will be building an application that illustrates the serialization and deserialization process by using the XmlSerializer class. The application user interface is shown in Figure 8-1.

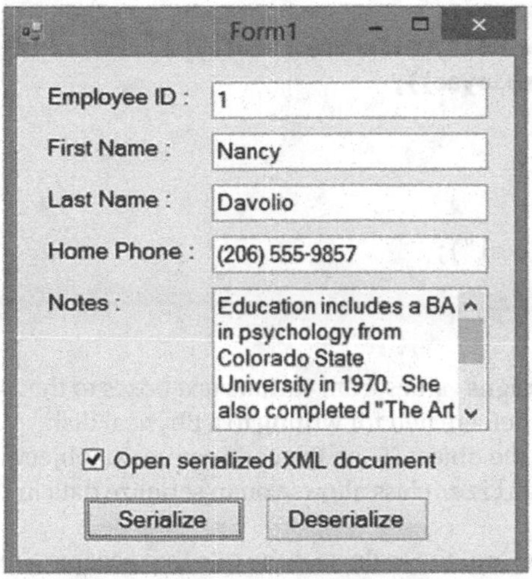

Figure 8-1. *Application for illustrating XML serialization*

The application consists of a class called `Employee` with five public properties: `EmployeeID`, `FirstName`, `LastName`, `HomePhone`, and `Notes`. There are five text boxes that accept values for these properties. The two buttons, Serialize and Deserialize, do the job of serializing and deserializing the `Employee` object, respectively. The check box determines whether the serialized XML document will be opened in a browser for viewing.

Before you can use the `XmlSerializer` class, you should create the `Employee` class shown in Listing 8-1.

Listing 8-1. The Employee Class

```
public class Employee
{
    public int EmployeeID { get; set; }
    public string FirstName { get; set; }
    public string LastName { get; set; }
    public string HomePhone { get; set; }
    public string Notes { get; set; }
}
```

The class consists of five public properties for storing various pieces of information about an employee, namely `EmployeeID`, `FirstName`, `LastName`, `HomePhone`, and `Notes`.

The `Click` event handler of the Serialize button contains the code shown in Listing 8-2.

Listing 8-2. Serializing Objects in XML Format

```
private void button1_Click(object sender, EventArgs e)
{
    Employee emp = new Employee();
    emp.EmployeeID = int.Parse(textBox1.Text);
    emp.FirstName = textBox2.Text;
    emp.LastName = textBox3.Text;
    emp.HomePhone = textBox4.Text;
    emp.Notes = textBox5.Text;
```

```
FileStream stream =
  new FileStream($"{Application.StartupPath}\\employee.xml", FileMode.Create);
XmlSerializer serializer = new XmlSerializer(typeof(Employee));
serializer.Serialize(stream, emp);
stream.Close();
if (checkBox1.Checked)
{
    Process.Start($"{Application.StartupPath}\\employee.xml");
}
}
```

The code creates an instance of the Employee class. It then assigns values from various text boxes to the corresponding properties of the Employee class. A FileStream is then created for writing to a physical disk file (Employee.xml). This stream is used while actually serializing the object. Then the code creates an object of the XmlSerializer class. As mentioned previously, the XmlSerializer class allows you to serialize data in XML format.

There are several overloads of the XmlSerializer constructor, and the code uses the one that accepts the type of class whose objects are to be serialized. The type information about the Employee class is obtained by using the typeof keyword. The Serialize() method of XmlSerializer serializes an object to a specified stream, TextWriter, or XmlWriter.

Because our example uses a FileStream to serialize the Employee object, after serialization is complete, the stream is closed. Finally, the serialized data from the XML file is displayed in a browser by using the Start() method of the Process class.

The Click event handler of the Deserialize button contains the code shown in Listing 8-3.

Listing 8-3. Deserializing by Using the XmlSerializer Class

```
private void button2_Click(object sender, EventArgs e)
{
  FileStream stream =
    new FileStream($"{Application.StartupPath}\\employee.xml", FileMode.Open);
  XmlSerializer serializer = new XmlSerializer(typeof(Employee));
  Employee emp = (Employee)serializer.Deserialize(stream);
  stream.Close();
  textBox1.Text = emp.EmployeeID.ToString();
  textBox2.Text = emp.FirstName;
  textBox3.Text = emp.LastName;
  textBox4.Text = emp.HomePhone;
  textBox5.Text = emp.Notes;
}
```

The code creates a FileStream pointing to the same file that was created during the serialization process. Note that this time the file is opened in Open mode and not in Create mode. Then an object of XmlSerializer is created as before.

The Deserialize() method of the XmlSerializer class accepts a Stream, a TextReader, or an XmlReader from which the object is to be read for deserialization. It then returns the deserialized object. The deserialized data is always returned as an object and needs to be casted to the Employee type. Then various property values of the deserialized object are assigned to respective text boxes.

To test the application, you run it, enter some values in the text boxes, and click the Serialize button. Figure 8-2 shows a sample XML document obtained by running the preceding application.

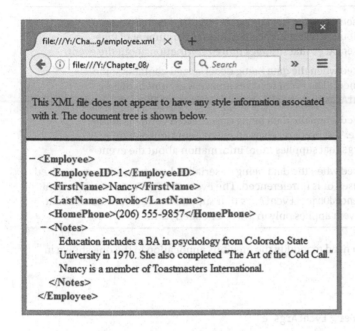

Figure 8-2. *Employee object serialized as an XML document*

Examine the resultant XML markup carefully. The class name (Employee) has become the name of the root element. The elements such as <EmployeeID>, <FirstName>, and <LastName> have the same name as the corresponding properties of the Employee class. Now close the application and run it again. This time click the Deserialize button. You will find that the text boxes show the property values that you specified during the last run of the application.

Handling Events Raised During Deserialization

Imagine a case where one application is serializing objects and the other is deserializing them. What if the serialized objects contain some extra attributes and elements? The application that is deserializing such objects must have some way to signal this discrepancy. Fortunately, the XmlSerializer class comes with certain events to handle such situations. These events are raised during the deserialization process when the structure of the class and the serialized XML don't match. Table 8-1 lists these events.

Table 8-1. *Events of the XmlSerializer Class*

Event Name	Description
UnknownAttribute	This event is raised when the data being deserialized contains some unexpected attribute. The event receives an event argument of type XmlAttributeEventArgs that supplies more information about the event.
UnknownElement	This event is raised when the data being deserialized contains some unexpected element. The event receives an event argument of type XmlElementEventArgs that supplies more information about the event.
UnknownNode	This event is raised when the data being deserialized contains some unexpected node. The event receives an event argument of type XmlNodeEventArgs that supplies more information about the event.
UnreferencedObject	This event is raised when the data being deserialized contains some recognized type that is not used or is unreferenced. The event receives an event argument of type UnreferencedObjectEventArgs that supplies more information about the event. This event applies only to SOAP-encoded XML.

To illustrate the use of these events, you need to modify the previous application to the one shown in Listing 8-4.

Listing 8-4. Events of the XmlSerializer Class

```
private void button2_Click(object sender, EventArgs e)
{
  FileStream stream =
    new FileStream($"{Application.StartupPath}\\employee.xml", FileMode.Open);
  XmlSerializer serializer = new XmlSerializer(typeof(Employee));
  serializer.UnknownAttribute +=
    new XmlAttributeEventHandler(serializer_UnknownAttribute);
  serializer.UnknownElement +=
    new XmlElementEventHandler(serializer_UnknownElement);
  serializer.UnknownNode += new XmlNodeEventHandler(serializer_UnknownNode);
  Employee emp = (Employee)serializer.Deserialize(stream);
  stream.Close();
  textBox1.Text = emp.EmployeeID.ToString();
  textBox2.Text = emp.FirstName;
  textBox3.Text = emp.LastName;
  textBox4.Text = emp.HomePhone;
  textBox5.Text = emp.Notes;
}

void serializer_UnknownNode(object sender, XmlNodeEventArgs e)
{
  MessageBox.Show($"Unknown Node {e.Name} found at Line {e.LineNumber}");
}
void serializer_UnknownElement(object sender, XmlElementEventArgs e)
{
  MessageBox.Show($"Unknown Element {e.Element.Name} found at Line {e.LineNumber}");
}
```

```
void serializer_UnknownAttribute(object sender, XmlAttributeEventArgs e)
{
  MessageBox.Show($"Unknown Attribute {e.Attr.Name} found at Line {e.LineNumber}");
}
```

Notice the code marked in bold. After declaring the instance of the XmlSerializer class, it wires up three event handlers—UnknownAttribute, UnknownElement, and UnknownNode—that simply display a message box showing the name of the attribute, element, or node and the line number at which the attribute, element, or node is encountered. Notice how the event argument parameter is used to extract information about the unexpected content.

To test these events, modify the serialized XML file manually, as shown in Listing 8-5.

Listing 8-5. Modifying the Serialized XML Manually

```
<?xml version="1.0"?>
<Employee xmlns:xsi="http://www.w3.org/2001/XMLSchema-instance"
 xmlns:xsd="http://www.w3.org/2001/XMLSchema" EmpCode="E001">
  <EmployeeID>1</EmployeeID>
  <FirstName>Nancy</FirstName>
  <LastName>Davolio</LastName>
  <HomePhone>(206) 555-9857</HomePhone>
  <Notes>Education includes a BA in psychology from Colorado State University in 1970.
She also completed "The Art of the Cold Call." Nancy is a member of Toastmasters
International.</Notes>
  <OfficePhone>(206) 555-1234</OfficePhone>
</Employee>
```

Notice the markup in bold. We added an EmpCode attribute and an <OfficePhone> element manually to the XML file. Save the file and run the application. This time when you click the Deserialize button, you will see message boxes informing you of the discrepancies. Figure 8-3 shows one such message box.

Figure 8-3. *Unexpected content encountered during the deserialization process*

Serializing and Deserializing Complex Types

In the preceding example, we serialized simple types; the members of the Employee class were simple types such as an integer and a string. However, real-world classes are often complex ones. They may contain members that are class types, enumerated types, or even arrays. The XmlSerializer class provides support for such complex types, and that is what you are going to see in the next example.

The user interface of the application now changes to look like the one shown in Figure 8-4.

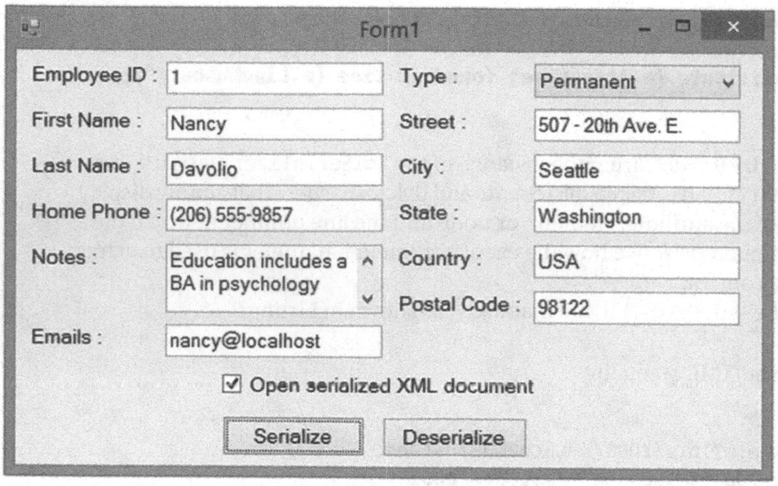

***Figure 8-4.** Application for illustrating XML serialization of complex types*

The first five text boxes remain the same as in the previous example. However, six text boxes and one combo box are new. The newly added text boxes capture the e-mail, street, city, state, country, and postal code information of the employee. The combo box captures the employee type (permanent or contract).

To store the address information of employees, you need to add a property called Address to the Employee class. The Address property itself is of type Address. The Address class is shown in Listing 8-6.

***Listing 8-6.** The Address Class*

```
public class Address
{
    public string Street { get; set; }
    public string City { get; set; }
    public string State { get; set; }
    public string Country { get; set; }
    public string PostalCode { get; set; }
}
```

This class has five public properties for storing street address, city, state, country, and postal code, respectively.

To store the employee type, you need to add a property called Type to the Employee class. The Type property will be an enumeration of type EmployeeType, which contains two values: Permanent and Contract. The EmployeeType enumeration is shown in Listing 8-7.

***Listing 8-7.** The EmployeeType Enumeration*

```
public enum EmployeeType
{
  Permanent, Contract
}
```

The e-mail information is stored in a property called Emails. An employee can have more than one e-mail address and hence this property is of the string array type. Listing 8-8 shows the modified version of the Employee class.

Listing 8-8. The Employee Class After Adding Address, Type, and Emails Properties

```
public class Employee
{
    public int EmployeeID { get; set; }
    public string FirstName { get; set; }
    public string LastName { get; set; }
    public string HomePhone { get; set; }
    public string Notes { get; set; }
    public string[] Emails { get; set; }
    public EmployeeType Type { get; set; }
    public Address Address { get; set; } = new Address();
}
```

Notice the property definitions marked in bold. The three public properties—Address, Type, and Emails—are of type Address, EmployeeType, and string array, respectively. The code in the Click event handler of the Serialize button now changes to the code shown in Listing 8-9.

Listing 8-9. Serializing Complex Types

```
private void button1_Click(object sender, EventArgs e)
{
  Employee emp = new Employee();
  emp.EmployeeID = int.Parse(textBox1.Text);
  emp.FirstName = textBox2.Text;
  emp.LastName = textBox3.Text;
  emp.HomePhone = textBox4.Text;
  emp.Notes = textBox5.Text;
  emp.Type =
    (comboBox1.SelectedIndex == 0 ? EmployeeType.Permanent :
    EmployeeType.Contract);
  emp.Address.Street = textBox6.Text;
  emp.Address.City = textBox7.Text;
  emp.Address.State = textBox8.Text;
  emp.Address.Country = textBox9.Text;
  emp.Address.PostalCode = textBox10.Text;
  emp.Emails = textBox11.Text.Split(',');
  FileStream stream =
    new FileStream($"{Application.StartupPath}\\employee.xml", FileMode.Create);
  XmlSerializer serializer = new XmlSerializer(typeof(Employee));
  serializer.Serialize(stream, emp);
  stream.Close();
  if (checkBox1.Checked)
  {
    Process.Start($"{Application.StartupPath}\\employee.xml");
  }
}
```

The code is essentially the same as in the preceding examples. However, it sets the newly added properties to corresponding values from the text boxes and combo box. Notice how the complex property Address is set. Also, notice how comma-separated emails entered in the e-mail text box are converted into a string array by using the Split() method. After the Employee object is serialized by calling Serialize(), the serialized XML document looks like the one shown in Figure 8-5.

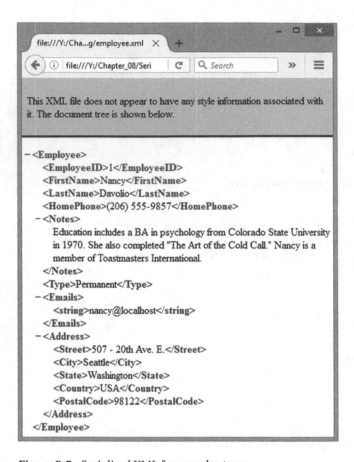

Figure 8-5. Serialized XML for complex types

Examine the serialized XML data carefully. The address is represented by the <Address> node, the name of which is derived from the Address property of the Employee class. The <Address> node has five child nodes: <Street>, <City>, <State>, <Country>, and <PostalCode>. Their names are derived from the respective properties of the Address class.

The <Type> element represents the Type property of the Employee class. The enumeration value, Permanent, is stored in the XML markup. Finally, the <Emails> node represents the Emails property, and its child nodes are nothing but individual array elements. Because the e-mails are stored in a string array, the individual values are enclosed in <string></string> elements.

Listing 8-10 shows the code in the Click event of the Deserialize button.

Listing 8-10. Deserializing Complex Types

```
private void button2_Click(object sender, EventArgs e)
{
  FileStream stream = new FileStream($"{Application.StartupPath}\\employee.xml", FileMode.
  Open);
  XmlSerializer serializer = new XmlSerializer(typeof(Employee));
  Employee emp=(Employee)serializer.Deserialize(stream);
  stream.Close();
  textBox1.Text = emp.EmployeeID.ToString();
```

```
    textBox2.Text = emp.FirstName;
    textBox3.Text = emp.LastName;
    textBox4.Text = emp.HomePhone;
    textBox5.Text = emp.Notes;
    comboBox1.SelectedIndex = (emp.Type == EmployeeType.Permanent?0:1);
    textBox6.Text=emp.Address.Street;
    textBox7.Text=emp.Address.City;
    textBox8.Text=emp.Address.State;
    textBox9.Text=emp.Address.Country;
    textBox10.Text=emp.Address.PostalCode;
    textBox11.Text = string.Join(",", emp.Emails);
    stream.Close();
}
```

The code is very much the same as in previous examples. It deserializes the previously serialized
Employee object by using the XmlSerializer class. The property values are then assigned to various controls
on the form. Notice how the Emails property is converted into a comma-separated string by using the
Join() method of the string class. The following points are worth noting when serializing complex types:

- To serialize and deserialize enumerated values, the application that serializes the
  object and the application that deserializes it must define the same enumeration
  under consideration.

- While serializing object properties, all the public members of the object are
  serialized. The member names are assigned to the child elements in the
  resultant XML.

- During the deserialization process, XmlSerializer instantiates the main class
  (Employee) as well as all the subclasses (Address) and assigns values to the
  respective properties.

- While serializing arrays, an XML element represents the array. The individual array
  elements form the child element of this element. The individual array elements are
  enclosed in an element depending on the data type of the array.

- While deserializing, XmlSerializer creates an array with the same number of
  elements as the serialized elements. It then assigns the array element values
  accordingly.

Serialization and Inheritance

Serialization is not limited to simple and complex types. It is equally applicable to inherited classes. Assume
that you have a class called Manager that inherits from our Employee class. Now when you serialize Manager,
all the public properties of the Employee base class and Manager are serialized. This is also true in the case of
a long chain of inheritance.

To demonstrate how inherited classes are serialized, we need to add a class called Manager to our
application. The Manager class inherits from the Employee class (see Listing 8-1) and extends it by adding an
integer property NoOfSubordinates. The Manager class is shown in Listing 8-11.

Listing 8-11. The Manager Class

```
public class Manager : Employee
{
    public int NoOfSubordinates { get; set; }
}
```

The code creates a class named Manager that inherits from the Employee class. It then adds an integer property—NoOfSubordinates—to store the number of subordinates of a manager. To accommodate the additional property, the user interface of the application changes, as shown in Figure 8-6.

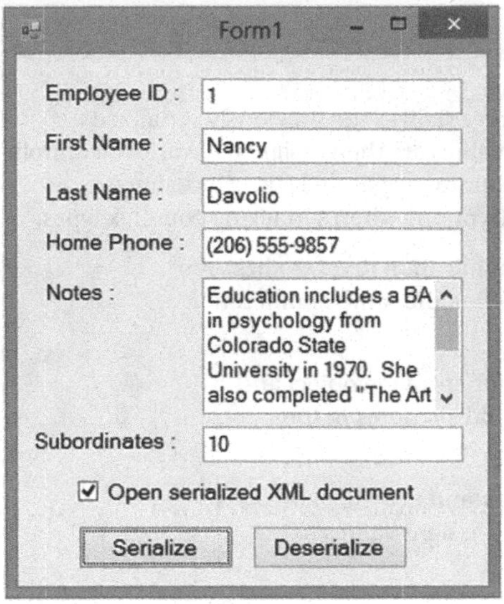

Figure 8-6. *Application to demonstrate serialization of inherited classes*

The application is almost the same as in Figure 8-1, but there is an extra text box for accepting the number of subordinates of the manager. Listing 8-12 shows the Click event handler of the Serialize button.

Listing 8-12. Serializing the Inherited Manager Class

```
private void button1_Click(object sender, EventArgs e)
{
    Manager manager = new Manager();
    manager.EmployeeID = int.Parse(textBox1.Text);
    manager.FirstName = textBox2.Text;
    manager.LastName = textBox3.Text;
    manager.HomePhone = textBox4.Text;
    manager.Notes = textBox5.Text;
    manager.NoOfSubordinates = int.Parse(textBox6.Text);
    FileStream stream =
      new FileStream($"{Application.StartupPath}\\employee.xml", FileMode.Create);
    XmlSerializer serializer = new XmlSerializer(typeof(Manager));
    serializer.Serialize(stream, manager);
    stream.Close();
```

```
  if (checkBox1.Checked)
  {
    Process.Start($"{Application.StartupPath}\\employee.xml");
  }
}
```

The code is essentially the same as we have been using up until now, but it uses the Manager class instead of the Employee class. An instance of Manager is created, and all its properties are set. Then an instance of XmlSerializer is created by passing the Type information of the Manager class. Finally, the Manager instance is serialized by calling the Serialize() method of XmlSerializer. Figure 8-7 shows the resultant XML output.

Figure 8-7. *Serialized XML of the Manager class*

Notice how all the public properties from the Employee base class as well as the one from Manager are serialized. The code to deserialize the Manager class is very similar to the one we used previously. Listing 8-13 shows this code.

Listing 8-13. Deserializing the Manager Class

```
private void button2_Click(object sender, EventArgs e)
{
  FileStream stream =
    new FileStream($"{Application.StartupPath}\\employee.xml", FileMode.Open);
  XmlSerializer serializer = new XmlSerializer(typeof(Manager));
  Manager manager = (Manager)serializer.Deserialize(stream);
  stream.Close();
  textBox1.Text = manager.EmployeeID.ToString();
  textBox2.Text = manager.FirstName;
  textBox3.Text = manager.LastName;
```

```
  textBox4.Text = manager.HomePhone;
  textBox5.Text = manager.Notes;
  textBox6.Text = manager.NoOfSubordinates.ToString();
}
```

The only difference in this code is that it uses Manager in the deserialization process instead of Employee.

Customizing the Serialized XML

The XmlSerializer class automatically uses the name of the public members as the names for the resultant XML elements. This is what is required in many cases. However, sometimes you may need to customize the serialized XML data to suit your needs. In the previous example illustrating the serialization of complex types, we got the XML document shown in Listing 8-14.

Listing 8-14. Serialized XML Document Without Any Customization

```
<?xml version="1.0"?>
<Employee xmlns:xsi="http://www.w3.org/2001/XMLSchema-instance"
xmlns:xsd="http://www.w3.org/2001/XMLSchema">
  <EmployeeID>1</EmployeeID>
  <FirstName>Nancy</FirstName>
  <LastName>Davolio</LastName>
  <HomePhone>(206) 555-9857</HomePhone>
  <Notes>Education includes a BA in psychology from Colorado State University in 1970.
  She also completed "The Art of the Cold Call." Nancy is a member of Toastmasters
  International.</Notes>
  <Type>Permanent</Type>
  <Emails>
    <string>nancy@localhost</string>
  </Emails>
  <Address>
    <Street>507 - 20th Ave. E. Apt. 2A</Street>
    <City>Seattle</City>
    <State>Washington</State>
    <Country>USA</Country>
    <PostalCode>98122</PostalCode>
  </Address>
</Employee>
```

However, what if you want the resultant XML structure to resemble Listing 8-15?

Listing 8-15. Serialized XML After Customization

```
<?xml version="1.0"?>
<MyEmployee xmlns:xsi="http://www.w3.org/2001/XMLSchema-instance"
xmlns:xsd="http://www.w3.org/2001/XMLSchema" EmployeeCode="1">
  <FName>Nancy</FName>
  <LName>Davolio</LName>
```

```
  <Remarks>
Education includes a BA in psychology from Colorado State University in 1970. She also
completed "The Art of the Cold Call." Nancy is a member of Toastmasters International.
  </Remarks>
  <EmployeeType>Permanent Employee</EmployeeType>
  <EmailAddresses>
    <Email>nancy@localhost</Email>
  </EmailAddresses>
  <Address>
    <Street>507 - 20th Ave. E. Apt. 2A</Street>
    <City>Seattle</City>
    <State>Washington</State>
    <Country>USA</Country>
    <PostalCode>98122</PostalCode>
  </Address>
</MyEmployee>
```

Observe Listing 8-15 carefully. There are some significant changes:

- The root element of the document is <MyEmployee> and not <Employee>.

- The element names are totally different from the public property names.

- The employee ID is stored as the EmployeeCode attribute.

- The EmployeeType enumeration value is different from the actual enumeration item text.

- E-mail addresses are stored as <Email> elements and not as <string> elements.

- The HomePhone property value is not serialized even if it is a public member of the class.

To achieve such customization, the System.Xml.Serialization namespace provides several attributes. You are required to decorate your classes, enumerations, and properties with these attributes to customize the way they are serialized. Listing 8-16 shows the Employee class and the EmployeeType enumeration after applying many of these attributes.

Listing 8-16. Customizing Serialization by Using Attributes

```
[XmlRoot(ElementName="MyEmployee")]
public class Employee
{
    [XmlAttribute(AttributeName = "EmployeeCode")]
    public int EmployeeID { get; set; }

    [XmlElement(ElementName = "FName")]
    public string FirstName { get; set; }

    [XmlElement(ElementName = "LName")]
    public string LastName { get; set; }

    [XmlIgnore]
    public string HomePhone { get; set; }
```

```
[XmlElement(ElementName = "Remarks")]
public string Notes { get; set; }

[XmlArray(ElementName = "EmailAddresses")]
    [XmlArrayItem(ElementName = "Email")]
public string[] Emails { get; set; }

[XmlElement(ElementName = "EmployeeType")]
public EmployeeType Type { get; set; }

[XmlElement(IsNullable = true)]
public Address Address { get; set; } = new Address();
}

public enum EmployeeType
{
    [XmlEnum(Name="Permanent Employee")]
    Permanent,
    [XmlEnum(Name = "Employee on contract")]
    Contract
}
```

Let's dissect the preceding listing step by step and see the significance of each attribute used.

Changing the XML Document Root

By default, the XmlSerializer class uses the name of the class as the name of the XML root element. To alter this behavior, you can decorate your class with the [XmlRoot] attribute. The [XmlRoot] attribute has a property called ElementName that indicates the new name of the XML document root element. The [XmlRoot] attribute must be applied to a class definition and hence we've placed it on top of the Employee class.

Changing the Element Names

By default, the XmlSerializer class uses the names of the public members to assign to the output XML elements. For example, the FirstName property gets serialized as the <FirstName> element. This default behavior can be altered by using the [XmlElement] attribute. The [XmlElement] attribute has a property called ElementName that specifies the name of the resulting XML element. The [XmlElement] attribute is applied to the public member that will be serialized, and thus the FirstName, LastName, Notes, Type, and Address properties are decorated with the [XmlElement] attribute.

Serializing Members As Attributes

By default, all the public members of your class are serialized as XML elements in the output document. The [XmlAttribute] attribute allows you to change this default behavior. The AttributeName property of the [XmlAttribute] attribute indicates the name that will be given to the resultant XML attribute. [XmlAttribute] is applied to the public member that you want to serialize as an attribute. In our example, we add the [XmlAttribute] attribute to the EmployeeID property.

Ignoring Public Members in the Serialization Process

By default, all the public members of a class are serialized, but sometimes this is not what you want. For example, if you are storing credit card information in a public property, you may not want to serialize it for obvious security reasons. A public member can be ignored during the serialization process by decorating it with the [XmlIgnore] attribute. In our example, the HomePhone property is marked with this attribute.

Changing Array and Array Element Names

The Employee class has a property called Emails that is of type string array. Under the default naming scheme, when this property is serialized, an XML node is created with the name Emails. This node further contains child nodes, each containing the array element value. The names of the child elements are the same as the data type of the array (<string> in our example). You can alter this behavior with the help of the [XmlArray] and [XmlArrayElement] attributes. The former marks public members that are array types and specifies the XML element name for the member. The latter attribute governs the name of the XML element assigned to the individual array members. In our example, the Emails property will be serialized as <EmailAddresses>, and each array element will be enclosed within an <Email> element.

Ignoring Null Objects in the Serialization Process

The Employee class has an Address property that is an object type. If this property is null, XmlSerializer still emits an empty XML element for it, but you can use the [XmlElement] attribute to change this behavior. The IsNullable Boolean property of the [XmlElement] attribute indicates whether the empty XML element will be emitted when the member is null. Setting this property to true will not emit the empty XML element if the Address property is null.

Changing Enumeration Identifiers

The EmployeeType enumeration has two values: Permanent and Contract. By default when a member of the EmployeeType type is serialized, the value of these enumeration identifiers is emitted in the serialized XML. The [XmlEnum] attribute specifies the alternate value to serialize instead of the actual identifier name, and is applied on enumeration identifiers. The Name property of the [XmlEnum] attribute specifies the text that will be serialized instead of the identifier name.

Serializing and Deserializing Objects Using DataContractSerializer

In the preceding section, you used the XmlSerializer class to serialize and deserialize objects. The XmlSerializer has been available since version 1.1 of the .NET Framework. Along with Windows Communication Foundation (WCF) another class, called DataContractSerializer, was added that can also be used for XML serialization. The DataContractSerializer class is the default serializer for WCF services, but you can also use it to serialize and deserialize your objects as you did with the XmlSerializer.

In order to use DataContractSerializer, you need to add a couple of attributes to your classes:

- The class must be decorated with the [DataContract] attribute.

- Every member of the class that you want to be serialized must be marked with [DataMember] attribute. Members not decorated with [DataMember] will be ignored during the serialization process.

■ **Note** We are going to revisit the [DataContract] and [DataMember] attributes in Chapter 10 when we discuss WCF services. At that time, it will be more clear to you as to how these attributes are used by WCF. Here it suffices to say that they are necessary to serialize an object using the DataContractSerializer class.

To illustrate the use of DataContractSerializer class, you will develop a similar application as for XmlSerializer (see Figure 8-1). Of course, you will need to modify the Employee class and the code that serializes and deserializes the Employee object, as discussed next.

First of all, open the Employee class and modify it, as shown in Listing 8-17.

Listing 8-17. Marking a Class with the [DataContract] and [DataMember] Attributes

```
[DataContract]
public class Employee
{
    [DataMember]
    public int EmployeeID { get; set; }
    [DataMember]
    public string FirstName { get; set; }
    [DataMember]
    public string LastName { get; set; }
    [DataMember]
    public string HomePhone { get; set; }
    [DataMember]
    public string Notes { get; set; }
}
```

The [DataContract] attribute added to the Employee class indicates that the Employee class is a data contract and can be serialized by DataContractSerializer. The [DataMember] attribute added to the properties of Employee class indicates that the member under consideration is part of a data contract and can be serialized by the DataContractSerializer.

Next, modify the Click event handler of the Serialize button, as shown in Listing 8-18.

Listing 8-18. Serialize Data Using DataContractSerializer

```
private void button1_Click(object sender, EventArgs e)
{
    Employee emp = new Employee();
    emp.EmployeeID = int.Parse(textBox1.Text);
    emp.FirstName = textBox2.Text;
    emp.LastName = textBox3.Text;
    emp.HomePhone = textBox4.Text;
    emp.Notes = textBox5.Text;
    FileStream stream = new FileStream($"{Application.StartupPath}\\employee.xml", FileMode.
    Create);

    DataContractSerializer serializer = new DataContractSerializer(typeof(Employee));
        serializer.WriteObject(stream, emp);
```

```
        stream.Close();
        if (checkBox1.Checked)
        {
            Process.Start($"{Application.StartupPath}\\employee.xml");
        }
    }
}
```

Most of the code shown in Listing 8-18 should look familiar to you except the lines marked in bold. The first line marked in bold creates an instance of DataContractSerializer by passing the type information of the Employee class. The second line calls the WriteObject() method of DataContractSerializer. The WriteObject() method accepts two parameters—a stream object to write the data and the object to be serialized.

If you run the application and click on the Serialize button after filling various text boxes, the resultant XML document should resemble Figure 8-8.

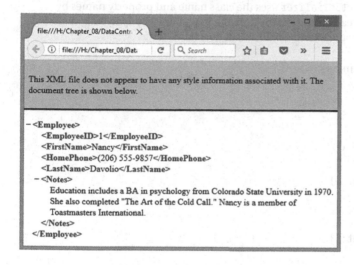

Figure 8-8. *XML serialized by DataContractSerializer*

In order to deserialize XML previously serialized using DataContractSerializer, you can use the ReadObject() method. Listing 8-19 shows the Click event handler of the Deserialize button that illustrates the use of ReadObject().

Listing 8-19. Serialize Data Using DataContractSerializer

```
private void button2_Click(object sender, EventArgs e)
{
    FileStream stream = new FileStream($"{Application.StartupPath}\\employee.xml",
    FileMode.Open);

    DataContractSerializer serializer = new DataContractSerializer(typeof(Employee));
    Employee emp = (Employee)serializer.ReadObject(stream);

    stream.Close();
    textBox1.Text = emp.EmployeeID.ToString();
    textBox2.Text = emp.FirstName;
```

```
    textBox3.Text = emp.LastName;
    textBox4.Text = emp.HomePhone;
    textBox5.Text = emp.Notes;
}
```

Notice the code marked in bold. The first line creates an instance of DataContractSerializer by passing the type information of Employee class. The second line then calls the ReadObject() method on the DataContractSerializer. The stream to read is supplied as the parameter to ReadObject(). The ReadObject() reads an object, which is then casted to the Employee type.

If you run the application again and click on the Deserialize button, you will find that all the text boxes are filled with the correct values.

Customizing the Serialized XML

As you must have observed, the DataContractSerializer uses the class name and property names by default for the resultant XML elements. You can customize the XML element names by specifying them in the [DataContract] and [DataMember] attributes. Listing 8-20 shows how this is done.

Listing 8-20. Customizing XML Element Names

```
[DataContract(Name ="MyEmployee")]
public class Employee
{
    [DataMember(Name ="EmployeeCode")]
    public int EmployeeID { get; set; }
    [DataMember(Name = "FName")]
    public string FirstName { get; set; }
    [DataMember(Name = "LName")]
    public string LastName { get; set; }
    [IgnoreDataMember]
    public string HomePhone { get; set; }
    [DataMember(Name = "Remarks")]
    public string Notes { get; set; }
}
```

The [DataContract] attribute now specifies its Name property to be MyEmployee. Thus the root element name will be MyEmployee. The [DataMember] attributes added to the EmployeeID, FirstName, LastName and Notes properties set their Name properties to EmployeeCode, FName, LName, and Remarks, respectively. The HomePhone property is decorated with the [IgnoreDataMember] attribute, indicating that HomePhone won't be serialized.

Figure 8-9 shows a sample XML generated after the customization just discussed.

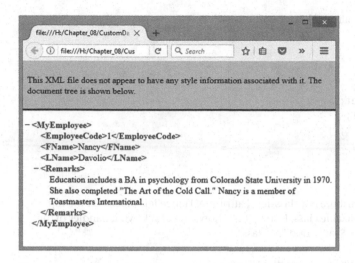

Figure 8-9. *XML element names are now customized*

As you can see, the XML element names are now as per our Name property. Also, the HomePhone has not been serialized. If you deserialize this XML, you will find that all the text boxes except HomePhone are populated as expected. The HomePhone text box remains empty for obvious reasons.

Serializing and Deserializing Objects Using SoapFormatter

In the beginning of this chapter, you learned that there are three flavors of serialization based on the format (binary, XML, and SOAP). Serializing objects into binary format is outside the scope of this book, and you have already learned how to serialize objects in XML format using the XmlSerializer and DataContractSerializer classes. Now it's time to learn how objects can be serialized in SOAP format using the SoapFormatter class.

■ **Note**   The SoapFormatter class used in this section is now considered obsolete. We discuss it here because some older applications might still be using it. Also, it gives you chance to become familiar with the SOAP format without going into the details of ASMX web services or WCF services.

SOAP is an industry standard that forms one of the pillars of web services. Though SOAP is used extensively along with web services, you can use it as an encoding format for object serialization.

When you serialize objects by using the XmlSerializer class, you need not do anything special to the classes themselves. However, when you want to use SOAP as a serialization format, you must mark your classes with the [Serializable] attribute. Only then can your classes be serialized.

The SoapFormatter class takes care of all the intricacies of serializing your objects in SOAP format. The SoapFormatter class resides in the System.Runtime.Serialization.Formatters.Soap namespace, which physically resides in the System.Runtime.Serialization.Formatters.Soap.dll assembly.

Let's revisit the application that we developed when we began this chapter (see Figure 8-1) and modify it to use SoapFormatter instead of XmlSerializer. The user interface of the application remains unchanged, but the way we serialize and deserialize the objects differs.

First, you need to mark the Employee class with the [Serializable] attribute. The modified Employee class is shown in Listing 8-21.

Listing 8-21. Marking a Class with the [Serializable] Attribute

```
[Serializable]
public class Employee
{
    public int EmployeeID { get; set; }
    public string FirstName { get; set; }
    public string LastName { get; set; }
    public string HomePhone { get; set; }
    public string Notes { get; set; }

}
```

As you can see, the [Serializable] attribute is a class-level attribute. Hence it is placed on the top of the Employee class and marked as a serializable class. Listing 8-22 shows the Click event handler of the Serialize button. This time the code uses the SoapFormatter class.

Listing 8-22. Serializing Objects by Using the SoapFormatter Class

```
private void button1_Click(object sender, EventArgs e)
{
  Employee emp = new Employee();
  emp.EmployeeID = int.Parse(textBox1.Text);
  emp.FirstName = textBox2.Text;
  emp.LastName = textBox3.Text;
  emp.HomePhone = textBox4.Text;
  emp.Notes = textBox5.Text;
  FileStream stream =
    new FileStream($"{Application.StartupPath}\\employee.xml", FileMode.Create);

  SoapFormatter formatter = new SoapFormatter();
  formatter.Serialize(stream, emp);
  stream.Close();
  if (checkBox1.Checked)
  {
    Process.Start($"{Application.StartupPath}\\employee.xml");
  }
}
```

The code creates an instance of the Employee class and sets its properties to the values entered in the text boxes. A FileStream object is then created and creates a file to which the serialized data is to be written. Then a SoapFormatter object is created. The Serialize() method of SoapFormatter accepts two parameters: a stream to which the serialized data is to be written and the object that is to be serialized. The counterpart of this operation is performed in the Click event handler of the Deserialize button and is shown in Listing 8-23.

Listing 8-23. Deserialization by Using the SoapFormatter Class

```
private void button2_Click(object sender, EventArgs e)
{
  FileStream stream =
    new FileStream($"{Application.StartupPath}\\employee.xml", FileMode.Open);
  SoapFormatter formatter = new SoapFormatter();
  Employee emp=(Employee)formatter.Deserialize(stream);
  textBox1.Text = emp.EmployeeID.ToString();
  textBox2.Text = emp.FirstName;
  textBox3.Text = emp.LastName;
  textBox4.Text = emp.HomePhone;
  textBox5.Text = emp.Notes;
  stream.Close();
}
```

The code opens a stream pointing to the same file to which the object was serialized before. An instance of SoapFormatter is then created. The Deserialize() method of SoapFormatter reads the stream and deserializes the object. The return value of Deserialize() is of type object and hence it is type converted to the Employee class. After the Employee object is retrieved, its property values are assigned to the corresponding text boxes. If you run the application and serialize the Employee object, you should see output similar to Figure 8-10.

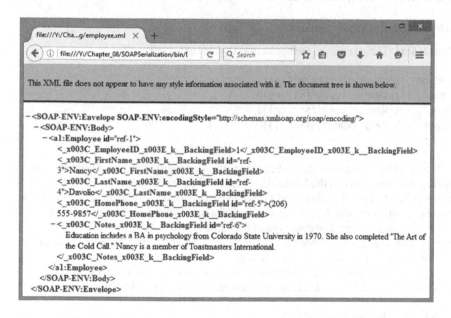

Figure 8-10. Object serialized in SOAP format

As you can see, the XML output is now in SOAP format. There is also mention of some namespaces related to SOAP. Notice that the XML element names are not same as the property names, instead unique element names are formed using the property names. Unlike XML serialization, which is shallow by nature, SOAP serialization done via the SoapFormatter class is deep serialization. It serializes private, protected, and public members of an object.

Customizing SOAP Serialization

In the preceding section, you used the default behavior of SOAP serialization to serialize and deserialize objects. You can also customize the SOAP serialization process if you want. There are two ways to achieve this:

- Implement the ISerializable interface.

- Use certain serialization and deserialization attributes.

The first method has been available since .NET Framework 1.1. The latter method was introduced in .NET 2.0. In our example, we are going to use both the methods to customize the serialization process.

We will use the same application that we developed in the previous section while illustrating the use of the SoapFormatter class. Suppose that you want to customize the names of the elements in the resultant SOAP message. You also want to control which properties are being serialized.

Finally, also suppose that you want to protect the serialized XML data from casual users. You want to implement Base64 encoding to the data that is being serialized so that casual readers cannot easily read the file content. That data needs to be encoded in a Base64 encoding scheme and decoded when deserialized.

Open the Employee class you created earlier and implement the ISerializable interface on it. As a part of the implementation, you need to to do two things:

- Implement the GetObjectData() method.

- Add a constructor that handles deserialization.

Listing 8-24 shows the GetObjectData() method added to the Employee class.

Listing 8-24. GetObjectData() Added to Employee Class

```
public void GetObjectData(SerializationInfo info, StreamingContext context)
{
    info.AddValue("EmpCode", EmployeeID, typeof(int));
    info.AddValue("FName", FirstName, typeof(string));
    info.AddValue("LName", LastName, typeof(string));
    info.AddValue("Remarks", Notes, typeof(string));
}
```

The GetObjectData() method has two parameters—SerializationInfo and StreamingContext. The GetObjectData() method is called after you call the Serialize() method on the SoapFormatter object.

The code inside GetObjectData() uses the AddValue() method of the SerializationInfo object to decide what values will be serialized. For example, the first call to AddValue() specifies that EmployeeID value will be serialized as an EmpCode element. The data type of the value is also specified using the third parameter. Notice that we don't serialize the HomePhone property of the Employee class. The other properties are serialized as EmpCode, FName, LName, and Remarks, respectively.

Next, add a constructor to the Employee class that matches the signature shown in Listing 8-25. This constructor will be called when you call the Deserialize() method of the SoapFormatter object.

Listing 8-25. Constructor That Handles the Deserialization

```
protected Employee(SerializationInfo info, StreamingContext context)
{
    EmployeeID = (int)info.GetValue("EmpCode", typeof(int));
    FirstName = (string)info.GetValue("FName", typeof(string));
    LastName = (string)info.GetValue("LName", typeof(string));
    Notes = (string)info.GetValue("Remarks", typeof(string));
    HomePhone = "";
}
```

234

The constructor accepts the same two parameters as the GetObjectData() method. The purpose of this constructor is to retrieve previously serialized values and assign them to properties.

This is done using the GetValue() method of SerializationInfo class. The GetValue() method accepts the name associated with the value to be retrieved and its data type. Upon retrieving the value it is casted and assigned to the corresponding property of the Employee object being constructed. Notice that the HomePhone property is assigned an empty string value since we have ignored it during serialization process.

Now add two helper functions called Encode() and Decode() to the preceding application, as shown in Listing 8-26.

Listing 8-26. Encoding and Decoding Data by Using Base64 Encoding

```
private string Encode(string str)
{
  byte[] data = ASCIIEncoding.ASCII.GetBytes(str);
  return Convert.ToBase64String(data);
}

private string Decode(string str)
{
  byte[] data=Convert.FromBase64String(str);
  return ASCIIEncoding.ASCII.GetString(data);
}
```

Make sure to add these helper methods to the Employee class. The Encode() function accepts a string that is to be encoded in Base64 format. It then converts the string into a byte array by using the GetBytes() method of the ASCIIEncoding class. The byte array is then fed to the ToBase64String() method of the Convert class, which returns a Base64-encoded string representing the supplied array of bytes.

The Decode() function accepts a Base64-encoded string that is to be decoded back to a plain string representation. It then calls the FromBase64String() method of the Convert class and passes the supplied Base64 string to it. The FromBase64String() method returns a byte array representing the decoded version of the supplied string. The byte array is converted to a string by using the GetString() method of the ASCIIEncoding class.

Now we need to add four methods to the Employee class, as shown in Listing 8-27.

Listing 8-27. Customizing SOAP Serialization and Deserialization

```
[OnSerializing]
public void OnSerializing(StreamingContext context)
{
    FirstName = Encode(FirstName);
    LastName = Encode(LastName);
    HomePhone = Encode(HomePhone);
    Notes = Encode(Notes);
}


[OnSerialized]
public void OnSerialized(StreamingContext context)
{
    FirstName = Decode(FirstName);
    LastName = Decode(LastName);
    HomePhone = Decode(HomePhone);
    Notes = Decode(Notes);
}
```

```
[OnDeserializing]
public void OnDeserializing(StreamingContext context)
{
    //no code here
}

[OnDeserialized]
public void OnDeserialized(StreamingContext context)
{
    FirstName = Decode(FirstName);
    LastName = Decode(LastName);
    HomePhone = Decode(HomePhone);
    Notes = Decode(Notes);
}
```

The four methods are marked with the [OnSerializing], [OnSerialized], [OnDeserializing], and [OnDeserialized] attributes. These attributes allow you to customize the serialization and deserialization process by using pre- and post-methods:

- The method marked with [OnSerializing] is automatically called by the serialization framework before the data is serialized.

- The method marked with [OnSerialized] is called when the serialization is complete.

- Similarly, the methods marked with [OnDeserializing] and [OnDeserialized] are called before and after the deserialization operation.

All these methods must accept a parameter of type StreamingContext. The StreamingContext parameter provides additional information about the serialization or deserialization process.

In our example, the OnSerializing() method calls the Encode() helper method that we created earlier to encode the property values into Base64 format. Thus the data being serialized is not a plain string but a Base64 string. After the serialization is complete, we may still need the same data in plain-string format. That is why the Decode() method is called in the OnSerialized() method.

The OnDeserializing() method doesn't include any code in our example. However, if you want to execute some code before deserialization takes place, you can add your custom logic in this method. After the previously serialized data is deserialized, it should give us the values in plain-string format and not in Base64 format. Hence the OnDeserialized() method calls Decode() and converts the Base64 values into plain text. Figure 8-11 shows a sample SOAP data post serialization.

Figure 8-11. *Base64-encoded data after serialization*

Notice how the entire data is serialized in Base64 format. Also notice how element names are picked from the values specified in the GetObjectData() method.

If you click on the Deserialize button, you will find that all the text boxes except HomePhone are populated with correct values. This is because we ignored HomePhone during the serialization.

Summary

In this chapter, we examined the XML serialization process in detail. The .NET Framework itself uses serialization in many places including web services and WCF services. The three classes, namely XmlSerializer, DataContractSerializer, and SoapFormatter, allow you to serialize your objects in XML and SOAP. The XmlSerializer is used by XML web services to perform the serialization. DataContractSerializer is used by WCF services and Web API to perform the serialization.

The XML serialization done using XmlSerializer can be customized with the help of various attributes such as [XmlRoot] and [XmlElement]. The XML serialization done using DataContractSerializer can be customized with the help of attributes such as [DataContract] and [DataMember]. The SOAP serialization done using SoapFormatter can be customized by implementing the ISerializable interface. You can also use attributes such as [OnSerializing] and [OnDeserialized] to control the pre- and post-processing of the data.

In the next chapter, you are going to learn about XML web services. You will also learn more about the SOAP protocol and related standards.

■ ■ ■

CHAPTER 9

XML in Web Services

The idea of distributed application development is not new. Distributed technologies such as Distributed Component Object Model (DCOM), Remote Method Invocation (RMI), and Common Object Request Broker Architecture (CORBA) have existed for years. However, none of these technologies is an unambiguous industry standard. That is where standards based services step in. A service exposes some functionality as an API (Application Programming Interface) that the clients can consume. The data transfer between the client and the service usually happens in a format known to both the parties (such binary, SOAP, XML, and JSON).

The .NET Framework allows you to build services using three main ways—Web Services (also called ASMX web services or XML web services), Windows Communication Foundation (WCF), and Web API. These frameworks have been developed at different points in time based on the industry trends and demands prevalent at those respective times. Web services allow you to build SOAP based services over HTTP. WCF is a generic service development framework that can deal with variety of communication channels such as TCP and HTTP and formats such as binary, SOAP, XML, and JSON. Web API is a framework for building HTTP based RESTful services. This chapter discusses the first flavor—the web services. The other two flavors are discussed in the next chapter.

It should be noted that web services are now considered an older way of developing services. Although .NET Framework and Visual Studio still support them, modern applications prefer WCF and Web API over web services. However, this chapter still discusses web services because that will allow you to become familiar with XML-based protocols and standards such as SOAP and WSDL.

Keep in mind that this chapter is not aimed at teaching you web service development in detail. It primarily focuses on building basic data driven ASMX web services and the role played by XML. Specifically, you learn about the following topics:

- What web services are

- Creating and consuming web services using the .NET Framework

- What SOAP is and how web services use it

- What WSDL is and what's its purpose

What Are Web Services?

The concept of web services can be best understood with the help of components that you might have built using the .NET Framework. What is a component? A *component* is a reusable piece of software that provides certain functionality to your application. For example, a component developed for a banking application might be providing services such as loan calculation, interest calculation, and so forth. If you need the same business logic at any other place, such a component will be of great use. Components also isolate your business logic from the rest of the application. Such components do not provide any user interface to your application. They simply provide the required services to you.

© Bipin Joshi 2017

B. Joshi, *Beginning XML with C# 7*, https://doi.org/10.1007/978-1-4842-3105-0_9

Generally, components reside on the same machine as your application. What if they are to be located on a separate server altogether? What if the network involved is not a LAN but the Internet? What if you want to host the components on a Unix box and consume them from a Windows machine? That is where web services come into the picture.

You can think of web services as components that reside on a web server, while applications consume them over a network. More formally, web services can be defined as a set of programmable APIs that can be called over a network using XML, SOAP, and HTTP.

Web services are an industry standard, and no single company owns web services. The three standards—XML, SOAP, and HTTP—are the pillars of the web service infrastructure. The following are some points to be remembered about web services:

- Web service standards are platform-independent industry standards.

- Web services do not provide any user interface. They provide only functionality or services to your application.

- Web services use XML, SOAP, and HTTP as the communication protocols.

- Web services use the same request-response model as used by web applications.

- All communication between a web service and its client happens in a plain-text format.

- Web services can reside on any web server as long as the client has network connectivity with that server.

- A web service and its client can be developed using completely different platforms. For example, you may develop a web service using the .NET Framework and consume it in a Java application.

- Web services under .NET Framework are also called ASMX web services due to the file extension used by the web service files (`*.asmx`).

Creating and Consuming Web Services

Building web services requires three essential steps:

- Creating a web service

- Creating a proxy for the web service

- Creating a client application that consumes the web service

Modern software development platforms often introduce the concept of a proxy while performing remote communication. A *proxy* is an entity that stands in for some other entity and pretends to your client application that the proxy itself is the actual web service. In doing so, the proxy shields you from low-level network programming details (such as socket programming, underlying protocols, communication formats, and security). Your client application never talks with the web service directly. All the communication (request as well as response) is routed through the proxy.

If the proxy wants to pretend that the proxy itself is the web service, it must look like the web service. This requires the detailed description or metadata of a web service. The web service standards provide what is known as Web Services Description Language (WSDL). WSDL is an XML dialect that describes the web service, listing details such as the functions exposed by the web service, their parameters, data types, and return values. The proxy is generated using this WSDL document of a web service.

The file extension used by .NET Framework web services is `.asmx`. The web service `.asmx` files can have code-behind files just like ASP.NET Web Forms.

Creating a Web Service

To create a web service using Visual Studio, you need to create a new web application named EmployeeWebService and then add an ASMX web service to it. Figure 9-1 shows the New Project dialog of Visual Studio.

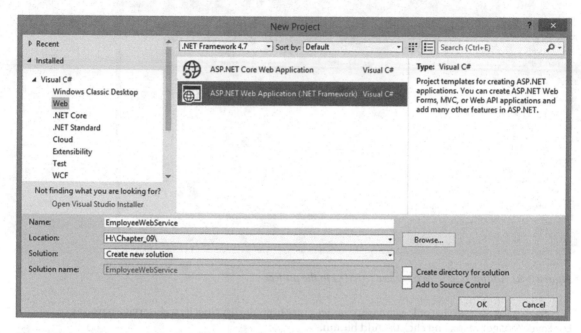

Figure 9-1. *Creating a new web application project in Visual Studio*

Once you select ASP.NET Web Application as the project type and click OK, select Empty as the project template. Also make sure to check the Web Forms checkbox. This dialog is shown in Figure 9-2.

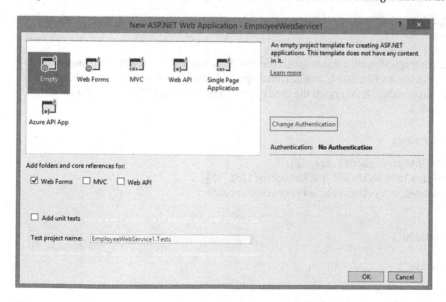

Figure 9-2. *Creating a Web Forms project using the Empty project template*

After you create the project, add a folder under the project root folder named Services. Then right-click on the Services folder and choose Add ➤ New Item. This will open the Add New Item dialog, as shown in Figure 9-3.

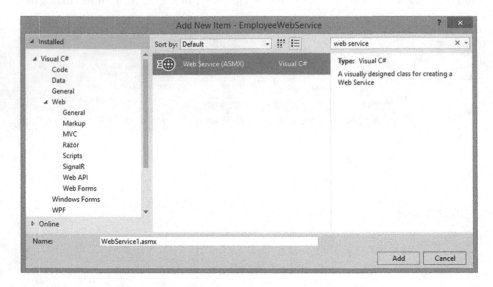

Figure 9-3. *Adding a new Web Service (ASMX) to the project*

Search for web service or locate a web service entry from the list. Specify web service name as EmployeeManager.asmx and click the Add button.

Now you should see the EmployeeManager.asmx as well as its code-behind file—EmployeeManager.asmx.cs. The .asmx file contains the markup shown in Listing 9-1.

Listing 9-1. @WebService Directive

```
<%@ WebService Language="C#" CodeBehind="EmployeeManager.asmx.cs" Class="EmployeeWebService.Services.EmployeeManager" %>
```

The @WebService directive specifies that this is a web service. Note that the CodeBehind attribute points the EmployeeManager.asmx.cs file. The Class attribute specifies the class from the CodeBehind file that contains web service functionality. If you open the EmployeeManager.asmx.cs file, you should see something similar to Listing 9-2.

Listing 9-2. The Web Service Class

```
[WebService(Namespace = "http://tempuri.org/")]
[WebServiceBinding(ConformsTo = WsiProfiles.BasicProfile1_1)]
public class EmployeeManager : System.Web.Services.WebService
{
    [WebMethod]
    public string HelloWorld()
    {
        return "Hello World";
    }
}
```

Here we have a class called EmployeeManager that inherits from System.Web.Services.WebService class. Actually, inheriting from the WebService class is not mandatory, but doing so will give you added facilities such as state maintenance. Inside this class we have a public method called HelloWorld(). The method by itself does not contain anything special—you must have written many such methods in your own applications. What makes it special, however, is the WebMethod attribute, which makes the method web callable—that is, the client application can call this method over a network. Your class can contain any number of public or private methods. However, only the methods that are public and decorated with the WebMethod attribute are web callable.

Notice that the Service class is decorated with the [WebService] and [WebServiceBinding] attributes. The [WebService] attribute is used to specify some additional information about the web service such as its description and namespace. The Namespace property indicates the default XML namespace to use for the XML web service. The XML namespaces allow you to uniquely identify elements and attributes from an XML document. Every web service needs to have a unique XML namespace to identify itself so that client applications can distinguish it from other web services. By default, this namespace is set to http://tempuri.org/ but it is recommended that you change it to some other URI. For example, you can use the domain name of your company as the namespace. Note that although many times the XML namespaces are URLs, they need not point to actual resources on the Web. The [WebServiceBinding] attribute specifies a WSDL binding used by that service. You may think of a WSDL binding as an interface that defines a set of web service operations. The ConformsTo attribute specifies the Web Services Interoperability (WSI) specification. The WS-I organization provides guidelines for web services interoperability across multiple platforms.

Run the application and you should see something similar to Figure 9-4.

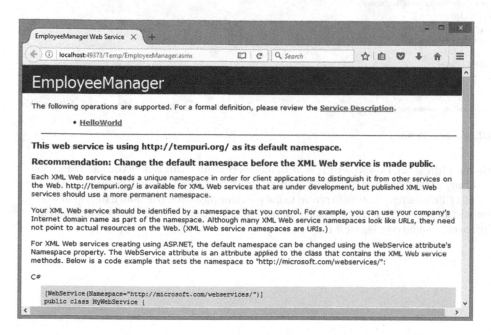

Figure 9-4. *Web service help page*

243

You might be wondering why our web service is showing this user interface when we know that web services do not have a user interface. Actually, this is not a user interface of the web service. This interface is called a *web service help page* and allows you to test your web services. Because web services by themselves do not have a user interface, how will you or your clients test them to see whether they function correctly? To help you in such cases, ASP.NET generates these help pages automatically. At the top of the help page, you will see a link titled Service Description. Just click on it and you will be presented with the WSDL of your web service (see Figure 9-5).

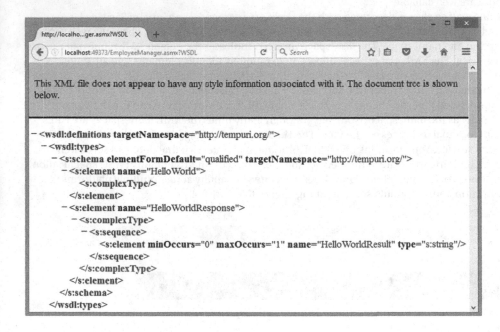

Figure 9-5. *WSDL of a web service*

Have a look in the address bar. Do you see the WSDL in the query string? This is how you can manually retrieve the WSDL of any ASP.NET web service. Simply attach *WSDL* at the end of the web service URL and you get the WSDL. Click the Back button to return to the previous page. You will notice the list of web methods (operations). Click the HelloWorld web method. You will be taken to another help page wherein you can execute this web method (see Figure 9-6).

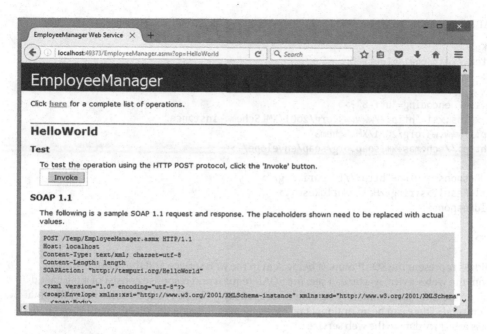

Figure 9-6. *Invoking a web method*

Before you click the Invoke button, have a look below it. You should see markup, as shown in Listings 9-3 and 9-4.

Listing 9-3. SOAP Request

```
POST /EmployeeWebService/EmployeeManager.asmx HTTP/1.1
Host: localhost
Content-Type: text/xml; charset=utf-8
Content-Length: length
SOAPAction: "http://tempuri.org/HelloWorld"

<?xml version="1.0" encoding="utf-8"?>
<soap:Envelope xmlns:xsi="http://www.w3.org/2001/XMLSchema-instance"
xmlns:xsd="http://www.w3.org/2001/XMLSchema"
xmlns:soap="http://schemas.xmlsoap.org/soap/envelope/">
  <soap:Body>
    <HelloWorld xmlns="http://tempuri.org/" />
  </soap:Body>
</soap:Envelope>
```

Listing 9-4. SOAP Response

```
HTTP/1.1 200 OK
Content-Type: text/xml; charset=utf-8
Content-Length: length

<?xml version="1.0" encoding="utf-8"?>
<soap:Envelope xmlns:xsi="http://www.w3.org/2001/XMLSchema-instance"
xmlns:xsd="http://www.w3.org/2001/XMLSchema"
  xmlns:soap="http://schemas.xmlsoap.org/soap/envelope/">
  <soap:Body>
    <HelloWorldResponse xmlns="http://tempuri.org/">
      <HelloWorldResult>string</HelloWorldResult>
    </HelloWorldResponse>
  </soap:Body>
</soap:Envelope>
```

These two blocks represent the SOAP request being sent to the web service and the SOAP response being received from the web service. As you can see, the SOAP request and response consist of a tag called `<soap:Envelope>`. Inside there is a mandatory tag called `<soap:Body>`. The Body tag contains the XML data being passed or returned. There can be an optional tag, `<soap:Header>`, inside the `<soap:Envelope>` tag that can be used to pass arbitrary data to the web service.

Now click the Invoke button. The help page will execute the web method and open another window to show the web method response (see Figure 9-7).

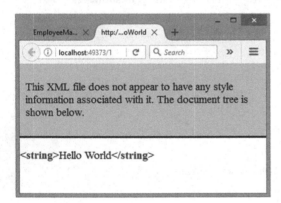

Figure 9-7. *Hello World response*

Now close the browser and return to Visual Studio. Modify the `HelloWorld()` method, as shown in Listing 9-5.

Listing 9-5. Web Method with a String Parameter

```
[WebMethod]
public string HelloWorld(string name)
{
  return "Hello " + name;
}
```

Here we have added one string parameter to the HelloWorld() method. The method now returns Hello concatenated with the name supplied. Run the web service again. This time you should see a help page, as shown in Figure 9-8, for invoking the web method.

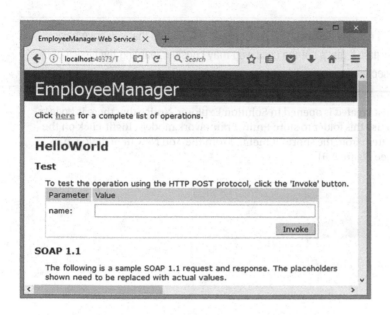

Figure 9-8. *Invoking a web method with a string parameter*

ASP.NET automatically generates a text box for you to enter the parameter. Of course, this works only for primitive data types such as strings and integers. ASP.NET will not be able to do so for array, object, or collection parameters.

Setting a Description for a Web Method

You can set a description for a web method by using the Description property of the WebMethod attribute. This description will be displayed on the help page. The code in Listing 9-6 illustrates its use.

Listing 9-6. Using the Description Property

```
[WebMethod(Description = "This is description for web method")]
public string HelloWorld()
{
  return "Hello World";
}
```

Adding Web Methods for CRUD Functionality

Now let's add a few web methods that are more meaningful and perform some database operations.

In this section you will add five web methods to the EmployeeManager web service. These methods will implement the CRUD (Create, Read, Update and Delete) functionality and perform the respective database operations on the Employees table of the Northwind database.

247

This example will use Entity Framework (EF) code-first approach to perform the database operations. Many modern applications use Entity Framework for database tasks. We use EF here just to save some time and to simplify our code. If you want, you can use ADO.NET code instead of Entity Framework.

■ **Note** Although this section doesn't use any advanced EF concepts, it is assumed that you have basic familiarity with Entity Framework code-first. If that's not the case, you may consider learning the basics of EF code-first before continuing with this section.

Make sure that the project you just created is opened in Solution Explorer. Notice that there is Models folder under the project root. We will use this folder to store Entity Framework models. Right-click on the Models folder and select Add ➤ New Item from the shortcut menu. From the Add New Item dialog, pick ADO.NET Entity Data Model entry (see Figure 9-9).

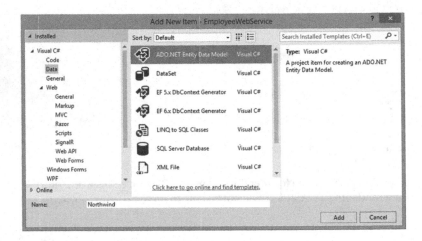

Figure 9-9. Adding an EF data model

Specify the model name to be **Northwind** and click the Add button. This will open a wizard, as shown in Figure 9-10.

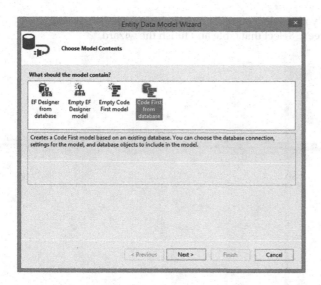

Figure 9-10. *Generating a context using code-first approach*

This dialog allows you to pick how the context is to be created. Select Code First from database option and click Next.

The next dialog (see Figure 9-11) allows you to specify the database connection string information. Go ahead and enter these details as per your database setup and security credentials. Click Next when you're ready.

Figure 9-11. *Specifying database connection string details*

The next wizard step (see Figure 9-12) allows you to select one or more database tables you want to use. In our example, you need only one table—Employees. Select that table and finish the wizard.

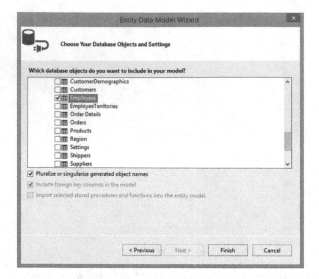

Figure 9-12. Selecting the Employees table

Successfully completing the wizard will add two files to the Models folder—Northwind.cs and Employee.cs. The former file contains a class that inherits from DbContext and the latter file contains the Employee entity class.

Since we are interested only in the five columns—EmployeeID, FirstName, LastName, HomePhone, and Notes—remove all the other properties from the Employee entity class. Listing 9-7 shows the final Employee class.

Listing 9-7. Final Employee Entity Class

```
public partial class Employee
{
    public int EmployeeID { get; set; }
    public string LastName { get; set; }
    public string FirstName { get; set; }
    public string HomePhone { get; set; }
    public string Notes { get; set; }
}
```

The Employee class contains five public properties that map to the respective columns of the Employees table. Also, modify the Northwind context class to match Listing 9-8.

Listing 9-8. Northwind Context Class

```
public partial class Northwind : DbContext
{
    public Northwind()
        : base("name=Northwind")
    {
    }

    public virtual DbSet<Employee> Employees { get; set; }
}
```

The Northwind context contains a single DbSet called Employees. This completes our EF model and we are ready to add the CRUD functionality to the EmployeeManager web service.

Now we will add five web methods to the EmployeeManager web service. These web methods are SelectAll(), SelectByID(), Insert(), Update(), and Delete(). These web methods do the respective operation. Let's discuss them one-by-one.

Listing 9-9 shows the SelectAll() web method.

Listing 9-9. SelectAll() Web Method

```
[WebMethod]
public List<Employee> SelectAll()
{
    using (Northwind db = new Northwind())
    {
        return db.Employees.OrderBy(e => e.EmployeeID).ToList();
    }
}
```

The SelectAll() web method returns a List of Employee objects. Inside, it creates a Northwind context object. It then selects all the Employee objects using the Employees DbSet, orders them on EmployeeID and then returns the list to the caller. Notice that SelectAll()—and all the other methods—is decorated with the [WebMethod] attribute.

Next, add the SelectByID() web method, as shown in Listing 9-10.

Listing 9-10. SelectByID() Web Method

```
[WebMethod]
public Employee SelectByID(int id)
{
    using (Northwind db = new Northwind())
    {
        return db.Employees.Find(id);
    }
}
```

The SelectByID() web method accepts an integer ID parameter representing an EmployeeID and returns an Employee object matching that value. Inside, it uses the Find() method on the Employees DbSet to grab the Employee object with the matching ID.

Now add Insert() web method, as shown in Listing 9-11.

Listing 9-11. Insert() Web Method

```
[WebMethod]
public string Insert(Employee obj)
{
    using (Northwind db = new Northwind())
    {
        db.Employees.Add(obj);
        db.SaveChanges();
        return "Employee added successfully!";
    }
}
```

The Insert() web method accepts an Employee object containing the details of an employee to be added to the database and returns a success message. Inside, it adds the obj to the Employees DbSet using the Add() method. The SaveChanges() method is then called to persist the changes to the database. Finally, a success message is returned to the caller.

Now it's time to add the Update() web method, as shown in Listing 9-12.

Listing 9-12. Update() Web Method

```
[WebMethod]
public string Update(Employee emp)
{
    using (Northwind db = new Northwind())
    {
        db.Entry(emp).State = EntityState.Modified;
        db.SaveChanges();
        return "Employee modified successfully!";
    }
}
```

The Update() web method accepts an Employee object that needs to be updated in the database. Inside, it changes the State property of the entity to Modified. This is done using the Entry() method of the context and EntityState enumeration. As before, SaveChanges() is called to save the changes to the physical database. Finally, a success message is returned to the caller.

Complete the EmployeeManager web service by adding the Delete() web method, as shown in Listing 9-13.

Listing 9-13. Delete() Web Method

```
[WebMethod]
public string Delete(int id)
{
    using (Northwind db = new Northwind())
    {
        Employee emp = db.Employees.Find(id);
        db.Employees.Remove(emp);
        db.SaveChanges();
        return "Employee deleted successfully!";
    }
}
```

The Delete() web method accepts an EmployeeID of an employee to be deleted. Inside, it finds the employee using the Find() method of Employees DbSet. It then removes that employee from the Employees DbSet using the Remove() method. SaveChanges() is called to save the changes to the physical database. Finally, a success message is sent to the caller.

This completes the EmployeeManager web service. Run it in the browser to display its help page. This time you will see the newly added five web methods, as shown in Figure 9-13.

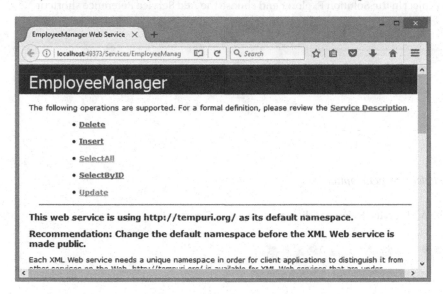

Figure 9-13. *Web service help page listing all the CRUD web methods*

Although you can't invoke all of them using the help page (because some of them need the Employee object as a parameter), you can try executing the SelectAll(), SelectByID(), and Delete() web methods. A sample outcome after running SelectByID() for EmployeeID of 1 is shown in Figure 9-14.

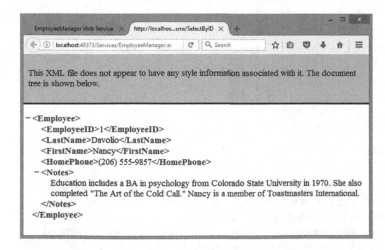

Figure 9-14. *SelectByID() returning a single employee*

As you can see, the data is being sent over the wire as an XML document.

Creating a Proxy for a Web Service

To create a proxy for the web service by using Visual Studio, you must first create the client application because the proxy always resides there. Though any type of application can act as a client to the web service, as an example we will create a Windows Forms application that consumes the EmployeeManager web service.

Add a new Windows Forms project to the current Visual Studio solution. Right-click on the the References folder of this project in the Solution Explorer and choose the Add Service Reference shortcut menu option (see Figure 9-15).

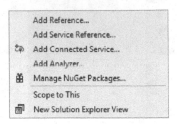

Figure 9-15. *Add Service Reference menu option*

Doing so will open the Add Service Reference dialog, as shown in Figure 9-16.

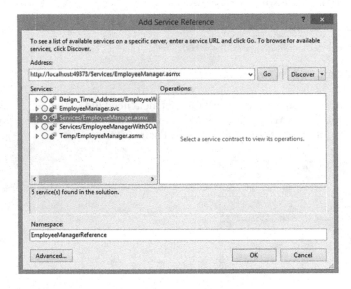

Figure 9-16. *Add Service Reference dialog*

Clicking on the Discover button will list all the services (including the EmployeeManager.asmx) under the Services section. Selecting EmployeeManager.asmx will reveal its URL under the Address area. If your service is external to the solution, you would have manually typed its URL here.

The Namespace text box allows you to specify a namespace name for the proxy class being generated. Enter **EmployeeManagerReference** in this text box and click the OK button. This will generate a "WCF style" proxy for your web service and place it under the Service References folder (see Figure 9-17).

Figure 9-17. *EmployeeManagerReference is placed inside the Service References folder*

There is an alternate way to generate the proxy through the same Add Service References option—using Web Reference. Let's see how that works. Open the same Add Service Reference dialog. There is Advanced button located at the bottom of the dialog. Clicking on it opens Service Reference Settings dialog, as shown in Figure 9-18.

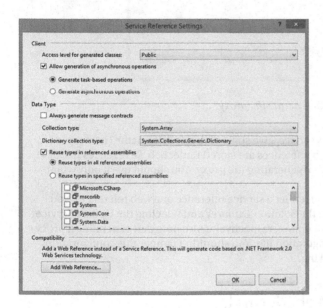

Figure 9-18. *Service Reference Settings dialog*

There is Add Web Reference button at the bottom of this dialog (under the Compatibility section). Clicking it opens another dialog—Add Web Reference (see Figure 9-19).

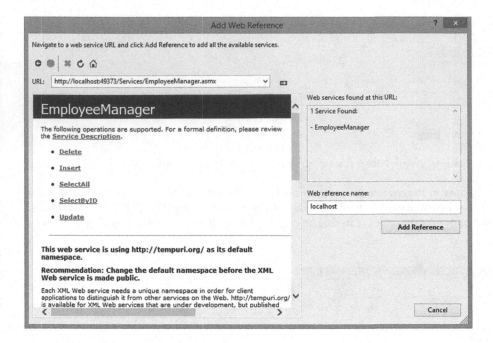

Figure 9-19. *Using the Add Web Reference dialog to generate the proxy*

You can navigate to the EmployeeManager web service, give some web reference name (namespace name), and click on the Add Reference button. Web references are stored under Web References folder. It should be noted that web reference is an older way of generating the proxy. You should use it only when backward compatibility is necessary.

Irrespective of the way you generated the proxy (either a service reference or a web reference), you can always update a proxy by right-clicking on it in the Solution Explorer and selecting the Update Service Reference or Update Web Reference shortcut menu option, respectively. Also note that generating a proxy also adds certain markup in the application's configuration file. You shouldn't tamper this configuration unless you are sure about the changes you are making.

Creating a Form That Calls the Web Methods

To demonstrate how to call web methods, you will need to create a form that will allow you to add, modify, and delete employees from the Employees table. The form should look like Figure 9-20.

Figure 9-20. *Application that calls the web methods*

The form displays a list of existing EmployeeIDs in a dropdown list. If you select an EmployeeID from the dropdown list, its details—such as first name, lastname, home phone, and notes—are displayed in the respective text boxes. You can then either modify the details, and click the Update button, or you can delete that employee by clicking the Delete button. To add a new employee, you need to fill in the details in the respective fields (EmployeeID is an identity column and hence will be autogenerated by the database). Clicking on the Insert button saves the new employee details into the database. A success message as returned by the web methods is displayed in a label below the buttons.

The dropdown list is filled with a list of existing EmployeeIDs in the Load event of the form. Listing 9-14 shows how this is done.

Listing 9-14. Filling EmployeeIDs in the Dropdown List

```
private void Form1_Load(object sender, EventArgs e)
{
    EmployeeManagerSoapClient proxy = new EmployeeManagerSoapClient();
    Employee[] data = proxy.SelectAll();
    foreach(Employee emp in data)
    {
        comboBox1.Items.Add(emp.EmployeeID);
    }
}
```

The code creates an instance of the proxy class—EmployeeManagerSoapClient. This class (and also the Employee class in the client application) comes from the EmployeeWebServiceClient. EmployeeManagerReference namespace and hence you need to import the namespace before using this class. Note that we discussed two ways of generating the proxy. Here the code is using the "WCF style" proxy to call the web service. The name of the generated proxy class is formed by appending SoapClient to the end of the original web service class (EmployeeManager).

Then the code calls the SelectAll() method on the proxy. The SelectAll() method of the web service returns a List of Employee objects. That list is received as an array in the client code. You can fine-tune this behavior while generating the proxy (the Advanced Settings dialog). Here we will stick to the default settings since they are sufficient to demonstrate the functioning of the web service. A foreach loop iterates through the array and fills the dropdown list with all the EmployeeID values.

Upon selecting an EmployeeID, its details are populated in the other text boxes. This is done in the SelectedIndexChanged event of the dropdown list (see Listing 9-15) by invoking the SelectByID() web method.

Listing 9-15. Calling the SelectByID() Web Method

```
private void comboBox1_SelectedIndexChanged(object sender, EventArgs e)
{
    EmployeeManagerSoapClient proxy = new EmployeeManagerSoapClient();
    Employee data = proxy.SelectByID((int)comboBox1.SelectedItem);
    textBox1.Text = data.FirstName;
    textBox2.Text = data.LastName;
    textBox3.Text = data.HomePhone;
    textBox4.Text = data.Notes;
    label6.Text = "";
}
```

The code creates a proxy object as before. It then calls the SelectByID() method on the proxy by passing the selected EmployeeID. The SelectByID() method returns an Employee object. Details of the employee—such as FirstName, LastName, HomePhone, and Notes—are populated in the respective text boxes.

To add a new employee, you need to fill all the text boxes with the corresponding values and click the Insert button. The Click event handler of the Insert button then calls the Insert() web method. This is shown in Listing 9-16.

Listing 9-16. Calling the Insert() Web Method

```
private void button2_Click(object sender, EventArgs e)
{
    EmployeeManagerSoapClient proxy = new EmployeeManagerSoapClient();
    Employee data = new Employee();
    data.FirstName = textBox1.Text;
    data.LastName = textBox2.Text;
    data.HomePhone = textBox3.Text;
    data.Notes = textBox4.Text;
    label6.Text = proxy.Insert(data);
}
```

The code creates a proxy object and a new Employee object. This Employee object represents a new employee to be added into the database. Properties such as FirstName, LastName, HomePhone, and Notes are set to the values entered into the respective text boxes. Finally, the Insert() method is called on the proxy to add the employee. The Insert() method returns a success message (assuming that there was no exception) that is then displayed in a Label.

To modify an employee's details, you need to select the EmployeeID from the dropdown list and then change the values from the text boxes. Once you've added the changes, clicking on the Update button attempts to save the modified details by calling the Update() web method. This is shown in Listing 9-17.

Listing 9-17. Calling the Update() Web Method

```
private void button1_Click(object sender, EventArgs e)
{
    EmployeeManagerSoapClient proxy = new EmployeeManagerSoapClient();
    Employee data = new Employee();
    data.EmployeeID = (int)comboBox1.SelectedItem;
    data.FirstName = textBox1.Text;
    data.LastName = textBox2.Text;
    data.HomePhone = textBox3.Text;
    data.Notes = textBox4.Text;
    label6.Text=proxy.Update(data);
}
```

The code is almost identical to the insert operation discussed earlier. The only difference is that it picks an EmployeeID from the dropdown list instead of the text box (since an existing employee is being modified). And the Update() method is called on the proxy after assigning all the properties of the Employee object.

Removing an employee is straightforward. All you need to do is select an EmployeeID from the dropdown list and click on the Delete button. The code that removes an employee is shown in Listing 9-18.

Listing 9-18. Calling the Delete() Web Method

```
private void button3_Click(object sender, EventArgs e)
{
    EmployeeManagerSoapClient proxy = new EmployeeManagerSoapClient();
    int id = (int)comboBox1.SelectedItem;
    label6.Text = proxy.Delete(id);
}
```

The code simply calls the Delete() method on the proxy by passing an EmployeeID to be deleted.

This completes the client application. Run the application and test whether CRUD operations are working as expected. To better understand the flow of execution, you can set breakpoints in various event handlers as well as in the web methods.

Understanding SOAP

In the previous section, you learned that SOAP is a lightweight XML-based protocol that forms one of the building blocks of the web service infrastructure. You also learned how web service requests and responses are encoded in SOAP format. Now it's time to peek inside SOAP in a bit of detail. Have a look at Listing 9-19.

Listing 9-19. SOAP Request

```
POST /WebServiceDemos/Service.asmx HTTP/1.1
Host: localhost
Content-Type: text/xml; charset=utf-8
Content-Length: length
SOAPAction: "http://tempuri.org/HelloWorld"
<?xml version="1.0" encoding="utf-8"?>
<soap:Envelope xmlns:xsi="http://www.w3.org/2001/XMLSchema-instance"
xmlns:xsd="http://www.w3.org/2001/XMLSchema"
```

```
xmlns:soap="http://schemas.xmlsoap.org/soap/envelope/">
  <soap:Body>
    <HelloWorld xmlns="http://tempuri.org/" />
  </soap:Body>
</soap:Envelope>
```

As you might have guessed, Listing 9-20 represents a SOAP request. If you observe this markup carefully, you will find that the request consists of an envelope (`<soap:Envelope>`) and body (`<soap:Body>`). In fact, a SOAP request or response can contain four possible parts. Each of these parts is described in Table 9-1.

Table 9-1. *Parts of a SOAP Message*

Part	Description
Envelope	Wraps the SOAP request or response. It is the root element of the SOAP message and is represented by the `<soap:Envelope>` markup tag. All SOAP messages must have an envelope.
Header	Optional parts of a SOAP message. They are used to pass arbitrary data to and from the web service and its client. For example, you can use them to pass authentication information to the web service. A SOAP header is represented by the `<soap:Header>` markup tag.
Body	A mandatory part of a SOAP message. It includes the actual request or response data in XML format. The SOAP body is represented by the `<soap:Body>` markup tag.
Fault	An optional part of a SOAP message. It comes into the picture whenever there is a runtime exception in the web service. The exception details are enclosed in the `<soap:Fault>` tag and sent back to the client application.

Using SOAP Headers

In this section, you will modify the `EmployeeManager` web service and the client application to use SOAP headers. Let's assume that in order to successfully call the `EmployeeManager` web service, the client is supposed to send a secret Key to the web service. With every call to a web method, the web service needs to check for the existence of a valid Key.

Now the question is—how would you pass the secret key from the client to the service? One option would be to include it in the signature of all the web methods. But this will complicate the web methods and make future changes difficult. A better alternative is to pass the secret key via a custom SOAP header. The web service will authenticate a call on the basis of this SOAP header and return the requested data only if the key is validated.

To begin the modification, add a class called `EmployeeManagerHeader` in the `Services` folder (you can place it in any other folder if you so wish). This class wraps the secret key and consists of just a single property: `ClientKey`. Listing 9-20 shows the completed `User` class.

Listing 9-20. Creating a Class That Inherits from the SoapHeader Class

```
public class EmployeeManagerHeader:SoapHeader
{
    public string ClientKey { get; set; }
}
```

Notice that the EmployeeManagerHeader class inherits from the SoapHeader base class, which resides in the System.Web.Services.Protocols namespace and represents a basic SOAP header. All the custom SOAP header classes must inherit directly or indirectly from the SoapHeader class. Make sure that you have imported the System.Web.Services.Protocols namespace before creating the User class.

The User class simply contains a string property—ClientKey. After you create the EmployeeManagerHeader class, modify the EmployeeManager web service as shown in Listing 9-21.

Listing 9-21. Using a SOAP Header

```
public class EmployeeManager : System.Web.Services.WebService
{
    public EmployeeManagerHeader Header;

    [WebMethod]
    [SoapHeader("Header", Direction = SoapHeaderDirection.In)]
    public List<Employee> SelectAll()
    {
        if (Header==null)
        {
            throw new SoapHeaderException("SOAP header was not found!", SoapException.
            ClientFaultCode);
        }

        if(Header.ClientKey != "KEY001")
        {
            throw new SoapException("Invalid client key!", SoapException.ClientFaultCode);
        }

        using (Northwind db = new Northwind())
        {
            return db.Employees.OrderBy(e => e.EmployeeID).ToList();
        }
    }
    ....
    ....,
}
```

Examine the web service class carefully. At the top it declares a variable of type EmployeeManagerHeader. The SelectAll() web method is now decorated with an additional attribute called [SoapHeader]. This is how you specify information about a SOAP header.

The [SoapHeader] attribute specifies one parameter and one property. The first parameter specifies the name of the SOAP header member that we want to use. In our example, the name of the EmployeeManagerHeader variable is Header and hence that is what we pass to the web method. This member must be available publicly in the web service class. The Direction property indicates the direction of the SoapHeader and is of enumeration type SoapHeaderDirection. The possible values of the SoapHeaderDirection enumeration are as follows:

- In: The direction of In indicates that the SOAP header is passed from the client to the web service.

- Out: The direction of Out indicates that the SOAP header is passed from the web service to the client.

- InOut: The direction of InOut indicates that the SOAP header is passed to and from the web service and its client.

- Fault: The direction of Fault indicates that a SOAP header is to be sent to the client when the web method throws an exception.

Inside the SelectAll() web method, we check whether the SOAP header is null. If so, this indicates that the client key was not sent and hence the code raises a SoapHeaderException. The SoapHeaderException class is used to represent an error in the SOAP header. The first parameter of the SoapHeaderException constructor is the error message, and the second parameter is the SOAP fault code for the client call.

The code then checks the ClientKey property of the SOAP header. If the client key is incorrect, a SoapException is raised. The SoapException class is used to represent an error with the SOAP request processing. The constructor of SoapException takes the same two parameters as the SoapHeaderException class.

■ **Note**   For the sake of simplicity the code uses a hard-coded string value for a client key. In a more realistic case you would check the key against some datastore. And the key might be encrypted for security reasons. Also, here we added the [SoapHeader] attributed to the SelectAll() web method. Repeat the same process for all the other web methods of the EmployeeManager web service.

To successfully consume the EmployeeManager web service you just modified, you need to modify the client application also. Listing 9-22 shows how the SOAP header required by the SelectAll() web method can be passed from the client application.

Listing 9-22. Passing a SOAP Header from the Client Application

```
private void Form2_Load(object sender, EventArgs e)
{
    EmployeeManagerSoapClient proxy = new EmployeeManagerSoapClient();

    EmployeeManagerHeader header = new EmployeeManagerHeader();
    header.ClientKey = "KEY001";

    try
    {
        Employee[] data = proxy.SelectAll(header);
        foreach (Employee emp in data)
        {
            comboBox1.Items.Add(emp.EmployeeID);
        }
    }
    catch(Exception ex)
    {
        MessageBox.Show(ex.Message);
    }
}
```

Before you write this code, make sure to update the proxy by right-clicking on it and selecting the Update Service Reference option. This is required because we have now changed the web service to use SOAP headers. And the proxy should know those details.

Notice the code marked in bold letters. The first line in bold letters creates an object of EmployeeManagerHeader and sets its ClientKey property. This class gets created on the client side during the proxy generation and placed in the same namespace as that of the proxy.

The second line in bold letters calls the SelectAll() method on the proxy. This time the SOAP header object—header—is passed as the method parameter. This way the SelectAll() web method will receive it from the client. Although here we will discuss only the SelectAll() method, you should modify all the other event handlers in the client application to use the SOAP header.

To test the client application, run it and check whether CRUD operations can be performed as before. Now, stop the application and explicitly set the EmployeeManagerHeader object to null. Then run the application again. You should get a message box, as shown in Figure 9-21, that informs you about the SoapHeaderException.

Figure 9-21. *Catching a SoapHeaderException*

Stop the application and revert the code that sets the header to null. Set the ClientKey property to some invalid key. Run the application again. This time the message box (see Figure 9-22) should inform you about the SoapException being thrown.

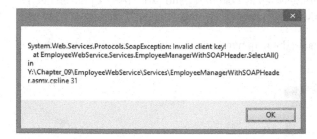

Figure 9-22. *Catching SoapException*

■ **Note**   In the example that we just discussed, it was assumed that you are using a service reference. If you are using a web reference instead, the SOAP header is passed a bit differently. We won't discuss those differences here, but you can easily figure that out with the help of Visual Studio IntelliSense.

Customizing the XML Serialization

In the previous chapter it was mentioned that web services use XmlSerializer to serialize the XML data involved in the web service communication. This also means that you can use the attributes such as [XmlRoot] and [XmlElement] to customize the serialized outcome. Although we won't go into too much detail about this customization process, a simple illustration will give you some idea.

Consider the Employee class shown in Listing 9-23.

Listing 9-23. Customizing XML Serialization in Web Services

```
[XmlRoot(ElementName ="EmployeeRoot")]
public partial class Employee
{
    [XmlElement(ElementName ="EmpCode")]
    public int EmployeeID { get; set; }

    [XmlElement(ElementName = "LName")]
    public string LastName { get; set; }

    [XmlElement(ElementName = "FName")]
    public string FirstName { get; set; }

    [XmlIgnore]
    public string HomePhone { get; set; }

    [XmlElement(ElementName = "Remarks")]
    public string Notes { get; set; }
}
```

It is the same Employee class but this time attributes such as [XmlRoot] and [XmlElement] haven been added to customize the XML element names. The HomePhone property is decorated with [XmlIgnore] so as to ignore it from the serialization process.

If you invoke the SelectByID() web method using the help page, you should see something similar to Figure 9-23.

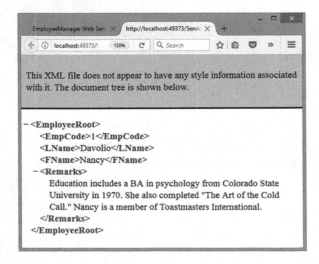

Figure 9-23. *Customizing element names for serialization*

As you can see, the serialized Employee object now uses element names such as <EmployeeRoot>, <FName>, <LName>, and <Remarks>. There is no HomePhone entry because we ignored it using [XmlIgnore].

Understanding the WSDL Document

While developing your first web service in this chapter, you learned that WSDL is an XML vocabulary that describes the web service in terms of web methods exposed, their parameters, data types, and return values. Though you will rarely modify or construct WSDL yourself (at least when you are using Visual Studio), it is helpful to understand the internal structure of the WSDL document. This way, your understanding of the web service metadata will broaden. You will also find the knowledge of WSDL useful while learning Windows Communication Foundation services, which are covered in Chapter 12.

Let's see the WSDL of a simple Hello World web service that we created initially in this chapter. We will be using this web service only as a sample. The discussion that follows is applicable to any other WSDL document. The WSDL of the preceding EmployeeManager web service, as shown in a browser, is shown in Figure 9-24.

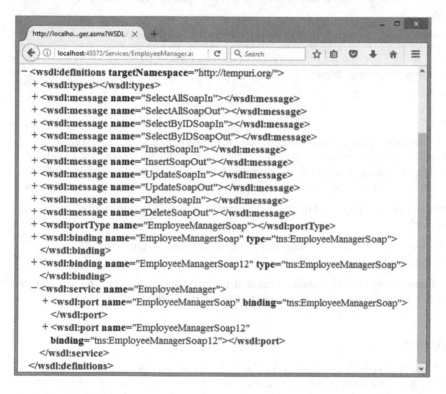

Figure 9-24. *WSDL of the EmployeeManager web service*

If you observe this WSDL markup, you can identify six main parts of the document. These six parts are the core elements of any WSDL document and are listed in Table 9-2.

Table 9-2. Parts of WSDL

Part	Description
types	The `<wsdl:types>` element encloses all the type definitions from the web service.
message	The XML data that is being carried between the web service and its client. The `<wsdl:message>` element represents this message.
portType	The `<wsdl:portType>` section defines a group of operations (web methods) exposed by the web service. You may think of it as an interface that contains a series of `<wsdl:operation>` elements.
binding	The protocol and format used by the portType. It is represented by the `<wsdl:binding>` markup tag.
port	An endpoint of a web service communication. It is represented by the `<wsdl:port>` markup tag.
service	The collection of one or more ports. It is represented by the `<wsdl:service>` markup tag.

Let's look at each of these parts in more detail.

The Messages

You learned previously that web service communication works on the basis of a request and response model. A web service request as well as response consists of SOAP data. This SOAP data is called a *SOAP message*. Each web method has a message that represents a request for the web method and a message that represents the response from that web method. Thus our SelectAll() web method will have two messages:

- The name of the request message is of the form XXXXSoapIn, where XXXX is the name of the web method.

- Similarly, the name of the response message is of the form XXXXSoapOut, where XXXX is the name of the web method.

The WSDL message elements provide a consolidated list of all the messages exposed by the web service. The message names provided by this list are used everywhere else in the WSDL document.

The Type Definitions

Each message in a web service has a specific structure, or schema. This schema is specified by the types element of the WSDL document. If you observe the types section in the WSDL mentioned earlier, you will find that it specifies a schema for all the messages. You will also notice that the data type of the parameters and return values are specified here. This schema closely matches the XSD Schema you learned about in the earlier chapters.

The Port Types

A web service consists of one or more operations. In simple terms, an *operation* is analogous to a function or method. Each operation has an input message (request) and an output message (response). All the operations of a web service are listed under the portType section. The port name is of the form XXXXSoap, where XXXX is the name of the web service class. The EmployeeManager web service has five operations. Each operation consists of two messages—input message and output message. Recollect that messages are defined in the message section.

The Binding

A *binding* specifies the message format and protocol for each port type. For example, in our web service there is a binding defined for the EmployeeManagerSoap port type. The linking between a binding and port type is the type attribute of the <wsdl:binding> element. The binding name is of the form XXXXSoap, where XXXX is the name of the web service class.

The Service

A *service* is a set of ports and bindings. A web service port is a logical endpoint for a web service. A service has the same name as the web service class. In our example, the service element defines a port called EmployeeManagerSoap and links it with the EmployeeManagerSoap binding.

A Summary of WSDL

To summarize what we have discussed:

- A web service consists of one or more operations.

- Each operation typically has a request message and a response message.

- Each message is listed in the message section of the WSDL.

- The schema of all the messages is defined by the types section of the WSDL.

- All the operations exposed by a web service are listed under the portType section of the WSDL.

- For each port type, a transport format and protocol needs to be specified. This is referred to as *binding*.

- The binding for a port type is specified by the binding section of the WSDL.

- The service section of the WSDL defines an endpoint for the web service called a *port*.

- A port has a specific binding associated with it.

Summary

In this chapter, you learned about one of the powerful features of the .NET Framework: web services. Web services are a programmable set of APIs that can be called over a network by using industry standards such as XML, SOAP, and HTTP. Web services can prove to be very beneficial in areas such as application integration, cross-platform communication, and distributed communication over the Internet.

You learned to create web services, a proxy for the web service, and a client that consumes the web service. Finally, you peeked into the internal structure of SOAP and WSDL.

CHAPTER 10

■ ■ ■

XML in WCF and Web API

Chapter 9 introduced you to web services and you learned to develop service based applications. Web services are based on certain standards and protocols such as SOAP, XML and WSDL. They are great when it comes to developing standards based services that are accessed on the internet. However, at times your needs are different. For example, you may want to develop services for an intranet application and want to use binary format over TCP for performance reasons. Or you want to use some highly secure communication mechanism that uses some custom encryption strategies. Web services may not serve your purpose in such cases.

Recognizing the need to bridge the gap between various component technologies, Microsoft developed what is known as the *Windows Communication Foundation (WCF)*. WCF is a generic framework that provides a unified model for developing service-oriented software components. Under WCF you can employ the same piece of software regardless of whether you are using it over the Internet or an intranet. You can design and develop your software initially for TCP networks and later use it over HTTP. This can be achieved with no changes to the source code. What is more interesting for us is the fact that by default WCF uses XML (SOAP) as the data transfer format. That means data that is sent between the client and the server is in XML (SOAP) format. You can also customize how your objects are serialized on the wire.

WCF is a general purpose framework for developing services. It requires good amount of configuration. And many developers find this configuration tedious. Especially for web application where the underlying communication channel is HTTP and the data transfer is in some text-based format (XML, SOAP, JSON and so on) the extensive feature set and configuration of WCF is unnecessary. That's how Web API came into existence. Web API is a framework for building RESTful services. Web API framework is developed specifically keeping web applications and HTTP in mind and offers a simple programming model to the developers.

This chapter introduces you to the following topics:

- Common terms used in relation to WCF

- Creating and consuming a WCF service

- The role of XML in WCF services

- Creating and consuming a service using Web API

- Configuring the Web API to use XML format

■ **Note**   This chapter is not intended to teach you the basics of WCF and Web API. It focuses more on how XML is related to these service development frameworks. If you are unfamiliar with WCF and Web API, consider learning their basics from the Microsoft's official documentation.

© Bipin Joshi 2017

B. Joshi, *Beginning XML with C# 7*, https://doi.org/10.1007/978-1-4842-3105-0_10

Operations Based Services vs. Resource Based Services

Broadly speaking, a service can be categorized either as an operation based service or a resource based service. What does that mean? Consider the EmployeeManager web service you developed in Chapter 9. You essentially added methods into the web service as per your requirement. In that example you added five methods to implement CRUD operations. But you could have added as many as you want depending on your requirement. Later you invoked those methods by calling them on the proxy. Thus you explicitly invoked operations of a service. This was an example of operations based service.

Resource based services are resource oriented. A resource could be anything, say, business objects, a database or a file. A resource based service allows you to perform actions on a resource such as adding a resource, updating a resource, removing a resource and fetching a resource. Thus a resource based service confines itself to a resource. This is different than operations based service where the service is free to do anything of your choice. RESTful services are resource based services (you will learn more about REST in later sections).

Each approach of developing a service has its own pros and cons. We won't go into those details in this book. Suffice it to say that WCF allows you to develop both kinds of services, whereas Web API allows you to build RESTful services. In the later sections of this chapter, you will develop both kinds of services. You will also observe where XML fits into this whole picture.

Understanding WCF Vocabulary

In Chapter 9, you learned about the Web Services Description Language (WSDL). WSDL uses terms such as *port*, *message*, *service type*, *binding*, and *service*. WCF vocabulary is similar to WSDL with a few differences. In this section, you will learn the WCF vocabulary:

- *Service model*: The model provided by WCF to build software components.

- *Channel layer*: That part of WCF that deals with low-level network programming. The classes from the channel layer are used by high-level classes of WCF.

- *Service*: A piece of software that responds to communication over a network. A service has one or more endpoints. Communication with the service is redirected to one of these endpoints.

- *Endpoint*: Where the actual request for a service is redirected. An endpoint consists of an address, a binding, and a contract.

- *Address*: Nothing but the unique location of the underlying service on a network. Clients use this address to talk with the service. An address takes the form of a Uniform Resource Locator (URL)—for example, http://localhost:8000/ MyService.

- *Binding*: An address is just a URL where the service can be located. However, that's not enough. You also need to know the protocol used for communication such as TCP or HTTP. This is specified with the help of a binding. The binding specifies the protocol for encoding the request and response as well as the protocol for transporting them over the network.

- *Contract*: A set of operations that are exposed by the service. In other words, a contract is a set of operations available at a given endpoint. At the code level, a contract is defined with the help of an interface.

- *Service type*: A class that implements a contract.

Creating and Consuming a WCF Service

To create and consume WCF services, you essentially need to develop three pieces of software:

- One or more service types

- A host that publishes the services exposed by the service types on a network

- A client application that consumes the functionality exposed by the service types

All the core functionality of WCF is available in the `System.ServiceModel.dll` assembly.

The `System.ServiceModel` namespaces contain many classes and attributes related to WCF. So, you must reference this assembly and import the `System.ServiceModel` namespace as and when needed. In the next few sections, you learn how to develop each of the three parts.

Creating the Service

Creating a WCF service requires the following steps:

1. Define a contract for the service.

2. Implement the service contract.

3. Define the data structures (if any) to carry data from the service to the client.

Now that you have a brief idea about what's involved in creating WCF services, let's create a service. Begin by creating a new project of type WCF Service Library named `EmployeeWCFService` (see Figure 10-1).

Figure 10-1. *Creating a new WCF service library*

Then add an interface to the project by using the Add New Item dialog box and name it `IEmployeeManager`.

■ **Note**   When you create a new project of type WCF Service Library, Visual Studio adds a template for creating a new service by default. Additionally the Add New Item dialog of Visual Studio also provides a template for adding a new WCF Service. However, for the sake of clear understanding, I am not going to use the default code templates.

Import the System.ServiceModel namespace at the top of the interface file and add the code shown in Listing 10-1 in the interface.

Listing 10-1. Creating the IEmployeeManager Interface

```
using System;
using System.Collections.Generic;
using System.Text;
using System.ServiceModel;
using System.Data;

namespace EmployeeWCFService
{
  [ServiceContract]
  public interface IEmployeeManager
  {
    [OperationContract]
    List<EmployeeDataContract> SelectAll();

    [OperationContract]
    EmployeeDataContract SelectByID(int id);

    [OperationContract]
    string Update(EmployeeDataContract emp);
  }
}
```

The IEmployeeManager interface acts as a WCF contract. The IEmployeeManager interface defines three methods: SelectAll(), SelectByID(), and Update(). The SelectAll() method when implemented will return a list of all the employees from the Employees table of the Northwind database. The SelectByID() method when implemented will return details of a specific employee. The EmployeeDataContract class is defined and explained later in this section. Notice two things about the IEmployeeManager WCF contract:

- The interface must be decorated with the [ServiceContract] attribute. This attribute indicates that the interface decorated by it is a WCF service contract.

- Each method signature in the interface must be marked with the [OperationContract] attribute, which indicates that the method decorated by it will be exposed as a part of the service. Methods are referred to as *operations* in WCF.

After you define a contract, you need to implement it. You do this by creating a class that implements the contract interface. You need not do anything special with the service type apart from implementing the service contract.

In our example, the EmployeeDataContract class is used to carry details of an employee from the service to the client. This is the *data contract* of the service. So, add the EmployeeDataContract class to the project. Also add a reference to the System.Runtime.Serialization assembly. Then import the System.ServiceModel and System.Runtime.Serialization namespaces at the top of the EmployeeDataContract class. Listing 10-2 shows the complete code that makes up the Employee class.

Listing 10-2. The EmployeeDataContract Class

```
using System;
using System.Collections.Generic;
using System.Text;
using System.ServiceModel;
using System.Runtime.Serialization;
using System.Data;

namespace EmployeeWCFService
{
    [DataContract]
    public class EmployeeDataContract
    {
        [DataMember]
        public int EmployeeID { get; set; }
        [DataMember]
        public string LastName { get; set; }
        [DataMember]
        public string FirstName { get; set; }
        [DataMember]
        public string HomePhone { get; set; }
        [DataMember]
        public string Notes { get; set; }
    }
}
```

The EmployeeDataContract class consists of five public properties: EmployeeID, FirstName, LastName, HomePhone, and Notes. Notice how the class is marked with the [DataContract] attribute, and individual properties with the [DataMember] attribute. This way, the class and its state information are serialized to the client. Anytime you want to return custom objects from your service methods, you need to mark such classes with the [DataContract] attribute. Further, each member of the class that will be transferred to the client must be marked with the [DataMember] attribute. You may notice that the use of the [DataContract] attribute is similar to the [Serializable] attribute.

■ **Note**   You will find this code familiar because you used [DataContract] and [DataMember] attributes in Chapter 8 while learning XML serialization.

The EmployeeDataContract simply defines the data contract needed by the EmployeeManager service. However, you need to write code that fetches the data from the Northwind database. You can, of course, use plain ADO.NET code to accomplish this task. But to save us some time and code we will use Entity Framework code-first for this purpose. To generate EF model and context, add a new folder into the project root named Models, right-click on it and open the Add New Item dialog. Then under the Data section, select ADO.NET Entity Data Model (Figure 10-2).

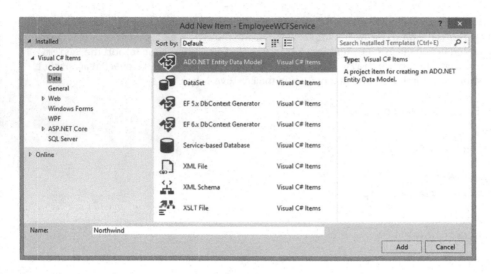

Figure 10-2. *Adding ADO.NET Entity Data Model*

Name and model **Northwind** and click Add. This will start a wizard. Pick Code First from database option (Figure 10-3) and simply follow the wizard to generate the context and entity classes.

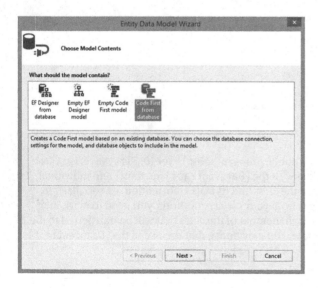

Figure 10-3. *Generating a model using the code-first approach*

Successful run of the wizard will add Northwind.cs and Employee.cs files to the Models folder. The former file contains the context class whereas the latter file contains the Employee entity class. Since these classes are autogenerated for you, they are not discussed here.

The last step in creating this service is to implement the service contract in a class called EmployeeManager. Listing 10-3 shows the complete code of the EmployeeService class.

Listing 10-3. The EmployeeService Class

```csharp
public class EmployeeManager:IEmployeeManager
{
    public List<EmployeeDataContract> SelectAll()
    {
        using (Northwind db = new Northwind())
        {
            var query = from e in db.Employees
                        orderby e.EmployeeID ascending
                        select new EmployeeDataContract()
                        {
                            EmployeeID = e.EmployeeID,
                            FirstName = e.FirstName,
                            LastName = e.LastName,
                            HomePhone = e.HomePhone,
                            Notes = e.Notes
                        };
            return query.ToList();
        }
    }
    public EmployeeDataContract SelectByID(int id)
    {
        using (Northwind db = new Northwind())
        {
            var query = from e in db.Employees
                        where e.EmployeeID == id
                        select new EmployeeDataContract()
                        {
                            EmployeeID = e.EmployeeID,
                            FirstName = e.FirstName,
                            LastName = e.LastName,
                            HomePhone = e.HomePhone,
                            Notes = e.Notes
                        };
            return query.SingleOrDefault();
        }
    }

    public string Update(EmployeeDataContract emp)
    {
        using (Northwind db = new Northwind())
        {
            Employee existing = db.Employees.Find(emp.EmployeeID);
            existing.FirstName = emp.FirstName;
            existing.LastName = emp.LastName;
            existing.HomePhone = emp.HomePhone;
            existing.Notes = emp.Notes;
            db.SaveChanges();
            return "Employee modified successfully!";
        }
    } }
```

275

The EmployeeManager class implements the IEmployeeManager interface. The SelectAll() method fills a list with all the employees and returns it to the caller. Notice that SelectAll() method needs to return EmployeeDataContract objects. This is done by mapping data from the Employee objects to EmployeeDataContract objects using the LINQ to Entities query.

The SelectByID() method accepts an employee ID. It then fetches details of that employee from the database using LINQ to Entities query. The EmployeeDataContract object is then returned to the caller.

The Update() method accepts an EmployeeDataContract object. Inside, it finds an existing employee based on its EmployeeID. The properties of the existing employee are then modified using the values from the EmployeeDataContract. The SaveChanges() method saves the changes to the database. A message is sent back to the caller indicating that the employee has been successfully modified.

Compile the EmployeeWCFService project so as to produce the EmployeeWCFService.dll assembly.

Hosting the Service

Now that you have created the service type, it's time to think about hosting it. Hosting the service will make it available on a network so that client applications can consume it. To host the service, you have multiple options. Some of them include:

- Create a console application and use it as a host.

- Host the WCF service in IIS.

- Host the WCF service in a Windows service application.

In this example, we use a console application as a host. In later sections, you learn to use IIS to host WCF services.

Add a new project of the type console application in the same solution as the service and name it EmployeeWCFServiceHost. See Figure 10-4.

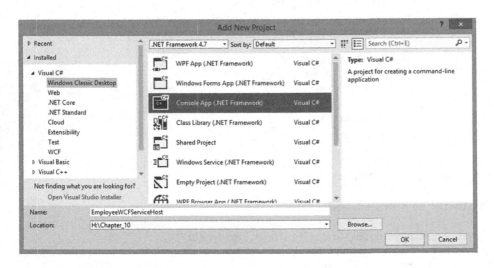

Figure 10-4. *Creating a console application to host the WCF service*

Add a reference to the System.ServiceModel and EmployeeWCFService assemblies. The newly created console application project will already contain an App.config file. Open the App.config file in Visual Studio Editor and enter the markup shown in Listing 10-4 inside the <configuration> root element.

Listing 10-4. Configuring the Service

```
<system.serviceModel>
  <services>
    <service name="EmployeeWCFService.EmployeeManager"
             behaviorConfiguration="EmployeeWCFServiceBehavior">
      <endpoint address="EmployeeManager"
                binding="basicHttpBinding"
                contract="EmployeeWCFService.IEmployeeManager">
      </endpoint>
    </service>
  </services>
  <behaviors>
    <serviceBehaviors>
      <behavior name="EmployeeWCFServiceBehavior">
        <serviceMetadata httpGetEnabled="True"/>
        <serviceDebug includeExceptionDetailInFaults="true" />
      </behavior>
    </serviceBehaviors>
  </behaviors>
</system.serviceModel>
```

The `<system.serviceModel>` section of the configuration file contains all the configuration settings related to hosting WCF services. There are two subsections: `<services>` and `<behaviors>`.

The former contains configuration information about one or more services in terms of name, endpoints, and addresses. The latter contains configuration information about behavior exhibited by the services defined in the `<services>` section. A *behavior* is a class that modifies or extends the service or client functionality. It can also modify channel settings.

Each service from the `<services>` section is configured via a `<service>` section:

- The name attribute specifies the fully qualified name of the service type (`EmployeeWCFService.EmployeeManager` in our case).

- The behaviorConfiguration attribute points to the name of the service behavior as defined in the `<serviceBehaviors>` section.

- The `<endpoint>` element details one or more endpoints where the service is available.

- The address attribute of the `<endpoint>` element specifies the address of the service.

- The binding attribute specifies the protocol to be used for communication. The two commonly used bindings are `net.tcp` for TCP and `basicHttpBinding` for HTTP. There are several other bindings provided, such as `netMsmqBinding`, `netNamedPipeBinding`, and so on.

- Finally, the contract attribute specifies the fully qualified name of the interface that provides the service contract (`IEmployeeManager` in our case).

In our example, we created an endpoint for HTTP-based communication.
The <serviceBehaviors> section contains one or more <behavior> elements:

- The name attribute of the <behavior> element specifies the name of that behavior.
  This name is used in the behaviorConfiguration attribute of the <service>
  element.

- The <serviceMetadata> element indicates that the metadata of the service can be
  retrieved by using an HTTP GET request. You will find this feature analogous to web
  services, where you retrieve WSDL by using a query string (that is, a GET request).

Now open the Main() method of the console application and type in the code shown in Listing 10-5.

Listing 10-5. Hosting the WCF Service

```
static void Main(string[] args)
{
    try
    {
        Type t = typeof(EmployeeManager);
        Uri http = new Uri("http://localhost:8000/EmployeeWCFService");
        ServiceHost host = new ServiceHost(t, tcp, http);
        host.Open();
        Console.WriteLine("Employee Manager Service Published.");
        Console.ReadLine();
        host.Close();
    }
    catch (Exception ex)
    {
        Console.WriteLine(ex.Message);
        Console.ReadLine();
    }
}
```

The code retrieves the Type of the service type class by using the typeof() expression. It then creates
an instance of the Uri class pointing to the HTTP-based URL where the service is to be published. Note how
the port number is set as 8000. You could use any port number but ensure that it's not used by any other
applications and is not blocked on a network.

Then an instance of the ServiceHost class is created. The ServiceHost class hosts the service by
publishing the service type at the specified URIs. Note that the constructor of the ServiceHost class takes
a parameter array of URIs. In our example, we have passed two, but you can pass more if you want. The
following constructor signature will make it clear:

```
public ServiceHost (Type serviceType, params Uri[] baseAddresses)
{
    ...
}
```

The Open() method of the ServiceHost class is then called. This method actually hosts the service
depending on the configuration information. The service will remain published so long as the host
application is live. That is why the ReadLine() method of the Console class is called. It keeps the application
live until the user presses the Enter key. Finally, the Close() method of the ServiceHost class is called. This
completes the host application.

■ **Note**   During development, you can also use Visual Studio's built-in WCF service host, skipping the host application altogether. However, for the sake of clear understanding of all the steps involved, we won't use the built-in host in this example.

Consuming the Service

In this section, you create a client application that consumes the EmployeeWCFService we created previously. To begin, you need to create a Windows application called EmployeeWCFServiceClient, like the one shown in Figure 10-5.

Figure 10-5. The client consuming the WCF service

The application consists of a list box containing a list of all the employees. Clicking a particular employee will display their details in text boxes placed below. You can change the details such as first name, last name, home phone and notes. Clicking on the Update button will save the changes to the database. A success message is also displayed to the user using a Label.

Before you consume the service, you should create a proxy for it. Run the service host application that you developed earlier (make sure to run the application from outside of Visual Studio so that you can complete the next step). Then right-click the client application project and choose the Add Service Reference menu option. This will open a dialog like the one shown in Figure 10-6.

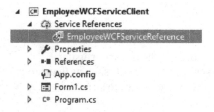

(Add Service Reference dialog)

Figure 10-6. *Adding a service reference*

Enter the HTTP endpoint address of the WCF service (i.e., `http://localhost:8000/EmployeeWCFService`) and `EmployeeWCFServiceReference` as the namespace name for the proxy class.

This will create a service reference for the service. All the service references added to a project are listed in the Solution Explorer, as shown in Figure 10-7.

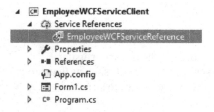

Figure 10-7. *Service reference as shown in the Solution Explorer*

Adding a service reference will also add some markup in the client's application configuration file. Now you can call the service from your client code. Listing 10-6 shows the `Load` event handler of the form.

Listing 10-6. Retrieving the List of Employees

```
private string endPoint = "BasicHttpBinding_IEmployeeManager";

private void Form1_Load(object sender, EventArgs e)
{
    EmployeeManagerClient proxy = new EmployeeManagerClient(endPoint);
    EmployeeDataContract[] data = proxy.SelectAll();
```

```
    foreach(EmployeeDataContract emp in data)
    {
        comboBox1.Items.Add(emp.EmployeeID);
    }
  proxy.Close();
}
```

The code declares a local variable—endpoint—to store the name of the service endpoint. You can figure out the endpoint configuration name from the client's application configuration file.

The code then creates a new instance of the proxy class. Notice how the proxy class is named XXXXClient (EmployeeManagerClient in our case), where XXXX is the name of the original service class. In the constructor of the proxy class, you pass the desired endpoint configuration name.

The code then calls the SelectAll() method on the proxy object to retrieve details of all the employees. Notice that the SelectAll() method called on the proxy returns an array of EmployeeDataContract objects. A foreach loop then fills the EmployeeIDs into the combo box. Finally, the underlying communication channel is closed by calling the Close() method of the proxy.

When a user clicks any of the employees listed in the combo box, details of that employee are to be displayed in the other text boxes. This is done in the SelectedIndexChanged event handler of the combo box (see Listing 10-7).

Listing 10-7. Retrieving the Details of an Employee

```
private void comboBox1_SelectedIndexChanged(object sender, EventArgs e)
{
    EmployeeManagerClient proxy = new EmployeeManagerClient(endPoint);
    EmployeeDataContract data = proxy.SelectByID((int)comboBox1.SelectedItem);
    textBox1.Text = data.FirstName;
    textBox2.Text = data.LastName;
    textBox3.Text = data.HomePhone;
    textBox4.Text = data.Notes;
    label6.Text = "";
    proxy.Close();
}
```

The code is very similar to what you saw earlier. This time it calls the SelectByID() method on the proxy by passing the selected EmployeeID. The SelectByID() method returns an EmployeeDataContract object filled with the required details. The details such as EmployeeID, FirstName, LastName, HomePhone, and Notes are then displayed in respective text boxes.

Once the details of an employee are displayed in the text boxes, you can change them and click on Update to save them to the database. The Click event handler of the Update button is shown in Listing 10-8.

Listing 10-8. Saving the Modifications to the Database

```
private void button1_Click(object sender, EventArgs e)
{
    EmployeeManagerClient proxy = new EmployeeManagerClient(endPoint);
    EmployeeDataContract data = new EmployeeDataContract();
    data.EmployeeID = (int)comboBox1.SelectedItem;
    data.FirstName = textBox1.Text;
    data.LastName = textBox2.Text;
    data.HomePhone = textBox3.Text;
```

```
    data.Notes = textBox4.Text;
    label6.Text=proxy.Update(data);
    proxy.Close();
}
```

The code is straightforward—it creates a proxy object as before. This time it also creates a new EmployeeDataContract object and fills it with the modified details of an employee. The Update() method of the proxy is then called in an attempt to save the changes to the database. A Label control displays the success message returned by the Update() method.

Testing the Host and Client

Now that you have coded all three parts (service, host, and client), let's test them. First, compile all the projects from the solution. Then run the host console application. If everything goes well, you should see a command prompt like the one shown in Figure 10-8.

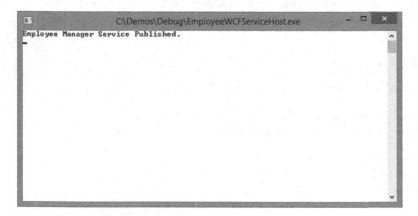

Figure 10-8. *Running the host application*

Next open a browser and enter the URL of the service endpoint (http:// localhost:8000/ EmployeeWCFService) in the address bar. You should get a web page like the one shown in Figure 10-9.

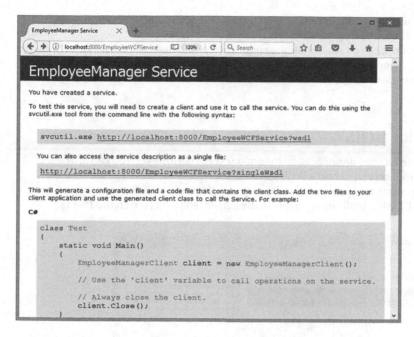

Figure 10-9. *Testing to see whether the service is hosted properly*

If you get this page, the service is hosted correctly. Click on the URL specified at the top of the web page and you should see the WSDL of the service, as shown in Figure 10-10.

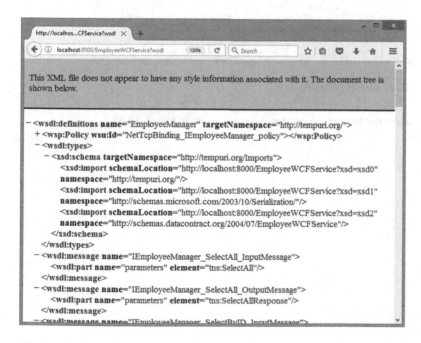

Figure 10-10. *WSDL of the service*

You will find this mechanism very similar to web services, where you retrieved the WSDL of a web service just by specifying the `wsdl` query string parameter.

Now run the client application, and you should see the combo box populated with the list of all the employees. Click individual employee names, and their details will be displayed in various text boxes. Also test whether any modifications to the employee details are saved in the database after clicking the Update button.

Hosting a WCF Service in IIS

In the preceding example, we used a console application to host our service. However, you can also use IIS (or Visual Studio development web server) to host a WCF services. This way, your service is automatically started when the IIS application starts, and you also get all the security features of IIS for your service.

To begin, add a new ASP.NET Web Application project to the current solution (see Figure 10-11).

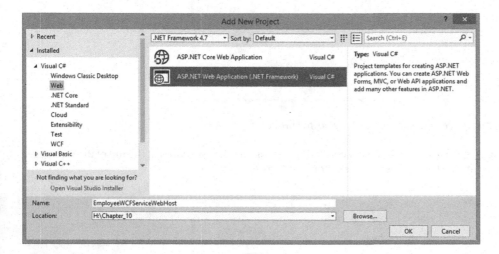

Figure 10-11. *Adding a new ASP.NET web application*

While creating the project, select the Empty project template, as shown in Figure 10-12.

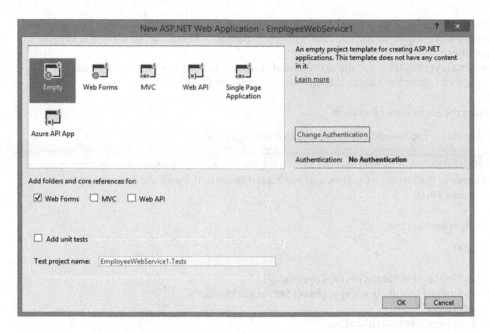

Figure 10-12. *Project based on the Empty template*

This way, you will have a project with just the basic project items such as web.config. Next, add a reference to the EmployeeWCFService assembly as you did in the earlier examples. Now, add a new WCF service to the project using the Add New Item dialog (see Figure 10-13).

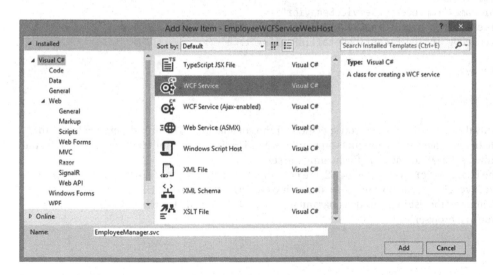

Figure 10-13. *Adding a new WCF service*

This will add a new .svc file to the project and also its code-behind. The .svc file contains information about the WCF service being exposed. You can delete the code-behind file because our service is already bundled in an assembly.

Then open the EmployeeManager.svc file in the Visual Studio text editor. You will find that the .svc file contains the @ServiceHost directive. Modify this directive as shown in Listing 10-9.

Listing 10-9. Adding the ServiceHost Directive

```
<%@ServiceHost Service="EmployeeWCFService.EmployeeManager" %>
```

The @ServiceHost directive indicates that the file is a WCF service host. The Service attribute specifies the fully qualified name of the service type. Now add a web.config file to the web site and type in the markup shown in Listing 10-10.

Listing 10-10. Configuring the Host

```
<system.serviceModel>
  <services>
    <service name="EmployeeWCFService.EmployeeManager"
             behaviorConfiguration="EmployeeWCFServiceBehavior">
      <endpoint address=""
                binding="basicHttpBinding"
                contract="EmployeeWCFService.IEmployeeManager">
      </endpoint>
    </service>
  </services>
  <behaviors>
    <serviceBehaviors>
      <behavior name="EmployeeWCFServiceBehavior">
        <serviceMetadata httpGetEnabled="True"/>
        <serviceDebug includeExceptionDetailInFaults="true" />
      </behavior>
    </serviceBehaviors>
  </behaviors>
</system.serviceModel>
```

It is essentially the same markup that you specified for the console host. The only difference is that the address attribute of the <endpoint> element is an empty string. This is because for an IIS-hosted service, the address is the same as the URI of the .svc file hosting the service.

To access the EmployeeService hosted in IIS, the endpoint URL will be http://localhost:49303/EmployeeManager.svc (change the port number to match yours). Observe that the URL points to the .svc file. You can also append the wsdl query string parameter to extract its WSDL. Figure 10-14 shows a sample run of the .svc file in a browser.

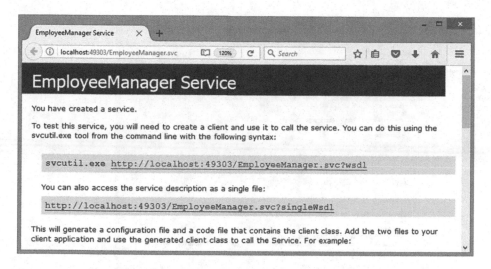

Figure 10-14. Navigating to the .svc file in a browser

You can feed this URL to the proxy generator and the proxy will be generated for you. The overall process of proxy creation and invoking the service remains the same as in the previous example.

Understanding the Role of XML in WCF Services

From what you have learned up until now, it is clear that WCF uses XML for configuring various pieces of services. However, there is more to the story.

In the preceding example that you just developed, the employee data from the EmployeeManager service magically appeared in the client application. However, how did that happen? How was the data sent on the wire? As far as basic HTTP binding is concerned, the data is serialized on the wire as a SOAP message. This means XML data in the form of a SOAP envelop is being sent to the client.

■ **Note** SOAP based communication can cause a performance penalty due to its bulky nature. However, SOAP is a natural choice when interoperability is more important for your application. WCF also allows you to use binary communication over TCP. Such a communication can give performance benefits to your application. Discussion of these details is beyond the scope of this book.

Just to understand what has just been said, go to the EmployeeWCFService project and press F5. Doing so will open WCF Test Client, as shown in Figure 10-15.

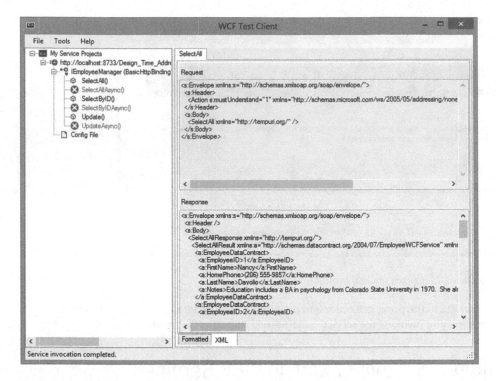

Figure 10-15. *Observing a message in WCF test client*

The WCF test client allows you to invoke service methods. On the left side, double-click on the SelectAll() method. Then click on the Invoke button on the right side of the panel. This will invoke the method and all the EmployeeDataContract objects will be returned. Switch to XML tab and you will see the SOAP request and SOAP response messages.

In case of WCF RESTful services (you will learn about them in later sections), the data is serialized as plain XML rather than a SOAP message.

Using XmlSerializer Instead of DataContractSerializer

The WCF framework can use two approaches while serializing the XML data:

- By default, WCF uses the DataContractSerializer class (an implementation of XmlObjectSerializer) for serializing the XML data. You already learned about the DataContractSerializer class in Chapter 8.

- You can also instruct WCF to use XmlSerializer for the XML serialization. Doing so will give you more control of how the data is serialized. You can customize the serialization process by using various attributes such as [XmlAttribute] and [XmlElement]. You already learned about the XmlSerializer class in Chapter 8.

To instruct the WCF framework that it should use XmlSerializer instead of DataContractSerializer, all you need to do is decorate the service contract interface with the [XmlSerializerFormat] attribute. The IEmployeeManager interface after applying the [XmlSerializerFormat] attribute is shown in Listing 10-11.

Listing 10-11. Applying the [XmlSerializerFormat] Attribute

```
[ServiceContract]
[XmlSerializerFormat]
public interface IEmployeeManager
{
  ....
  ....
}
```

Understanding REST Services

The WCF services we discussed so far were operations-based, in that you always explicitly invoked a specific method or operation of the service. Modern web applications often create and consume RESTful services. From our earlier discussion you know that REST services are resource-based services. Although this chapter doesn't attempt to teach you the fundamental of REST services as such, a brief discussion REST is worthwhile.

REST stands for REpresentational State Transfer. REST is not a standard; it's a way of architecting your services. Unlike ASMX web services or WCF operations-based services that use protocols and standards such as Simple Object Access Protocol (SOAP) and Web Services Description Language (WSDL), RESTful services harness the simplicity and power of HTTP.

Here are some fundamental characteristics of RESTful services:

- REST services use the HTTP protocol.

- REST services make HTTP requests (using meaningful HTTP verbs such as GET, POST, PUT, and DELETE) to fetch and submit data.

- REST services are stateless in nature.

- REST exposes services as resources that are accessible and discoverable through URLs.

- REST services typically transfer data in JSON or XML format.

As far as the .NET Framework is concerned there are two ways for creating RESTful services—WCF REST services and Web API. Nowadays, it is more common for web applications to use JSON (JavaScript Object Notation) as a format for data transfer between a service and its client, but you can use XML also. Our interest is, of course, is to see how XML can be used along with these frameworks.

The HTTP verbs such as GET, POST, PUT, and DELETE indicate the desired action to be performed on a resource. If a service performs create, read, update, and delete (CRUD) operations on a database, you could use POST to indicate an INSERT operation, GET to indicate a SELECT operation, PUT to indicate an UPDATE operation, and DELETE to indicate a DELETE operation. However, merely using a specific verb won't enforce a particular type of operation. It's up to you to implement these verbs in a service depending on application's requirements.

Now that you have an idea about what REST services are, you'll see how to create them, first using WCF and then using Web API.

Creating a REST Service Using WCF

Creating a RESTful service using WCF requires the same steps that you are familiar with. However, two major changes are:

- Since REST services use HTTP verbs to invoke methods, you use webHttpBinding. It is also common to host such a service in IIS or a web server (as discussed earlier).

- The mapping between HTTP verbs and service methods is specified in the service contract.

Apart from these changes, the remaining parts of a service are more or less the same as before.

Begin by creating a new ASP.NET Web Application based on the empty project template. As you did with the EmployeeWCFService project, add a Models folder and generate the Entity Framework context and entity class (Employee). Also add EmployeeDataContract class as before.

Next, add an interface—IEmployeeManager—to the project. The completed IEmployeeManager interface is shown in Listing 10-12.

Listing 10-12. IEmployeeManager Interface

```
[ServiceContract]
public interface IEmployeeManager
{
    [OperationContract]
    [WebGet(UriTemplate = "/employees",
            ResponseFormat =WebMessageFormat.Xml)]
    List<EmployeeDataContract> SelectAll();

    [OperationContract]
    [WebGet(UriTemplate = "/employees/{id}",
        ResponseFormat = WebMessageFormat.Xml)]
    EmployeeDataContract SelectByID(string id);

    [OperationContract]
    [WebInvoke(Method = "POST",
            UriTemplate = "/employees",
            RequestFormat =WebMessageFormat.Xml ,
            ResponseFormat = WebMessageFormat.Xml)]
    string Insert(EmployeeDataContract emp);

    [OperationContract]
    [WebInvoke(Method = "PUT",
            UriTemplate = "/employees/{id}",
            RequestFormat =WebMessageFormat.Xml,
            ResponseFormat = WebMessageFormat.Xml)]
    string Update(string id,EmployeeDataContract emp);

    [OperationContract]
    [WebInvoke(Method = "DELETE",
            UriTemplate = "/employees/{id}",
            ResponseFormat = WebMessageFormat.Xml)]
    string Delete(string id);
}
```

Observe the IEmployeeManager interface carefully. It looks quite similar to the previous example but with a few more operations. Now it has total five operations—SelectAll(), SelectByID(), Insert(), Update(), and Delete().

The operations are decorated with the [OperationContract] attribute. Additionally, they have either the [WebGet] or [WebInvoke] attribute on them. These attributes come from the System.ServiceModel.Web namespace and indicate that the WCF service is following the REST programming model.

The [WebGet] attribute indicates that SelectAll() and SelectByID() are retrieval operations. The [WebInvoke] attribute indicates that Insert(), Update(), and Delete() are invoke operations.

The properties of [WebGet] and [WebInvoke] configure the REST service. These properties are discussed next:

- Method: The Method property indicates the HTTP verb that invokes an operation. Common verbs are GET, POST, PUT, and DELETE.

- UriTemplate: Indicates the template of the endpoint URL that is used to invoke a method. For example, http://localhost/employees or http://localhost/employees/1. Notice how the EmployeeID is parameterized using the {id} syntax. This id value is considered as a string and hence all the underlying operations specify id parameter as a string type.

- RequestFormat: Indicates the format of the data accompanying a request. Possible values are Xml and Json (WebMessageFormat enumeration).

- ResponseFormat: Indicates the format of the data accompanying a response. Possible values are Xml and Json (WebMessageFormat enumeration).

Now that the IEmployeeManager interface is ready, add a WCF service to the project called EmployeeManager.svc. The code-behind file of the .svc file will house the EmployeeManager class. This class implements the IEmployeeManager interface as before. The complete code of the EmployeeManager class is shown in Listing 10-13.

Listing 10-13. EmployeeManager Class Implements IEmployeeManager

```
public class EmployeeManager:IEmployeeManager
{
    public List<EmployeeDataContract> SelectAll()
    {
        using (Northwind db = new Northwind())
        {
            var query = from e in db.Employees
                        orderby e.EmployeeID ascending
                        select new EmployeeDataContract()
                        {
                            EmployeeID = e.EmployeeID,
                            FirstName = e.FirstName,
                            LastName = e.LastName,
                            HomePhone = e.HomePhone,
                            Notes = e.Notes
                        };
            return query.ToList();
        }
    }
```

```
public EmployeeDataContract SelectByID(string id)
{
    using (Northwind db = new Northwind())
    {
        int empId = int.Parse(id);
        var query = from e in db.Employees
                    where e.EmployeeID == empId
                    select new EmployeeDataContract()
                    {
                        EmployeeID = e.EmployeeID,
                        FirstName = e.FirstName,
                        LastName = e.LastName,
                        HomePhone = e.HomePhone,
                        Notes = e.Notes
                    };
        return query.SingleOrDefault();
    }
}

public string Insert(EmployeeDataContract obj)
{
    using (Northwind db = new Northwind())
    {
        Employee emp = new Employee();
        Emp.EmployeeID = obj.EmployeeID;
        emp.FirstName = emp.FirstName;
        emp.LastName = emp.LastName;
        emp.HomePhone = emp.HomePhone;
        emp.Notes = emp.Notes;
        db.Employees.Add(emp);
        db.SaveChanges();
        return "Employee added successfully!";
    }
}

public string Update(string id,EmployeeDataContract obj)
{
    using (Northwind db = new Northwind())
    {
        Employee emp = db.Employees.Find(int.Parse(id));
        emp.FirstName = obj.FirstName;
        emp.LastName = obj.LastName;
        emp.HomePhone = obj.HomePhone;
        emp.Notes = obj.Notes;
        db.SaveChanges();
        return "Employee modified successfully!";
    }
}

public string Delete(string id)
{
    using (Northwind db = new Northwind())
```

```
        {
            Employee emp = db.Employees.Find(int.Parse(id));
            db.Employees.Remove(emp);
            db.SaveChanges();
            return "Employee deleted successfully!";
        }
    }
}
```

This implementation should be familiar to you because SelectAll(), SelectByID(), and Update() are quite similar to the previous example.

The Insert() method accepts a new EmployeeDataContract object and constructs a new employee from it. It then adds the newly created employee to the Employees DbSet. The SaveChanges() method saves the data to the database.

The Delete() method accepts an EmployeeID to be deleted. Inside, it finds that employee and removes them from the Employees DbSet using Remove() method. The SaveChanges() method saves the changes to the database.

Now, open the web.config file and add the configuration shown in Listing 10-14.

Listing 10-14. Configuring of the EmployeeManager Service

```xml
<system.serviceModel>
  <services>
    <service name="EmployeeWCFServiceREST.EmployeeManager"
            behaviorConfiguration="EmployeeWCFServiceRESTBehavior">
      <endpoint address=""
                binding="webHttpBinding"
                contract="EmployeeWCFServiceREST.IEmployeeManager"
                behaviorConfiguration="web">
      </endpoint>
    </service>
  </services>

  <behaviors>
    <serviceBehaviors>
      <behavior name="EmployeeWCFServiceRESTBehavior">
        <serviceMetadata httpGetEnabled="true" httpsGetEnabled="true" />
        <serviceDebug includeExceptionDetailInFaults="false" />
      </behavior>
      <behavior>
        <serviceMetadata httpGetEnabled="true" httpsGetEnabled="true" />
        <serviceDebug includeExceptionDetailInFaults="false" />
      </behavior>
    </serviceBehaviors>
    <endpointBehaviors>
      <behavior name="web">
        <webHttp/>
      </behavior>
    </endpointBehaviors>
  </behaviors>
</system.serviceModel>
```

This configuration is quite similar to what you used in the previous host applications. The main difference is it uses webHttpBinding binding rather than basicHttpBinding.

This completes the EmployeeManager REST service. And now it's time to consume it from a client application.

Creating a Client That Consumes the EmployeeManager REST Service

The client application that consumes the EmployeeManager REST service will be a Windows Forms application. This application is shown in Figure 10-16.

Figure 10-16. *Client application consuming the REST service*

The client application looks quite similar to the one you developed in the earlier example. But now it has two more buttons—Insert and Delete—for invoking the respective operations. Entering details of a new employee except EmployeeID and clicking the Insert button adds that employee. Since EmployeeID is an identity column, you don't need to specify it from the user interface. Selecting an EmployeeID from the combo box and clicking on the Delete button deletes that employee. The success message returned from insert, update, and delete operations is displayed in a Label control placed below the buttons.

Although the client application's user interface resembles the previous example, the internal workings are totally different. Previously you created a proxy in the client application and then invoked the desired methods on the proxy. That was alright since the service was operations-based. Now this client application wants to consume a REST service. Here, HTTP verbs decide what methods of the service are to be invoked. So, no proxy generation is necessary. Instead, this application will use the HttpClient component from the System.Net.Http namespace. Let's see how.

The Load event handler of the form is shown in Listing 10-15.

Listing 10-15. Getting Employee Data When the Form Loads

```
private HttpClient client;

private void Form1_Load(object sender, EventArgs e)
{
    client = new HttpClient();
    client.BaseAddress = new Uri("http://localhost:49833");
    client.DefaultRequestHeaders.Accept.Add(new MediaTypeWithQualityHeaderValue
    ("application/xml"));
    HttpResponseMessage response = client.GetAsync("/EmployeeManager.svc/employees").Result;
    string xmlData = response.Content.ReadAsStringAsync().Result;
    XmlDocument doc = new XmlDocument();
    doc.LoadXml(xmlData);
    XmlNodeList list = doc.GetElementsByTagName("EmployeeID");
    foreach(XmlNode item in list)
    {
        comboBox1.Items.Add(item.InnerText);
    }
}
```

The code declares an HttpClient variable—client—for calling the REST service. Since we want to call the services from multiple places, this object is created at form level rather than a local variable of the event handler.

The Load event handler instantiates the HttpClient and sets its BaseAddress property to the base URL, where the REST service is located. In our case this is the URL of the web application where we added the EmployeeManager.svc file. Make sure to change the port number as per your setup. You can easily get this URL by viewing the .svc file in a browser.

The next line adds the Accept header to the DefaultRequestHeaders collection. The Accept header value of application/xml means the service should return data in XML format.

Then the code calls the SelectAll() of the service. Notice that nowhere the operation name is mentioned. The code uses the GetAsync() method of the HttpClient object and specifies the endpoint URL of the service. Recollect that IEmployeeManager specifies this UriTemplate. The GetAsync() method uses GET verb to make the request. All the methods of HttpClient are asynchronous in nature. Accessing the Result property blocks the current thread until the method completes.

The GetAsync() method returns HttpResponseMessage—an object that wraps the actual return value. To grab the actual value, you use the ReadAsStringAsync() method. The ReadAsStringAsync() method returns the XML representation of the data returned by the REST service. This XML fragment is then loaded in an XmlDocument. Since we want to fill the combo box with EmployeeID values, all the <EmployeeID> elements are retrieved using the GetElementsByTagName() method. A foreach loop iterates through the retrieved elements and fills the combo box as desired.

If you observe the xmlData string variable in the Quick Watch window of Visual Studio, you will see XML markup as shown in Listing 10-16.

Listing 10-16. REST Service Returns Data in XML Format

```
<ArrayOfEmployeeDataContract xmlns="http://schemas.datacontract.org/2004/07/
EmployeeWCFServiceREST" xmlns:i="http://www.w3.org/2001/XMLSchema-instance">
<EmployeeDataContract>
<EmployeeID>1</EmployeeID>
<FirstName>Nancy</FirstName>
<HomePhone>(206) 555-9857</HomePhone>
```

```
<LastName>Davolio</LastName>
<Notes>Education includes a BA in psychology from Colorado State University in
1970.  She also completed "The Art of the Cold Call."  Nancy is a member of Toastmasters
International.</Notes>
</EmployeeDataContract>
....
....
</ArrayOfEmployeeDataContract>
```

■ **Note**   Here we use the raw XML returned by the WCF REST service. If you want, you can load this XML data into Employee/EmployeeDataContract objects in the client application (you will need to create these classes in the client application). This way, the client application can process these objects as needed. We won't do that here because our primary interest is to see how the XML data format is used by these frameworks.

Okay, now let's see how `SelectByID()` can be called in the `SelectedIndexChanged` event handler of the combo box (see Listing 10-17).

Listing 10-17. Calling the SelectByID() Method

```
private void comboBox1_SelectedIndexChanged(object sender, EventArgs e)
{
    HttpResponseMessage response = client.GetAsync("/EmployeeManager.svc/employees/" +
    comboBox1.SelectedItem).Result;
    string xmlData = response.Content.ReadAsStringAsync().Result;
    XmlDocument doc = new XmlDocument();
    doc.LoadXml(xmlData);
    textBox1.Text = doc.GetElementsByTagName("FirstName")[0].InnerText;
    textBox2.Text = doc.GetElementsByTagName("LastName")[0].InnerText;
    textBox3.Text = doc.GetElementsByTagName("HomePhone")[0].InnerText;
    textBox4.Text = doc.GetElementsByTagName("Notes")[0].InnerText;
    label6.Text = "";
}
```

This code is similar to the previous listing. However, the `GetAsync()` method also passes an EmployeeID in the URL. This way `SelectByID()` method of the REST service is called. The remaining code simply reads the returned XML data and fills various text boxes with FirstName, LastName, HomePhone and Notes values.

The `Click` event handler of the Insert button is responsible for calling the `Insert()` method of the REST service. This event handler is shown in Listing 10-18.

Listing 10-18. Calling the Insert() Method of the REST Service

```
private void button1_Click(object sender, EventArgs e)
{
    string xmlEmp = $"<EmployeeDataContract xmlns='http://schemas.datacontract.
    org/2004/07/EmployeeWCFServiceREST' xmlns:i='http://www.w3.org/2001/XMLSchema-
    instance'><FirstName>{textBox1.Text}</FirstName><HomePhone>{textBox3.Text}</
    HomePhone><LastName>{textBox2.Text}</LastName><Notes>{textBox4.Text}</Notes></
    EmployeeDataContract>";

    HttpContent content = new StringContent(xmlEmp, Encoding.UTF8, "application/xml");

    HttpResponseMessage response = client.PostAsync("/EmployeeManager.svc/employees",
    content).Result;

    string xmlMsg = response.Content.ReadAsStringAsync().Result;

    XmlDocument doc = new XmlDocument();
    doc.LoadXml(xmlMsg);
    label6.Text = doc.DocumentElement.InnerText;

}
```

We have configured the REST service to use XML format for the request as well as the response. While adding an employee, we first need to form an XML fragment that represents an EmployeeDataContract object. This is done by creating an XML fragment as shown. The XML fragment basically creates a <EmployeeDataContract></EmployeeDataContract> element with four child elements—<FirstName>, <LastName>, <HomePhone>, and <Notes>. The values of these child elements are set from the respective text boxes. As you can see, the name of the root element matches the name of the data contract class and the names of the child elements correspond to the names of the data members.

Then the XML fragment is wrapped inside a StringContent object. And then PostAsync() method of HttpClient is called. The PostAsync() method makes a POST request to the specified service. The StringContent object containing the employee details also accompanies the request.

The Insert() method of the service returns a success message. This message is unpacked from HttpResponseMessage using the ReadAsStringAsync() method. This message is then displayed in a Label control.

The Client event handler of the Update button is similar and is shown in Listing 10-19.

Listing 10-19. Calling the Update() Method of the REST Service

```
private void button2_Click(object sender, EventArgs e)
{
    string xmlEmp = $"<EmployeeDataContract xmlns='http://schemas.datacontract.
    org/2004/07/EmployeeWCFServiceREST' xmlns:i='http://www.w3.org/2001/XMLSchema-in
    stance'><EmployeeID>{comboBox1.SelectedItem}</EmployeeID><FirstName>{textBox1.
    Text}</FirstName><HomePhone>{textBox3.Text}</HomePhone><LastName>{textBox2.Text}</
    LastName><Notes>{textBox4.Text}</Notes></EmployeeDataContract>";

    HttpContent content = new StringContent(xmlEmp, Encoding.UTF8, "application/xml");

    HttpResponseMessage response = client.PutAsync("/EmployeeManager.svc/employees/" +
    comboBox1.SelectedItem, content).Result;
```

```
    string xmlMsg = response.Content.ReadAsStringAsync().Result;

    XmlDocument doc = new XmlDocument();
    doc.LoadXml(xmlMsg);
    label6.Text = doc.DocumentElement.InnerText;
}
```

The main difference here is that PutAsync() method of HttpClient has been called. Doing so makes a PUT request to the service. The request URL also includes the EmployeeID to be modified.

Finally, the Click event handler of the Delete button does the job of calling the Delete() method of the service and is shown in Listing 10-20.

Listing 10-20. Calling Delete() Method of the REST Service

```
private void button3_Click(object sender, EventArgs e)
{
    HttpResponseMessage response = client.DeleteAsync("/EmployeeManager.svc/employees/" +
    comboBox1.SelectedItem).Result;
    string xmlMsg = response.Content.ReadAsStringAsync().Result;
    XmlDocument doc = new XmlDocument();
    doc.LoadXml(xmlMsg);
    label6.Text = doc.DocumentElement.InnerText;
}
```

Here, the code calls the DeleteAsync() method of HttpClient. The EmployeeID to be deleted is passed as a part of the URL.

This completes the client application. Run the client and see whether the combo box gets filled with the existing EmployeeID values. Also try adding, modifying, and deleting employees to confirm the workings of the EmployeeManager REST service.

Creating a REST Service Using Web API

Now that you know what it takes to create a REST service using WCF, let's see how Web API can be put to use for that purpose. In this section, you create a Web API service that exposes the CRUD functionality just as the WCF service you created in the previous section. A Windows Forms-based client application then consumes the service.

Begin by creating a new ASP.NET web application based on the Web API project template (see Figure 10-17).

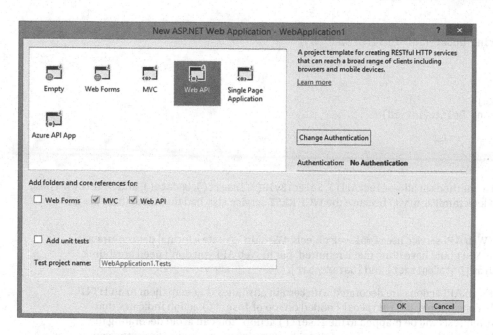

Figure 10-17. *Creating a project based on Web API template*

The newly created project contains a Web API service. Rename that service (file as well as the class) to EmployeeManagerController. Next, generate the Entity Framework model for the Employees table of the Northwind database, as you did in the previous examples.

Open the EmployeeManagerController in the Visual Studio Editor. You will notice that the EmployeeManagerController class inherits from ApiController. Then write the actions that perform the CRUD operations in the EmployeeManagerController. The skeleton of these actions is shown in Listing 10-21.

Listing 10-21. Skeleton of the Web API Service

```
public class EmployeeManagerController : ApiController
{
    [HttpGet]
    public List<Employee> SelectAll()
    {
    }

    [HttpGet]
    public Employee SelectByID(int id)
    {
    }

    [HttpPost]
    public string Insert(Employee obj)
    {
    }
```

```
[HttpPut]
public string Update(int id, Employee obj)
{
}

[HttpDelete]
public string Delete(int id)
{
}
}
```

There are five methods in all—SelectAll(), SelectByID(), Insert(), Update(), and Delete(). These methods should look familiar to you because the WCF REST service also had them. But there are a few differences:

- The Web API service uses Employee objects. We didn't create a formal data contract here. You could have done that if required, but in Web API you don't need attributes such as [DataContract] and [DataMember].

- The Web API actions are decorated with certain attributes that map them to an HTTP verb. For example, the [HttpPost] added on top of Insert() action indicates that POST requests will be mapped to the Insert() action. You can avoid decorating the actions with these attributes if you follow the default naming convention—the action name begins with the HTTP verb it handles. For example, Get() is automatically mapped to the GET verb, Post() is automatically mapped to the POST verb, and so on.

The inside code of these actions is very similar to the EmployeeManager WCF service. So, we won't discuss all of them here. For the sake of clarity, only SelectAll() and Post() are shown in Listing 10-22.

Listing 10-22. The SelectAll() and Post() Web API Actions

```
[HttpGet]
public List<Employee> SelectAll()
{
    using (Northwind db = new Northwind())
    {
        var query = from e in db.Employees
                    orderby e.EmployeeID ascending
                    select e;
        return query.ToList();
    }
}

[HttpPost]
public string Insert(Employee obj)
{
    using (Northwind db = new Northwind())
    {
        Employee emp = db.Employees.Find(obj.EmployeeID);
        emp.FirstName = emp.FirstName;
        emp.LastName = emp.LastName;
        emp.HomePhone = emp.HomePhone;
        emp.Notes = emp.Notes;
```

```
        db.Employees.Add(emp);
        db.SaveChanges();
        return "Employee added successfully!";
    }
}
```

Unlike WCF, Web API doesn't require any host configuration to be added to web.config. That's the benefit of the simple programming model offered by Web API.

Creating a Client That Consumes the EmployeeManager Web API Service

The client application that consumes the Web API is quite similar to the WCF client application you created earlier and is shown in Figure 10-18.

Figure 10-18. *Client application that calls the Web API*

Although the client application is quite similar to what you developed earlier, there are two differences:

- The endpoint URL to the REST service will now change and will follow the Web API conventions.

- Since the Web API is now returning and accepting Employee objects, the XML data received and sent from the client will be wrapped inside an <Employee> element.

To understand how these changes are reflected in the code, Listing 10-23 shows the Load event handler of the form.

Listing 10-23. Load Event Handler Receives Employee Objects in XML Format

```
private void Form1_Load(object sender, EventArgs e)
{
    client = new HttpClient();
    client.BaseAddress = new Uri("http://localhost:49443");
    client.DefaultRequestHeaders.Accept.Add(new MediaTypeWithQualityHeaderValue("applicati
on/xml"));

    HttpResponseMessage response = client.GetAsync("/api/EmployeeManager").Result;
    string xmlData = response.Content.ReadAsStringAsync().Result;

    XmlDocument doc = new XmlDocument();
    doc.LoadXml(xmlData);

    XmlNodeList list = doc.GetElementsByTagName("EmployeeID");
    foreach(XmlNode item in list)
    {
        comboBox1.Items.Add(item.InnerText);
    }

}
```

Notice the lines marked in bold. The `BaseAddress` property now points to the address of Web API application. You should change the port number as per your setup.

The second bold line specifies the URL of the Web API. Notice that the URL takes the form / `api/<api_controller>`. This pattern comes from the default route of Web API and you can change it in the `WebApiConfig.cs` file of the Web API project.

If you observe the `xmlData` returned from the Web API, you should see something like this:

```
<ArrayOfEmployee xmlns:i="http://www.w3.org/2001/XMLSchema-instance" xmlns="http://schemas.
datacontract.org/2004/07/EmployeeWebAPIService.Models">
<Employee>
  <EmployeeID>1</EmployeeID>
  <FirstName>Nancy</FirstName>
  <HomePhone>(206) 555-9857</HomePhone>
  <LastName>Davolio</LastName>
  <Notes>Education includes a BA in psychology from Colorado State University in 1970.
  She also completed "The Art of the Cold Call." Nancy is a member of Toastmasters
  International.</Notes>
</Employee>
....
</ArrayOfEmployee>
```

As you can see, the employee details are now wrapped inside an `<Employee>` element.

This also means that during POST and PUT operations, you should send the data wrapped inside an `<Employee>` element. For example, consider the code shown in Listing 10-24, which shows the `Click` event handler of the Update button.

Listing 10-24. Calling PutAsync() to Modify an Employee

```
private void button2_Click(object sender, EventArgs e)
{
    string xmlEmp = $"<Employee xmlns='http://schemas.datacontract.org/2004/07/
    EmployeeWebAPIService.Models' xmlns:i='http://www.w3.org/2001/XMLSchema-instance'>
    <EmployeeID>{comboBox1.SelectedItem}</EmployeeID><FirstName>{textBox1.Text}
    </FirstName><HomePhone>{textBox3.Text}</HomePhone><LastName>{textBox2.Text}
    </LastName><Notes>{textBox4.Text}</Notes></Employee>";

    HttpContent content = new StringContent(xmlEmp, Encoding.UTF8, "application/xml");
    HttpResponseMessage response = client.PutAsync("/api/EmployeeManager/" + comboBox1.
    SelectedItem, content).Result;
    string xmlMsg = response.Content.ReadAsStringAsync().Result;
    XmlDocument doc = new XmlDocument();
    doc.LoadXml(xmlMsg);
    label6.Text = doc.DocumentElement.InnerText;
}
```

The modified employee details are now wrapped inside the <Employee> element along with the namespace details.

Other event handlers are not discussed here since they are quite similar to the previous examples. Just take care of these couple of differences and complete them on your own (or grab them from the book's source code).

Once the client application is ready, run the application and test whether CRUD operations work as expected.

Using XmlSerializer Instead of DataContractSerializer

Just like WCF services, Web API also uses DataContractSerializer for the sake of performing XML serialization. If you want to use XmlSerializer instead, you need to configure the Web API accordingly.

To configure the Web API to use XmlSerializer instead of DataContractSerializer, open the WebApiConfig.cs file from the App_Start folder. Then add the code shown in Listing 10-25.

Listing 10-25. Configuring Web API to Use XmlSerializer

```
public static void Register(HttpConfiguration config)
{
    config.MapHttpAttributeRoutes();
    config.Formatters.XmlFormatter.UseXmlSerializer = true;
    config.Routes.MapHttpRoute(
        name: "DefaultApi",
        routeTemplate: "api/{controller}/{id}",
        defaults: new { id = RouteParameter.Optional }
    );
}
```

Notice the code shown in bold. The UseXmlSerializer property of the XmlFormatter (XmlFormatter is an object of XmlMediaTypeFormatter) is set to true. Since the Web API is now configured to use XmlSerializer, you no longer need to specify those data contract XML namespaces while sending data to the Web API.

Summary

This chapter introduced you to two service development frameworks—Windows Communication Foundation (WCF) and Web API. WCF allows you to develop operations-based as well as resource-based REST services. On the other hand, Web API allows you to build resource based REST services. WCF and Web API can deal with variety of data formats, although JSON and XML are quite popular these days. Our interest was to see how data can be sent and received in XML format using these frameworks.

Creating an operations-based WCF service involves three pieces—service, host, and client application. The client application generates a proxy for the service to invoke its operations. WCF uses XML configuration for configuring the service. Moreover, WCF uses SOAP messages to pass the data over HTTP.

Creating a REST service using WCF and Web API involves two pieces—service and the client application. Both of these frameworks can use XML format for transferring the data over the wire. The client application doesn't create any proxy, rather it calls the service directly using `HttpClient`. A simple way to access the XML data returned by a REST service is to load it in `XmlDocument`.

■ ■ ■

CHAPTER 11

XML in SQL Server

Most business applications store data in some kind of datastore, which is usually a relational database. To that end, SQL Server is one of Microsoft's flagship products. Since many applications rely on the XML data, that Microsoft found it necessary to incorporate strong support for XML in their database engine.

Because SQL Server is such a popular database, it is worth learning its XML features. Moreover, it would be interesting to see how these features can be consumed from the applications built on top of the .NET Framework. In this chapter, you learn about the following:

- Using XML extensions to the SELECT statement of the SQL Server

- Using SQLXML managed classes

- Working with the new XML data type

You should note, however, that an extensive examination of all the XML features of SQL Server is out of the scope of this book. The intention here is to make you familiar with the XML capabilities of SQL Server.

■ **Note** I used SQL Server 2012 Developer Edition to develop the examples of this chapter. Many of the examples should work with earlier versions (such as SQL Server 2010) of the product also, but I suggest you install the latest versions to avoid any mismatch. You'll also need to install the SQLXML managed classes. You can download SQLXML from Microsoft's official web site.

Using XML Extensions to the SELECT Statement

In SQL Server, you can execute SELECT statements that return the results in XML format. In Chapter 7, you got a taste of this feature while using the ExecuteXmlReader() method of the SqlCommand class. Now it's time to look at these extensions in detail.

The FOR XML Clause

To fetch the FOR XML clause SQL Server data in XML format, you need to use the FOR XML clause with the SELECT statement. The FOR XML clause has four modes that allow you to return the XML results in different formats. The modes of the FOR XML clause are listed in Table 11-1.

Table 11-1. *Modes of the FOR XML Clause*

Mode	Description
AUTO	Returns the results of the SELECT query as XML fragments. By default it returns the data as XML elements. The name of the XML element is the same as the table name, and column values are returned as XML attributes. You have the option to return all the columns as elements instead of attributes.
RAW	Returns the results as a `<row>` element. The column values are returned as XML attributes.
PATH	Allows you to define the nesting of the returned XML by using simple XPath syntax.
EXPLICIT	Defines a schema for the returned results explicitly in the SELECT query.

To test these modes of the FOR XML clause, you will execute some SELECT queries against the Northwind database. To execute the queries, you can either use SQL Server Management Studio or Server Explorer of Visual Studio (shown in Figure 11-1).

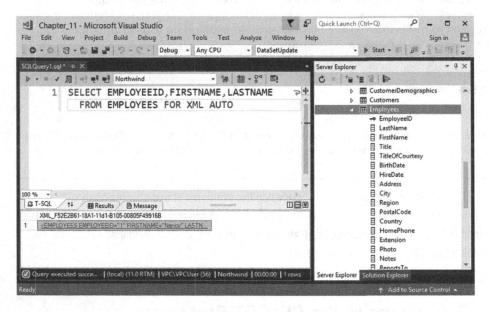

Figure 11-1. *The Server Explorer of Visual Studio with Query window*

The AUTO Mode

Open SQL Server Management Studio and issue the SELECT statement shown in Listing 11-1.

Listing 11-1. Using the AUTO Mode of the FOR XML Clause

```
SELECT EMPLOYEEID,FIRSTNAME,LASTNAME FROM EMPLOYEES FOR XML AUTO
```

```
<EMPLOYEES EMPLOYEEID="1" FIRSTNAME="Nancy" LASTNAME="Davolio"/>
<EMPLOYEES EMPLOYEEID="2" FIRSTNAME="Andrew" LASTNAME="Fuller"/>
<EMPLOYEES EMPLOYEEID="3" FIRSTNAME="Janet" LASTNAME="Leverling"/>
....
```

The SELECT statement from Listing 11-1 selects three columns—EmployeeID, FirstName, and LastName—from the Employees table. Listing 11-1 also shows the returned data in XML format. Notice how the table name is used for the XML element names (<EMPLOYEES>), and column names are used for attribute names.

Have you noticed something about the character casing of the returned XML? It depends totally on the table name and columns used in the SELECT statement. For example, if you specify column names in uppercase, the XML attributes will be in uppercase. You may need to keep this in mind while parsing the XML data in your application. By default, the AUTO mode returns all the column values as XML attributes. If you want, you can return them as elements instead. This is achieved by using the ELEMENTS clause with the AUTO mode. Listing 11-2 shows how the ELEMENTS clause works.

Listing 11-2. Using the ELEMENTS Clause of the AUTO Mode

```
SELECT EMPLOYEEID,FIRSTNAME,LASTNAME FROM EMPLOYEES FOR XML AUTO,ELEMENTS
```

```
<EMPLOYEES>
<EMPLOYEEID>1</EMPLOYEEID>
<FIRSTNAME>Nancy</FIRSTNAME>
<LASTNAME>Davolio</LASTNAME>
</EMPLOYEES>
....
```

As you can see, we specify the ELEMENTS clause after the AUTO mode. Notice how the column values are returned as elements this time. The names of the elements are the same as the column names.

■ **Note**   The XML data returned by the FOR XML clause in the preceding code is not well formed by default. It doesn't include the root element. However, as you will see later, you can specify the root element yourself.

The RAW Mode

The RAW mode of the FOR XML clause returns the XML data as zero or more XML elements. By default, the name of the elements is <row>. You can change this default behavior by specifying an element name yourself. The column values are returned as XML attributes. Listing 11-3 shows the use of RAW mode.

Listing 11-3. Using the RAW Mode of the FOR XML Clause

```
SELECT EmployeeID,FirstName,LastName FROM Employees FOR XML RAW
```

```
<row EmployeeID="1" FirstName="Nancy" LastName="Davolio"/>
<row EmployeeID="2" FirstName="Andrew" LastName="Fuller"/>
<row EmployeeID="3" FirstName="Janet" LastName="Leverling"/>
<row EmployeeID="4" FirstName="Margaret" LastName="Peacock"/>
....
```

As you can see, the FOR XML clause is followed by the RAW mode. The returned XML contains <row> elements with attributes holding the column values. If you want to change the default element name, you can specify your own element name, as shown in Listing 11-4.

Listing 11-4. Assigning a Custom Element Name to the Output of RAW Mode

```
SELECT EmployeeID,FirstName,LastName FROM Employees FOR XML RAW ('Employee')
```

```
<Employee EmployeeID="1" FirstName="Nancy" LastName="Davolio"/>
<Employee EmployeeID="2" FirstName="Andrew" LastName="Fuller"/>
<Employee EmployeeID="3" FirstName="Janet" LastName="Leverling"/>
<Employee EmployeeID="4" FirstName="Margaret" LastName="Peacock"/>
....
```

As you can see, we've now specified Employee as the element name in parentheses. This element name is given to all the returned rows.

Returning the Schema of the XML

The XMLSCHEMA clause of the FOR XML clause allows you to return the XSD Schema of the XML data being returned. You may use this schema to validate your data further in your application. Listing 11-5 shows how the XMLSCHEMA clause is used.

Listing 11-5. Returning an XML Schema

```
SELECT EmployeeID,FirstName,LastName FROM Employees FOR XML AUTO, XMLSCHEMA
```

```xml
<xsd:schema targetNamespace="urn:schemas-microsoft-com:sql:SqlRowSet1"
xmlns:schema="urn:schemas-microsoft-com:sql:SqlRowSet1"
xmlns:xsd="http://www.w3.org/2001/XMLSchema"
xmlns:sqltypes="http://schemas.microsoft.com/sqlserver/2004/sqltypes"
elementFormDefault="qualified">
<xsd:import namespace="http://schemas.microsoft.com/sqlserver/2004/sqltypes"
schemaLocation="http://schemas.microsoft.com/sqlserver/2004/sqltypes/sqltypes.xsd"/>
<xsd:element name="Employees">
<xsd:complexType>
<xsd:attribute name="EmployeeID" type="sqltypes:int" use="required"/>
<xsd:attribute name="FirstName" use="required">
<xsd:simpleType><xsd:restriction base="sqltypes:nvarchar" sqltypes:localeId="1033"
sqltypes:sqlCompareOptions="IgnoreCase IgnoreKanaType IgnoreWidth"
sqltypes:sqlSortId="52">
<xsd:maxLength value="10"/>
</xsd:restriction>
</xsd:simpleType>
</xsd:attribute>
<xsd:attribute name="LastName" use="required">
<xsd:simpleType>
<xsd:restriction base="sqltypes:nvarchar" sqltypes:localeId="1033"
sqltypes:sqlCompareOptions="IgnoreCase IgnoreKanaType IgnoreWidth"
sqltypes:sqlSortId="52">
<xsd:maxLength value="20"/>
</xsd:restriction>
</xsd:simpleType>
</xsd:attribute>
```

```
</xsd:complexType>
</xsd:element>
</xsd:schema>
<Employees xmlns="urn:schemas-microsoft-com:sql:SqlRowSet1" EmployeeID="1"
FirstName="Nancy" LastName="Davolio"/>
<Employees xmlns="urn:schemas-microsoft-com:sql:SqlRowSet1" EmployeeID="2"
FirstName="Andrew" LastName="Fuller"/>
....
```

As you can see, the XMLSCHEMA clause returns the XML Schema along with the data.

The PATH Mode

Though the AUTO and RAW modes return data in XML format, you have very little control over the nesting and naming conventions of the returned data. The PATH mode, on the other hand, allows you to specify the nesting structure as well as element and attribute names by using simple XPath syntax. Suppose you want to retrieve records from the Employees table in the format shown in Listing 11-6.

Listing 11-6. Custom Nesting and Naming

```
<Employee ID="1">
<Name>
<FirstName>Nancy</FirstName>
<LastName>Davolio</LastName>
</Name>
</Employee>
```

Each record is to be returned as an <Employee> element. The EmployeeID column value is to be returned as the ID attribute of the <Employee> element. There should be an element named <Name> with two sub-elements: <FirstName> and <LastName>. The <FirstName> and <LastName> elements should contain data from the FirstName and LastName columns, respectively. To retrieve XML data in this format, you can use the PATH mode, as shown in Listing 11-7.

Listing 11-7. Using the PATH Mode of the FOR XML Clause

```
SELECT EmployeeID "@ID",FirstName "Name/FirstName",LastName "Name/LastName"
FROM Employees FOR XML PATH ('Employee')
```

As you can see, the SELECT query now specifies certain extra pieces of information along with the column names. We want to return the EmployeeID column value as the ID attribute and hence the query adds @ID after the EmployeeID column. Similarly, the FirstName and the LastName columns are followed by the desired nesting and element names, that is, Name/FirstName and Name/LastName, respectively. The name of the element generated is specified after the PATH mode in parentheses. Notice how the XPath syntax (@, /) is used to specify the attributes and element nesting.

The EXPLICIT Mode

The EXPLICIT mode is possibly the most confusing mode of the FOR XML clause. On the one hand, it increases the complexity of the SELECT statement, but on the other, it gives much more fine-grained control on the resultant output.

■ **Note**   I discuss the EXPLICIT mode only to the extent of giving a feeling of how it renders the XML output. In no way does this book try to teach you the EXPLICIT mode apart from the basics. If you want to learn about the EXPLICIT mode in detail, you may consider reading the official product documentation.

Suppose that you want to return the XML content as shown in Listing 11-8.

Listing 11-8. Customized XML Output Using EXPLICIT Mode

```
<Employee EmpID="1">
<FirstName>Nancy</FirstName>
<LastName>Davolio</LastName>
</Employee>
```

You can identity two levels in this markup. Level 1 consists of the <Employee> element, and level 2 consists of the <FirstName> and <LastName> elements. The EmployeeID column is outputted as the EmpID attribute of the <Employee> element and hence belongs to level 1.

When using EXPLICIT mode to generate this XML output, we need to write two SELECT queries:

- The first query will outline the structure, nesting, and element names of the various columns involved.

- The second query will actually fetch the data. The results of the two queries will be merged with a UNION clause.

Let's look at the first SELECT query (see Listing 11-9).

Listing 11-9. Defining the Structure of the XML Output

```
SELECT
1 AS Tag,
NULL AS Parent,
EmployeeID AS [Employee!1!EmpID],
FirstName AS [Employee!1!FirstName!element],
LastName AS [Employee!1!LastName!element]
FROM Employees
```

The query selects five columns: 1, NULL, EmployeeID, FirstName, and LastName. The last three columns are obvious, but what are 1 and NULL? The Tag and Parent columns are implicit columns in the resultant table that are created by SQL Server internally:

- The Tag column specifies the nesting level of the current element. A Tag value of 1 indicates that this query is defining the structure for level 1 of the XML output.

- The Parent column specifies the parent level of the current tag. A Parent value of NULL indicates that this is the top-level element.

Each column specified after the Parent column has some metadata specifications enclosed in square brackets. Multiple pieces of metadata are separated by an exclamation character (!):

- The first part indicates the name of the parent element of the current element or attribute.

- The second part indicates the tag number of the element.

- The third part indicates the name of the current element or attribute.

- If you specify only these three parts, the column value will be outputted as an attribute. To specify that it should be outputted as an element, you must specify the fourth part. The fourth part is a predefined keyword called element.

In our example, the top-level element is <Employee>. This top-level element name is decided by the first real column in the SELECT list (in our case, EmployeeID). The top-level element name is picked up from the first piece of metadata information specified after the EmployeeID column. We want to output the EmployeeID column value as an attribute named EmpID. Thus the parent level of the EmpID attribute is tag 1. Finally, the third piece of metadata information specifies that the attribute name is EmpID.

The metadata for the FirstName and LastName columns specifies that their parent is the level 1 element and they are to be outputted as <FirstName> and <LastName> elements, respectively.

The second SELECT query is shown in Listing 11-10.

Listing 11-10. Fetching the Data for the Structure Defined in the Previous Query

```
SELECT
1,
NULL,
EmployeeID,
FirstName,
LastName
FROM Employees
ORDER BY
[Employee!1!EmpID],
[Employee!1!FirstName!element],
[Employee!1!LastName!element]
FOR XML EXPLICIT
```

The query selects data for tag 1 and selects the EmployeeID, FirstName, and LastName columns. The ORDER BY clause indicates the sequence in which the elements will appear in the resultant XML. Finally, the query adds a FOR XML EXPLICIT clause.

Now that you understand both queries, you can use the UNION ALL clause, as shown in Listing 11-11.

Listing 11-11. Using the UNION ALL Clause

```
SELECT
1 AS Tag,
NULL AS Parent,
EmployeeID AS [Employee!1!EmpID],
FirstName AS [Employee!1!FirstName!element],
LastName AS [Employee!1!LastName!element]
FROM Employees
UNION All
SELECT
1,NULL,
EmployeeID,
FirstName,
LastName
FROM Employees
ORDER BY [Employee!1!EmpID],
```

```
[Employee!1!FirstName!element],
[Employee!1!LastName!element]
FOR XML EXPLICIT
```

The UNION ALL clause combines the results of both of these queries, and you get the XML output shown in Listing 11-8. Let's go a bit further and assume that you want to retrieve XML in the format shown in Listing 11-12.

Listing 11-12. XML Output with Deeper Nesting

```
<Employee empid="1">
<Name>
<FName>Nancy</FName>
<LName>Davolio</LName>
</Name>
</Employee>
```

The XML output has one more level of nesting. The <FName> and <LName> elements are enclosed in the <Name> element, which in turn is enclosed in the <Employee> element. The EmployeeID column is outputted as an empid attribute. The SELECT queries required to generate this output are given in Listing 11-13.

Listing 11-13. SELECT Queries for Generating Output as Shown in Listing 11-12

```
SELECT
1 AS Tag,
NULL AS Parent,
EmployeeID AS [employee!1!empid],
FirstName AS [Name!2!FName!element],
LastName AS [Name!2!LName!element]
FROM Employees

UNION ALL

SELECT 2 AS Tag,
1 AS Parent,
EmployeeID,
FirstName,
LastName
FROM Employees
ORDER BY
[Employee!1!empid],
[Name!2!FName!element],
[Name!2!LName!element]
FOR XML EXPLICIT
```

The first SELECT statement defines the structure of the resultant XML output. Notice that this time, the FirstName and LastName columns define their parent element as <Name> and have a tag level of 2. They also define element names for the FirstName and LastName columns as <FName> and <LName>, respectively. The second query defines tag 2. It specifies that the parent of tag 2 is tag 1 via the Parent column. It orders the result set by using the ORDER BY clause as before. If you run this script in Management Studio, you should see the XML output shown in Listing 11-12.

Specifying the Root Element Name

In all the preceding queries, you obtained XML markup for an individual table row, but there was no root element specified for the markup. If you want, you can specify the root element by adding the ROOT clause, as shown in Listing 11-14.

Listing 11-14. Using the ROOT Clause

```
SELECT EmployeeID,FirstName,LastName FROM Employees FOR XML AUTO, ROOT('MyRoot')
```

```
<MyRoot>
<Employees EmployeeID="1" FirstName="Nancy" LastName="Davolio"/>
<Employees EmployeeID="2" FirstName="Andrew" LastName="Fuller"/>
....
</MyRoot>
```

As you can see, the ROOT clause is appended at the end of the query with the name of the root element in parentheses. The returned XML is now wrapped inside this root element.

Using OPENXML

As you've seen, the FOR XML clause of SQL Server allows you to retrieve relational data in XML format. However, there is another way to do it—the OPENXML function, which allows you to read XML data in a relational fashion. Suppose that you have XML markup that contains a list of employees, and your aim is to import this list into your Employees table. In the absence of something like OPENXML, accomplishing this task would be tedious. As you will soon see, the OPENXML function makes your job much easier. Listing 11-15 shows the source XML markup containing the employee listing.

Listing 11-15. The Source XML Markup

```
<Employees>
<Employee EmployeeID="10" FirstName="John" LastName="Moore" />
<Employee EmployeeID="11" FirstName="Bill" LastName="Short" />
</Employees>
```

As you can see, the root element of the markup is <Employees>. Further, it contains <Employee> elements representing employee records. The EmployeeID, FirstName, and LastName appear as attributes of the <Employee> element. To read any XML markup by using the OPENXML function, you need to perform the following steps:

1. Prepare and load the XML document for processing.

2. Call the OPENXML function as per your need.

3. Remove the loaded XML document from memory.

These three steps are illustrated in Listing 11-16.

Listing 11-16. Using the OPENXML Function

```
SET IDENTITY_INSERT Employees ON
DECLARE @hDoc INT
DECLARE @xml VARCHAR(1000)

SET @xml=
'<Employees>
<Employee EmployeeID="10" FirstName="John" LastName="Gates" />
<Employee EmployeeID="11" FirstName="Bill" LastName="Short" />
</Employees>'

EXEC sp_xml:preparedocument @hDoc OUTPUT, @xml

INSERT INTO EMPLOYEES (EMPLOYEEID,FIRSTNAME,LASTNAME)
(
SELECT * FROM
OPENXML(@hDoc,'Employees/Employee',0)
WITH (EmployeeID int,FirstName varchar(50),LastName varchar(50))
)

EXEC sp_xml:removedocument @hDoc
```

The script in Listing 11-16 declares two variables named hDoc and xml. The integer variable hDoc is used later for storing a handle to the loaded XML document. The VARCHAR variable xml is used to store the XML markup shown in Listing 11-15 as a string. The SET statement assigns the XML markup to the xml variable. Then we call the sp_xml:preparedocument system stored procedure, which parses and loads the supplied XML markup in memory. It returns a handle to the loaded document in the form of an integer.

Next, this handle is collected in the hDoc variable that we declared earlier. Then an INSERT statement is executed, making use of the OPENXML function. Observe the call to OPENXML carefully. The OPENXML function is used in a SELECT statement as if it were a table. It accepts three parameters:

- The first parameter is a handle to the XML data loaded by using sp_xml:preparedocument.

- The second parameter is an XPath pattern pointing to the node of the XML data that is to be treated as a row. In our example, this base path is Employees/Employee.

- The third parameter is a flag indicating the mapping between the XML data and the relational rowset. The third parameter can take the values shown in Table 11-2.

Table 11-2. *Mapping Between XML Data and a Relational Rowset*

Flag Value	Description
0	Specifies that attributes of the XML elements are supplying column values for the relational rowset. This is the default.
1	Specifies that attributes of the XML elements are supplying column values for the relational rowset. When combined with a flag value of 2, attributes are picked up as column values and then element values are assigned to the remaining columns.
2	Specifies that elements of the source XML are supplying column values for the relational rowset.
8	This flag can be combined with 1 or 2 and indicates that the consumed data should not be copied to the overflow property @mp:xmltext.

Further, the WITH clause of OPENXML specifies the structure of the resultant rowset. The structure can be specified as a comma-separated list of column names and their data types. In our example, we have three columns: EmployeeID, FirstName, and LastName. Note that these column names are the same as the attribute names in the source XML markup.

Thus the rowset returned from the SELECT statement and OPENXML is fed to the INSERT statement. The INSERT statement then adds the data to the Employees table. In our example, it will add two rows.

After the INSERT operation is done, the XML document is removed from memory by using another system stored procedure: sp_xml:removedocument. This accepts the handle of an XML document loaded previously by using sp_xml:preparedocument and cleans up the memory consumed by the document. Calling sp_xml:removedocument is very important because failing to do so can waste valuable memory of your application.

■ **Note**   A thorough discussion of the OPENXML clause is outside the scope of this book. The aim here is to give you a basic understanding of the XML functionality of SQL Server.

Using SQLXML Features

SQLXML provides you with a set of managed classes, which you can use in your .NET applications to query the SQL Server database and read the returned results in XML format. You can also send updates from the client application in special XML formats, and SQL Server can update the database.

■ **Note**   Make sure to download and install SQLXML 4.0 SP1 before you continue with the remaining examples of this chapter.

The SQLXML Managed Classes

SQLXML provides you with a set of managed classes that can be used to execute queries against the database and return results in XML form. The classes provided by SQLXML physically reside in an assembly, called Microsoft.Data.SqlXml. The three core classes exposed by SQLXML are listed in Table 11-3.

Table 11-3. *SQLXML Managed Classes*

Class Name	Description
SqlXmlCommand	Allows you to execute queries as well as nonqueries against the database. This class exposes methods such as ExecuteNonQuery(), ExecuteStream(), and ExecuteXmlReader(). This class is analogous to the ADO.NET SqlCommand class.
SqlXmlParameter	Represents parameters to the queries executed by using the SqlXmlCommand class. This class is analogous to the ADO.NET SqlParameter class.
SqlXmlAdapter	Used to interact with the ADO.NET DataSet class. This class is analogous to the ADO.NET SqlDataAdapter class.

All the preceding classes can use the SQL Server OLEDB (SQLOLEDB) provider or the SQL Native Client to communicate with the underlying database. In the next few sections, you learn how the SQLXML classes can be used in your .NET applications.

Executing SELECT Queries

Let's begin by developing an application that will allow you to execute SELECT queries against the SQL Server database. The application user interface is shown in Figure 11-2.

Figure 11-2. *Application for executing SELECT queries via SqlXmlCommand*

The application consists of a text box for entering SELECT queries. Note that these SELECT queries must use some mode of the FOR XML clause you learned earlier. The Execute button executes the query and displays the results in a Web Browser control. The Click event handler of the Execute button is shown in Listing 11-17.

Listing 11-17. Using the SqlXmlCommand Class

```
private void button1_Click(object sender, EventArgs e)
{
  string strConn =
    @"Provider=SQLOLEDB;server=.\sqlexpress;database=northwind;integrated ➡
security=SSPI";
  SqlXmlCommand cmd = new SqlXmlCommand(strConn);
  cmd.CommandText = textBox1.Text;
  Stream stream= cmd.ExecuteStream();
  StreamReader reader=new StreamReader(stream);
  StreamWriter writer =
    File.CreateText($"{Application.StartupPath}\\sqlxmlresults.xml");
  writer.Write(reader.ReadToEnd());
  writer.Close();
  webBrowser1.Navigate($"{Application.StartupPath}\\sqlxmlresults.xml");
}
```

■ **Note**   Make sure to change the database connection string to match your development environment before running the preceding code.

The code declares a string variable for storing the database connection string. Notice the Provider parameter of the connection string, which specifies the SQLOLEDB provider. Then the code creates an instance of the SqlXmlCommand class by passing the connection string in its constructor. The CommandText property of SqlXmlCommand is set to the SELECT query entered in the text box, and the query is executed by calling the ExecuteStream() method of the SqlXmlCommand class.

The ExecuteStream() method executes your query and returns a Stream object containing the XML results. This Stream can then be used further to read the data. In the preceding code, the Stream is fed to a StreamReader class. We could have read the Stream byte by byte, but the StreamReader class makes our job easy.

The CreateText() method of the File class creates a new XML file at the specified location and returns a StreamWriter pointing to it. The XML returned from the database is read by using the ReadToEnd() method of the StreamReader class and is then written to the XML file. Finally, the Navigate() method of the Web Browser control is called to show the user the XML file.

There is an alternative way to do the same task. Have a look at Listing 11-18.

Listing 11-18. Using the ExecuteToStream() Method

```
private void button1_Click(object sender, EventArgs e)
{
string strConn =
  @"Provider=SQLOLEDB;server=.\sqlexpress;database=northwind;integrated ➡
security=SSPI";
  SqlXmlCommand cmd = new SqlXmlCommand(strConn);
  cmd.CommandText = textBox1.Text;
  StreamWriter writer =
    File.CreateText($"{Application.StartupPath}\\sqlxmlresults.xml");
  cmd.ExecuteToStream(writer.BaseStream);
  writer.Close();
  webBrowser1.Navigate($"{Application.StartupPath}\\sqlxmlresults.xml");
}
```

The code in Listing 11-18 looks very similar to that in Listing 11-17. The difference is that it calls the ExecuteToStream() method instead of ExecuteStream(), and by doing so emits the XML output to an existing Stream. The BaseStream property of the StreamWriter class returns the underlying Stream, which is then supplied to the ExecuteToStream() method.

■ **Note** You can also use the ExecuteXmlReader() method of the SqlXmlCommand class. This method is identical to the ExecuteXmlReader() method of the SqlCommand class that you learned about in Chapter 7.

Executing Parameterized SELECT Queries

It is quite common for your SELECT queries to have some parameters, and the technique to execute parameterized queries is similar to ADO.NET. However, there are a few differences. First, a parameter is represented by the SqlXmlParameter class. Second, the SqlXmlCommand class doesn't have a Parameters collection as does the SqlCommand class, so you need to call the CreateParameter() method of the SqlXmlCommand class to create a new parameter that belongs to the command. The value of the parameter can then be set. To illustrate the use of the SqlXmlParameter class, we will create an application like the one shown in Figure 11-3.

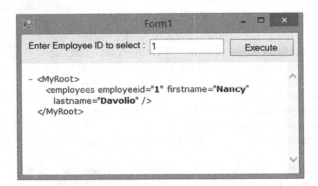

Figure 11-3. *Application for executing parameterized queries*

The application allows you to fetch details of only one employee whose EmployeeID is specified in the text box. The returned XML data is displayed in the Web Browser control as before. Listing 11-19 shows the Click event handler of the Execute button.

Listing 11-19. Using the SqlXmlParameter Class

```
private void button1_Click(object sender, EventArgs e)
{
  string strConn =
    @"Provider=SQLOLEDB;server=.\sqlexpress;database=northwind;integrated ➡
security=SSPI";
  string sql = "SELECT employeeid,firstname,lastname FROM employees
                WHERE employeeid=? FOR XML AUTO,ROOT('MyRoot')";
  SqlXmlCommand cmd = new SqlXmlCommand(strConn);
  cmd.CommandText = sql;
```

```
SqlXmlParameter param = cmd.CreateParameter();
param.Value = textBox1.Text;
StreamWriter writer =
  File.CreateText($"{Application.StartupPath}\\sqlxmlresults.xml");
cmd.ExecuteToStream(writer.BaseStream);
writer.Close();
webBrowser1.Navigate($"{Application.StartupPath}\\sqlxmlresults.xml");
}
```

Examine the SELECT query carefully. It has a WHERE clause with a parameter marked with a question mark (?). Further, the CreateParameter() method is called on the SqlXmlCommand class. The CreateParameter() method creates and returns a new SqlXmlParameter. You can then set the Value property of this SqlXmlParameter class. If your query has more than one parameter, you will need to call the CreateParameter() method once for each parameter. Note that the sequence of parameters in the query and the sequence in which you create SqlXmlParameter objects must be the same. After creating the required parameter, the XML output is saved to a FileStream by using the ExecuteToStream() method of SqlXmlCommand.

Filling a DataSet

A DataSet is one of the most commonly used objects for data binding and disconnected processing. It is obvious that the SQLXML object model must provide some mechanism to populate DataSet objects, and the SqlXmlAdapter fits the bill. It allows you to populate a DataSet and reflect the changes made to the DataSet back in the database. To illustrate the use of SqlXmlAdapter in populating a DataSet, you need to create an application like the one shown in Figure 11-4.

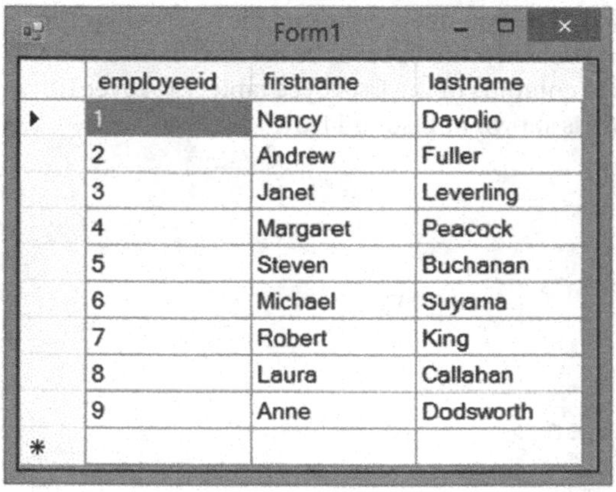

employeeid	firstname	lastname
1	Nancy	Davolio
2	Andrew	Fuller
3	Janet	Leverling
4	Margaret	Peacock
5	Steven	Buchanan
6	Michael	Suyama
7	Robert	King
8	Laura	Callahan
9	Anne	Dodsworth
*		

Figure 11-4. *Application that fills a DataSet by using SqlXmlAdapter*

The application consists of a DataGridView control. When the form loads, a DataSet is filled with all the records from the Employees table and the resultant DataSet is bound to the DataGridView control. The Load event handler that does this job is shown in Listing 11-20.

Listing 11-20. Filling a DataSet with SqlXmlAdapter

```
private void Form1_Load(object sender, EventArgs e)
{
  string strConn =
    @"Provider=SQLOLEDB;server=.\sqlexpress;database=northwind;integrated ➡
security=SSPI";
  string sql = "SELECT employeeid,firstname,lastname FROM employees FOR XML AUTO";
  SqlXmlCommand cmd = new SqlXmlCommand(strConn);
  cmd.CommandText = sql;
  DataSet ds = new DataSet();
  SqlXmlAdapter da = new SqlXmlAdapter(cmd);
  da.Fill(ds);
  dataGridView1.DataSource - ds.Tables[0].DefaultView;
}
```

The code creates a SqlXmlCommand object as before. It then creates a new instance of the DataSet and SqlXmlAdapter classes. The SqlXmlAdapter accepts the SqlXmlCommand object as a parameter and thus the SELECT query (or stored procedure) is passed to it. The Fill() method of SqlXmlAdapter is then called by passing a DataSet object as a parameter. The Fill() method populates the DataSet with the results returned from the query. Finally, the DataSet is bound to the DataGridView control.

Updating a DataSet by Using SqlXmlAdapter

In the preceding example, we simply populated a DataSet with the help of the SqlXmlAdapter class. What if you make changes to the DataSet data and want to save those changes in the database? The SqlXmlAdapter does provide the Update() method that updates the database with any changes to your DataSet. However, you need to do a bit more work than that. While filling the DataSet, you need to specify the XSD Schema for the DataTable being created. This schema provides mapping between the DataTable column names and the actual table column names. In our example, we retrieve three columns of the Employee table: EmployeeID, FirstName, and LastName. The schema for this data structure is shown in Listing 11-21.

Listing 11-21. Schema—Employees.xsd—for Our Data

```
<?xml version="1.0" encoding="utf-8" ?>
<xs:schema xmlns:xs="http://www.w3.org/2001/XMLSchema">
  <xs:element name="Employees">
    <xs:complexType>
      <xs:sequence>
        <xs:element name="EmployeeID" type="xs:integer"/>
        <xs:element name="FirstName" type="xs:string"/>
        <xs:element name="LastName" type="xs:string"/>
      </xs:sequence>
    </xs:complexType>
  </xs:element>
</xs:schema>
```

The schema defines a root element called <Employees>, which has three child elements: <EmployeeID>, <FirstName>, and <LastName>. Note that the schema defines the columns as elements and not as attributes. To see the SqlXmlAdapter class in action, you need to develop an application as shown in Figure 11-5.

Figure 11-5. *Application for illustrating the Update() method of SqlXmlAdapter*

The application consists of a DataGridView control that displays all the employees from the Employees table. You can change the data in the DataGridView and click the Update button to save the changes back to the database. The complete code that makes this application work is shown in Listing 11-22.

Listing 11-22. Saving Changes Made to a DataSet

```
DataSet ds = new DataSet();
SqlXmlAdapter da;
SqlXmlCommand cmd;
string strConn =
  @"Provider=SQLOLEDB;server=.\sqlexpress;database=northwind;integrated ➦
security=SSPI";

private void Form1_Load(object sender, EventArgs e)
{
  cmd = new SqlXmlCommand(strConn);
  cmd.RootTag = "ROOT";
  cmd.CommandText = "Employees";
  cmd.CommandType = SqlXmlCommandType.XPath;
  cmd.SchemaPath = $"{Application.StartupPath}\\employees.xsd";
  ds = new DataSet();
  da = new SqlXmlAdapter(cmd);
  da.Fill(ds);
  dataGridView1.DataSource = ds.Tables[0].DefaultView;
}

private void button1_Click(object sender, EventArgs e)
{
  da.Update(ds);
}
```

The code in Listing 11-22 shows several interesting things. The `SqlXmlCommand`, `DataSet`, and `SqlXmlAdapter` variables are declared at the form level because we will be using them in more than one place. Notice the code marked in bold. It sets the `RootTag` property of the `SqlXmlCommand` property. The AUTO mode of the FOR XML clause doesn't return data along with a root element by default, so this property is used to indicate the name of the root element inside which the rest of the XML data will be wrapped.

The `CommandType` property is set to XPath, indicating that the `CommandText` property is an XPath expression. This means that this time the `CommandText` property is not a SELECT query, but is the XPath expression Employees, which will return various `<Employees>` elements.

The `CommandType` property of the `SqlXmlCommand` class is of type `SqlXmlCommandType`. The possible values of the `SqlXmlCommandType` enumeration are listed in Table 11-4.

Table 11-4. Values of the SqlXmlCommandType Enumeration

Value	Description
DiffGram	Indicates that `CommandText` is a DiffGram
Sql	Indicates that `CommandText` is a SQL statement (default)
Template	Indicates that `CommandText` is a template
TemplateFile	Indicates that `CommandText` is a template file
UpdateGram	Indicates that `CommandText` is an UpdateGram
XPath	Indicates that `CommandText` is a valid XPath expression

Further, the `SchemaPath` property specifies the path of the schema file that we created earlier. Then the `SqlXmlAdapter` populates a `DataSet`, which is bound to the `DataGridView`.

After the data is displayed in the `DataGridView`, you can modify it. After the modifications are complete, you need to click the Update button. The `Click` event of the Update button calls the `Update()` method of `SqlXmlAdapter`, which accepts the `DataSet` whose changes are to be reflected in the database. In Chapter 7, you learned that the `DataSet` class internally tracks the changes made to the data by using the DiffGram format. The same DiffGram is used by the `SqlXmlAdapter` class to propagate the changes back to the database.

Applying XSLT Templates

In Chapter 6, you learned to apply XSLT style sheets to XML data. You saw that XSLT allows you to transform XML data from one form to another. The same concept also can be applied in SQLXML, where you may want to apply XSLT templates to whatever data you receive in your client application. This is accomplished by using the `XslPath` property of the `SqlXmlCommand` class. To demonstrate the use of `XslPath`, you need to develop an application like the one shown in Figure 11-6.

Figure 11-6. *Application to illustrate the use of the XslPath property*

The application consists of a Web Browser control. When the form loads, a SELECT query is executed by using SqlXmlCommand. An XSLT style sheet is then applied to the returned XML data to transform it into HTML. The resultant HTML document is then displayed in the Web Browser control.

Before you write any code, you must create an XSLT style sheet named Employees.xslt as shown in Listing 11-23.

Listing 11-23. Employees.xslt Markup

```
<?xml version="1.0" encoding="UTF-8" ?>
<xsl:stylesheet version="1.0" xmlns:xsl="http://www.w3.org/1999/XSL/Transform">
  <xsl:template match="/">
    <html>
      <body>
        <h1>Employee Listing</h1>
        <table border="1">
          <tr>
            <th>Employee ID</th>
            <th>First Name</th>
            <th>Last Name</th>
          </tr>
          <xsl:for-each select="root/employees">
            <tr>
              <td>
                <xsl:value-of select="@EmployeeID"/>
              </td>
              <td>
                <xsl:value-of select="@FirstName"/>
              </td>
```

```
        <td>
          <xsl:value-of select="@LastName"/>
        </td>
      </tr>
    </xsl:for-each>
  </table>
</body>
</html>
</xsl:template>
</xsl:stylesheet>
```

The style sheet iterates through all the <Employees> elements and renders an HTML table. The HTML table displays the attribute values in various cells. Note that we will be using the AUTO mode of the FOR XML clause, which returns column values as XML attributes. That is why the style sheet uses attribute names (@ EmployeeID, @FirstName, and @LastName). The code that actually executes the SELECT query and performs the transformation is shown in Listing 11-24.

Listing 11-24. Applying an XSLT Style Sheet

```
private void Form1_Load(object sender, EventArgs e)
{
string strConn =
  @"Provider=SQLOLEDB;server=.\sqlexpress;database=northwind;integrated ➡
security=SSPI";
  SqlXmlCommand cmd = new SqlXmlCommand(strConn);
  cmd.CommandText = "SELECT EmployeeID,FirstName,LastName
                        FROM employees FOR XML AUTO";
  cmd.RootTag = "root";
  cmd.XslPath = $"{Application.StartupPath}\\employees.xslt";
  StreamWriter writer =
    File.CreateText($"{Application.StartupPath}\\sqlxmlresults.htm");
  cmd.ExecuteToStream(writer.BaseStream);
  writer.Close();
  webBrowser1.Navigate($"{Application.StartupPath}\\sqlxmlresults.htm");
}
```

Notice the code marked in bold. This time the SELECT statement doesn't contain a ROOT clause. We could indeed have used it, but the code achieves the same thing with the help of the RootTag property of the SqlXmlCommand class. Recollect that in the absence of a ROOT clause in the FOR XML query, the returned XML data doesn't contain a root element. The RootTag property of SqlXmlCommand specifies the name of the root tag inside which the output of the SELECT query will be wrapped.

The XSLT style sheet to be used for transformation is specified via the XslPath property of the SqlXmlCommand class. This way, the SqlXmlCommand class knows which style sheet to apply to the returned XML data. The rest of the code should be familiar to you, as we discussed it in previous examples. It simply saves the transformed XML data into a disk file and displays that file in the Web Browser control.

Writing Template Queries

In the preceding example, we specified the SELECT query directly in code. There is an alternative to this too: you can store the queries in an XML file and specify the path of this XML file as the CommandText of the SqlXmlCommand class. These XML files are called *XML templates*. The structure of this XML file can be seen in Listing 11-25.

Listing 11-25. Creating an XML Template

```xml
<?xml version="1.0" encoding="utf-8" ?>
<ROOT xmlns:sql="urn:schemas-microsoft-com:xml-sql">
  <sql:header>
    <sql:param name='EmpID'>1</sql:param>
  </sql:header>
  <sql:query>
    SELECT EmployeeID,FirstName,LastName FROM Employees
    WHERE employeeid>@Empid FOR XML AUTO
  </sql:query>
</ROOT>
```

The root element <ROOT> is a user-defined element, but the namespace urn:schemas-microsoft-com:xml-sql is necessary. The <ROOT> element contains an optional section called <sql:header>, which is used to define parameters used by your query (if any). Each parameter is specified by using a <sql:param> element. The name attribute of the <sql:param> element indicates the name of the parameter, while the value of the parameter is stored within the <sql:param> and </sql:param> tags. The actual query is stored in the <sql:query> section. The query uses the parameter by prefixing its name with the @ symbol.

To use this XML template file, you need to create an application like the one shown in Figure 11-7.

	EmployeeID	FirstName	LastName
▶	2	Andrew	Fuller
	3	Janet	Leverling
	4	Margaret	Peacock
	5	Steven	Buchanan
	6	Michael	Suyama
	7	Robert	King
	8	Laura	Callahan
	9	Anne	Dodsworth
✳			

Figure 11-7. *Application that illustrates the use of XML templates*

The application consists of a DataGridView that displays all the records from the Employees table. The Load event of the form contains all the code necessary to use the XML template (see Listing 11-26).

Listing 11-26. Using XML Templates

```
private void Form1_Load(object sender, EventArgs e)
{
  string strConn =
    @"Provider=SQLOLEDB;server=.\sqlexpress;database=northwind;integrated ➥
security=SSPI";
  SqlXmlCommand cmd = new SqlXmlCommand(strConn);
  cmd.CommandType = SqlXmlCommandType.TemplateFile;
  cmd.CommandText = $"{Application.StartupPath}\\querytemplate.xml";
  DataSet ds = new DataSet();
  SqlXmlAdapter da = new SqlXmlAdapter(cmd);
  da.Fill(ds);
  dataGridView1.DataSource = ds.Tables[0].DefaultView;
}
```

Notice the code marked in bold. This time the CommandType property of the SqlXmlCommand class is set to TemplateFile. This indicates that the CommandText property will be specifying the path of the XML template file. Then the CommandText property is set to the path of the XML template file we just created in Listing 11-25. The instance of SqlXmlAdapter is used as before to populate a DataSet. The DataSet is finally bound to the DataGridView control.

Updating Data with DiffGrams

In Chapter 7, you learned that DataSet objects can be serialized as XML documents. While serializing a DataSet object, we used an XmlWriteMode enumeration to specify how the data is to be written. Now, one of the options of XmlWriteMode was DiffGram, which persisted the DataSet contents in DiffGram format. Imagine that you have such a DiffGram containing inserts, updates, and deletes and you want to save these changes back to the database. One way to do this is to use DataSet and SqlXmlAdapter, which you've already seen.

There is another technique that also involves the SqlXmlCommand class. The SqlXmlCommand class can come in handy if you have a raw DiffGram that is not necessarily loaded in a DataSet. To illustrate the use of the SqlXmlCommand class, you need to develop an application like the one shown in Figure 11-8.

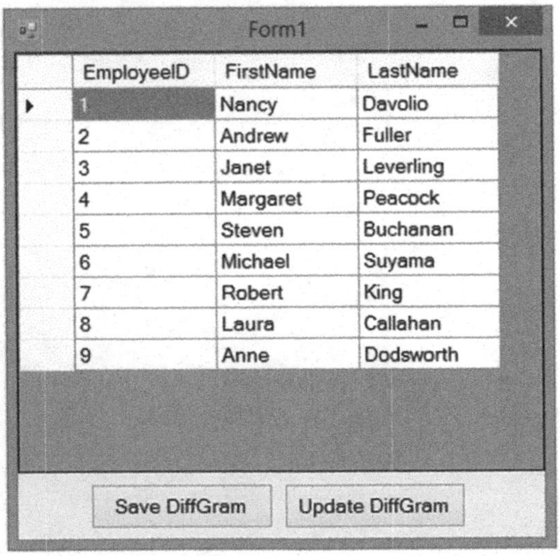

Figure 11-8. Application for updating DiffGrams

The application consists of a DataGridView control for displaying all the records from the Employees table. There are two buttons: Save DiffGram and Update DiffGram. The former saves the contents of the DataSet to a disk file in DiffGram format. The latter button reads the previously saved DiffGram and updates the database.

The Load event handler of the form contains the code shown in Listing 11-27.

Listing 11-27. Filling a DataSet

```
string strConn = @"Provider=SQLOLEDB;server=.; ➥
database=northwind;user id=sa;password=sa";
DataSet ds = new DataSet();

private void Form1_Load(object sender, EventArgs e)
{
  SqlXmlCommand cmd = new SqlXmlCommand(strConn);
  cmd.RootTag = "ROOT";
  cmd.CommandText = "Employees";
  cmd.CommandType = SqlXmlCommandType.XPath;
  cmd.SchemaPath = $"{Application.StartupPath}\\employees.xsd";
  SqlXmlAdapter da = new SqlXmlAdapter(cmd);
  da.Fill(ds);
  dataGridView1.DataSource = ds.Tables[0].DefaultView;
}
```

The code should be familiar to you, as you used it in previous examples. It simply populates a DataSet by using the SqlXmlAdapter class. The DataSet acts as the DataSource for the DataGridView control. The code that saves this DataSet as a DiffGram goes in the Click event of the Save DiffGram button and is shown in Listing 11-28.

Listing 11-28. Saving a DataSet as a DiffGram

```
private void button2_Click(object sender, EventArgs e)
{
  StreamWriter writer=File.CreateText($"{Application.StartupPath}\\employees.xml");
  ds.WriteXml(writer, XmlWriteMode.DiffGram);
  writer.Close();
}
```

The code calls the WriteXml() method of DataSet to save its contents to an XML file (Employees.xml). The XmlWriteMode parameter of WriteXml() indicates that DiffGram format is to be used while writing the data. This DiffGram is executed against the database when you click the Update DiffGram button. The Click event handler of the Update DiffGram button is shown in Listing 11-29.

Listing 11-29. Updating a DiffGram in a Database

```
private void button1_Click(object sender, EventArgs e)
{
  StreamReader reader = File.OpenText($"{Application.StartupPath}\\employees.xml");
  SqlXmlCommand cmd = new SqlXmlCommand(strConn);
  cmd.CommandType = SqlXmlCommandType.DiffGram;
  cmd.CommandText = reader.ReadToEnd();
  cmd.SchemaPath = $"{Application.StartupPath}\\employees.xsd";
```

```
    cmd.ExecuteNonQuery();
    MessageBox.Show("DiffGram updated to database successfully!");
}
```

The code opens the `Employees.xml` file in a `StreamReader` object. It then creates an instance of the `SqlXmlCommand` class and sets the `CommandType` property of the `SqlXmlCommand` instance to `DiffGram`. This is how you tell `SqlXmlCommand` about your intention to update a DiffGram. When the `CommandType` is `DiffGram`, the `CommandText` property must contain the DiffGram itself. The `ReadToEnd()` method of `StreamReader` reads the complete DiffGram and assigns it to the `CommandText` property.

If you want to update the database by using the DiffGram method, you must specify the `SchemaPath` property also. In this case, the schema is the same as we created in Listing 11-21 earlier. Finally, the `ExecuteNonQuery()` method of the `SqlXmlCommand` is called to save all the changes to the database. The `ExecuteNonQuery()` method is used for executing queries that do not return anything. In our example, we simply wanted to update the DiffGram to the database and hence we used the `ExecuteNonQuery()` method.

■ **Note**   Just like DiffGram, the `SqlXmlCommand` object also allows you to update UpdateGrams. The UpdateGram format is similar to DiffGram in that it keeps the differential versions of the data. However, the `DataSet` class doesn't have any methods to serialize itself in UpdateGram format. You can think of DiffGram as a subset of UpdateGram.

The XML Data Type

Up until now, you've seen various features of SQL Server that provide a strong integration between relational and XML data. But that's not all. This section gives the next installment of the XML features of SQL Server: the XML data type. Prior to SQL Server 2005, storing XML data in a table essentially meant that you had to use a VARCHAR or TEXT column for the data. From the point of view of storage, this was fine; but from a data-manipulation point of view, it was tedious. The XML data was treated just like any other text data. The new XML data type introduced in SQL Server 2005 is exclusively for storing XML documents and fragments.

■ **Note**   An XML document is markup that contains the root element, whereas an XML fragment is markup without any root element. Remember that the FOR XML clause by default returns XML fragments and not documents.

As well as storing XML data, you can also execute XQuery operations and special XML data-manipulation statements on the data. The XML data can have an XSD Schema attached to it so that data validations can be performed. You can also index tables on the basis of an XML column.

■ **Note**   XQuery is a W3C recommendation that deals with querying XML documents. You can think of XQuery as SQL for XML data. The XQuery syntax is based on XPath expression syntax.

To begin, let's see how to add a column of type XML to a SQL Server table.

Creating a Table with an XML Column

To see how a column of type XML can be added to a SQL Server table, you will create a new table in the Northwind database called XMLDocs. Figure 11-9 shows the XMLDocs table in design mode.

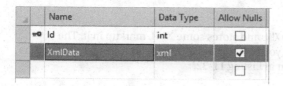

	Name	Data Type	Allow Nulls
🔑	Id	int	☐
	XmlData	xml	☑
			☐

Figure 11-9. *Creating a table with an XML column*

The XMLDocs table consists of two columns: Id and XmlData. The former column is the primary and is marked as an identity column, and the latter is of type XML.

Inserting, Modifying, and Deleting XML Data

Inserting, modifying, or deleting XML data is similar to any other data type. However, there are some points to keep in mind. Listing 11-30 shows how to use INSERT and UPDATE statements against a column of type XML.

Listing 11-30. Inserting and Updating XML Columns

```
-- Here goes INSERT
INSERT INTO xmldocs(xmldata)
VALUES(
'<Employee EmployeeID="1">
<FirstName>Nancy</FirstName>
<LastName>Davolio</LastName>
</Employee>')

-- Here goes UPDATE
UPDATE xmldocs
SET xmldata='
<Employee EmployeeID="1">
<FirstName>Nancy</FirstName>
<LastName>Davolio</LastName>
</Employee>'
WHERE Id=1
```

As you can see, for an INSERT or an UPDATE against a column of the XML data type, you can use XML data in string format. You can also declare a variable of type XML in your Transact-SQL (T-SQL) scripts, as shown in Listing 11-31.

Listing 11-31. Declaring a Variable of Type XML

```
DECLARE @xmldata xml
SET @xmldata='
<Employee EmployeeID="2">
<FirstName>Nancy</FirstName>
```

```
<LastName> Davolio</LastName>
</Employee>'

UPDATE xmldocs
SET xmldata=@xmldata
WHERE Id=1
```

The script declares a variable called xmldata of type XML and stores some XML markup in it. The xmldata variable is then used in the UPDATE statement. If you want to explicitly convert a string value into the XML data type, you can use the CONVERT function as shown in Listing 11-32.

Listing 11-32. Converting String Values to an XML Data Type

```
DECLARE @xmldata VARCHAR(255)
SET @xmldata='
<Employee EmployeeID="2">
<FirstName>Nancy</FirstName>
<LastName> Davolio</LastName>
</Employee>'

UPDATE xmldocs
SET xmldata=CONVERT(xml,@xmldata,0)
WHERE Id=1
```

The first parameter to the CONVERT function is the target data type. The second parameter is the source data to be converted, and the third parameter is the style. The value of 0 indicates that insignificant whitespace will be discarded. You might be wondering—if XML data can be represented as a string, why would we want to use XML variables at all? The answer is, using the XML data type is recommended because the XML data type checks that the XML data is well formed.

Methods of the XML Data Type

The XML data type provides some methods to query XML columns or variables. Some of these methods are listed in Table 11-5.

Table 11-5. *Methods of the XML Data Type*

Method	Description
query()	Queries an XML column or variable based on some XQuery expression and returns the results of the query.
value()	Queries an XML column or variable and returns a scalar value of the SQL data type.
exist()	Tells you whether the given XQuery expression returns any results.
modify()	Modifies the content of an XML data type column or variable with the help of XML Data Modification Language, discussed later in this chapter.
nodes()	Returns XML data as relational data.

Some of these methods are discussed in the following sections.

Using the query() Method

The query() method is used to query XML data by using XQuery expressions. Listing 11-33 illustrates how this method is used.

Listing 11-33. Using the query() Method

```
SELECT xmldata.query('/Employee[@EmployeeID=2]') FROM xmldocs
```

```
<Employee EmployeeID="2">
<FirstName>Nancy</FirstName>
<LastName> Davolio</LastName>
</Employee>
```

The SELECT query uses the query() method on the XmlData column. The query() method accepts a valid XQuery expression and returns the matching nodes. In our example, we fetch the <Employee> element whose EmployeeID attribute value is 1. As you can see, the XQuery syntax is based on XPath syntax.

Using the value() Method

The value() method accepts an XQuery expression and returns a scalar (single) value. Listing 11-34 shows the use of this method.

Listing 11-34. Using the value() Method

```
SELECT xmldata.value('(/Employee/@EmployeeID)[1]','int') FROM xmldocs WHERE id=1
```

```
-----------
1
```

The value() method accepts two parameters:

- The first parameter is an XQuery.

- The second parameter is the target SQL Server data type.

In this example, we are trying to select the EmployeeID attribute value of the first employee. Note that the expression /Employee/@EmployeeID returns multiple rows, and hence we specify the row index to access by using array notation. The EmployeeID scalar value is to be represented as an integer, and hence the second parameter is int. Note that the data type name must be enclosed in quotes.

Using the exist() Method

The exist() method checks whether there are any nodes matching the supplied XQuery expression. Listing 11-35 illustrates the use of the exist() method.

Listing 11-35. Using the exist() Method

```
SELECT xmldata.exist('/Employee[@EmployeeID=1]') FROM xmldocs
```

The exist() method returns 1 if the XQuery expression returns at least one node, 0 if the XQuery expression returns zero nodes, and NULL if the XML column is null.

XML Data Modification Language (XML DML)

As SQL provides data-manipulation statements for relational data, so the XML DML of SQL Server allows you to insert, replace, and delete data from an XML column. The XML DML statements are used along with the modify() method mentioned in Table 11-5. Listing 11-36 shows a script that inserts, replaces, and deletes XML data from the XmlData column of the XMLDocs table.

Listing 11-36. Inserting, Replacing, and Deleting Content from an XML Column

```
-- Here goes insert
UPDATE xmldocs
SET xmldata.modify
('
insert <Employee EmployeeID="3">
<FirstName>Janet</FirstName>
<LastName>Leverling</LastName>
</Employee> after (/Employee)[2]')

-- Here goes replace

UPDATE xmldocs
SET xmldata.modify
('
replace value of
(/Employee/@EmployeeID)[1] with "10"')

-- Here goes delete

UPDATE xmldocs
SET xmldata.modify
('
delete (/Employee[@EmployeeID=3])
')
```

The first UPDATE query uses the modify() method of the XML column to specify an insert XML DML statement that inserts a new <Employee> node at the end of the existing markup. Observe this syntax carefully. The whole insert statement is enclosed within quotes and acts as a parameter to the modify() method. The first expression in the insert statement is the new XML markup to be inserted followed by the after clause. In our example, we want to insert the new <Employee> after the second <Employee> node and hence we specify (/Employee)[2]. You can also use the before, as first, and as last clauses.

The second UPDATE query uses the modify() method along with the replace value of XML DML statement. The replace value of statement takes two expressions:

- The first specifies the markup to be replaced. In our example, we want to replace the EmployeeID attribute of the first <Employee> node.

- The second expression is the new value to be replaced. In our example, we want to assign a value of 10 to the EmployeeID attribute.

Finally, the third UPDATE statement uses the modify() method along with the delete XML DML statement. The delete statement takes the expression on the basis of which the markup is to be deleted. In our example, we want to delete an employee with EmployeeID equal to 3.

XQuery Support in the XML Data Type

While working with the XML data type, you saw that it heavily uses XQuery expressions. The XQuery expressions are in turn based on XPath syntax. In Chapter 4, you were introduced to XPath functions. The XQuery specifications support almost all the functions that you learned earlier.

Summary

SQL Server provides strong integration with XML. This chapter introduced you to many of the XML features of SQL Server, which allows you to view relational data as XML. This is done with the help of the FOR XML clause of the SELECT statement. You can also look at XML data in a relational way by using the OPENXML function.

You also saw how SQL Server makes it easy to retrieve data in a client application with the help of the SQLXML managed classes. These classes allow you to select data as a stream, an XmlReader, or a DataSet. They also allow you to update UpdateGrams and DiffGrams in the database. The XML data type of SQL Server can be used to store whole XML documents or fragments and allows you to manipulate them via XML DML.

■ ■ ■

CHAPTER 12

XML in .NET Framework

Up until now, you have learned how to work with your own XML data. This includes reading, writing, validating, serializing, and querying XML data. Microsoft has used XML extensively in the .NET Framework. This use of XML comes in different flavors, such as XAML markup of note, server control markup of ASP.NET, and configuration system of the .NET Framework. Understanding the use of XML in the .NET Framework is therefore essential for any .NET developer. This chapter introduces you to many of these features. Specifically, you learn about the following topics:

- Using XAML in defining the WPF user interfaces

- Using ASP.NET server controls to define the web user interface

- Understanding ASP.NET server controls such as the XML, XML data source, TreeView, Menu, and SiteMap

- Using the configuration system of the .NET Framework

- Understanding the XML documentation

Note that although this chapter covers a broad range of topics, by no means does it give an exhaustive treatment to these topics. The focus here is to briefly point at the use of XML in various areas of the .NET Framework.

Using XAML to Define the WPF User Interface

You have been developing Windows Forms applications throughout this book. As you are aware, a Windows Forms are classes that contain all the code required to display the form and the event handlers. Thus two concerns—user interface and functioning (event handlers)—are mixed together. A better programming approach would be to separate these two concerns into their own units.

Windows Presentation Foundation (WPF) applications do just that. WPF uses a special vocabulary of XML called XAML (Extensible Application Markup Language) to define a user interface. The XAML markup typically resides in files with an .xaml extension. The code responsible for the functioning of the application (runtime logic such as event handlers and methods) is housed in a C# class. When you design a user interface of a Windows Forms application, the UI is translated into C# code. That's not the case with WPF applications. When you design a WPF user interface in Visual Studio, the UI is translated into XAML markup (and not into C# code).

The XAML markup is an XML markup and hence follows all the rules of XML grammar. You can create/edit an XAML markup in any XML/text editor, but Visual Studio provides a rich editor to work with it.

Just to understand how the XAML markup looks, you will create a WPF application as shown in Figure 12-1.

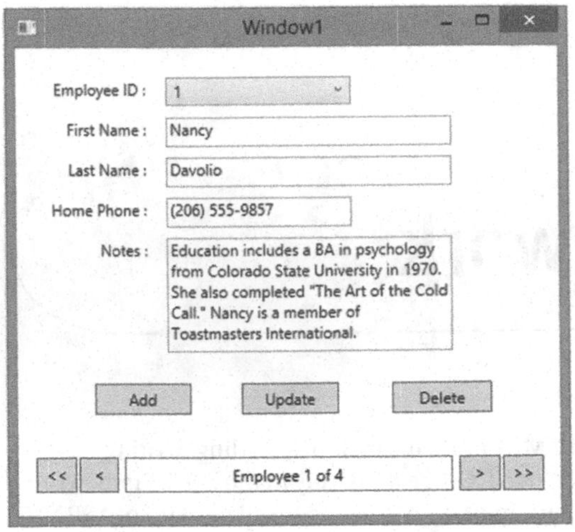

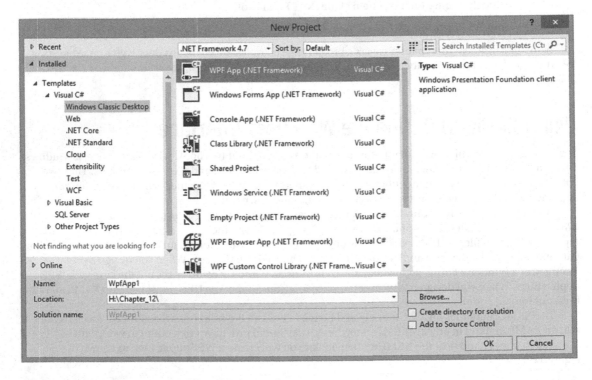

Figure 12-1. *A WPF application for managing Employees.xml*

This application should sound familiar to you because you developed a similar Windows Forms application in Chapter 2. As far as the functionality of the application is concerned, it's exactly same—add, update, and delete employees from the Employees.xml file. We are not going to discuss the functionality again to save some space. Our primary interest here is the XAML markup. You can grab the complete source code of this application from this book's source code download.

To develop this application, create a new WPF application project using Visual Studio (see Figure 12-2).

Figure 12-2. *Creating a new WPF application project*

Once the project is created, you will notice two .xaml files in it called App.xaml and MainWindow.xaml. Our interest is the MainWindow.xaml file, since it defines the user interface of our application. You can add WPF windows using the Add New Item dialog.

You can open the MainWindow.xaml file in the Visual Studio Designer (see Figure 12-3) and edit it in two ways:

- Drag and drop WPF controls from the toolbox onto the design surface and set their properties. Doing so will generate certain XAML markup for you.

- Manually edit the .xaml file and add the markup (primarily consisting of certain elements and their attributes) into it directly. The design surface will also reflect the relevant changes.

The MainWindow.xaml file ready for editing is shown in Figure 12-3. Figure 12-4 shows the toolbox with WPF controls.

Figure 12-3. *MainWindow.xaml in the Visual Studio Designer*

Figure 12-4. Toolbox showing WPF controls

You can try playing with the designer just to get some familiarity. And try to design a user interface of the application as shown earlier. We won't go into the details of the UI designing process here. The XAML markup responsible for the user interface is shown in Listing 12-1 (to save some space, some of the markup has been omitted from the listing).

Listing 12-1. XAML Markup Responsible for the User Interface

```
<Window x:Class="WpfAndXaml.MainWindow"
        xmlns="http://schemas.microsoft.com/winfx/2006/xaml/presentation"
        xmlns:x="http://schemas.microsoft.com/winfx/2006/xaml"
        xmlns:d="http://schemas.microsoft.com/expression/blend/2008"
        xmlns:mc="http://schemas.openxmlformats.org/markup-compatibility/2006"
        xmlns:local="clr-namespace:WpfAndXaml"
        mc:Ignorable="d"
        Title="Window1" Height="400.2" Width="433.431" Loaded="Window_Loaded">
....
        <Grid HorizontalAlignment="Center" Height="367" VerticalAlignment="Center"
        Width="396" Margin="10,10,9,10">
            <Label Content="Employee ID :" HorizontalAlignment="Left" Margin="13,22,0,0"
            VerticalAlignment="Top" RenderTransformOrigin="-0.575,0.017"/>
            <Label Content="First Name :" HorizontalAlignment="Left" Margin="23,53,0,0"
            VerticalAlignment="Top" RenderTransformOrigin="-0.575,0.017"/>
            <Label Content="Last Name :" HorizontalAlignment="Left" Margin="24,84,0,0"
            VerticalAlignment="Top" RenderTransformOrigin="-0.575,0.017"/>
            <Label Content="Home Phone :" HorizontalAlignment="Left" Margin="11,115,0,0"
            VerticalAlignment="Top" RenderTransformOrigin="-0.575,0.017"/>
            <Label Content="Notes :" HorizontalAlignment="Left" Margin="49,146,0,0"
            VerticalAlignment="Top" RenderTransformOrigin="-0.575,0.017"/>
            <ComboBox x:Name="comboBox1" HorizontalAlignment="Left" Margin="106,26,0,0"
            VerticalAlignment="Top" Width="143"/>
            <TextBox x:Name="textBox1" HorizontalAlignment="Left" Height="23"
            Margin="106,57,0,0" TextWrapping="Wrap" Text="TextBox" VerticalAlignment="Top"
            Width="219" RenderTransformOrigin="0.439,-0.159"/>
```

```
    <TextBox x:Name="textBox2" HorizontalAlignment="Left" Height="23"
    TextWrapping="Wrap" Text="TextBox" VerticalAlignment="Top" Width="219"
    Margin="106,88,0,0"/>
    <TextBox x:Name="textBox3" HorizontalAlignment="Left" Height="23"
    TextWrapping="Wrap" Text="TextBox" VerticalAlignment="Top" Width="143"
    Margin="106,119,0,0"/>
    <TextBox x:Name="textBox4" HorizontalAlignment="Left" Height="88"
    TextWrapping="Wrap" Text="TextBox" VerticalAlignment="Top" Width="219"
    Margin="106,150,0,0"/>
    <Button x:Name="button1" Content="Add" HorizontalAlignment="Left"
    VerticalAlignment="Top" Width="75" Margin="49,262,0,0" Click="button1_Click"
    Height="24"/>
    <Button x:Name="button2" Content="Update" HorizontalAlignment="Left"
    VerticalAlignment="Top" Width="75" Margin="163,262,0,0" Click="button2_Click"
    Height="24"/>
    <Button x:Name="button3" Content="Delete" HorizontalAlignment="Left"
    VerticalAlignment="Top" Width="75" Margin="279,262,0,0" Click="button3_Click"
    Height="24"/>
.... ....
        </Grid>
    </Grid>
</Window>
```

Although we are not going to understand the markup from WPF point of view, let's quickly inspect it from the XML point of view.

The markup has the Window root element indicating that it's a window. There are certain namespaces as used by the WPF applications. Two of them are worth knowing because you will find them in every WPF XAML document:

- http://schemas.microsoft.com/winfx/2006/xaml/presentation is the main WPF namespace. It contains all the WPF classes, including the controls used on the user interfaces. As you can see, it is the default namespace for the entire XAML document.

- http://schemas.microsoft.com/winfx/2006/xaml is the XAML namespace. It has the namespace prefix of x. It includes various XAML features that are needed by all the applications.

The x:Class attribute specifies that a C# class named MainWindow is going to contain the code such as event handlers. The MainWindow class inherits from Window class (indicated by the <Window> element). This class is often called a code-behind class.

The <Grid> section acts as a layout scheme for the container for the WPF controls housed in the window. Inside, there are markup elements such as <ComboBox>, <Label>, <TextBox>, and <Button> that represent the respective user interface elements. Each of the elements has its own set of attributes (such as Content, Text, HorizontalAlignment, VerticalAlignment, and Margin).

These elements actually map to certain classes defined by the WPF framework and are often called *backing types*. For example, the <Button> element maps to the System.Windows.Controls.Button class. The Margin and FontSize attributes of the <Button> element correspond to the Margin and FontSize properties of the Button class, respectively.

So far so good. Now, let's see how to add event handlers to the buttons. Double-click on any of the Button controls to open the MainWindow class (the MainWindow.xaml.cs file) and the Click event handler of that button. The Click event handler of button1 (Add) is shown in Listing 12-2.

Listing 12-2. Click Event Handler of the Button Control

```
public partial class MainWindow : Window
{

    public MainWindow()
    {
        InitializeComponent();
    }

    private void button1_Click(object sender, RoutedEventArgs e)
    {
      //your code here
    }
}
```

The button1_Click() method represents the Click event handler of the button. After generating this empty event handler, look at the XAML markup again.

```
<Button x:Name="button1"
Content="Add"
HorizontalAlignment="Left"
VerticalAlignment="Top"
Width="75"
Margin="49,262,0,0"
Click="button1_Click"
Height="24"/>
```

As you can see that Click attribute has been added to the <Button> element that points to the Click event handler.

As mentioned, we won't discuss the code responsible for the working this application since it is quite similar to the example you developed in Chapter 2. You can get the complete source code from the book's source code download. You may even copy and paste the event handler code into your project to make the application work as expected.

When you compile the application the XAML markup is translated into a CLR type and is merged with the code-behind class (notice that the code-behind class is a partial class) to form a single unit of code. You can now run the application and see if it works as expected.

Displaying XML Data in a WPF Application

In the preceding section, you learned that WPF uses XAML to define its user interface elements. However, it would be more interesting to see how XML data can be displayed in WPF applications. To see how that's done, you build another WPF application, as shown in Figure 12-5.

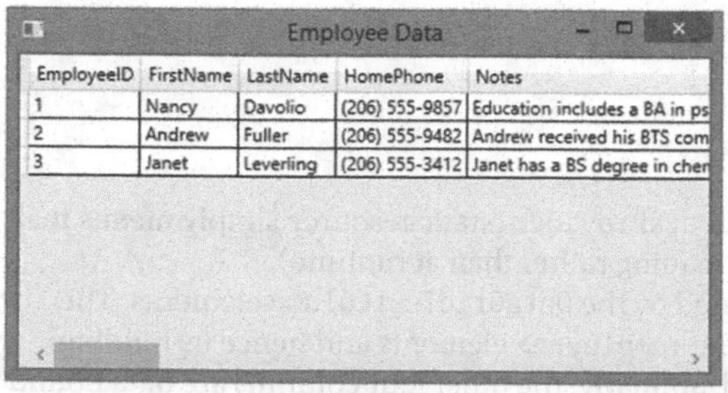

Figure 12-5. Employee XML data displayed in a grid

The application's user interface consists of a DataGrid that displays XML data from the Employees.xml file. The DataGrid has five columns that display EmployeeID, FirstName, LastName, HomePhone, and Notes.

To develop this application, create a new WPF project as before and drag and drop a Grid control on it. Then configure a resource for the grid (not to be confused with DataGrid), as shown in Listing 12-3.

Listing 12-3. Configuring XmlDataProvider

```
<Grid.Resources>
  <XmlDataProvider x:Key="EmployeeData"
    Source="Employees.xml"
    XPath="/employees/employee"/>
</Grid.Resources>
```

A resource is an object that you want to use often in an application. Here you configure XmlDataProvider as a resource. An XmlDataProvider object can point to an XML file or contain inline XML data. In our example, the employee data is stored in Employees.xml file and hence the Source property of the XmlDataProvider is set to Employees.xml. The key specifies a name by which a resource is identified, EmployeeData in this case. The XPath property specifies an XPath query that gives us the desired data. In this case, we want to fill grid rows with data from the <employee> nodes. So, the XPath query is set to / employees/employee.

Drag and drop a DataGrid control from the toolbox and change its XAML (you can do that using the XAML Editor pane of the designer) to resemble Listing 12-4.

Listing 12-4. DataGrid Columns Are Bound to XML Data

```
<DataGrid x:Name="grid1" DataContext="{StaticResource EmployeeData}"
 ItemsSource="{Binding XPath=/employees/employee}"
 AutoGenerateColumns="False" HorizontalAlignment="Stretch"
 VerticalAlignment="Stretch">
<DataGrid.Columns>
  <DataGridTextColumn Header="EmployeeID"
   Binding="{Binding XPath=@employeeid}" />
  <DataGridTextColumn Header="FirstName"
   Binding="{Binding XPath=firstname}" />
  <DataGridTextColumn Header="LastName"
   Binding="{Binding XPath=lastname}" />
  <DataGridTextColumn Header="HomePhone"
   Binding="{Binding XPath=homephone}" />
```

```
<DataGridTextColumn Header="Notes"
  Binding="{Binding XPath=notes}" />
</DataGrid.Columns>
</DataGrid>
```

The DataContext property of the DataGrid is set to XmlDataProvider (static resource simply means that the resource under consideration is resolved at the time of loading rather than at runtime).

Also notice that the DataGrid has five columns as defined by the DataGridTextColumn elements. The EmployeeID column binds to the employeeid attribute of the <employee> elements and hence its binding property is configured to use the XPath query @employeeid. Similarly, the other four columns are data bound to the firstname, lastname, homephone, and notes elements.

■ **Note**   The data binding syntax used by WPF may look slightly odd if you haven't worked with WPF before. Although we won't go into the details of this syntax in this book, you can read the MSDN documentation to learn more.

Once the XAML markup is ready, run the application and see if the DataGrid is filled with the employee data.

Using XML in ASP.NET

ASP.NET is a framework for building dynamic and data-driven web applications. In ASP.NET, web pages are called *Web Forms*. Web Forms use the .aspx extension and contain HTML markup, server control markup, and optionally code. Every Web Form is a class that inherits directly or indirectly from the System.Web. UI.Page base class.

■ **Note**   Your ASP.NET applications may use Web Forms or MVC. You may also use the new framework—ASP. NET Core—to build web applications. The discussion and examples discussed in the following sections use ASP.NET Web Forms. My aim is merely to show you how ASP.NET uses XML and XML-based syntax in several places. So, when I say ASP.NET, I mean ASP.NET Web Forms.

Server controls are object-oriented wrappers over traditional HTML elements. They are processed by ASP.NET on the server side, which is why they are called server controls. They provide many advantages over traditional HTML controls, including rich functionality, data binding, object-oriented features, and many others. An ASP.NET web site is a collection of Web Forms and related resources such as images, JavaScript files, and compiled components.

XML and ASP.NET

ASP.NET uses XML in several places. Some of the main areas where XML is used extensively are as follows:

- Server control markup

- XML data source control

- Navigational controls such as TreeView, Menu, and SiteMap

- XML control

- Web site configuration

You learn about all these features in the following sections.

Server Control Markup

As mentioned previously, ASP.NET Web Forms primarily consist of HTML and server control markup. The server control markup is actually a special vocabulary of XML. Each server control has a predefined tag name, tag prefix, and attributes. Some server controls are empty elements (they do not contain any child elements), whereas others can contain markup or text.

To better understand server controls, you will develop an ASP.NET web site with a Web Form. The Web Form represents a typical Contact Us page. The page will be used by end users to contact you with any questions, feedback, or comments about your web site.

Creating a Web Site

To create a new web site using Visual Studio, you need to choose the File ➤ New ➤ Web Site menu option. This option opens the New Web Site dialog box shown in Figure 12-6.

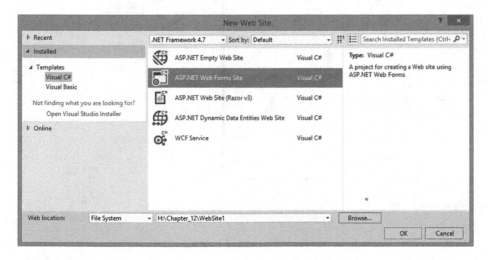

Figure 12-6. *Creating a new web site*

The ASP.NET Web Forms Site template allows you to create a web site. The Web location dropdown list indicates the target location where the web site will be created. Possible locations are file system, web server (HTTP), and FTP folder (FTP). In our example, we will choose file system. The path specified after the Location dropdown is the target folder where the web site will be created. Make sure to select Visual C# as the language. Click the OK button to create the web site. Visual Studio will create the web site with a certain folder structure and there will also be a Web Form named Default.aspx.

■ **Note**   In most of our examples, we don't need various items created by the default project template. You may simply remove them from the project to reduce the clutter. You may also use ASP.NET Empty Web Site project template to create an empty project and add the items as needed.

Designing the Web Form

The next task is to design the Contact Us Web Form. To do so, switch to Design view, choose Table ➤ Insert Table from the menu, and insert a table with 11 rows and 2 columns in the default Web Form. Now you need to drag and drop various controls and arrange them in the cells of this table, as detailed in the following steps. Figure 12-7 shows Default.aspx after the designing is complete.

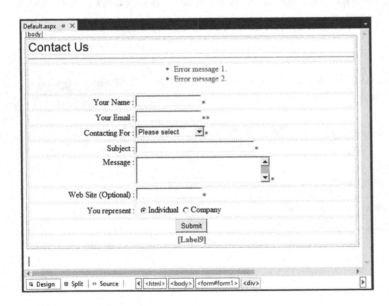

Figure 12-7. *Designing a Web Form*

The Web Form consists of many server controls such as Label, TextBox, DropDownList, RadioButtonList, Button, RequiredFieldValidator, RegularExpressionValidator, and ValidationSummary. To begin designing the Web Form, use the following steps:

1.   Drag and drop a Label control to the first row of the table. Set its Text property to **Contact Us**. Set its Font property to your choice. Also, drag and drop a Horizontal Rule HTML control below the Contact Us label.

2.   Drag and drop a ValidationSummary control in the second row. The ValidationSummary control is available in the Validation node of the toolbox and is used to display a consolidated list of validation errors from the current Web Form.

3.   Drag and drop seven Label controls in rows 3 through 9. Set their Text properties to **Your Name :**, **Your Email :**, **Contacting For :**, **Subject :**, **Message :**, **Web Site (Optional) :**, and **You represent :**, respectively.

4.   Drag and drop a TextBox control after the Your Name, Your Email, Subject, Message, and Web Site (Optional) labels, respectively. Set the TextMode property of the Message text box to **MultiLine**.

5.   Drag and drop a DropDownList control after the Contacting For label.

6.   Drag and drop a RadioButtonList after the You Represent label.

7.   Drag and drop a Button control to row 10 and set its Text property to **Submit**.

8.   Drag and drop a Label control to row 11 and set its Text property to a blank string. This label will be used to display a success message to the user.

9.   Select the DropDownList control. Open its property window and locate the Items property. Add four items in the DropDownList: **Please Select**, **Sales Quotation**, **Technical Problem**, and **Other**.

10. Select the RadioButtonList control. Open its property window and locate the Items property. Add two items in the RadioButtonList: **Individual** and **Company**.

11. Drag and drop a RequiredFieldValidator control in front of the controls that accept a name, e-mail, reason for contact, subject, and message. The RequiredFieldValidator control is used to validate that the control to which it has been attached contains some value. Set the ControlToValidate property of all the RequiredFieldValidator controls to the ID property of the respective text boxes or **DropDownList**.

12. Set the InitialValue property of the RequiredFieldValidator attached to the Contacting For dropdown to **Please Select**. This way, the user will need to choose an option other than Please Select.

13. Drag and drop a RegularExpressionValidator control in front of the controls that accept an e-mail and web site. The RegularExpressionValidator control validates the entered value for a specific pattern. The pattern is set by using regular expression syntax. Set the ControlToValidate property of both the RegularExpressionValidator controls to the ID property of the respective text boxes. Set the ValidationExpression property of the first RegularExpressionValidator control to **Internet Email Address**. Similarly, set the ValidationExpression property of the second RegularExpressionValidator control to **Internet URL**.

14. Set the Text property of all the validation controls (RequiredFieldValidator and Regular-ExpressionValidator) to *. This text will be displayed in place of the validation control whenever there is a validation error. Also, set the ErrorMessage property of all the validation controls to some meaningful error message. The ErrorMessage will be displayed in the ValidationSummary control in the event of any validation error.

Our Web Form design is now over. At the bottom of the Web Form Designer, you will find a tab named Source. Click on it to see the markup generated for our Web Form. The relevant markup of Default.aspx is shown in Listing 12-5.

Listing 12-5. Server Control Markup from Default.aspx

```
<%@ Page Language="C#" AutoEventWireup="true"
CodeFile="Default.aspx.cs" Inherits="_Default" %>

<!DOCTYPE html>

...
<form id="form1" runat="server">
...
<asp:Label ID="Label1" runat="server" Font-Names="Arial"
Font-Size="X-Large" Text="Contact Us">
</asp:Label>
...
<asp:ValidationSummary ID="ValidationSummary1" runat="server" />
...
<asp:Label ID="Label2" runat="server" Text="Your Name :"></asp:Label>
...
<asp:TextBox ID="TextBox1" runat="server"></asp:TextBox>
<asp:RequiredFieldValidator
            ID="RequiredFieldValidator1"
            runat="server" ControlToValidate="TextBox1"
            Display="Dynamic"
            ErrorMessage="Please enter your name">*
</asp:RequiredFieldValidator>
...
<asp:Label ID="Label3" runat="server" Text="Your Email :"></asp:Label>
...
<asp:TextBox ID="TextBox2" runat="server"></asp:TextBox>
<asp:RequiredFieldValidator
            ID="RequiredFieldValidator2" runat="server"
            ControlToValidate="TextBox2"
```

```
                Display="Dynamic"
                ErrorMessage="Please enter your email">*
</asp:RequiredFieldValidator>
<asp:RegularExpressionValidator
                ID="RegularExpressionValidator1"
                runat="server"
                ControlToValidate="TextBox2"
                Display="Dynamic"
                ErrorMessage="Please enter a valid email address"
                ValidationExpression="\w+([-+.']\w+)*@\w+([-.]\w+)*\.\w+([-.]\w+)*">*
</asp:RegularExpressionValidator></td>
...
<asp:Label ID="Label4" runat="server" Text="Contacting For :"></asp:Label>
...
<asp:DropDownList ID="DropDownList1" runat="server">
<asp:ListItem Value=" Please select ">Please select</asp:ListItem>
<asp:ListItem Value=" Sales Quotation ">Sales Quotation</asp:ListItem>
<asp:ListItem Value=" Technical Problem ">Technical Problem</asp:ListItem>
<asp:ListItem Value=" Other ">Other</asp:ListItem>
</asp:DropDownList>
<asp:RequiredFieldValidator ID="RequiredFieldValidator3" runat="server"
ControlToValidate="DropDownList1" Display="Dynamic"
ErrorMessage="Please select a reason for contacting us"
InitialValue="PS">*
</asp:RequiredFieldValidator>
...
<asp:Label ID="Label5" runat="server" Text="Subject :"></asp:Label>
...
<asp:TextBox ID="TextBox3" runat="server" Columns="37"></asp:TextBox>
<asp:RequiredFieldValidator
                ID="RequiredFieldValidator4" runat="server" ControlToValidate="TextBox3"
                Display="Dynamic" ErrorMessage="Please enter subject">*
</asp:RequiredFieldValidator>
...
<asp:Label ID="Label6" runat="server" Text="Message :"></asp:Label>
...
<asp:TextBox ID="TextBox4" runat="server" Columns="30" Rows="3"
 TextMode="MultiLine"></asp:TextBox>
<asp:RequiredFieldValidator
ID="RequiredFieldValidator5" runat="server" ControlToValidate="TextBox4"
Display="Dynamic" ErrorMessage="Please enter message">*
</asp:RequiredFieldValidator>
...
<asp:Label ID="Label7" runat="server" Text="Web Site (Optional) :"></asp:Label>
...
<asp:TextBox ID="TextBox5" runat="server"></asp:TextBox>
<asp:RegularExpressionValidator
ID="RegularExpressionValidator2" runat="server" ControlToValidate="TextBox5"
Display="Dynamic" ErrorMessage="Please enter a valid URL"
ValidationExpression="http(s)?://([\w-]+\.)+[\w-]+(/[\w- ./?%&=]*)?">
*</asp:RegularExpressionValidator>
...
```

```
<asp:Label ID="Label8" runat="server" Text="You represent :"></asp:Label>
...
<asp:RadioButtonList ID="RadioButtonList1" runat="server"
RepeatDirection="Horizontal">
<asp:ListItem Selected="True" Value="Individual">Individual</asp:ListItem>
<asp:ListItem Value="ListItem">Company</asp:ListItem>
</asp:RadioButtonList>
...
<asp:Button ID="Button1" runat="server" OnClick="Button1_Click" Text="Submit" />
...
<asp:Label ID="Label9" runat="server" Font-Bold="True" ForeColor="Red"></asp:Label>
...
</html>
```

Observe the markup carefully. At the top, you have a directive called @Page. A directive gives information about some entity to the ASP.NET processing engine. The @Page directive gives details about the current Web Form such as language of coding, code filename, and the class from the code file that represents this Web Form.

Next, there is a <!DOCTYPE> declaration that indicates that this document is an HTML5 document.

If you observe further, you will notice that every server control is represented by special XML markup. For example, a Label control is represented by an <asp:Label> tag, and a TextBox control is represented by an <asp:TextBox> tag. The part prior to the colon (:)—in other words, asp—is called a *tag prefix*. The part after the colon—Label or TextBox—is called a *tag name*.

Each server control has its ID attribute set to a unique value. The ID of a control is used to access it programmatically. Similarly, every server control has a runat attribute, which must have the value of server and indicates that the tag is server control markup. You will also observe that all the properties that you set via the Properties window are represented either as attributes or child elements in the server control markup. Thus ASP.NET server control markup is a special vocabulary of XML.

Writing Code

In this section, you will write some code so that when a user enters valid data and clicks the Submit button, the data is e-mailed to you. To accomplish this requirement, you need to handle the Click event of the Submit button. Double-click on Submit and you will be taken to the code-behind file (Default.aspx.cs), where you can write the code. Listing 12-6 shows the Web Form class and the skeleton of the Click event handler. We'll fill that in next.

Listing 12-6. Web Form Class and the Click Event Handler

```
public partial class _Default : System.Web.UI.Page
{
    protected void Button1_Click(object sender, EventArgs e)
    {

    }
}
```

The code-behind file contains a partial class named _Default that inherits from the System.Web. UI.Page base class, which provides basic functionality to your Web Form. Remember that the @Page directive has an attribute called Inherits that refers to this class. The _Default class is marked as partial because only when the markup file (.aspx) and code-behind file (.cs) are combined, the complete class is generated. This merging happens at runtime and is the job of the ASP.NET Framework. Also, notice several namespaces that are imported at the top of the code-behind file. All the namespaces that start with System.Web are physically located in an assembly, System.Web.dll. This is the main assembly for ASP.NET Web Forms.

■ **Note**   A thorough discussion of ASP.NET server controls and related concepts is beyond the scope of this book. If you are interested in ASP.NET web application development using Web Forms, consider visiting https://www.asp.net/web-forms to learn more.

To code the functionality, you need to import two namespaces: System.Net and System.Net.Mail. The latter namespace provides classes for sending e-mails. Listing 12-7 shows the Click event handler after adding the necessary code.

Listing 12-7. Sending E-Mail from the Code-Behind File

```
protected void Button1_Click(object sender, EventArgs e)
{
  SmtpClient client = new SmtpClient("localhost");
  client.Credentials = CredentialCache.DefaultNetworkCredentials;
  MailMessage msg = new MailMessage();
  msg.From = new MailAddress(TextBox2.Text);
  msg.To.Add("user@localhost");
  msg.Subject = TextBox3.Text;
  msg.Body =
    "[" + DropDownList1.SelectedItem.Text + "]" + TextBox4.Text + "\r\n" +
      TextBox1.Text + "\r\n" + TextBox5.Text;
  client.Send(msg);
  Label9.Text = "Your message has been sent. Thank you!";
}
```

The code declares an object of the SmtpClient class. The SmtpClient class allows you to send e-mails based on Simple Mail Transfer Protocol (SMTP). The constructor of the SmtpClient class accepts the IP address or name of the machine used for SMTP operations. In our example, it is assumed that you are using a local installation of IIS for sending e-mails and hence localhost is passed as the parameter. The Credentials property of the SmtpClient class indicates the network credentials of a user for authenticating the sender. The DefaultNetworkCredentials property of the CredentialCache class indicates the authentication credentials of the current Windows user.

After the credentials have been set, a new MailMessage is created. The MailMessage class represents an e-mail message. The From and To properties of this class represent the sender and receiver, respectively, and are of type MailAddress (make sure to change the e-mail address to suit your setup). The Subject and Body properties indicate the subject and body of the e-mail, respectively. All these properties are assigned by using the values entered in various Web Form controls. Finally, the Send() method of the SmtpClient class sends the supplied MailMessage to one or more recipients. A success message is displayed in a label informing the user that the message has been received.

Running the Web Application

To run the web application that you just finished, you need to choose the Debug ➤ Start Debugging menu option (or just press F5). Visual Studio will start the development web server in the background and will host your web site in it. It will also open a browser and load the `Default.aspx`. Figure 12-8 shows the `Default.aspx` Web Form in the browser.

Figure 12-8. *Default.aspx in a browser*

If you try to click the Submit button without entering any values, you should see validation error messages, as shown in Figure 12-9.

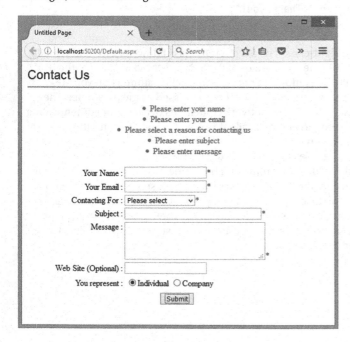

Figure 12-9. *Web form showing validation errors*

Notice how the ValidationSummary displays a collective list of error messages, whereas an asterisk is displayed in place of individual validation controls. If you enter valid values in the controls and click Submit, the code will send an e-mail to your e-mail address and will display a success message, as shown in Figure 12-10.

Figure 12-10. *Successful execution of the Web Form*

■ **Note**   Since this was the first ASP.NET example, I outlined all the steps required to develop and run the application. Now that you are familiar with the web site projects, future examples focus on the primary topic being discussed, skipping detailing of these steps.

The XML Data Source Control

One of the strengths of server controls is their ability to perform data binding with relational or hierarchical data. ASP.NET data source controls are a set of web server controls that automate common data-access tasks such as fetching records and displaying them in other data bound controls. All of this is achieved without any code being written by the developer. As we are looking at XML in this book, it is the XML data source control we are interested in. This control is very useful when you are using server controls such as TreeView that essentially display hierarchical data. Let's see how the XML data source control can be used along with a TreeView control.

Begin by creating a new web site via Visual Studio. Add a new XML file to your web site by using the Add New Item dialog box and name it Navigation.xml. The Navigation.xml file contains XML markup representing the web site navigation structure. The XML markup from Navigation.xml is shown in Listing 12-8.

Listing 12-8. XML Markup from the Navigation.xml File

```xml
<?xml version="1.0" encoding="utf-8" ?>
<node text="Home" url="default.aspx">
  <node text="Products" url="products.aspx">
    <node text="Product 1" url="product1.aspx"></node>
    <node text="Product 2" url="product2.aspx"></node>
    <node text="Product 3" url="product3.aspx"></node>
  </node>
  <node text="Services" url="services.aspx">
    <node text="Service 1" url="service1.aspx"></node>
    <node text="Service 2" url="service2.aspx"></node>
    <node text="Service 3" url="service3.aspx"></node>
  </node>
  <node text="About Us" url="about.aspx"></node>
  <node text="Contact Us" url="contact.aspx"></node>
</node>
```

The root tag of the document is <node>, which further contains various <node> tags. Each <node> element represents a node of the TreeView control and has two attributes, text and url:

- The text attribute specifies the text to be displayed in the TreeView node.

- The url attribute points to a URL where the user should be navigated.

The nesting of the <node> elements decides the nesting of the TreeView rendered. Thus the root node of the TreeView will be Home. The Home node will have four immediate children: Products, Services, About Us, and Contact Us. Similarly, the Products and Services nodes will have three children each.

Now drag and drop an XmlDataSource control from the toolbox onto the Web Form Designer. Set its DataFile property to Navigation.xml. The DataFile property points to an XML file that will be supplying data to the XML data source control. Next, drag and drop a TreeView control onto the Web Form and set its DataSourceID property to the ID of the XmlDataSource control you just configured. Now locate the DataBindings property of the TreeView and open the TreeView DataBindings Editor (see Figure 12-11).

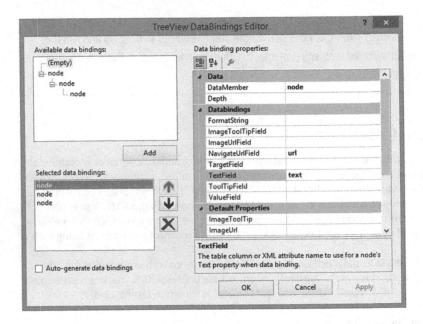

Figure 12-11. *TreeView DataBindings Editor*

In the Available Data Bindings area, you will see all the nodes at each level from the XML file. Select the node at each level and click the Add button. You will now have three entries in the Selected Data Bindings area. Select the first data binding and set its TextField and NavigateUrlField properties to text and url, respectively. As you might have guessed, text and url are the attributes of the <node> element. The DataMember property indicates the name of the element from the XML document that is supplying the data and is automatically set to node. Repeat the same process for the remaining two data bindings. Listing 12-9 shows the complete markup of Default.aspx.

Listing 12-9. Markup Containing the XmlDataSource and the TreeView

```
<%@ Page Language="C#" AutoEventWireup="true" CodeFile="Default.aspx.cs"
Inherits="_Default" %>

<!DOCTYPE html>

<html xmlns="http://www.w3.org/1999/xhtml" >
  <head runat="server">
    <title>Untitled Page</title>
  </head>
  <body>
    <form id="form1" runat="server">
      <asp:XmlDataSource ID="XmlDataSource1" runat="server"
                         DataFile="~/Navigation.xml">
      </asp:XmlDataSource>
      <asp:TreeView ID="TreeView1" runat="server" AutoGenerateDataBindings="False"
                    DataSourceID="XmlDataSource1" Font-Bold="True" Font-Size="Large"
                    ShowLines="True">
        <DataBindings>
          <asp:TreeNodeBinding DataMember="node" NavigateUrlField="url"
                               TextField="text" />
          <asp:TreeNodeBinding DataMember="node" NavigateUrlField="url"
                               TargetField="text" />
          <asp:TreeNodeBinding DataMember="node" NavigateUrlField="url"
                               TargetField="text" />
        </DataBindings>
      </asp:TreeView>
    </form>
  </body>
</html>
```

As you can see, the XML data source control and the TreeView control are represented by the `<asp:XmlDataSource>` and `<asp:TreeView>` markup tags, respectively. Each TreeView node binding is represented by an `<asp:TreeNodeBinding>` tag. The `DataMember`, `NavigateUrlField`, and `TextField` attributes of the `TreeNodeBinding` element represent the properties that you assigned previously.

Now run the web site as before and see how the TreeView control renders the various nodes based on the structure specified in the `Navigation.xml` file. Figure 12-12 shows a sample run of the Web Form.

Figure 12-12. A TreeView populated by using an XML data source control

Applying Transformations

In the preceding example, you supplied the XML file as is to the XML data source control. What if you want to apply an XSLT transformation to the XML file and then bind it with the TreeView? Fortunately, the XML data source control has a built-in facility to do just that: the TransformFile property, which points to an XSLT file. Before supplying the XML data to other controls such as a TreeView, the XSLT style sheet is applied to the XML data and then the transformed data is passed on. Suppose that you bound a TreeView control to an XML document, as shown in Listing 12-10.

Listing 12-10. XML Document to Be Bound to a TreeView

```xml
<?xml version="1.0" encoding="utf-8"?>
<MenuItem Title="Home" URL="default.aspx">
  <MenuItem Title="Products" URL="products.aspx">
    <MenuItem Title="Product 1" URL="product1.aspx" />
    <MenuItem Title="Product 2" URL="product2.aspx" />
    <MenuItem Title="Product 3" URL="product3.aspx" />
  </MenuItem>
  <MenuItem Title="Services" URL="services.aspx">
    <MenuItem Title="Service 1" URL="service1.aspx" />
    <MenuItem Title="Service 2" URL="service2.aspx" />
    <MenuItem Title="Service 3" URL="service3.aspx" />
  </MenuItem>
  <MenuItem Title="About Us" URL="about.aspx" />
  <MenuItem Title="Contact Us" URL="contact.aspx" />
</MenuItem>
```

As you can see, this XML document uses the `<MenuItem>` element to represent a TreeView node. The `Title` and `URL` attributes represent the `Text` and `NavigateUrlField` properties of individual TreeView nodes. Now suppose that for some reason, you want to bind the same TreeView to another XML document, as shown in Listing 12-11.

Listing 12-11. XML Markup from the New XML File

```
<?xml version="1.0" encoding="utf-8" ?>
<node text="Home" url="default.aspx">
  <node text="Products" url="products.aspx">
    <node text="Product 1" url="product1.aspx"></node>
    <node text="Product 2" url="product2.aspx"></node>
    <node text="Product 3" url="product3.aspx"></node>
  </node>
  <node text="Services" url="services.aspx">
    <node text="Service 1" url="service1.aspx"></node>
    <node text="Service 2" url="service2.aspx"></node>
    <node text="Service 3" url="service3.aspx"></node>
  </node>
  <node text="About Us" url="about.aspx"></node>
  <node text="Contact Us" url="contact.aspx"></node>
</node>
```

You might have noticed that this is the same XML file that we used in the previous example. To cater to the change, you need to reconfigure the TreeView node data bindings to suit the new XML document. If the underlying data binding has complex nesting, this may not be an easy task. This situation can be avoided if you apply an XSLT style sheet to the XML from Listing 12-11 and transform it to match the XML in Listing 12-10. The XSLT style sheet that can do this transformation is shown in Listing 12-12.

Listing 12-12. An XSLT Style Sheet for Transforming the New XML Markup

```
<?xml version="1.0" encoding="UTF-8" ?>
<xsl:stylesheet version="1.0" xmlns:xsl="http://www.w3.org/1999/XSL/Transform">
  <xsl:template match="/">
    <xsl:for-each select=".">
      <xsl:apply-templates/>
    </xsl:for-each>
  </xsl:template>
  <xsl:template match="node">
    <xsl:element name="MenuItem">
      <xsl:attribute name="Title">
        <xsl:value-of select="@text"/>
      </xsl:attribute>
      <xsl:attribute name="URL">
        <xsl:value-of select="@url"/>
      </xsl:attribute>
      <xsl:apply-templates />
    </xsl:element>
  </xsl:template>
</xsl:stylesheet>
```

The style sheet transforms a `<node>` element to a `<MenuItem>` element. Further, it transforms the `text` and `url` attributes to the `Title` and `URL` attributes, respectively.

To test how the `TransformFile` property works, you need to modify the preceding example by following these steps:

1. Add a new XSLT file named `Navigation.xslt` to the web site.

2. Key in the markup shown in Listing 12-12.

3. Set the `TransformFile` property of the XML data source control to `Navigation.xslt`.

4. Open the TreeView DataBindings Editor of the TreeView and modify the data bindings to use the MenuItem node as `DataMember`, Title as `TextField`, and URL as `NavigateUrlField`.

This time, the TreeView DataBindings Editor looks like Figure 12-13.

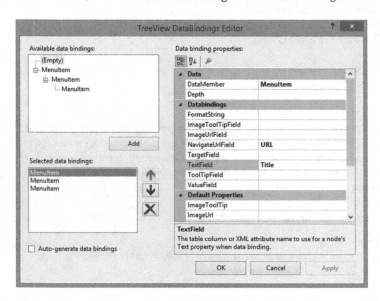

Figure 12-13. *TreeView DataBindings Editor showing transformed nodes*

You will observe that although the `DataFile` property is still `Navigation.xml`, the data bindings shown are as per the transformation specified in the XSLT style sheet. If you run the Web Form again, the output should be the same as in Figure 12-12 earlier.

Filtering Data by Using XPath Expressions

At times you may want to filter the data from the source XML file and bind the filtered data to other controls. This is where the XPath property of the XML data source control comes in. The XPath property takes a valid XPath expression and applies it to the source XML data.

Suppose, for example, that you want to display only product-related nodes in the TreeView. You can achieve this by setting the XPath property of the XML data source to `/node/node[@text="Products"]`. This way, only the product-related nodes (Products, Product 1, Product 2, and Product 3) will be filtered. The TreeView will have nesting up to two levels only (Products as the top node, and the other three nodes as child nodes). Figure 12-14 shows a sample run of the same Web Form after setting the XPath property.

Figure 12-14. *TreeView after applying the XPath filter*

Binding an XML Data Source to a Menu Control

In the previous examples, you used a TreeView to display data supplied by an XML data source control. ASP. NET also provides a Menu control that can be used to display hierarchical data. The Menu control closely matches the TreeView control with respect to XML data binding. However, it differs in its look and feel. The Menu control renders dynamic pulldown menus in your Web Forms similar to traditional Windows applications. Let's see an example of how it can be used.

Create a new web site in Visual Studio. Add the `Navigation.xml` file that you created previously to the web site by using the Add Existing Item dialog box. Drag and drop an `XmlDataSource` control onto the default Web Form and set its `DataFile` property to `Navigation.xml`. Now drag and drop a Menu control onto the form and set its `DataSourceID` property to the ID of the `XmlDataSource` control you just configured.

Now, locate the Menu control's `DataBindings` property. Similar to the TreeView, the Menu control opens the Menu DataBindings Editor, wherein you can configure the data bindings.

The process of configuring data bindings is exactly the same as before. You need to select the required data bindings and set their `DataMember`, `TextField`, and `NavigateUrl` properties to `node`, `text`, and `url`, respectively. Figure 12-15 shows the Menu DataBindings Editor with required data bindings added.

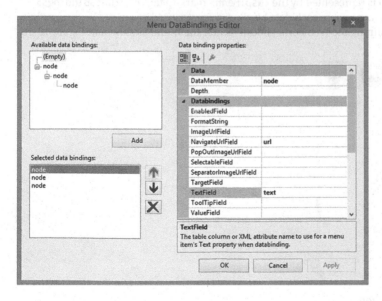

Figure 12-15. *Menu DataBindings Editor*

The complete markup of the Web Form is shown in Listing 12-13.

Listing 12-13. Markup of the Menu Control

```
<%@ Page Language="C#" AutoEventWireup="true" CodeFile="Default.aspx.cs"
        Inherits="_Default" %>

<!DOCTYPE html>
<html xmlns="http://www.w3.org/1999/xhtml" >
  <head runat="server">
    <title>Untitled Page</title>
  </head>
  <body>
    <form id="form1" runat="server">
      <asp:XmlDataSource ID="XmlDataSource1" runat="server"
                         DataFile="~/Navigation.xml"></asp:XmlDataSource>
      <asp:Menu ID="Menu1" runat="server" BackColor="#E3EAEB"
              DataSourceID="XmlDataSource1"
        <DataBindings>
          <asp:MenuItemBinding DataMember="node" NavigateUrlField="url"
                             TextField="text" />
          <asp:MenuItemBinding DataMember="node" NavigateUrlField="url"
                             TextField="text" />
          <asp:MenuItemBinding DataMember="node" NavigateUrlField="url"
                             TextField="text" />
        </DataBindings>
      </asp:Menu>
    </form>
  </body>
</html>
```

As you can see, the Menu control is represented by the `<asp:Menu>` markup tag. The `<DataBindings>` section defines one or more data bindings, where each data binding is represented by an `<asp:MenuItemBinding>` element. Running the Web Form should render the menu as shown in Figure 12-16.

Figure 12-16. *The Menu control in action*

Working with Site Maps

A *site map* is an XML file that details the overall navigational layout of your web site. You can then consume this site map file as required. The site map file has an extension of .sitemap. Let's examine site map files via an example. Have a look at Figure 12-17.

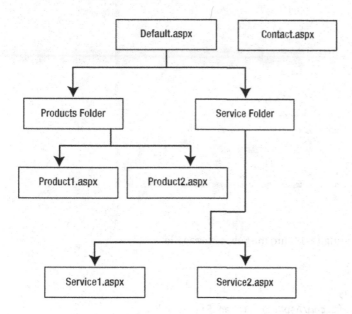

Figure 12-17. *Structure of a web site*

Figure 12-17 shows the directory structure of a sample web site. The home page (Default.aspx) and Contact Us page (contact.aspx) reside in the root folder of the web site. There are two subfolders called Products and Services. Each of them contains two Web Forms—Product1.aspx and Product2.aspx, and Service1.aspx and Service2.aspx—respectively. Now let's represent this web site structure by using a site map.

Create a new web site by using Visual Studio. Add a new site map file by using the Add New Item dialog box (see Figure 12-18). Name the site map file Web.sitemap.

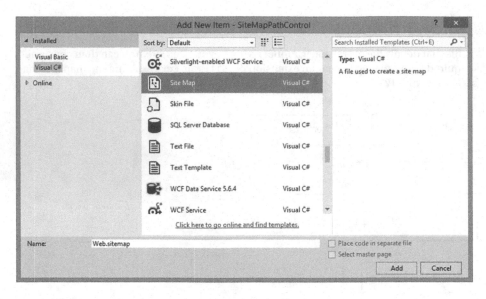

Figure 12-18. *Adding a new site map*

Now type the XML markup shown in Listing 12-14 into the `Web.sitemap` file.

Listing 12-14. Contents of the Web.sitemap File

```
<?xml version="1.0" encoding="utf-8" ?>
<siteMap xmlns="http://schemas.microsoft.com/AspNet/SiteMap-File-1.0" >
<siteMapNode url="default.aspx" title="Home" description="My Web Site">
  <siteMapNode url="~/products/default.aspx" title="Products">
    <siteMapNode url="~/products/product1.aspx" title="First Product" />
    <siteMapNode url="~/products/product2.aspx" title="Second Product" />
  </siteMapNode>
  <siteMapNode url="~/services/default.aspx" title="Services">
    <siteMapNode url="~/services/service1.aspx" title="First Service" />
    <siteMapNode url="~/services/service2.aspx" title="Second Service" />
  </siteMapNode>
<siteMapNode url="contact.aspx" title="Contact Us" />
</siteMapNode>
</siteMap>
```

The site map file contains a set of predefined tags and attributes. The root node of a site map file is `<siteMap>`. It further contains several `<siteMapNodes>` tags depending on your web site structure. The `<siteMapNode>` tag has four important attributes. They are listed in Table 12-1.

Table 12-1. *Attributes of a Site Map Node*

Attribute	Description
title	Indicates the title of the page. This attribute is often used by navigational controls to display the title for the URL.
url	Indicates the URL of the page that this node represents.
description	Specifies the description of the destination page. You can use this description to show ToolTips.
roles	While using security trimming, this attribute specifies the roles that are allowed to access this page.

■ **Note** *Security trimming* is a feature that implements role-based security by rendering only the nodes that are allowed for the current user. In other words, a particular `<siteMapNode>` will be accessible to a user only if the user's role is specified in the `roles` attribute of the `<siteMapNode>` element.

Site map files are often used to render some kind of navigational structure. There are two common ways in which you can consume the site map file you just created:

- In a `SiteMapPath` control
- In a `SiteMapDataSource` control

In the following sections, you are going to see both of them.

Using a SiteMapPath Control

The `SiteMapPath` control allows you to render what are often called *breadcrumbs*. Figure 12-19 shows what breadcrumbs are.

Figure 12-19. *Breadcrumbs*

The `SiteMapPath` control displays various levels of navigation. You can click on the parent or root levels to navigate back or to the top level. Before we delve into the details, let's first create the required directory structure and Web Forms. Begin by adding two folders to the web site called `Products` and `Services`. Add the Web Forms as shown in Table 12-2.

Table 12-2. *Folders and Web Forms*

Web Form Name	Folder
Default.aspx	Root folder
Contact.aspx	Root folder
Product1.aspx	Products
Product2.aspx	Products
Service1.aspx	Services
Service2.aspx	Services

Now drag and drop a SiteMapPath control onto each Web Form. Run Service2.aspx in the browser, and you should see something similar to Figure 12-19. The SiteMapPath control automatically renders breadcrumbs for the current Web Form based on its location in the site map file.

Using a SiteMapDataSource Control

The use of site maps is not limited just to the SiteMapPath control. You can also attach the site map to navigational controls such as a TreeView. In this example, we will use the same site map file to bind to a TreeView.

Create a new web site by using Visual Studio. Add the same Web.sitemap file to it. This time drag and drop a SiteMapDataSource control onto the Web Form. The SiteMapDataSource control automatically picks up the Web.sitemap file and supplies it to other controls. Further, drag and drop a TreeView control and set its DataSourceID property to the ID attribute of the SiteMapDataSource. That's it. Run the Web Form, and it should resemble Figure 12-20.

Figure 12-20. *TreeView bound with SiteMapDataSource control*

Using the XML Control

In Chapter 6, you learned to apply XSLT style sheets to XML data and transform them from one vocabulary to another. You achieved this by creating an instance of the XslCompiledTransform class. You then loaded an XSLT style sheet into it by using its Load() method. Finally, you did the transformation by using its Transform() method. ASP.NET provides an easy alternative to this manual coding: the XML control. The XML control accepts an XML document and XSLT style sheet. It then applies the style sheet to the XML data and renders the content on the web page. The most common use of the XML control is to transform XML data into HTML, though of course it doesn't have to be HTML.

To illustrate the use of the XML control, create a new web site. Add a new XML file named Employees.xml and type in the markup shown in Listing 12-15.

Listing 12-15. XML File That Supplies Data to the XML Control

```
<?xml version="1.0" encoding="utf-8" ?>
<?xml-stylesheet type="text/xsl" href="Employees.xslt"?>
<!-- This is list of employees -->
<employees>
  <employee employeeid="1">
    <firstname>Nancy</firstname>
    <lastname>Davolio</lastname>
    <homephone>(206) 555-9857</homephone>
    <notes>
      <![CDATA[Education includes a BA in psychology from Colorado State University in 1970.
      She also completed "The Art of the Cold Call." Nancy is a member of Toastmasters
      International.]]>
    </notes>
  </employee>
  <employee employeeid="2">
    <firstname>Andrew</firstname>
    <lastname>Fuller</lastname>
    <homephone>(206) 555-9482</homephone>
    <notes>
      <![CDATA[Andrew received his BTS commercial in 1974 and a Ph.D. in
international marketing from the University of Dallas in 1981. He is fluent in
French and Italian and reads German. He joined the company as a sales
representative, was promoted to sales manager in January 1992 and to vice
president of sales in March 1993. Andrew is a member of the Sales Management
Roundtable, the Seattle Chamber of Commerce, and the Pacific Rim Importers
Association.]]>
    </notes>
  </employee>
  <employee employeeid="3">
    <firstname>Janet</firstname>
    <lastname>Leverling</lastname>
    <homephone>(206) 555-3412</homephone>
    <notes>
      <![CDATA[Janet has a BS degree in chemistry from Boston College (1984).
```

She has also completed a certificate program in food retailing management. Janet was hired as a sales associate in 1991 and promoted to sales representative in February 1992.]]>
```
    </notes>
  </employee>
</employees>
```

Similarly, add a new XSLT style sheet named Employees.xsl and type in the markup shown in Listing 12-16.

Listing 12-16. XSLT Style Sheet to Be Applied

```
<?xml version="1.0" encoding="UTF-8" ?>
<xsl:stylesheet version="1.0" xmlns:xsl="http://www.w3.org/1999/XSL/Transform">
  <xsl:template match="/">
    <html>
      <body>
        <h1>Employee Listing</h1>
        <table border="1">
          <tr>
            <th>Employee ID</th>
            <th>First Name</th>
            <th>Last Name</th>
            <th>Home Phone</th>
            <th>Notes</th>
          </tr>
          <xsl:for-each select="employees/employee">
            <tr>
              <td>
                <xsl:value-of select="@employeeid"/>
              </td>
              <td>
                <xsl:value-of select="firstname"/>
              </td>
              <td>
                <xsl:value-of select="lastname"/>
              </td>
              <td>
                <xsl:value-of select="homephone"/>
              </td>
              <td>
                <xsl:value-of select="notes"/>
              </td>
            </tr>
          </xsl:for-each>
        </table>
      </body>
    </html>
  </xsl:template>
</xsl:stylesheet>
```

■ **Note** These are the same files that you used in Chapter 6. If you want, you can add them to your web site instead of recreating them.

Now drag and drop an XML control onto the default Web Form. Set its DocumentSource property to Employees.xml and its TransformSource property to Employees.xsl. The former property points to the XML file that is to be transformed, whereas the latter property points to the XSLT style sheet that is to be applied to the DocumentSource. Now run the Web Form and you should see something similar to Figure 12-21.

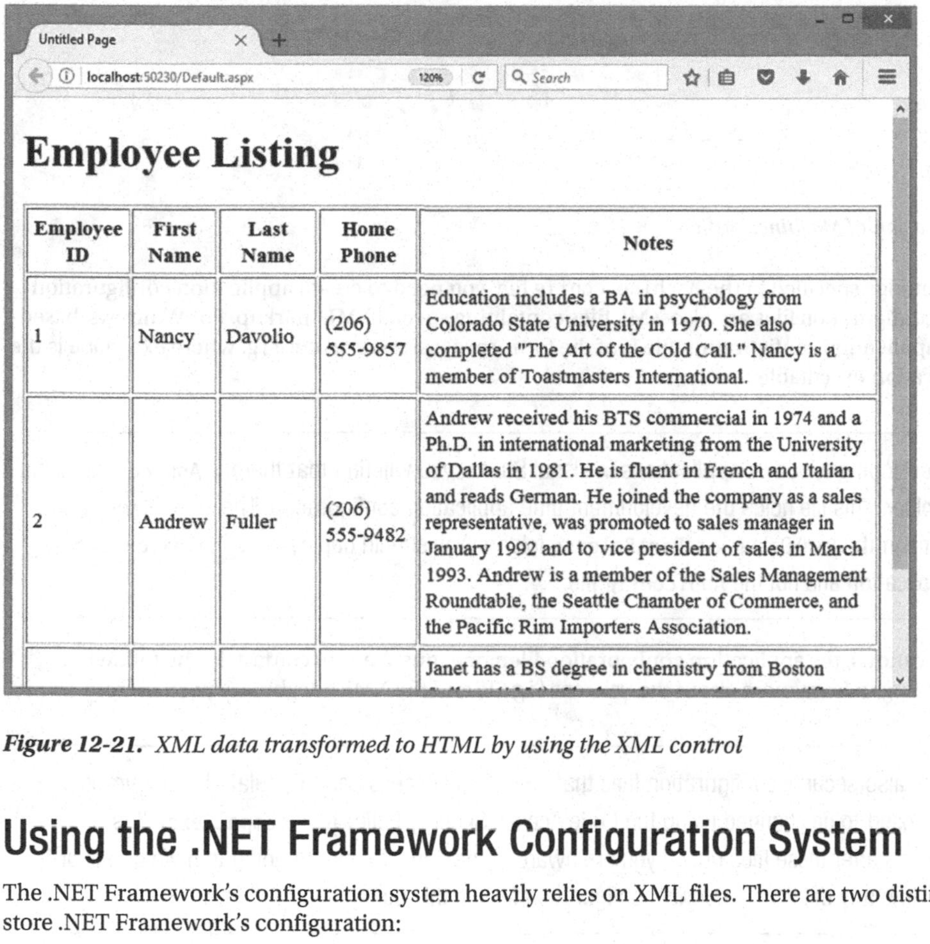

Figure 12-21. *XML data transformed to HTML by using the XML control*

Using the .NET Framework Configuration System

The .NET Framework's configuration system heavily relies on XML files. There are two distinct XML files that store .NET Framework's configuration:

- Machine configuration files

- Application configuration files

When you install the .NET Framework on a machine, an XML file named Machine.config gets created in the <installation_path>/Config folder. The Machine.config file is the master configuration file and contains configuration settings that are applied to all .NET applications running on that machine.

Though this file is in XML format and can be edited directly, you should do so with caution. That's because any change made to this file is going to affect all the applications running on that machine. Figure 12-22 shows location of Machine.config in a sample installation.

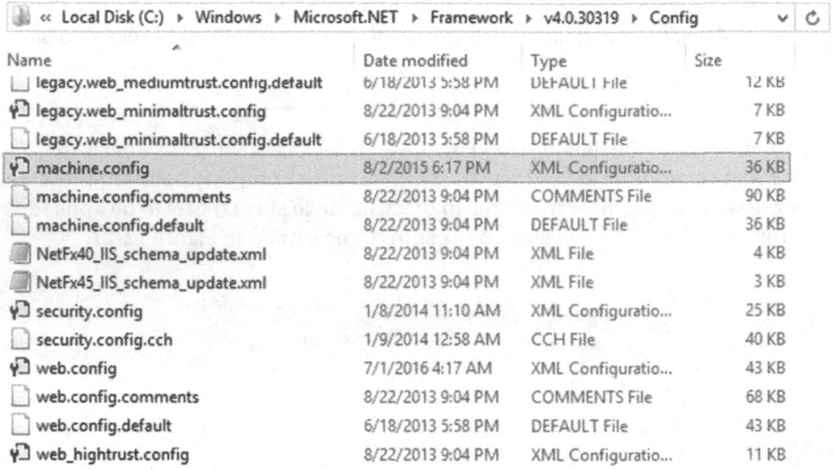

Figure 12-22. *Location of Machine.config*

To override settings specified in the Machine.config file, you need to create application configuration files. Application configuration files are also XML files containing special XML markup. For Windows-based applications, the application configuration file is of the form <exe_name>.exe.config, where exe_name is the name of the application executable.

■ **Note**   While developing windows applications in Visual Studio, you will find that there is App.config file in the project's root folder. This file holds the development time application configuration. The <exe_name>.exe. config can be found in the Bin\Debug or Bin\Release folders. You should deploy <exe_name>.exe.config along with your application and not the App.config file.

For web applications, the application configuration filename must be web.config. In the following sections, you are going to learn more about the web.config file and the XML vocabulary used therein.

■ **Note**   There are also security configuration files that store Code Access Security related configuration. These files are supposed to be changed using the Code Access Security Policy tool (Caspol.exe). It is recommended that you alter these files only if you are aware of the impact they are going to have on security policy. We won't go into any details of security configuration files in this book.

Structure of the web.config File

Listing 12-17 shows the general structural outline of a web.config file.

Listing 12-17. Structural Outline of web.config

```
<configuration>
    <appSettings />
    <connectionStrings />
    <system.web />
</configuration>
```

As you can see, the root node of the web.config file is <configuration>, and there are three main subsections:

- The <appSettings> section is used to specify application configuration settings.

- The <connectionStrings> section is used to store one or more database connection strings.

- The <system.web> section contains all the settings applicable to web applications.

All of these sections are optional. However, in most real-world cases you will have at least the <system.web> section.

■ **Note**   The web.config file contains many configuration sections. It isn't possible to cover every section here. I am going to discuss some commonly used sections only.

Web.config Inheritance

The web.config file exhibits what is often referred to as *inheritance behavior*. In a single web application, there can be one or more web.config files in different folders. The settings of one web.config file are applied to the folder in which it resides and all the subfolders. However, if the subfolders contain a web.config of their own, the settings specified in that web.config take precedence.

Using Web.config for Common Configuration Tasks

Now that we have a basic understanding of how web.config works, let's see how to perform some common configuration tasks. We are briefly going to cover the following tasks in particular:

- How to store and retrieve application configuration settings

- How to store and retrieve your database connection strings

- How to work with forms authentication

- How to deal with session state

- How to provide custom error pages in your web site

Storing and Retrieving Application Configuration Settings

Avoiding hard-coding values is a mandatory requirement in many real-world applications. Earlier in this chapter, we developed a Contact Us Web Form that sent messages from users to a specified e-mail address. In that example, we hard-coded an e-mail address in the code-behind file. What if the e-mail address changes after deployment? Obviously, you need to change the source code to match the new e-mail address and redeploy the application. This is not a recommended practice for real-world applications. Wouldn't it be nice if we could isolate the e-mail address from the application, store it in an external location, and retrieve it inside your code? Prior to .NET Framework, developers achieved this by using .INI files or the registry. In .NET, you have a nice alternative: the application configuration section of configuration files.

The <appSettings> section of web.config allows you to store such application-specific settings. You can then read these settings in your source code. If the settings change after deploying the application, you need to change just the web.config file and not the source code. Let's modify our Contact Us Web Form to use application configuration settings.

■ **Note**   Although the example discussed here uses the <appSettings> section in a web application, <appSettings> is equally applicable to Windows applications.

Open the same web site by choosing File ➤ Open ➤ Web Site from the menu. Open the web.config file and modify the <appSettings> section, as shown in Listing 12-18.

Listing 12-18. Storing Values in the <appSettings> Section

```
<appSettings>
    <add key="host" value="localhost"/>
    <add key="email" value="user@localhost"/>
</appSettings>
```

The <appSettings> section can contain one or more <add> elements. The <add> element has two attributes:

- The key attribute defines a key with which the value will be accessed in the code.

- The value attribute specifies the actual value of the key.

In our example, we defined two keys: host and email. The former key stores the value of the SMTP host, and the latter stores your e-mail address. Now open the code-behind of the Web Form and modify the Click event handler of the Submit button, as shown in Listing 12-19.

Listing 12-19. Retrieving Values from the <appSettings> Section

```
protected void Button1_Click(object sender, EventArgs e)
{
    string host = ConfigurationManager.AppSettings["host"];
    string email = ConfigurationManager.AppSettings["email"];
    SmtpClient client = new SmtpClient(host);
    client.Credentials = CredentialCache.DefaultNetworkCredentials;
    MailMessage msg = new MailMessage();
    msg.From = new MailAddress(TextBox2.Text);
    msg.To.Add(email);
    msg.Subject = TextBox3.Text;
```

```
msg.Body =
   "[" + DropDownList1.SelectedItem.Text + "]" + TextBox4.Text + "\r\n" +
     TextBox1.Text + "\r\n" + TextBox5.Text;
client.Send(msg);
Label9.Text = "Your message has been sent. Thank you!";
}
```

Observe the code marked in bold. The code uses a class called ConfigurationManager, which resides in the System.Configuration namespace. By default, System.Configuration is imported in the code-behind. The AppSettings property of the ConfigurationManager class exposes the entire <appSettings> section as a NameValueCollection. You can access individual values by using an index or a key name, though it is more common to access them by using key names.

The code retrieves the values of two keys—host and email—and stores them in a string variable. The constructor of the SmtpClient class now accepts the value stored in the host string variable instead of a hard-coded value. Similarly, the Add() method accepts the value stored in the email string variable and not a hard-coded value. If you run the application, you should get the results as before, but now you are free to change the host name and e-mail address without touching the source code.

Storing and Retrieving Database Connection Strings

Storing database connection strings outside the source code is probably the most common configuration task. The configuration file has a special section to store database connection strings called <connectionStrings>. The <connectionStrings> section allows you to store one or more database connection strings that can be retrieved later in your code. To retrieve the connection strings stored in the <connectionStrings> section, you again need to use the ConfigurationManager class.

To illustrate the use of the <connectionStrings> section, you will develop a simple employee listing Web Form. The Web Form will display a list of employees in a GridView control. To begin, create a new web site by using Visual Studio as before.

■ **Note**   Although the example discussed here uses the <connectionStrings> section in a web application, <connectionStrings> is equally applicable to Windows applications.

Open the web.config file in the IDE and modify the <connectionStrings> section, as shown in Listing 12-20.

Listing 12-20. Adding a Connection String to the <connectionStrings> Section

```
<connectionStrings>
  <add name="northwind"
       connectionString="data source=.;initial catalog=Northwind;
       integrated security=true"
       providerName="System.Data.SqlClient"/>
</connectionStrings>
```

The <connectionStrings> section can contain one or more <add> elements, each defining a database connection string:

- The name attribute of the <add> element defines a name for that connection string. This name is used later to access the connection string.

- The connectionString attribute specifies the actual database connection string.

- Finally, the providerName attribute indicates the .NET data provider that can be used to communicate with the database.

Now open the default Web Form and drag and drop a GridView control onto it. Then type in the code shown in Listing 12-21 in the Page_Load event of the Web Form.

Listing 12-21. Retrieving the Connection String

```
protected void Page_Load(object sender, EventArgs e)
{
  string strConn=
    ConfigurationManager.ConnectionStrings["northwind"].ConnectionString;
  SqlDataAdapter da =
    new SqlDataAdapter("SELECT EmployeeID,FirstName, LastName FROM Employees",
                       strConn);
  DataSet ds = new DataSet();
  da.Fill(ds, "employees");
  GridView1.DataSource = ds;
  GridView1.DataBind();
}
```

The code uses the ConfigurationManager class to retrieve the connection string value. The ConnectionStrings collection can be accessed by using an index or a connection string name. In our example, we access it with a name.

Each connection string stored in the <connectionStrings> section is represented by a ConnectionStringSettings class, and the ConnectionString property of this class returns the actual connection string. The connection string is then used as the second parameter of the SqlDataAdapter constructor, the first parameter being the SELECT query.

A DataSet is then filled by using the Fill() method of the SqlDataAdapter class. The DataSet thus created acts as a DataSource to the GridView control. The DataBind() method of the GridView control binds the data from the DataSet to the GridView. If you run the Web Form after writing the code, you should see something similar to Figure 12-23.

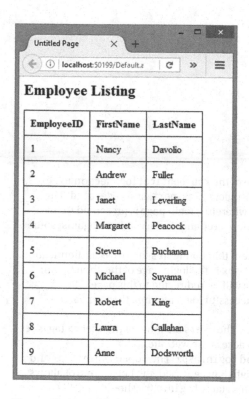

Figure 12-23. *Web Form displaying an employee listing*

Using Forms Authentication

While developing web sites, you may need to ensure that pages be accessible only to valid users of the application. Moreover, you may want that only the users belonging to certain role (say, Administrator) be allowed to access the pages. The later is often called *role-based security*. To implement such security features, you use authentication and authorization.

Authentication is a process by which you decide whether a person is a valid user of the application. Typically this validity is determined by a combination of username and password. Authorization is a process by which you decide whether an authenticated user can access a certain page or feature. A common way to authorize users is to add them to one or more roles.

The web.config file has two sections—<authentication> and <authorization>—that allow you to configure the respective security aspects for a web site. As an example, let's build a simple web site that authenticates a user and displays a welcome message upon a successful login attempt.

■ **Note** To keep things simple, we won't implement database-driven authentication and role-based security in this example. In a realistic case, you could either use ASP.NET Membership and Roles or, better yet, ASP.NET Identity to develop a full-fledge authentication and authorization scheme for your web site.

Create a new web site using Visual Studio as before. Then open the web.config file in the IDE and add the <authentication> and <authorization> sections, as shown in Listing 12-22.

Listing 12-22. Configuring Forms Authentication

```
<authentication mode="Forms">
  <forms loginUrl="~/login.aspx"
         defaultUrl="~/default.aspx">
  </forms>
</authentication>
<authorization>
  <deny users="?"/>
</authorization>
```

The markup shown in Listing 12-22 sets the mode attribute of the `<authentication>` section to Forms. The mode attribute can take one of these values—None, Forms, Windows, Passport, and Federated. The Forms authentication is a very common form of authentication wherein a login page is presented to the user, the user enters some username and password, and then those credentials are validated against some datastore (such as SQL Server).

The `<authentication>` section contains the `<forms>` element that configures the Forms authentication. The loginUrl attribute of the `<forms>` tag indicates that Login.aspx is the login page of the application. If any user tries to access other pages without logging in first, he will be redirected to this page. The defaultUrl attribute of the `<forms>` tag indicates that after a successful login attempt, the user can be redirected to the default page.

The `<authorization>` section contains the `<deny>` element. The users attribute of the `<deny>` tag is set to ?, indicating that anonymous users should not be allowed to access the web site.

Now add two Web Forms to the project—Default.aspx and Login.aspx. Then open Login.aspx and drag and drop a Login control on it from the toolbox. As you might have guessed, the Login control allows you to easily capture the username and password of a user. At this stage, Login.aspx should look like Figure 12-24.

Figure 12-24. *Login.aspx with Login control*

Now double-click on the Login control to go to its Authenticate event handler. The Authenticate event handler is a place for writing your code that validates the user credentials. In a real-world case you would have a database access involved here. For the sake of simplicity, our example uses a hard-coded username and password. The Authenticate event handler is shown in Listing 12-23.

Listing 12-23. Authenticate Event Handler

```
protected void Login1_Authenticate(object sender, AuthenticateEventArgs e)
{
    if(Login1.UserName=="admin" && Login1.Password=="password")
    {
        FormsAuthentication.SetAuthCookie(Login1.UserName, Login1.RememberMeSet);
        e.Authenticated = true;
        Response.Redirect(FormsAuthentication.DefaultUrl);
    }
    else
    {
        e.Authenticated = false;
    }
}
```

The Authenticate event handler checks the UserName and Password properties of the Login control. If they are admin and password respectively then it calls the SetAuthCookie() method of the FormsAuthentication class (System.Web.Security namespace). The Forms authentication works with the help of a cookie (by default). The presence of this cookie along with a request indicates that a user is an authenticated user. Absence of this cookie indicates that the user has not yet been authenticated. The SetAuthCookie() method issues this cookie to the user. The two parameters of the SetAuthCookie() method are username and whether to remember the logged-in status even after closing the browser (persistent cookie).

Once the authentication cookie is issued, the code redirects the user to the default page. Notice how the DefaultUrl property of FormsAuthentication class is used to retrieve the defaultUrl you set earlier in the configuration file.

If the username and password don't match the specified values, the Authenticated property of the AuthenticateEventArgs class is set to false. This way, the Login control will display an error message to the user.

Next, open the Default.aspx file and drag and drop two Label controls and a Button control on it. Set the Text property of the Button to Logout. The default page will display a welcome message to the user. To specify this message, write the code shown in Listing 12-24 in the Page_Load event handler.

Listing 12-24. Retrieving the Username

```
protected void Page_Load(object sender, EventArgs e)
{
    Label1.Text = $"Welcome {Page.User.Identity.Name}!";
    if (Request.IsAuthenticated)
    {
        Label2.Text = "You are an authenticated user.";
    }
}
```

The code retrieves the name of the currently logged in user using Page.User.Identity.Name and forms a welcome message based on it. The code then checks the IsAuthenticated property of the Request object. This property indicates whether a request is authenticated. If the request is authenticated, a message is shown in the second Label.

Now, double-click on the Button control to go in its Click event handler. Write the code shown in Listing 12-25 in the Click event handler.

Listing 12-25. Logging a User Out

```
protected void Button1_Click(object sender, EventArgs e)
{
    FormsAuthentication.SignOut();
    Response.Redirect(FormsAuthentication.LoginUrl);
}
```

The code calls the `SignOut()` method of the `FormsAuthentication` class. The `SignOut()` method removes the authentication cookie issued earlier. Once the cookie is removed, the user is taken back to the login page. This is done by redirecting the control to the page, as indicated by the `LoginUrl` property of `FormsAuthentication`.

If you run the application, you will be taken to the login page shown earlier. If you enter valid credentials, the default page will be displayed as shown in Figure 12-25.

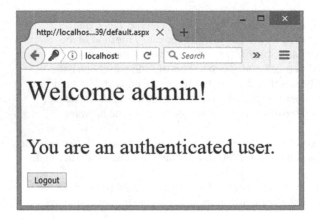

Figure 12-25. *Default page displaying welcome message*

As you can see, the welcome message is displaying the username. You can click on the Logout button to log out and return to the login page.

Configuring Session State

ASP.NET session allows you to store arbitrary pieces of information. Session state is maintained per user basis. Session is exposed as an intrinsic object—`Session`—that stores data as key-value pairs. To configure the behavior of the session, `web.config` has the `<sessionState>` element. Using the `<sessionState>` element you can fine-tune various aspects of session such as its storage mode, timeout, and cookieless nature.

To see how `<sessionState>` can be used, create a new ASP.NET web site as before. Open the `web.config` file and add the `<sessionState>` element, as shown in Listing 12-26.

Listing 12-26. The <sessionState> Element

```
<sessionState
        mode="InProc"
        timeout="2"
        cookieless="true">
</sessionState>
```

The `<sessionState>` element shown in Listing 12-26 sets the mode attribute to `InProc`. The mode attribute controls where the session data will be stored. The possible values are `Off`, `InProc`, `StateServer`, `SQLServer`, and `Custom`. If you set the mode to `Off`, the session is turned off and you can't store any data in the session. The value of `InProc` indicates that the session data is stored in the memory of the web server hosting the application. The `StateServer` and `SQLServer` modes allow you to store session state outside of the web server (we won't discuss them in this book).

The `timeout` attribute sets the idle time in minutes after which the session is emptied. The value of 2 means if you store some data in the session and thereafter don't use the application for 2 minutes, the data will be removed from the session. Default session timeout is 20 minutes.

By default, sessions require cookies enabled on the client browser. This cookie typically stores a session's ID. If you didn't want to use cookies for some reason, the `cookieless` attribute can come handy. Setting `cookieless` to `false` means that the session won't use cookies; instead ASP.NET will add something to the URL (you will see that in a minute).

Now, open `Default.aspx` and drag and drop a Label control on it. Then add the code shown in Listing 12-27 to the `Page_Load` event handler.

Listing 12-27. The Page_Load event handler

```
protected void Page_Load(object sender, EventArgs e)
{
    if(Session["timestamp"]==null)
    {
        Session["timestamp"] = DateTime.Now.ToString();
    }
    Label1.Text = Session["timestamp"].ToString();
}
```

The `Page_Load` event handler first checks whether `Session` contains a key named `timestamp`. If this key doesn't exist (the value is `null`), then current date and time values are stored into the session. The timestamp value is then assigned to the Label.

Run the web site; your Web Form should resemble Figure 12-26.

Figure 12-26. *Timestamp displayed from the session*

If you refresh the browser, you will find that the timestamp doesn't change. This indicates that the value stored in the session during the first run of the page is being used as expected. Now, keep the browser window idle for 3-4 minutes and then refresh it again. You will find that the timestamp has changed. This is due to the timeout value of 2 minutes. After 2 minutes of idle time, the timestamp key was removed from the session and hence a new timestamp was stored.

Also notice the browser's address bar. You will see some string segment inserted into the URL. This is the result of setting the `cookieless` attribute to `true`. Due to this setting, ASP.NET adds a session's ID into the URL rather than storing it in a cookie.

Displaying Custom Error Pages

Even after taking great care during the coding phase, errors can crop up at runtime in your web site. Users make typos in page URLs and try to access areas that are restricted, network failures can happen, and so on. As a robust programming practice, you should make provisions to trap all such unexpected errors. To that end, ASP.NET allows you to specify what is known as custom error pages in the web.config file. This is done using the <customErrors> element of web.config. Let's see how.

Create a new web site in Visual Studio. Add a new folder in it called Admin. This folder is supposed to contain administrative pages, and users are unauthorized to access it. Add the five Web Forms listed in Table 12-3.

Table 12-3. *Web Forms Arrangement*

Web Form	Folder	Description
Default.aspx	Root	The default page of the web site
FileNotFound.aspx	Root	Custom error page that is displayed for HTTP error code 404
UnAuthorized.aspx	Root	Custom error page that is displayed for HTTP error code 403
GlobalErrorPage.aspx	Root	Custom error page that is displayed for any other unhandled error in code or otherwise
Default.aspx	Admin	Represents the default page of the Admin folder

Now design Default.aspx from the root folder to look like the page shown in Figure 12-27.

Figure 12-27. *Design of Default.aspx*

Default.aspx contains two hyperlink controls titled Go to Admin Folder and Go to Nonexistent File. Set the NavigateUrl property of these hyperlink controls to ~/admin/default.aspx and ~/notexists.aspx, respectively. Note that we are deliberately setting the NavigateUrl of the second hyperlink to a nonexistent file. Now drag and drop a LinkButton control and set its Text property to Throw Exception. Add the code shown in Listing 12-28 in its Click event handler.

Listing 12-28. Throwing an Exception

```
protected void LinkButton1_Click(object sender, EventArgs e)
{
  throw new Exception("Unexpected Error");
}
```

The code simply throws a new exception. Because this is an unhandled exception, we will get a chance to trap it by using a custom error page. Now add a Label and a HyperLink control each on FileNotFound.aspx, UnAuthorized.aspx, and GlobalErrorPage.aspx. Set the Text property of the Label controls to a friendly error message. Point the HyperLink to Default.aspx so that users can easily navigate back to the home page.

Add the code shown in Listing 12-29 in the Page_Load event of the Admin/Default.aspx Web Form.

Listing 12-29. Throwing an HttpException

```
protected void Page_Load(object sender, EventArgs e)
{
  throw new HttpException(403, "Unauthorized");
}
```

The code raises an HttpException with a status code of 403 and a string message. The HttpException class represents an HTTP-specific exception. This way, we trigger an exception with status code 403 (unauthorized access).

Now open web.config in the IDE and add the markup shown in Listing 12-30 under the <system.web> section.

Listing 12-30. Specifying Custom Error Pages

```
<customErrors mode="On" defaultRedirect="GlobalErrorPage.aspx">
  <error statusCode="403" redirect="~/UnAuthorized.aspx"/>
  <error statusCode="404" redirect="~/FileNotFound.aspx"/>
</customErrors>
```

The <customErrors> section allows you to specify custom error pages for your web site. The mode attribute has three possible values:

- If the mode is On, custom error pages are enabled for all the machines browsing the web site.

- If the mode is Off, custom error pages are disabled for all the machines.

- If the mode is RemoteOnly, the custom errors are enabled only for remote machines browsing the web site, but they are turned off for local browsers.

During development, most commonly your web server and the browser will be running on the same machine and hence you should set the mode to On.

The defaultRedirect attribute points to a web page that is to be displayed in case there is any application-wide unhandled error.

The <customErrors> section can have a number of <error> tags. The statusCode attribute of the <error> tag specifies the web-server-level HTTP error code. The redirect attribute specifies the web page to be displayed in the event of that error. In our example, we configure two custom error pages: one for status code 403 (UnAuthorized.aspx) and the other for status code 404 (FileNotFound.aspx).

Now run Default.aspx and click all three links, one by one. You will notice that instead of displaying the default error page, this time ASP.NET displays the custom error pages as specified in web.config. Figure 12-28 shows one sample run of the web site.

Figure 12-28. *Custom error page for status code 403*

Documenting Code with XML Comments

Documenting your source code is a common requirement in any professional development. Everybody knows the importance of well-documented code. However, documenting your source code is just one part of the story. Often, you also need to generate professional help files that ship along with your application and are used by the end users.

There are various ways of creating documentation and help files. Most of them are manual in that somebody (a developer or a technical writer) needs to key in the help text in HTML or PDF format. Then a tool (such as Microsoft HTML Help Workshop) is used to compile the source files into a .CHM file. That means there is duplication of work. First, developers need to write comments in the source code. Then the same information is repeated in the help files.

Fortunately, the .NET Framework and Visual Studio support a feature called XML comments. By using this feature, you can add comments to your source code by using a specific XML vocabulary. Later you can extract these XML comments in a separate XML file and transform it into HTML or some other format. Thus documentation of code is automated and avoids duplication.

In C#, XML comments are indicated by three forward slashes (///). There are several XML tags that you can use in XML comments. In the following sections, you will learn many of them.

Creating a Class Library

To begin, you need to create a class library named XmlComments.dll. This class library represents a simple mathematical calculator and consists of a single class called Calculator. The Calculator class allows you to add, subtract, divide, and multiply numbers. Though this example may sound too simple (and indeed it is), your aim here is to learn XML commenting syntax.

Create a new class library project in Visual Studio. Name the project XmlComments and the class Calculator. Type the code from Listing 12-31 into the Calculator class.

Listing 12-31. The Calculator Class

```
public class Calculator
{
  public int Add(int a, int b)
  {
    return (a + b);
  }
}
```

```
public int Subtract(int a, int b)
{
  return (a - b);
}
public int Divide(int a, int b)
{
  return (a / b);
}
public int Multiply(int a, int b)
{
  return (a * b);
}
}
```

The class consists of four methods: Add(), Subtract(), Divide(), and Multiply(). Each method accepts two parameters and performs the corresponding action on them. The result of the calculation is returned to the caller. Now that you have the class ready, let's add XML documentation comments to it.

Documenting the Summary and Remarks

To describe your classes and members therein, you can use two tags: <summary> and <remarks>. The <summary> tag is used to describe a type or its members. The <remarks> tag is used to specify additional information about the type or member other than that specified in <summary>. Listing 12-32 shows the Calculator class after adding <summary> and <remarks> tags.

Listing 12-32. Adding <summary> and <remarks>

```
/// <summary>
/// This is a class that represents
/// a simple mathematical calculator.
/// </summary>
/// <remarks>
/// This class is developed on .NET Framework 4.7
/// </remarks>
public class Calculator
{
...
```

Adding Paragraphs

The summary or remarks may consist of multiple paragraphs of text. Each paragraph is represented by a <para> tag. Note that a <para> tag is always a child element of <summary> or <remarks>. Listing 12-33 shows the use of a <para> tag.

Listing 12-33. Using a <para> Tag

```
/// <summary>
/// This is a class that represents
/// a simple mathematical calculator.
/// <para>
/// You can use it to add, subtract,
```

```
/// divide and multiply integers and
/// fractional numbers.
/// </para>
/// </summary>
/// <remarks>
/// This class is developed on .NET Framework 4.7
/// </remarks>
```

Documenting Method Parameters and Return Values

Methods often take one or more parameters. They might also return some value to the caller. Parameters are represented by <param> tags, whereas return values are represented by <return> tags. The <param> tag has one attribute—name—that indicates the name of the parameter. Listing 12-34 shows the use of both of these tags on the Add() method.

Listing 12-34. Documenting Parameters and Return Values

```
/// <summary>
/// This method adds two integers.
/// </summary>
/// <param name="a">The first number</param>
/// <param name="b">The second number</param>
/// <returns>An integer representing addition of a and b</returns>
public int Add(int a, int b)
{
  return (a + b);
}
```

Specifying Scope and Permissions

Your class may contain private, protected, or public members. The scope of these members can be indicated by using the <permission> tag. The <permission> tag has one attribute, called cref, that specifies the name of the member in the given context. Listing 12-35 shows an example of using the <permission> tag.

Listing 12-35. Using the <permission> Tag

```
/// <summary>
/// This method adds two integers.
/// </summary>
/// <param name="a">The first number</param>
/// <param name="b">The second number</param>
/// <returns>An integer representing addition of a and b</returns>
/// <permission cref="Add">Public method</permission>
public int Add(int a, int b)
{
  return (a + b);
}
```

Specifying Links to Other Members

You may need to cross-reference members of your class. The MSDN library itself is a good example of this. At many places, documentation of one class points to another related class. Also, at the bottom of the documentation page, there appears a section called See Also. You can achieve the same thing for your documentation by using the <see> and <seealso> tags. The <see> tag must be used inside the <summary> or <remarks> tags. The <seealso> tag has an attribute called cref that points to another member and can be used outside the <summary> tag. Listing 12-36 illustrates the use of the <seealso> tag as an example.

Listing 12-36. Using the <seealso> Tag

```
/// <summary>
/// This method adds two integers.
/// </summary>
/// <param name="a">The first number</param>
/// <param name="b">The second number</param>
/// <returns>An integer representing addition of a and b</returns>
/// <permission cref="Add">Public method</permission>
/// <seealso cref="Subtract"/>
public int Add(int a, int b)
{
  return (a + b);
}
```

Adding Lists

Your documentation may need bulleted or numbered lists. This can be achieved by using three tags: <list>, <item>, and <listheader>. The <item> and <listheader> tags must appear inside the <list> tag. The <list> tag has an attribute named type that can take a value of bullet, number, or table. The <listheader> tag serves the purpose of supplying a header for the list. Finally, the <item> tag encapsulates a single item of the list. Listing 12-37 shows the use of these tags.

Listing 12-37. Using the <list>, <item>, and <listheader> Tags

```
/// <summary>
/// This is a class that represents
/// a simple mathematical calculator.
/// <para>
/// You can use it to add, subtract,
/// divide and multiply integers and
/// fractional numbers.
/// </para>
/// <list type="bullet">
/// <listheader>Supported Operations</listheader>
/// <item>Addition</item>
/// <item>Subtraction</item>
/// <item>Division</item>
/// <item>Multiplication</item>
/// </list>
/// </summary>
/// <remarks>
```

```
/// This class is developed on .NET Framework 4.7
/// </remarks>
public class Calculator
{
...
```

Generating XML Documentation from Comments

To generate XML documentation from source code comments, you need to open the project properties dialog box (see Figure 12-29).

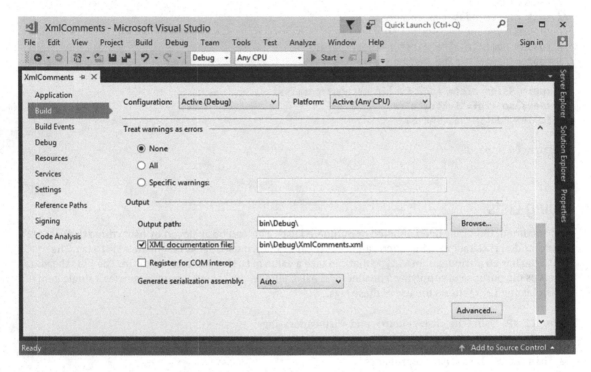

Figure 12-29. *Generating XML documentation*

The Output section of the Build tab allows you to specify whether to generate XML documentation and the filename. Specify the filename as XmlComments.xml and build the XmlComments class library. As a result of the compilation, you will get XmlComments.dll and XmlComments.xml in the output folder. Figure 12-30 shows XmlComments.xml opened in a browser.

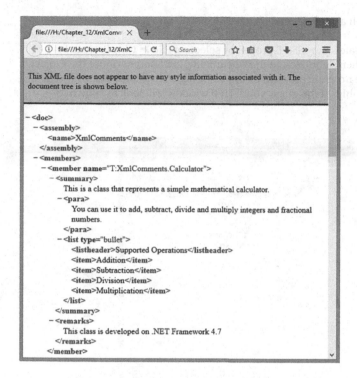

Figure 12-30. *XmlComments.xml viewed in browser*

As you might have guessed, documentation in XML is good but needs to be converted to a more readable format such as HTML or help files. There is no built-in way to do that in Visual Studio. Some of the ways to generate user-friendly documentation files include:

- Writing an XSLT style sheet that transforms XML documentation to HTML.

- Using a third-party tool that reads the XML comments or the XML documentation file and generates readable documentation for you.

In the next section, you will use the latter technique to generate documentation out of the XML comments.

Using Sandcastle Help File Builder to Generate Help Files

Sandcastle Help File Builder (SHFB) is a tool for generating documentation from the XML comments you learned in the previous section. This tool is available on GitHub at `https://github.com/EWSoftware/SHFB`. You can feed any .NET assembly to the tool and generate documentation in any of the following formats:

- HTML Help 1 (`.chm`)

- MS Help Viewer (`.mshc`)

- Open XML (`.docx`)

- Markdown (`.md`)

- HTML (`.htm`/`.html`)

In order to use SHFB, you must install it and its dependencies. The installation wizard guides you through all the steps.

Once you install SHFB, open it and create a new SHFB project by selecting File ➤ New Project. Save the newly created project in some folder. Then right-click on the Documentation Sources under the Project Explorer and pick the XmlComments.dll file from the previous example. Doing so indicates that you want to generate documentation from this assembly. At this stage, your SHFB window will look as shown in Figure 12-31.

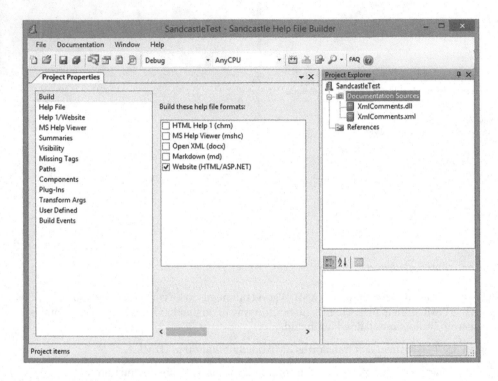

Figure 12-31. *Documentation sources added to SHFB*

Notice that the Documentation Sources also lists XmlComments.xml automatically. From the help file formats list, check the Only Website option. Selecting this option will generate documentation in HTML format and you can easily view it in any browser.

Next, select Documentation ➤ Build Project from the menu and let the tool generate the documentation for you. Once the documentation is generated, you can go to the Help folder under the SHFB project's folder and launch Index.html in any browser. Figure 12-32 shows the documentation generated for the XmlComments assembly.

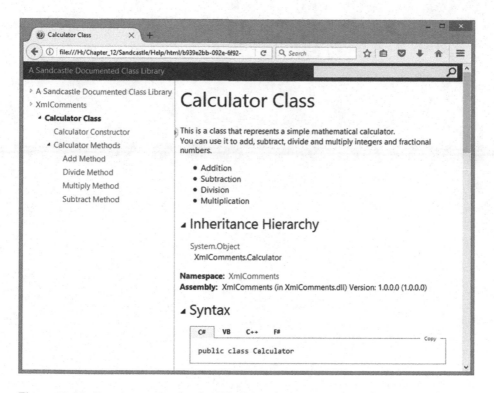

Figure 12-32. *Documentation for the Calculator class*

As you can see, SHFB converted your XML comments into nicely formatted and styled web pages. Try navigating to various parts of the documentation using the tree on the left.

Summary

The .NET Framework not only allows you to work with an array of XML technologies, but it also uses XML at many places itself. This chapter gave you an introduction to these areas.

You started with WPF applications, where the user interface is defined by XAML. You also displayed data from an XML document in a DataGrid of a WPF application.

ASP.NET uses XML heavily for server control markup and configuration. Then you learned about application configuration files. Specifically you learned to store and retrieve application configuration settings and database connection strings. The web.config file is an XML file that stores ASP.NET configuration information. You learned how to configure your web site to use forms authentication and session state. You also learned to configure custom error pages for dealing with unexpected errors in your web site.

Finally, you learned about XML comments—a feature that can assist documentation generation. You also used Sandcastle Help File Builder (SHFB) to convert the XML comments into HTML documentation.

CHAPTER 13

■ ■ ■

Working with LINQ to XML

Traditionally, software systems used different methods of accessing data from different datastores. For example, in order to access data from relational databases, flat files, and XML files, developers needed to learn and master different object models. These object models were often totally different from each other in terms of usage syntax and underlying philosophy. Beginning with the .NET Framework 3.5, Microsoft introduced Language Integrated Query (LINQ) technology that simplifies the hassle involved while consuming different sources of data. LINQ comes in three main flavors: LINQ to Objects, LINQ to ADO.NET, and LINQ to XML.

This chapter covers LINQ to XML features along with a brief primer on LINQ in general. Remember, however, that any detailed coverage of LINQ is beyond the scope of this book. This chapter restricts itself to the following topics:

- Brief introduction to LINQ expressions

- Capabilities of LINQ to XML

- When to use LINQ to XML

- Loading and saving XML documents using LINQ to XML

- Manipulating XML documents using LINQ to XML

- Validating XML documents using LINQ to XML

- Transforming XML documents using LINQ to XML

Overview of LINQ

Suppose that you are developing a complex application that deals with data stored in SQL Server, comma-separated files, in-memory collections, and XML files. You have been given a task to develop a set of classes that will take the data in and out of these datastores. As you might have guessed, you will probably end up with multiple data access strategies and object models, each specialized for a particular type of data source. Wouldn't it be nice if you could use just one unified way of accessing data for all your data sources? That's what LINQ is all about. LINQ provides a unified way of accessing data residing in in-memory collections, databases, and XML files. Figure 13-1 shows the overall architecture of LINQ.

© Bipin Joshi 2017
B. Joshi, *Beginning XML with C# 7*, https://doi.org/10.1007/978-1-4842-3105-0_13

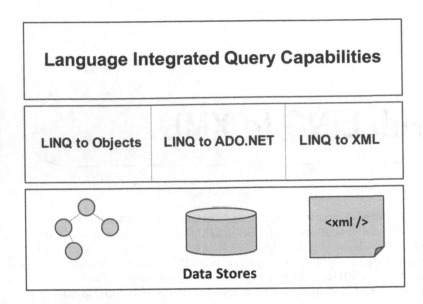

Figure 13-1. *Architecture of LINQ*

The bottom layer of the LINQ architecture consists of LINQ-enabled data sources. A LINQ-enabled data source is typically an object that implements the IEnumerable<T> or IQueryable<T> generic interfaces. You may wonder how relational databases and XML files will implement these interfaces; the LINQ to ADO.NET and LINQ to XML classes provide all the necessary infrastructure required to pull the data from such sources to a collection that implements the IEnumerable<T> or IQueryable<T> interfaces.

The .NET Framework provides what are known as *standard query operators* that work against any LINQ-enabled data source and provide facilities such as querying, filtering, sorting, and grouping the data. One can use the standard query operators directly on the LINQ data sources. However, to make life still easier, C# provides language keywords and constructs to perform LINQ tasks natively. That means querying the underlying datastore is now a feature integrated in the C# programming language itself. Using these features, you can write what are known as LINQ query expressions or LINQ queries.

■ **Note**   Though you can use standard query operators to work with LINQ-enabled data sources, in this chapter I am going to use C# language keywords for writing the LINQ queries.

Working with LINQ Queries

To get a feel of how LINQ works at code level, let's develop a simple example. Through this example you will learn to group, sort, filter, and select data from generic collection. The example application is shown in Figure 13-2.

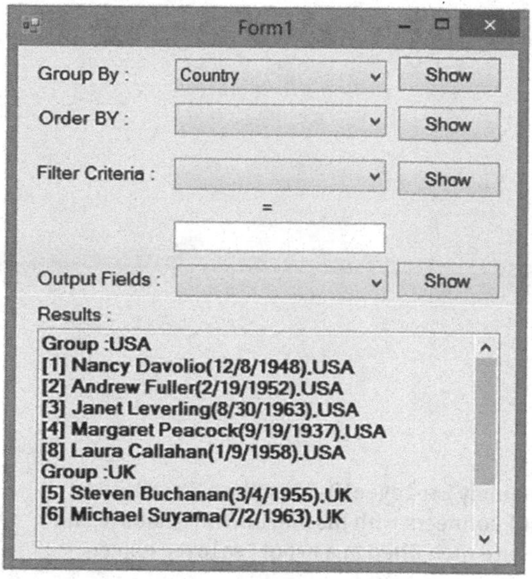

Figure 13-2. Basic LINQ operations

The application fills a generic list of Employee objects with data from the Employees table. The application user interface consists of a series of combo boxes that list columns of the Employee table (EmployeeID, FirstName, LastName, BirthDate, and Country). To group, sort, filter, and select data from the list, you can choose the desired field from the combo box and click the Show button. The results of the corresponding operation are shown in a read-only TextBox control.

Before you go into the details of LINQ queries, you first need to create the Employee class. Listing 13-1 shows the complete code of the Employee class.

Listing 13-1. The Employee Class

```
public class Employee
{
  public int EmployeeID { get; set; }
  public string FirstName { get; set; }
  public string LastName { get; set; }
  public DateTime BirthDate { get; set; }
  public string Country { get; set; }
  public static List<Employee> GetEmployees()
  {
    SqlConnection cnn = new SqlConnection(@"data source=.\sqlexpress;
      initial catalog=northwind;integrated security=true");
    cnn.Open();
    SqlCommand cmd = new SqlCommand(
    "SELECT employeeid,firstname,lastname,birthdate,country FROM employees");
    cmd.Connection = cnn;
    SqlDataReader reader = cmd.ExecuteReader();
    List<Employee> items = new List<Employee>();
```

```
    while (reader.Read())
    {
      Employee item = new Employee();
      item.EmployeeID = reader.GetInt32(0);
      item.FirstName = reader.GetString(1);
      item.LastName = reader.GetString(2);
      item.BirthDate = reader.GetDateTime(3);
      item.Country = reader.GetString(4);
      items.Add(item);
    }
    reader.Close();
    cnn.Close();
    return items;
  }
}
```

The Employee class consists of five public properties, namely EmployeeID, FirstName, LastName, BirthDate, and Country. The static method GetEmployees() connects with the Northwind database and fetches all the records from the Employees table. The values are then filled in a list of Employee objects. Finally, the list is returned to the caller.

Once you create the Employee class, you can call its GetEmployees() method from the Load event of the form (see Listing 13-2).

Listing 13-2. Storing Employee Objects into a Generic List

```
List<Employee> employees = null;
private void Form1_Load(object sender, EventArgs e)
{
  employees = Employee.GetEmployees();
}
```

Notice that in Listing 13-2 the generic list is declared at class level because multiple functions need to access the data. The Load event handler of the form simply calls the GetEmployees() method and stores the returned data in the list.

Grouping Data Using LINQ

Listing 13-3 shows the Click event handler of the Show button that groups the data based on the selected field.

Listing 13-3. Grouping Data Using LINQ

```
private void button1_Click(object sender, EventArgs e)
{
  txtResults.Clear();
  if (comboBox1.SelectedItem.ToString() == "Country")
  {
    var result = from employee in employees
                    group employee by employee.Country;
```

```
    foreach (var group in result)
    {
      OutputResults("Group :" + group.Key);
      foreach (Employee emp in group)
      {
        OutputResults(emp);
      }
    }
  }
  ...
}
```

The code first decides which field is to be used for the purpose of grouping (we see the code that deals with the country field here). Then it forms a LINQ query expression that groups the items from the list based on that field. Notice the use of C# language extensions to LINQ in the form of the var, from, and group keywords. When you work with LINQ, the return type of the queries is often unknown at the time of writing the query. To indicate such an anonymous type, C# uses the var keyword. The LINQ query that follows indicates that you want to fetch all the items from the employees collection and want to group them by Country values. At runtime, this LINQ query returns a dictionary.

The outer foreach loop iterates through all the items of this dictionary. With each iteration, the key of the dictionary item is outputted in the text box using the OutputResults() helper method (discussed next). The inner foreach loop iterates through all the employees from a group and emits their details in the text box. Listing 13-3 shows the code only for the Country field, but the other fields will follow the same structure. The OutputResults() helper method has two overloads, as shown in Listing 13-4.

Listing 13-4. Outputting Results to a Text Box

```
private void OutputResults(Employee emp)
{
  txtResults.Text += "[" + emp.EmployeeID + "] ";
  txtResults.Text += emp.FirstName + " " + emp.LastName +
    "(" + emp.BirthDate.ToShortDateString() + ")," +
    emp.Country + "\r\n";
}

private void OutputResults(string msg)
{
    txtResults.Text += msg + "\r\n";
}
```

The first overload of the OutputResults() helper method accepts an Employee object and appends its property values to the text box contents. The second overload simply accepts a string value and appends it to the text box contents.

Sorting Data Using LINQ

Now let's implement the sorting functionality. The sorting operation is done in the Click event handler of the second Show button. The part of the event handler is shown in Listing 13-5.

Listing 13-5. Sorting Data Using LINQ

```
private void button2_Click(object sender, EventArgs e)
{
  txtResults.Clear();
  if (comboBox2.SelectedItem.ToString() == "Country")
  {
    var result = from employee in employees
                      orderby employee.Country
                      select employee;
    foreach (var employee in result)
    {
      OutputResults(employee);
    }
  }
  ...
}
```

The orderby clause of a LINQ query sorts the results based on the indicated fields. The code in Listing 13-5 sorts the data on the basis of Country values. Notice the use of the select keyword that decides what to fetch. We will revisit the select keyword in later sections. The foreach loop then iterates the results and emits them in the text box.

Filtering Data Using LINQ

The employees list contains details about all the employees in the system. Often you need to work with a subset of the total data based on some criteria. The where clause of LINQ queries allows you to filter the data based on some condition. In our example, the Click event handler of the third Show button filters the employees list based on the criteria entered in the corresponding text box. A part of the relevant code is shown in Listing 13-6.

Listing 13-6. Filtering Data Using LINQ

```
private void button3_Click(object sender, EventArgs e)
{
  txtResults.Clear();
  if (comboBox3.SelectedItem.ToString() == "Country")
  {
    var result = from employee in employees
                      where employee.Country==textBox1.Text
                      select employee;
    foreach (var employee in result)
    {
      OutputResults(employee);
    }
  }
  ...
}
```

The code from Listing 13-6 filters the employees list for a specific country as supplied in the text box. Our example uses the == operator of C#. You can also use the && (AND) and | | (OR) operators to create more complex conditions. The results are then outputted to the text box as before.

Shaping Data Using LINQ

In all the LINQ queries so far, we fetched the entire Employee instance. What if we want only a part of the Employee instance or some computed data? That is where the select clause comes in handy. The select clause can be used to control the shape of the result (also known as the projection). In our examples, the output field's combo box governs which of the fields will be returned in the output. The actual shape of the output is decided by LINQ queries that go inside the Click event of the fourth Show button (see Listing 13-7).

Listing 13-7. Selecting Data Using LINQ

```
private void button4_Click(object sender, EventArgs e)
{
  txtResults.Clear();
  if(comboBox4.SelectedIndex==0)
  {
    var result = from employee in employees
                       select new
                   { employee.EmployeeID, employee.FirstName, employee.LastName };
    foreach (var emp in result)
    {
      OutputResults("[" + emp.EmployeeID + "] " +
      emp.FirstName + " " + emp.LastName);
    }
  }
  ...
}
```

The code first decides which of the fields of the Employee object are to be selected. It then constructs a new anonymous object that includes EmployeeID, FirstName, and LastName properties. The results are then outputted in the text box.

You can now run the application and test how these LINQ queries work.

Classic XML Technologies vs. LINQ to XML

Now that you have some idea about LINQ, let's focus on LINQ to XML. Before you delve into the actual coding, it would be beneficial to understand the key differences between classic XML technologies (XML DOM, XSLT, XSD, etc.) and LINQ to XML. The following sections summarize these key differences.

Working with XML Fragments

In classic XML technologies such as XML DOM, you essentially work with an XML document, so you access the XML data from top to bottom. This mechanism may not be ideal in each and every scenario, because while working with XML, your main focus is on elements and attributes. However, with a traditional DOM approach, you add an additional layer of complexity. LINQ for XML allows you to work with XML elements and attributes directly without bothering about the document node. This direct access allows you to work with XML fragments consisting of elements and attributes more easily.

Visual Construction of XML Trees

While working with XML DOM, you create various parts of an XML document (elements, attributes, text nodes, and so on) and then add them to the document. This style of creating XML documents does not give any visual clue about the document nesting. LINQ to XML provides what is known as *functional construction*, which allows you to create XML trees in a way that gives a visual clue about the nesting of the XML structure, as you'll see later in this chapter.

Ease in Namespace Handling

Dealing with XML namespaces and namespace prefixes is tedious in classic XML technologies. LINQ to XML takes away the complexity of dealing with namespace prefixes from developers by automatically doing the appropriate substitution at runtime.

Renaming XML Nodes

In DOM, you cannot directly rename a node. You need to create a new node and copy children of the older node to the new one. LINQ to XML simplifies this task by allowing you to rename nodes directly.

Static Methods to Load XML

While working with DOM, you must instantiate the XmlDocument class first and then load the XML document. LINQ to XML, however, allows you to load XML data via static methods, simplifying your code.

Whitespace Handling

When you read an XML file from disk, often it contains whitespace in the form of indentions. Such whitespace is not at all your focus as far as XML processing is concerned. However, while saving the data back, you may want to preserve the indentions. LINQ to XML simplifies whitespace handling for you. By default, when you save an XML document, only significant whitespace is saved. You can, of course, change this default behavior if you so desire.

XML Transformation

XSLT provides a rule-based, declarative approach for XML data transformation. However, many developers find XSLT difficult to master and spend a significant amount of time developing XSLT style sheets. LINQ to XML provides a programming model that most developers are familiar with. You can transform your XML document by using functional construction, gathering data from various sources, and assembling it in a new form. This can reduce development and maintenance costs. XSLT is still better when dealing with complex, document-centric scenarios.

When to Use LINQ to XML

In general, we can say that classic XML technologies are better if we want our applications to adhere to W3C standards and want to modify existing applications that already use the classic approaches. LINQ to XML can be a choice for new development where W3C compliance is not the concern and you want to code with the familiar syntax of C# without spending too much time mastering the XML family of technologies.

LINQ to XML Class Hierarchy

LINQ to XML provides an extensive collection of classes for a variety of purposes. These classes reside in the System.Xml.Linq namespace from the System.Xml.Linq.dll assembly. Figure 13-3 shows some of the most commonly used classes from this hierarchy.

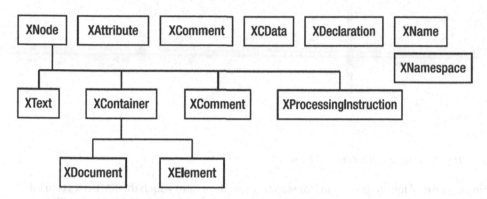

Figure 13-3. LINQ to XML class hierarchy

The XNode abstract class represents a node of an XML tree. The XContainer, XText, XComment, and XProcessingInstruction classes inherit from the XNode class. The XContainer class in turn acts as a base class for the XDocument and XElement classes. As you might have guessed, these classes represent a text node, comment, processing instruction, XML document, and element, respectively. The classes such as XAttribute, XComment, XCData, and XDeclaration are independent of the XNode hierarchy and represent attribute, comment, CDATA section, and XML declaration, respectively. The XName class represents the name of an element (XElement) or attribute (XAttribute). Similarly, the XNamespace class represents a namespace of an element or attribute.

Opening an Existing XML Document for Parsing

While working with classic XML DOM, you used the XmlDocument class to load an XML document. LINQ to XML offers two classes to load XML data: XDocument and XElement. In most situations, XElement is all you need to load XML files, streams, and fragments. However, in some rare cases, you may need to use XDocument instead. These special cases include the following:

- You want to add comments at the top level.

- You want to add processing instructions at the top level.

- You want to use a DTD for your XML document.

In any case, you can load XML data from a URI, a TextReader, an XmlReader, or even an XML string. To demonstrate the use of XElement in loading XML data, let's build an application like the one shown in Figure 13-4.

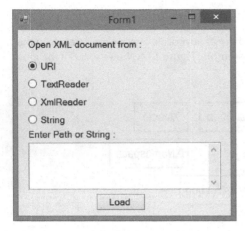

Figure 13-4. *Application that loads XML data in XElement*

The application consists of four radio buttons for selecting the place from which the XML data is to be loaded. The text box allows you to specify a URL where the XML file is located or raw XML markup. Clicking the Load button loads the data in an XElement and displays a message box with a success message. The Click event handler of the Load button is shown in Listing 13-8.

Listing 13-8. Loading XML Data Using XElement

```
private void button1_Click(object sender, EventArgs e)
{
  try
  {
    XElement root = null;
    if (radioButton1.Checked)
    {
      root = XElement.Load(textBox1.Text);
    }
    if (radioButton2.Checked)
    {
      StreamReader reader = File.OpenText(textBox1.Text);
      root = XElement.Load(reader);
    }
    if (radioButton3.Checked)
    {
      XmlReader reader = XmlReader.Create(textBox1.Text);
      root = XElement.Load(reader);
    }
    if (radioButton4.Checked)
    {
      root = XElement.Parse(textBox1.Text);
    }
    MessageBox.Show("XML Data Loaded Successfully!");
  }
```

```
catch (Exception ex)
{
    MessageBox.Show(ex.Message);
}
}
```

The code consists of a series of if blocks for checking the selected radio button. The first three if blocks use the Load() method of the XElement class. Notice that Load() is a static method of the XElement class and accepts a URI, a TextReader, or an XmlReader as a source of XML data. If the XML data is in the form of a raw string, the Parse() method is used instead of Load(). The Load() and Parse() methods return an instance of the XElement class that can be used for further processing.

■ **Note**   In order to compile the code from Listing 13-8, you must import the System.IO and System.Xml. Linq namespaces. This applies to most of the examples illustrated in this chapter.

To test the application, you can use the same Employees.xml file that we created in Chapter 2 (see Listing 2-2 for the complete XML markup).

Navigating Through an XML Tree

Under LINQ to XML, all the child nodes of an element can be accessed via the Nodes() method. The Nodes() method returns a sequence of IEnumerable<XNode> that can be iterated to access the individual nodes. If your interest is purely in elements, you can use the Elements() method that returns a sequence of IEnumerable<XElement>. The FirstNode and LastNode properties allow you to access the first and the last nodes, respectively. Similarly, the descendants can be accessed via the Descendants() method. To look at many of these methods in action, we will develop an application that populates a TreeView control with data from the Employees.xml file. The application user interface is shown in Figure 13-5.

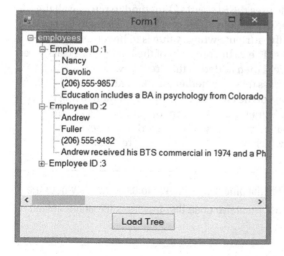

Figure 13-5. *Navigating through an XML tree using LINQ to XML*

The application consists of a TreeView control for displaying several <employee> elements. Each employee's TreeNode further displays information about that employee. The actual code to populate the tree view goes in the Click event handler of the Load Tree button (see Listing 13-9).

Listing 13-9. Loading the Tree with Employee Details

```
private void button1_Click(object sender, EventArgs e)
{
  XElement root = XElement.Load($"{Application.StartupPath}\\Employees.xml");
  TreeNode rootNode = new TreeNode(root.Name.LocalName);
  treeView1.Nodes.Add(rootNode);
  foreach(XElement employee in root.Elements())
  {
    TreeNode employeeNode = new TreeNode("Employee ID :" +
    employee.Attribute("employeeid").Value);
    rootNode.Nodes.Add(employeeNode);
    if (employee.HasElements)
    {
      foreach(XElement employeechild in employee.Descendants())
      {
        TreeNode childNode = new TreeNode(employeechild.Value);
        employeeNode.Nodes.Add(childNode);
      }
    }
  }
}
```

The code first loads the Employees.xml file into an instance of the XElement class. The Name property of the XElement class is of type XName and represents the name of the element. The LocalName property of the XName class returns the name of the underlying element without a namespace qualifier. This name is then used to add the root node of the TreeView.

Since we are interested only in the elements, the code uses the Elements() method to retrieve all the child elements of the <employees> element. The employeeid attribute of the <employee> element is accessed via the Attribute() method, which accepts the name of the attribute whose value is to be retrieved and returns an XAttribute instance representing that attribute. The Value property of the XAttribute class gives us the value of the attribute. A TreeNode for that employee is then added to the TreeView.

The HasElements Boolean property of the XElement class tells us whether an element has any child elements. If so, we iterate through all the descendants of the current <employee> element using its Descendants() method. In our example the Descendants() method will return four XElements for the <firstname>, <lastname>, <homephone>, and <notes> elements, respectively. The Value property of the XElement class returns the inner content of the element, which is then displayed in a TreeNode.

■ **Note**   In the preceding example, the structure of the XML document was known to us. In cases where the nesting of XML tags is not known at design time, you may use recursive code that traverses the entire nested hierarchy.

Looking for Specific Elements and Attributes

Searching XML data is a common requirement in many scenarios. LINQ to XML provides powerful ways to search your data. You can use all the features of LINQ to create your queries and look up the XML data. Most commonly we need to search:

- Elements matching a specific tag name
- Elements containing a specific value
- Attributes matching a specific value

In the sections that follow, we develop two applications: one allows you to search elements on the basis of their tag names, and the other allows you to grab one particular employee with a specific employee ID.

Retrieving Specific Elements Using the Descendants() Method

When you wish to retrieve a set of elements with a certain tag name, the `Descendants()` method can come in handy. In order to illustrate the use of the `Descendants()` method, we develop an application like the one shown in Figure 13-6.

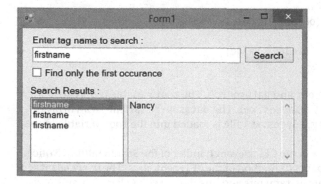

Figure 13-6. *Application for searching elements by tag name*

The application consists of a text box for specifying the tag name to search for. Upon clicking the Search button, the results will be displayed in a list box. Selecting a particular tag name from the list box will show its value in another read-only text box. The check box titled "Find Only the First Occurrence" determines whether to find all instances of the tag name or end the search after the first match is found.

The code that makes the application work is shown in Listing 13-10.

Listing 13-10. Using the Descendants() Method to Search Specific Elements

```
XElement root = null;
XElement[] datasource = null;

private void Form1_Load(object sender, EventArgs e)
{
  root = XElement.Load($"{Application.StartupPath}\\employees.xml");
}
```

```csharp
private void button1_Click(object sender, EventArgs e)
{
  textBox2.Text = "";
  var subset = from item in root.Descendants(textBox1.Text)
                        select item;

  if (!checkBox1.Checked)
  {
    datasource = subset.ToArray();
  }
  else
  {
    if (subset.Count() > 0)
    {
      datasource = new XElement[1];
      datasource[0] = subset.First();
    }
  }
  listBox1.DataSource = datasource;
  listBox1.DisplayMember = "Name";
}
private void listBox1_SelectedIndexChanged(object sender, EventArgs e)
{
  textBox2.Text= datasource[listBox1.SelectedIndex].Value;
}
```

The code declares two class-level variables: root and datasource. The root variable is of type XElement and holds a pointer to the root node of Employees.xml. The datasource variable is an array of type XElement and is used for data binding. The Employees.xml file is loaded into the root variable in the Load event of the form.

The main job of searching a tag name happens in the Click event handler of the Search button. Notice the LINQ query shown in bold. It uses the Descendants() method of the XElement class. The Descendants() method has two overloads: one that doesn't take any parameters and one that takes an element name as the parameter. The former overload returns all the descendant elements of the current node, whereas the latter overload returns all the descendant elements that match the specified tag name. If the check box is unchecked (i.e., we want to display all occurrences of the specified tag), then we convert the result into an array of XElement objects using the ToArray() method. Otherwise, we create an array of XElements manually and store the first occurrence of the element in it. Notice the use of the First() method to retrieve just the first instance of the element. The datasource variable is then bound with the list box.

In order to display the actual value of the element, the code handles the SelectedIndexChanged event of the list box. Inside it simply retrieves the selected XElement from the datasource array and displays its Value property in the text box.

To test the application, run it from Visual Studio. Type **firstname** in the search text box and click the Search button. The application should list three occurrences of the <firstname> tag in the list box. Click any of the instances, and you should see its value displayed in the other text box.

Searching on the Basis of Attribute Values

XML data often needs to be searched on the basis of attribute values and not just tag names. The Attributes() and Attribute() methods help you to do just that. To demonstrate the use of these methods, we will develop an application like the one shown in Figure 13-7.

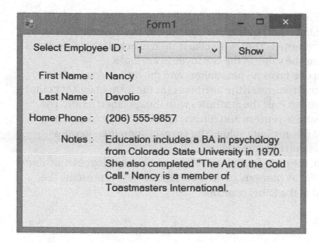

Figure 13-7. Application for searching attribute values

The application consists of a combo box that displays a list of employee IDs. Recollect that the Employees.xml file stores employee IDs in the employeeid attribute of the <employee> element. Upon selecting a specific employee ID and clicking the Show button, the details of that employee (first name, last name, home phone, and notes) are displayed. The code that does the searching is shown in Listing 13-11.

Listing 13-11. Searching Attribute Values

```
private void Form1_Load(object sender, EventArgs e)
{
  root = XElement.Load($"{Application.StartupPath}\\employees.xml");
  var result = from item in root.Elements("employee")
                        where item.Attributes("employeeid").Count() > 0
                        select item.Attribute("employeeid").Value;
  foreach (var obj in result)
  {
    comboBox1.Items.Add(obj);
  }
}

private void button1_Click(object sender, EventArgs e)
{
  var result = from item in root.Elements("employee")
                        where item.Attribute("employeeid").
                        Value == comboBox1.SelectedItem.ToString()
                        select item;
  foreach (var obj in result)
  {
    label6.Text = obj.Element("firstname").Value;
    label7.Text = obj.Element("lastname").Value;
    label8.Text = obj.Element("homephone").Value;
    label9.Text = obj.Element("notes").Value;
  }
}
```

401

The code loads the Employees.xml file into an instance of XElement in the Load event of the form. It then calls the Elements() method on the root element by supplying the tag name as employee. This way, only the elements with the employee tag name are returned. The where clause then checks if these elements contain the employeeid attribute and, if so, it returns the value of the employeeid attribute.

The Attributes() method has two overloads: one takes no parameters and the other accepts the attribute name as the parameter. The former overload returns all the attributes (in the form of an XAttribute collection) of an element, whereas the latter one returns only the attributes with the specified name. The Attribute() method accepts the name of an attribute to retrieve and returns an XAttribute instance associated with it. Notice that the query selects just the attribute value. The foreach loop then iterates through the results and populates the employee IDs into the combo box.

In the Click event handler of the Show button, the code fetches an element whose employeeid attribute matches the value selected in the combo box. The Value property of the XAttribute class represents the value of an attribute. The results are then displayed in the Label controls.

Modifying XML Data

LINQ to XML provides easy ways for adding, removing, and changing the content of an XML tree. These ways can be best seen with an example. Let's create an application like the one shown in Figure 13-8 that represents a data entry screen for the Employees.xml file.

Figure 13-8. *Data entry screen for the Employees.xml file*

The application displays <employee> elements from the Employees.xml file. You can navigate among various employees using the VCR controls provided at the bottom. You can also jump to an employee with a specific employee ID using the combo box. The Add, Update, and Delete buttons add, change, or remove an <employee> element from the underlying XML tree, respectively. The Save button saves the modified XML tree back to the Employees.xml file.

Loading the XML Document

When the application starts, it loads the Employees.xml file into an instance of the XElement class. This is done in the Load event of the form (see Listing 13-12).

Listing 13-12. Loading an XML Document

```
XElement doc = null;

private void Form1_Load(object sender, EventArgs e)
{
  doc=XElement.Load($"{Application.StartupPath}\\Employees.xml");
  var result=from item in doc.Descendants("employee")
                      select item.Attribute("employeeid").Value;
  foreach (var obj in result)
  {
    comboBox1.Items.Add(obj);
  }
  FillControls();
}
```

The code declares a variable of type XElement at form level. In the Load event, it loads Employees.xml into it. The descendant elements of the root node (i.e., all the <employee> elements) are retrieved using the Descendants() method, and their attributes are added to the combo box. The FillControls() method (discussed later) simply fetches the <employee> element matching the currently selected employee ID and displays its details (first name, last name, home phone, and notes) in the appropriate text boxes.

Navigating Between Various Nodes

The VCR arrangement at the bottom of the screen allows you to navigate among various <employee> elements. The Click event handlers of the next, previous, first, and last buttons (see Listing 13-13) essentially adjust the selected index of the combo box and call the FillControls() helper method to show the details of the selected employee.

Listing 13-13. Navigating Among Employee Elements

```
private void button4_Click(object sender, EventArgs e)
{
  comboBox1.SelectedIndex = 0;
  FillControls();
}

private void button5_Click(object sender, EventArgs e)
{
  if (comboBox1.SelectedIndex > 0)
  {
    comboBox1.SelectedIndex = comboBox1.SelectedIndex - 1;
  }
  FillControls();
}
```

```
private void button6_Click(object sender, EventArgs e)
{
  if (comboBox1.SelectedIndex < comboBox1.Items.Count - 1)
  {
    comboBox1.SelectedIndex = comboBox1.SelectedIndex + 1;
  }
  FillControls();
}

private void button7_Click(object sender, EventArgs e)
{
  comboBox1.SelectedIndex = comboBox1.Items.Count - 1;
  FillControls();
}
```

Adding New Content

In order to add a new employee, we need to specify employee ID, first name, last name, and notes in the respective controls and click the Add button. Inside the Click event of the Add button, we need to create new XElement instances that represent <employee>, <firstname>, <lastname>, <homephone>, and <notes> elements. Listing 13-14 shows how this is done.

Listing 13-14. Adding a New Employee Element

```
private void button1_Click(object sender, EventArgs e)
{
    XElement employee = new XElement("employee",
                                new XElement("firstname", textBox1.Text),
                                new XElement("lastname", textBox2.Text),
                                new XElement("homephone", textBox3.Text),
                                new XElement("notes",
                                        new XCData(textBox4.Text)));
    employee.SetAttributeValue("employeeid", comboBox1.Text);
    doc.Add(employee);
    comboBox1.Items.Add(comboBox1.Text);
    FillControls();
}
```

Notice the markup in Listing 13-14 carefully. The code creates a new instance of the XElement class using functional construction. The code written using functional construction gives a visual indication about the nesting of the XML tree. After looking at our code, you can easily identify that <firstname>, <lastname>, <homephone>, and <notes> are the child elements of the <employee> element. The constructor of the XElement class accepts a parameter array of content elements. The code supplies four new instances of the XElement class as the second parameter of the main XElement instance. Since the element representing notes can contain CDATA, its value is passed as an instance of the XCData class.

The employeeid attribute of the newly created <employee> element is assigned via the SetAttributeValue() method. The SetAttributeValue() method accepts an attribute name and its value as the parameter. If that attribute already exists, the method changes the attribute's value; otherwise, it adds the attribute.

The <employee> element is then added to the root element using the Add() method of the XElement class. The Add() method adds the supplied content as the child element of the current element.

Modifying Existing Content

Any changes to the values of the `<firstname>`, `<lastname>`, `<homephone>`, and `<notes>` elements are saved in the XML tree in the `Click` event of the Update button (see Listing 13-15).

Listing 13-15. Modifying an Existing Element

```
private void button2_Click(object sender, EventArgs e)
{
  string employeeid = comboBox1.SelectedItem.ToString();
  var employees = from item in doc.Descendants("employee")
                  where item.Attribute("employeeid").Value == employeeid
                  select item;
  foreach (var employee in employees)
  {
    employee.SetElementValue("firstname", textBox1.Text);
    employee.SetElementValue("lastname", textBox2.Text);
    employee.SetElementValue("homephone", textBox3.Text);
    employee.SetElementValue("notes", textBox4.Text);
  }
}
```

The code first selects only the `<employee>` element whose `employeeid` attribute matches the one selected in the combo box. It then calls the `SetElementValue()` method of the `XElement` class on the selected employee. The `SetElementValue()` method takes two parameters: the name of the element whose value is to be set and the new value of the element. If the element doesn't exist, it is added as a child element of the current element.

Deleting Existing Content

In order to delete an employee, we need to find it from the available `<employee>` elements and remove it from the XML tree. The `Click` event handler of the Delete button does this task (see Listing 13-16).

Listing 13-16. Deleting an Existing Element

```
private void button3_Click(object sender, EventArgs e)
{
  string employeeid = comboBox1.SelectedItem.ToString();
  var employees = from item in doc.Descendants("employee")
                  where item.Attribute("employeeid").Value == employeeid
                  select item;
  foreach (var employee in employees)
  {
    employee.Remove();
    break;
  }
  comboBox1.Items.Remove(employeeid);
  FillControls();
}
```

The code first finds the employee that is to be deleted. It then calls the `Remove()` method on the employee `XElement`. The `Remove()` method removes the current element from the tree.

Saving the Modified XML Tree to a File

The modified XML tree can be saved back to the disk using the Save() method of the XElement class. Listing 13-17 shows the relevant code.

Listing 13-17. Saving an XML Tree to a File

```
private void button8_Click(object sender, EventArgs e)
{
  doc.Save($"{Application.StartupPath}\\Employees.xml");
}
```

The Save() method simply accepts the path of the file where the XML tree is to be saved. In addition to saving an XML tree to a file, you can also use the Save() method to serialize an XML tree to XmlWriter or TextWriter objects.

Displaying Employee Details

In the preceding code, we use the FillControls() helper method to display details of the current employee. This method is shown in Listing 13-18.

Listing 13-18. Displaying the Current Employee's Details

```
private void FillControls()
{
  if (comboBox1.SelectedIndex == -1)
  {
    comboBox1.SelectedIndex = 0;
  }
  string employeeid = comboBox1.SelectedItem.ToString();
  var employees = from item in doc.Elements()
                  where item.Attribute("employeeid").Value == employeeid
                  select item;
  foreach (var employee in employees)
  {
    textBox1.Text = employee.Element("firstname").Value;
    textBox2.Text = employee.Element("lastname").Value;
    textBox3.Text = employee.Element("homephone").Value;
    textBox4.Text = employee.Element("notes").Value;
  }
  label6.Text = $"Employee {(comboBox1.SelectedIndex + 1)} of {comboBox1.Items.Count}";
}
```

The FillControls() helper method simply retrieves the <employee> element whose employeeid attribute is selected in the combo box. It then fills the text boxes with <firstname>, <lastname>, <homephone>, and <notes> element values. The Element() method accepts the name of an XML element and returns the first occurrence of that element as an XElement instance.

Finally, the status label of the VCR display is updated to reflect the current employee position.

■ **Note**   In addition to the `SetElementValue()` and `SetAttributeValue()` methods, you can also use the `Value` property of the `XElement` and `XAttribute` classes to set the value of an existing element or attribute, respectively. Similarly, in addition to the `Add()` method, you can use the `AddBeforeSelf()` and `AddAfterSelf()` methods to add content before and after the current element, respectively.

Events of the XElement Class

Whenever any of the elements is added, removed, or renamed, the `XElement` class raises `Changing` and `Changed` events. The `Changing` event is raised just before the actual change occurs, whereas the `Changed` event is raised after the change is made. These events give you a chance to perform pre-operations and post-operations related to the change.

To illustrate the use of these events, let's modify the preceding application to add support for `Changing` and `Changed` events.

Modify the `Load` event of the form to reflect the changes shown in Listing 13-19.

Listing 13-19. Wiring Changing and Changed Event Handlers

```
private void Form1_Load(object sender, EventArgs e)
{
  doc=XElement.Load($"{Application.StartupPath}\\employees.xml");

  doc.Changing += new EventHandler<XObjectChangeEventArgs>(doc_Changing);
  doc.Changed += new EventHandler<XObjectChangeEventArgs>(doc_Changed);

  var result=from item in doc.Descendants("employee")
                  select item.Attribute("employeeid").Value;
  foreach (var obj in result)
  {
    comboBox1.Items.Add(obj);
  }
  FillControls();
}
```

Notice the code marked in bold. The code wires the event handlers for `Changing` and `Changed` events. Both of these events receive an event argument parameter of type `XObjectChangeEventArgs`. The event handler for the doc_Changed event handler is shown in Listing 13-20.

Listing 13-20. Handling a Changed Event of XElement

```
void doc_Changed(object sender, XObjectChangeEventArgs e)
{
  string msg = "";
  switch (e.ObjectChange)
  {
    case XObjectChange.Add:
      msg = "A new element has been added";
      break;
```

```
    case XObjectChange.Remove:
      msg = "An element has been removed";
      break;
    case XObjectChange.Name:
      msg = "An element has been renamed";
      break;
    case XObjectChange.Value:
      msg = "Value has been changed";
      break;
  }
  MessageBox.Show(msg);
}
```

The XObjectChangeEventArgs class simply provides a hint about the cause of the event. The possible causes are adding an element (Add), removing an element (Remove), renaming an element (Name), and changing the value of an element (Value). Depending on the cause, the code may simply display a message to the user.

In order to test these events, run the application, change employee details, and click the Update button. You should see a series of message boxes informing you about the changes. Figure 13-9 shows a sample run of the application.

Figure 13-9. *Changed event raised after modifying an employee's information*

Dealing with Whitespace

The behavior of whitespace can be controlled when you call the Load(), Parse(), and Save() methods on XElement or XDocument. The Load() and Parse() methods provide overloads that accept a parameter of type LoadOptions. The LoadOptions enumeration allows you to specify whether or not to preserve whitespace while loading the XML tree. Similarly, the Save() method provides an overload that accepts a parameter of type SaveOptions. The SaveOptions enumeration allows you to specify whether spaces should be preserved while serializing the XML tree.

To illustrate the use of LoadOptions and SaveOptions enumerations, let's develop an application like the one shown in Figure 13-10.

Figure 13-10. *Application to demonstrate whitespace handling*

The application loads the Employees.xml file when you click the Load button. The Preserve White Spaces check box indicates whether we want to preserve whitespace during document loading and saving. The Click event handler of the Load button is shown in Listing 13-21.

Listing 13-21. Using LoadOptions and SaveOptions Enumerations

```
private void button1_Click(object sender, EventArgs e)
{
  XElement root = null;
  string path= $"{Application.StartupPath}\\employees.xml";
  if (!checkBox1.Checked)
  {
    root=XElement.Load(path, LoadOptions.None);
    MessageBox.Show(root.ToString());
    root.Save(path, SaveOptions.None);
  }
  else
  {
    root=XElement.Load(path, LoadOptions.PreserveWhitespace);
    MessageBox.Show(root.ToString());
    root.Save(path, SaveOptions.DisableFormatting);
  }
}
```

The code loads the Employees.xml file into an instance of the XElement class. Depending on the check box state, it decides the appropriate LoadOptions value. The value of None indicates that we do not intend to preserve insignificant whitespace, where the value of PreserveWhitespace indicates that we wish to preserve whitespace. Similarly, while saving the document back to the disk, the SaveOptions value governs the whitespace behavior. The value of None indicates that the document will be indented, and insignificant whitespace will not be preserved, whereas the value of DisableFormatting indicates that we do not want to indent the document, and whitespace will be preserved as they are. The XML content loaded in the XElement are displayed in a message box using the ToString() method of the XElement class.

Try running the application with the check box unchecked (see Figure 13-11) and checked (see Figure 13-12). Notice that the message box in Figure 13-12 has preserved the whitespace.

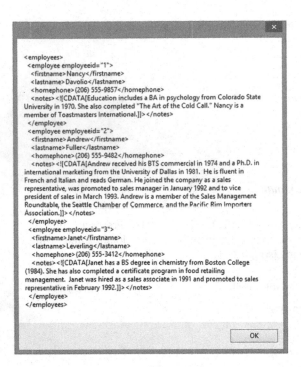

Figure 13-11. *Output with LoadOptions.None*

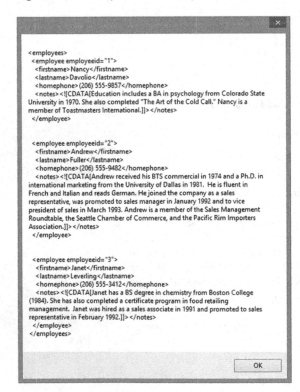

Figure 13-12. *Output with LoadOptions.PreserveWhitespace*

■ **Note**   Remember that just like XML DOM, the parsing process will be affected when you preserve whitespace (refer to the discussion from Chapter 2 in the "Dealing with Whitespace" section). However, since LINQ to XML allows you to query the XML tree in flexible ways, whitespace will not create any problem as long as you are not relying on the count of elements in your logic.

Dealing with Namespaces

At times the XML data that you are processing might be using XML namespaces. In such cases you may want to find out information about the namespace the XML data is using. The Name property of the XElement class provides a convenient place to obtain all the information about namespaces.

To illustrate the use of the Name property, we will create an application as shown in Figure 13-13.

Figure 13-13. *Obtaining namespace information*

The application consists of a Load button that loads the Employees.xml file. The namespace details are then displayed in the Label controls. In this example, we use the Employees.xml file from Listing 2-21 in Chapter 2. A part of the complete file is provided in Listing 13-22.

Listing 13-22. Employees.xml with a Namespace

```
<emp:employees xmlns:emp=" http://localhost/linqxml">
  <emp:employee employeeid="1">
    <emp:firstname>Nancy</emp:firstname>
    <emp:lastname>Davolio</emp:lastname>
    <emp:homephone>(206) 555-9857</emp:homephone>
...
```

Various markup tags of this listing are namespace qualified. The Click event handler of the Load button is shown in Listing 13-23.

Listing 13-23. Using the Name Property to Obtain Namespace Information

```
private void button1_Click(object sender, EventArgs e)
{
  XElement root = XElement.Load($"{Application.StartupPath}\\employees.xml");
  label4.Text = root.Name.NamespaceName;
  label5.Text = root.Name.LocalName;
  label6.Text = root.Name.ToString();
}
```

The code loads the Employees.xml file in an instance of the XElement class. The Name property of XElement is of type XName. The Namespace property of XName class gives the complete namespace name. The LocalName gives the name of the elements without the namespace qualifier, for example, employee, whereas calling the ToString() method returns the element name along with the namespace qualifier. Notice how the namespace-qualified element name is shown in Figure 13-13. The namespace is enclosed in braces ({ and }) followed by the local name of the element.

Specifying Namespaces While Constructing Elements

When you create an XML tree programmatically, you need to specify namespace information associated with it using the XNamespace class. To illustrate how this is done, we will develop an application like the one shown in Figure 13-14.

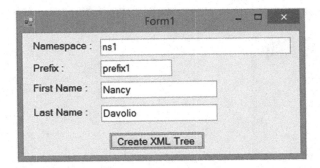

Figure 13-14. *Application that creates an XML tree with a namespace*

The application consists of four text boxes for entering a namespace name, a namespace prefix (if any), a first name, and a last name. Clicking the Create XML Tree button creates XElement and XAttribute instances as required and displays the resultant XML tree in a message box. The Click event handler of the button is shown in Listing 13-24.

Listing 13-24. Using XNamespace to Specify Namespace Information

```
private void button1_Click(object sender, EventArgs e)
{
  XNamespace ns = textBox1.Text;
  XElement root = new XElement(ns + "employee",
                              new XElement(ns + "firstname",textBox3.Text),
                              new XElement(ns + "lastname",textBox4.Text)
                              );
  if (textBox2.Text == "")
  {
    root.SetAttributeValue("xmlns", ns);
  }
  else
  {
    root.SetAttributeValue(XNamespace.Xmlns + textBox2.Text, ns);
  }
  MessageBox.Show(root.ToString());
}
```

The code creates an instance of the XNamespace class and sets the namespace name as indicated in the text box. Notice that the = operator is overloaded, and hence you can assign a string value directly to its instance. The <employee> element is then created. While specifying an element name, the code appends the element name to the namespace. If a namespace prefix is not specified, an attribute with the name xmlns is added to the root element. This way, the code defines a default namespace for the XML tree. If a namespace prefix is specified, that prefix is appended to the xmlns URI (see http://www.w3.org/2000/xmlns/ for more information on xmlns). Notice the use of the XNamespace.Xmlns property, which returns an XNamespace object corresponding to the xmlns URI. Finally, the resultant XML tree is shown using a message box. Figure 13-15 shows a sample generation of an XML tree.

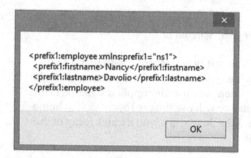

Figure 13-15. XML tree with namespace information

Validating XML Documents

XML documents are often validated against XML Schemas to ensure correctness of data. In Chapter 5, you learned validation techniques using XmlDocument, XmlReader, and XPathNavigator. Now it's time to see how LINQ to XML can be used to validate XML documents against XML Schemas. The XDocument as well as XElement classes provide an extension method named Validate() that does the job of validating the XML data against the XML Schema. Remember that, in order to access the Validate() extension method, you must import the System.Xml.Schema namespace in your code.

■ **Note**   Extension methods enable you to add methods to an existing class without inheriting or modifying the original class. They are a special kind of static methods that are called as if they were instance methods on the extended class.

To illustrate the use of the Validate() method, we will create an application like the one shown in Figure 13-16.

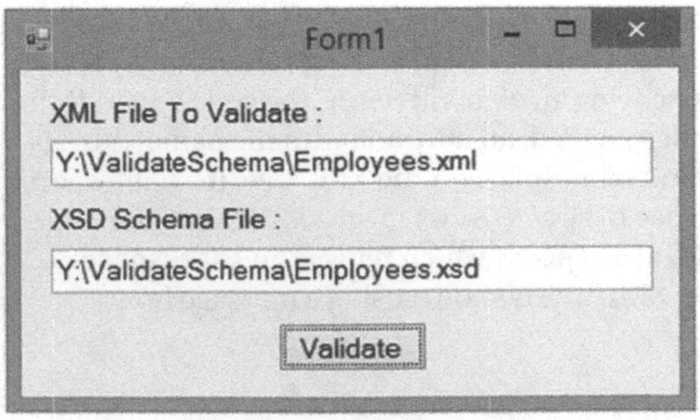

Figure 13-16. *Application that validates XDocument against an XML Schema*

The application consists of two text boxes and one button. The text boxes accept a path to the XML document that is to be validated and a path to the XML Schema file. Clicking the Validate button loads the XML document in an XDocument instance and validates the document against the supplied schema. Errors during validation (if any) are reported to the user. In this example, we will use the Employees.xsd schema file that we developed in Chapter 5 to validate the Employees.xml file. Just to give you a quick recap of the structure of the XSD Schema file, Listing 13-25 shows a part of it.

Listing 13-25. Partial Markup from Employees.xsd

```
<?xml version="1.0" encoding="utf-8"?>
<xs:schema attributeFormDefault="unqualified"
elementFormDefault="qualified"
xmlns:xs="http://www.w3.org/2001/XMLSchema">
  <xs:element name="employees">
    <xs:complexType>
      <xs:sequence>
        <xs:element name="employee" type="EmployeeType" minOccurs="0"
          maxOccurs="unbounded" />
      </xs:sequence>
    </xs:complexType>
  </xs:element>
  <xs:complexType name="EmployeeType">
    <xs:all>
      <xs:element name="firstname" type="NameSimpleType" />
      <xs:element name="notes" type="NotesSimpleType" />
      <xs:element name="lastname" type="NameSimpleType" />
      <xs:element name="homephone" type="PhoneSimpleType" />
    </xs:all>
...
```

The Click event handler of the Validate button is shown in Listing 13-26.

Listing 13-26. Validating Against the XSD Schema

```
private void button1_Click(object sender, EventArgs e)
{
  XDocument doc = XDocument.Load(textBox1.Text);
  XmlSchemaSet schema=new XmlSchemaSet();
```

414

```
schema.Add(null,textBox2.Text);
ValidationEventHandler handler = new ValidationEventHandler(MyHandler);
doc.Validate(schema, handler);
}

public void MyHandler(object sender, ValidationEventArgs e)
{
  MessageBox.Show(e.Message);
}
```

The code loads the source XML document in an instance of the XDocument class. It then creates an XmlSchemaSet and adds the specified XML Schema to it using the Add() method. The Validate() extension method of the XDocument class accepts two parameters: XmlSchemaSet and an event handler that gets called if validation fails. The event handler is of type ValidationEventHandler. The MyHandler() method acts as the event handler in our example. The validation is triggered by calling the Validate() method. If there are any validation errors, the MyHandler() event handler gets invoked. The MyHandler() event handler receives a parameter of type ValidationEventArgs. The Message property of the ValidationEventArgs class provides information about the validation errors.

In order to test the code, remove the employeeid attribute from the first <employee> element of the Employees.xml file and run the application. Figure 13-17 shows a validation error message after a sample run.

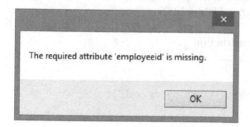

Figure 13-17. *A validation error*

Transforming XML Trees

In Chapter 6, we discussed how to transform XML data using XSLT style sheets. Though that approach still remains valid, LINQ to XML provides a new handy way of transforming XML data. Using this new approach, you can transform XML from one shape to another without knowing anything about XSLT.

■ **Note** The *shape* of an XML document refers to its element names, attribute names, and nesting of its hierarchy.

There are two common scenarios in transforming XML:

- You may want to transform an XML tree into an HTML tree. Similarly, you may want to transform an XML tree into another XML tree with an altogether different shape.

- You may want to project source XML code into an altogether different type.

In any case, LINQ to XML, along with its functional construction feature, provides an easy way to accomplish your task.

415

Changing the Shape of an XML Tree

Your transformation may call for a change in the shape of source XML tree. This is a common scenario when you want to transform XML into HTML for the purpose of displaying in the browser. This might also be needed while transferring XML data from one software system to another when the other system expects a different XML shape. To demonstrate how functional construction in LINQ to XML makes it easy to accomplish such changes in the shape, we will create an application like the one shown in Figure 13-18.

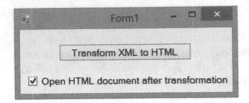

Figure 13-18. *Application that transforms XML into HTML*

The application consists of a button titled Transform XML to HTML and a check box. When you click the button, the XML data from Employees.xml is transformed into an HTML table and saved as Employees. htm. If the check box is checked, the Employees.htm file is displayed in the browser.

The code that does the job of transforming the data is shown in Listing 13-27.

Listing 13-27. Transforming an XML Tree Using Functional Construction

```
private void button1_Click(object sender, EventArgs e)
{
  XElement root = XElement.Load($"{Application.StartupPath}\\employees.xml");
  XElement html =
    new XElement("html",
                 new XElement("body",
                 new XElement("table",
                   new XAttribute("border",1),
                   new XElement("th", "Employee ID"),
                   new XElement("th", "First Name"),
                   new XElement("th", "LastName"),
                   new XElement("th", "Home Phone"),
                   new XElement("th", "Notes"),
                     from item in root.Descendants("employee")
                     select new XElement("tr",
                                         new XElement("td",
                                                 item.Attribute("employeeid").Value),
                                         new XElement("td",
                                                 item.Element("firstname").Value),
                                         new XElement("td",
                                                 item.Element("lastname").Value),
                                         new XElement("td",
                                                 item.Element("homephone").Value),
                                         new XElement("td",
                                                 item.Element("notes").Value)))));
  html.Save($"{Application.StartupPath}\\employees.htm");
```

```
    if (checkBox1.Checked)
    {
        Process.Start($"{Application.StartupPath}\\employees.htm");
    }
    else
    {
        MessageBox.Show($"Output saved as {Application.StartupPath}\\employees.htm");
    }
}
```

The code loads the Employees.xml file into an instance of the XElement class. It then creates another XElement named html using functional construction. Notice how the XML data is selected from descendant <employee> elements into the new XElement objects. Effectively, in just one statement, we are able to transform the source XML tree into HTML.

The new XElement formed after transformation is saved to the disk as the Employees.htm file. If the check box is checked, the code opens the Employees.htm file in the browser; otherwise, a success message box is displayed. Figure 13-19 shows the Employees.htm file generated as a result of a sample run of the application.

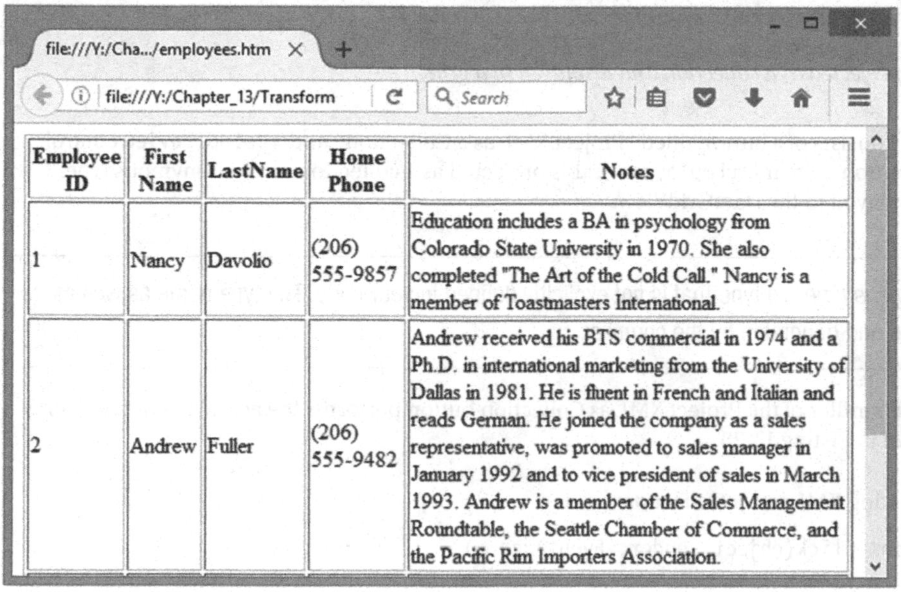

Figure 13-19. *Resultant HTML markup*

■ **Note** In addition to using functional construction, you can also create individual XElements and XAttributes and then create the required nesting. However, functional construction makes your code tidy and easy to read. If your XML data is generated as a result of some complex processing or logic, then you may need to create various elements and attributes as stand-alone entities and then associate them with each other. This process is very similar to the approach taken by XML DOM.

Projecting a New Type

Projection is the process by which source data is filtered, has its shape changed, or even has its type changed. For example, suppose that you want to load data from Employees.xml into a new collection of Employee objects such that each Employee object has the values filled from the <firstname>, <lastname>, <homephone>, and <notes> elements of the source XML.

In order to illustrate how projection works, we will create an application like the one shown in Figure 13-20.

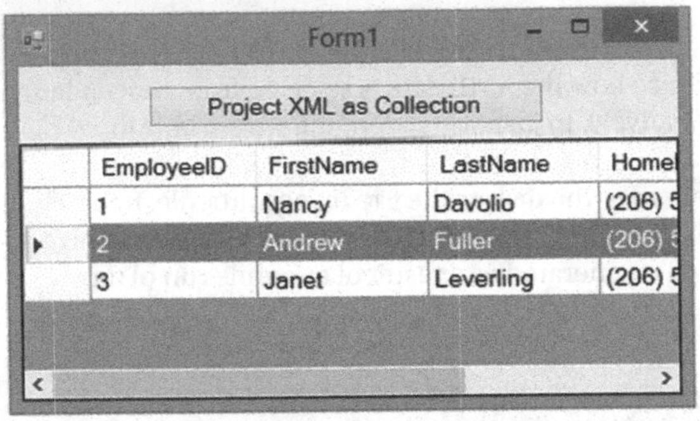

Figure 13-20. *Data projected as a collection and displayed in a grid*

The application consists of a button titled "Project XML as a Collection" and a DataGridView control. When you click the button, data from Employees.xml is projected as a collection of an anonymous type. The collection is then displayed in the DataGridView.

■ **Note** An *anonymous type* is a type that is not explicitly defined in your code. The type name as well as its properties are inferred and generated by the compiler.

The Click event handler of the Project XML as Collection button performs the actual job of projecting the XML and is shown in Listing 13-28.

Listing 13-28. Projecting XML into a Collection

```
private void button1_Click(object sender, EventArgs e)
{
  XElement root = XElement.Load($"{Application.StartupPath}\\employees.xml");
  var employees = from item in root.Descendants("employee")
                          select new
                          {
                              EmployeeID = item.Attribute("employeeid").Value,
                              FirstName = item.Element("firstname").Value,
                              LastName = item.Element("lastname").Value,
                              HomePhone = item.Element("homephone").Value,
                              Notes = item.Element("notes").Value
                          };
  dataGridView1.DataSource = employees.ToArray();
}
```

The code loads the `Employee.xml` file into an instance of the `XElement` class. It then selects the required data as an anonymous type with five properties, namely `EmployeeID`, `FirstName`, `LastName`, `HomePhone`, and `Notes`. Finally, the collection of the anonymous type is converted to an array for data binding with the `DataGridView` control.

Summary

LINQ to XML provides an altogether new way of processing XML data. This chapter examined many features of LINQ to XML in detail. You worked with classes such as `XElement` and `XDocument` that load XML trees for processing and learned how to deal with whitespace and namespaces in LINQ to XML. Common operations such as parsing, navigating, and modifying XML data were also covered. You also learned to validate XML documents against XML Schemas. Transforming XML data using LINQ to XML has its own advantages, and you used functional construction to transform the shape of the source XML. Finally, you projected an XML tree into a collection.

APPENDIX A

■ ■ ■

Creating a Custom XmlReader and XmlWriter

In Chapter 3, you learned about the XmlReader and XmlWriter classes. The abstract classes XmlReader and XmlWriter can be used in three ways:

- To call the Create() method of the respective classes that return an instance of the generic XmlReader or XmlWriter classes

- To use the concrete classes XmlTextReader and XmlTextWriter provided by the .NET Framework

- To create custom classes that inherit from the XmlReader and XmlWriter classes

You are already familiar with the first two approaches. In the following sections, you are going to learn how to create custom readers and writers from the abstract base classes XmlReader and XmlWriter.

Creating a Custom XmlReader

In this section, you will create a custom implementation of the XmlReader class. The SqlCommand class provides the ExecuteXmlReader() method that returns an instance of XmlReader to the caller. This works fine if your database is SQL Server, but what if your database is Microsoft Office Access or any other OLEDB-compliant database? Moreover, XML extensions such as the FOR XML clause may not be available for all databases. Does that mean that you cannot retrieve the data and read it by using an XmlReader? Of course not.

There is no out-of-the-box solution for this problem, but you can build your own mechanism to overcome this limitation, by creating a custom class that inherits from the XmlReader abstract class. You can then override the required properties and methods as per your need. The requirements for the custom XmlReader class are summarized here:

- It should accept the database connection string and table name to read.

- The column values should be treated as attribute values.

- It should allow iterating through the table to read each row.

- The column values should be accessible by specifying a column index or name.

© Bipin Joshi 2017

B. Joshi, *Beginning XML with C# 7*, https://doi.org/10.1007/978-1-4842-3105-0

Inheriting from XmlReader

The XmlReader class is an abstract class and provides several properties and methods that you need to override when you inherit from it. Listing A-1 shows signatures of these properties and methods.

Listing A-1. Properties and Methods of the XmlReader Class

```
public abstract int AttributeCount;
public abstract string BaseURI
{
  get;
}
public abstract void Close();
public abstract int Depth
{
  get;
}
public abstract bool EOF
{
  get;
}
public abstract string GetAttribute(int i);
public abstract string GetAttribute(string name, string namespaceURI);
public abstract string GetAttribute(string name);
public abstract bool HasValue
{
  get;
}
public abstract bool IsEmptyElement
{
  get;
}
public abstract string LocalName
{
  get;
}
public abstract string LookupNamespace(string prefix);
public abstract bool MoveToAttribute(string name, string ns);
public abstract bool MoveToAttribute(string name);
public abstract bool MoveToElement();
public abstract bool MoveToFirstAttribute();
public abstract bool MoveToNextAttribute();
public abstract XmlNameTable NameTable
{
  get;
}
public abstract string NamespaceURI
{
  get;
}
```

```
public abstract XmlNodeType NodeType
{
  get;
}
public abstract string Prefix
{
  get;
}
public abstract bool Read();
public abstract bool ReadAttributeValue();
public abstract ReadState ReadState
{
  get;
}
public abstract void ResolveEntity();
public abstract string Value
{
  get;
}
```

You can override these properties and methods and write your own data-manipulation logic. If you do not want to override a particular property or method, you still need to have its empty implementation. A better way is to throw an exception in such properties and methods so that the caller knows that these properties and methods are not implemented by you. I will not discuss every property here because you are already familiar with many of them (see Chapter 3 for more information).

Creating the TableReader Class

Now that you are familiar with the XmlReader abstract class, let's create our own implementation. To do so, create a new project of type class library by using Visual Studio. Add a class named TableReader. Make sure that references to the System.Xml and System.Data assemblies are added to the project. Import the namespaces as shown in Listing A-2 at the top of the TableReader class and ensure that the TableReader class inherits from the XmlReader class.

Listing A-2. Importing Namespaces and Setting Inheritance

```
using System.Xml;
using System.Data;
using System.Data.OleDb;

class TableReader:XmlReader
{
...
```

You need to add an implementation of each property and method mentioned. Visual Studio provides a shortcut for adding empty implementations of these members. Go to the class declaration line and look for the Quick Actions icon in the left margin. Open the Quick Actions list and choose the Implement Abstract Class option (see Figure A-1).

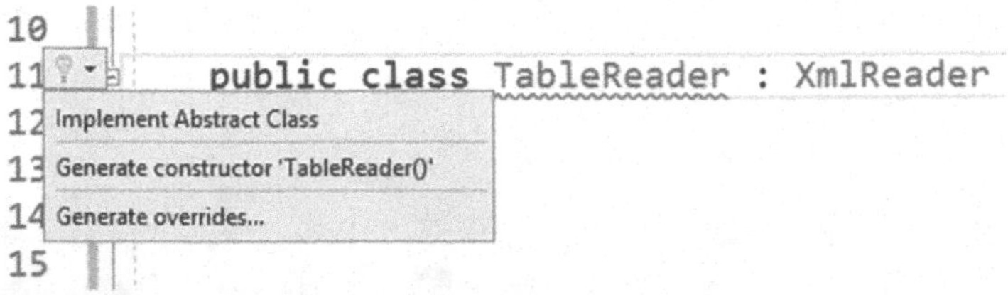

```
10
11       public class TableReader : XmlReader
12   Implement Abstract Class
13   Generate constructor 'TableReader()'
14   Generate overrides...
15
```

Figure A-1. *Adding empty implementations of properties and methods*

This will add dummy signatures of all the properties and methods that need to be overridden. Notice how the dummy implementation throws an exception by using the throw keyword. This way, if somebody tries to use unimplemented members, an exception will be thrown indicating that "the method or operation is not implemented." Code the TableReader class as shown in Listing A-3.

Listing A-3. The TableReader Class

```csharp
public class TableReader:XmlReader
{
        private OleDbConnection cnn;
        private OleDbCommand cmd;
        private OleDbDataReader reader;
        private int intColumnIndex = -1;
        private string strValue;

        public TableReader(string connectionString,string tableName)
        {
            cnn = new OleDbConnection(connectionString);
            cmd = new OleDbCommand();
            cmd.Connection = cnn;
            cmd.CommandText = tableName;
            cmd.CommandType = CommandType.TableDirect;
            cnn.Open();
            reader = cmd.ExecuteReader();
        }

        public override int AttributeCount
        {
            get
            {
                return reader.FieldCount;
            }
        }

        public override void Close()
        {
            reader.Close();
            cnn.Close();
        }
```

```csharp
public override int Depth
{
    get
    {
        return reader.Depth;
    }
}

public override string GetAttribute(int i)
{
    return reader.GetValue(i).ToString();
}

public override string GetAttribute(string name)
{
    return reader.GetValue(reader.GetOrdinal(name)).ToString();
}

public override bool MoveToAttribute(string name)
{
    intColumnIndex = reader.GetOrdinal(name);
    return true;
}

public override bool MoveToElement()
{
    intColumnIndex = -1;
    return true;
}

public override bool MoveToFirstAttribute()
{
    intColumnIndex = 0;
    return true;
}

public override bool MoveToNextAttribute()
{
    intColumnIndex++;
    if (intColumnIndex > reader.FieldCount - 1)
    {
        return false;
    }
    else
    {
        return true;
    }
}
```

```csharp
        public override bool Read()
        {
            intColumnIndex = -1;
            strValue = "";
            return reader.Read();
        }

        public override bool HasValue
        {
            get
            {
                return reader.IsDBNull(intColumnIndex);
            }
        }

        public override bool ReadAttributeValue()
        {
            if (intColumnIndex < reader.FieldCount)
            {
                strValue = reader.GetValue(intColumnIndex).ToString();
                return true;
            }
            else
            {
                return false;
            }
        }

        public string Name
        {
            get
            {
                if (intColumnIndex == -1)
                {
                    return cmd.CommandText;
                }
                else
                {
                    return reader.GetName(intColumnIndex);
                }
            }
        }

        public override string Value
        {
            get
            {
                return strValue;
            }
        }
...
}
```

In the following text, we dissect the code step by step.

Declaring Class-Level Variables

```
private OleDbConnection cnn;
private OleDbCommand cmd;
private OleDbDataReader reader;
private int intColumnIndex = -1;
private string strValue;
```

The TableReader class declares private variables of type OleDbConnection, OleDbCommand, and OleDbDataReader at the class level:

- The OleDbConnection class is used to establish a connection with any OLEDB-compliant databases.

- The OleDbCommand class is used to execute any query, SQL query, or stored procedures against a database.

- The OleDbDataReader class allows you to iterate through a result set in a cursor-oriented manner.

The intColumnIndex integer variable keeps track of the current column index whose value is to be read. Similarly, the strValue string variable stores the value from the column indicated by intColumnIndex.

Initializing the Variables

```
public TableReader(string connectionString,string tableName)
{
    cnn = new OleDbConnection(connectionString);
    cmd = new OleDbCommand();
    cmd.Connection = cnn;
    cmd.CommandText = tableName;
    cmd.CommandType = CommandType.TableDirect;
    cnn.Open();
    reader = cmd.ExecuteReader();
}
```

The constructor of the TableReader class accepts two parameters: the database connection string and the name of the table whose data is to be read. Using the connection string, the OleDbConnection is instantiated. The Connection property of the OleDbCommand class is set to the OleDbConnection class we just instantiated. The CommandText property of the OleDbCommand class is set to the name of the table whose data is to be read.

Have a look at the CommandType property. It is set to TableDirect, which returns all the rows from the table indicated by the CommandText property. In effect, it works as if we have specified SELECT * FROM <tableName> as the query. The database connection is then opened. The ExecuteReader() method of OleDbCommand is called and an OleDbDataReader is retrieved.

Retrieving the Total Number of Attributes

```
public override int AttributeCount
{
    get
    {
      return reader.FieldCount;
    }
}
```

The TableReader class is going to return column values as attributes in the resultant XML data. Hence, the AttributeCount read-only property returns the total number of columns in the underlying table. The total number of columns in the table is obtained by using the FieldCount property of the OleDbDataReader class.

Closing the Reader

```
public override void Close()
{
    reader.Close();
    cnn.Close();
}
public override int Depth
{
    get
    {
        return reader.Depth;
    }
}
```

The Close() method closes the OleDbDataReader as well as the OleDbConnection. The Depth property returns the Depth of the OleDbDataReader.

Reading Attributes

```
public override string GetAttribute(int i)
{
    return reader.GetValue(i).ToString();
}

    public override string GetAttribute(string name)
{
    return reader.GetValue(reader.GetOrdinal(name)).ToString();
}
```

The column values can be retrieved by using two overloads of the GetAttribute() method. The first overload accepts the attribute index. In our case, the attribute index is the same as the column index. The GetValue() method of the OleDbDataReader class accepts the column index and returns the column value as an object. The ToString() method returns a string representation of the object to the caller. The second overload accepts an attribute name. The GetOrdinal() method of OleDbDataReader accepts the column name and returns its index. The returned index is then passed to the GetValue() method as before.

Navigating Between the Attributes

```
public override bool MoveToAttribute(string name)
{
    intColumnIndex = reader.GetOrdinal(name);
    return true;
}

public override bool MoveToElement()
{
    intColumnIndex = -1;
    return true;
}

public override bool MoveToFirstAttribute()
{
    intColumnIndex = 0;
    return true;
}

public override bool MoveToNextAttribute()
{
    intColumnIndex++;
    if (intColumnIndex > reader.FieldCount - 1)
    {
        return false;
    }
    else
    {
        return true;
    }
}
```

The MoveToAttribute(), MoveToFirstAttribute(), MoveToNextAtribute(), and MoveToElement() methods allow you to navigate within the available attributes:

- The MoveToAttribute() method accepts the name of the column (which is the same as the attribute name) and sets the column index variable to the index of that column.

- The MoveToFirstAttribute() method sets the current column index to 0, whereas MoveToNextAttribute() increments it so that the next column value can be read.

- The MoveToElement() method simply sets the current column index to -1, indicating that no column value can be read. The MoveToElement() method is intended to move the reader to the element node from any of its attributes. By setting the column index to -1, we reset the column index counter and mimic this behavior.

Advancing the Reader

```
public override bool Read()
{
    intColumnIndex = -1;
    strValue = "";
    return reader.Read();
}
```

The Read() method allows you to iterate through the table. It calls the Read() method of the OleDbDataReader class and returns a Boolean value indicating whether the read operation was successful. As the record pointer is moving on to a new record, the current column index and value are reset.

Checking Whether the Value Is Empty

```
public override bool HasValue
{
    get
    {
        return reader.IsDBNull(intColumnIndex);
    }
}
```

The HasValue property indicates whether the TableReader contains any value. If the column contains a NULL value, HasValue should return false. The IsDbNull() method of the OleDbDataReader class accepts a column index and returns true if the column contains a NULL value.

Reading Values

```
public override bool ReadAttributeValue()
{
    if (intColumnIndex < reader.FieldCount)
    {
        strValue = reader.GetValue(intColumnIndex).ToString();
        return true;
    }
    else
    {
        return false;
    }
}
```

The ReadAttributeValue() method returns the value of the current column. It does so by using the GetValue() method of the OleDbDataReader class as before.

Returning the Table or Column Name

```
public string Name
{
    get
    {
        if (intColumnIndex == -1)
        {
            return cmd.CommandText;
        }
        else
        {
            return reader.GetName(intColumnIndex);
        }
    }
}
```

The Name property returns either the underlying table name or column name. This is useful to see which column is being read. The table name is obtained from the CommandText property of the OleDbCommand class, whereas the column name is obtained from the GetName() method of the OleDbDataReader class.

Returning Values

```
public override string Value
{
    get
    {
        return strValue;
    }
}
```

Finally, the Value property simply returns the value stored in the strValue variable. Note that strValue gets assigned in the ReadAttributeValue() method.

The remaining properties and methods are not implemented by the TableReader class. Compile the class library and you should get an assembly, TableReader.dll. This assembly can be used in client applications to work with OLEDB databases and XML.

Using the TableReader Class

To consume the TableReader class, you need to create a Windows Forms application like the one shown in Figure A-2.

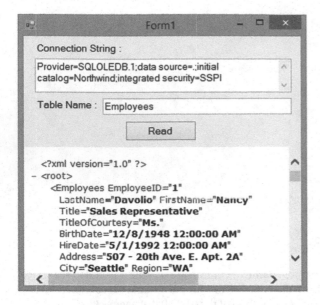

Figure A-2. *Application that consumes the TableReader class*

The application consists of text boxes for entering the database connection string and table name, respectively. After you click the Read button, the `TableReader` class is instantiated. It reads the table data and writes it to an XML file. The XML file thus created is displayed in a Web Browser control. The `Click` event handler of the Read button contains the code shown in Listing A-4.

Listing A-4. Using the TableReader Class

```
private void button1_Click(object sender, EventArgs e)
{
  TableReader tr = new TableReader(textBox1.Text, textBox2.Text);
  XmlTextWriter writer =
    new XmlTextWriter($"{Application.StartupPath}\\temp.xml", null);
  writer.WriteStartDocument();
  writer.WriteStartElement("root");
  int count = tr.AttributeCount;
  while (tr.Read())
  {
    writer.WriteStartElement(tr.Name);
    for (int i = 0; i < count; i++)
    {
      tr.MoveToAttribute(i);
      tr.ReadAttributeValue();
      writer.WriteAttributeString(tr.Name, tr.Value);
    }
    writer.WriteEndElement();
  }
```

```
    writer.WriteEndElement();
    tr.Close();
    writer.Close();
    webBrowser1.Navigate($"{Application.StartupPath}\\temp.xml");
}
```

Before you write the preceding code, add a reference to TableReader.dll in the Windows application and import the namespace at the top. The code creates an instance of the TableReader class by passing the database connection string and table name to its constructor. Then an XmlTextWriter is created that writes data to a temporary XML file called temp.xml. The TableReader class will return only the fragmented XML data; hence the root element is added by using the WriteStartElement() method of the XmlTextWriter class. The total number of columns in the supplied table is retrieved by using the AttributeCount property and is stored in a variable for later use.

A while loop calls the Read() method of the TableReader class. With each iteration, an element is added to the file with the same name as the table name. Recollect that the Name property of the TableReader class returns either the table name or column name depending on the current column index. Because we have just called the Read() method, the column index is going to be -1 and hence the table name will be returned.

Next, a for loop iterates through all the attributes—that is, columns. With each iteration of the for loop, the value of the attribute is read by using the ReadAttributeValue() method. An attribute is then written to the file along with its value by using the WriteAttributeString() method of the XmlTextWriter class. The WriteEndElement() method of the XmlTextWriter class writes end tags for the nearest open element. The TableReader and XmlTextReader are then closed by using their respective Close() methods. Finally, the Navigate() method of the web browser control shows the user the XML file.

Creating a Custom XmlWriter

Now that you have created a custom implementation of XmlReader, let's move further and see how to create a custom XmlWriter. As an example, we will create an RSS writer that emits RSS feeds.

Really Simple Syndication (RSS) is a standard way to share your web site content with others. It is nothing but standardized XML markup that describes the content you want to share. Because RSS is a widely accepted format, your content immediately becomes ready to be consumed by others. Listing A-5 illustrates an RSS document.

Listing A-5. Sample RSS Markup

```
<rss version="2.0">
  <channel>
    <title>My Web Site</title>
    <link>http://localhost/mywebsite</link>
    <description>Latest Articles from My Web Site</description>
    <copyright>Copyright (C) My Web Site. All rights reserved.</copyright>
    <generator>My RSS Generator</generator>
    <item>
      <title>Using WebRequest and WebResponse</title>
      <link>http://localhost/mywebsite/displayarticle.aspx?id=239</link>
      <description>Description goes here</description>
      <pubDate>Sun, 25 Jan 2004 12:00:00 AM GMT</pubDate>
    </item>
  </channel>
</rss>
```

Let's look at each markup tag closely:

- `<rss>` forms the root tag and has a `version` attribute. The version attribute specifies the RSS specification version used by the markup, 2.0 in this case.

- `<channel>` contains tags such as `<title>`, `<link>`, and `<item>` nodes. A channel represents metadata information from a particular source. It essentially acts as a container for the rest of the tags. An RSS document can contain one or more channels.

- `<title>` represents the title of this RSS feed.

- `<link>` represents the URL of the web site providing the RSS feed.

- `<description>` details more information about this feed.

- `<copyright>` specifies copyright information.

- `<generator>` specifies the application that generated this feed.

In addition to the preceding tags, there can be one or more `<item>` tags, each of which represents an actual item that you want to share (for example, an article or a blog entry). Each `<item>` tag further contains the following subnodes:

- `<title>` represents the title of this item (for example, the article title).

- `<link>` represents the URL of this item (for example, the article URL).

- `<description>` contains the description of the item (for example, a summary of the article).

- `<pubDate>` contains the publication date of the item. A typical date format is Sun 28 Dec 2003 12:00:00 AM GMT.

■ **Note** The RSS markup shown here is the basic markup. You may need to add additional tags to incorporate additional information. You can obtain more information about RSS at `https://en.wikipedia.org/wiki/RSS`.

The .NET Framework provides the `System.ServiceModel.Syndication` namespace, which contains classes for reading and writing an RSS feed. However, as an example we will create our own custom class called `RssWriter`. The `RssWriter` class will inherit from `XmlWriter` and allow you to emit RSS feeds easily.

To create `RssWriter`, you need to create a class library project. As before, be sure to add a reference to the `System.Xml` assembly.

Inheriting from XmlWriter

To create a custom implementation of `XmlWriter`, you need to inherit from it and override the properties and methods shown in Listing A-6.

Listing A-6. Properties and Methods of the XmlWriter Class

```
public abstract void Close();
public abstract void Flush();
public abstract string LookupPrefix(string ns);
public abstract void WriteBase64(byte[] buffer, int index, int count);
```

```
public abstract void WriteCData(string text);
public abstract void WriteCharEntity(char ch);
public abstract void WriteChars(char[] buffer, int index, int count);
public abstract void WriteComment(string text);
public abstract void
  WriteDocType(string name, string pubid, string sysid, string subset);
public abstract void WriteEndAttribute();
public abstract void WriteEndDocument();
public abstract void WriteEndElement();
public abstract void WriteEntityRef(string name);
public abstract void WriteFullEndElement();
public abstract void WriteProcessingInstruction(string name, string text);
public abstract void WriteRaw(string data);
public abstract void WriteRaw(char[] buffer, int index, int count);
public abstract void
  WriteStartAttribute(string prefix, string localName, string ns);
public abstract void WriteStartDocument(bool standalone);
public abstract void WriteStartDocument();
public abstract void WriteStartElement(string prefix, string localName, string ns);
public abstract WriteState WriteState
{
  get;
}
public abstract void WriteString(string text);
public abstract void WriteSurrogateCharEntity(char lowChar, char highChar);
public abstract void WriteWhitespace(string ws);
```

Many of these properties and methods should be familiar to you because we discussed them in Chapter 3.

Creating the RssWriter Class

To begin, we need to specify that the RssWriter class inherits from the XmlWriter base class. As shown in Figure A-1, add dummy definitions of the properties and methods that implement the abstract base class XmlWriter. Then add a couple of variables and a constructor to the RssWriter class, as shown in Listing A-7.

Listing A-7. The Constructor of RssWriter

```
public class RssWriter:XmlWriter
{
  private XmlWriter writer;
  private Stream objStream;
  public RssWriter(Stream stream)
  {
    objStream = stream;
    writer = XmlWriter.Create(objStream);
  }
}
```

The code declares class-level variables of XmlWriter and Stream types, respectively. The constructor takes a parameter of type Stream. This stream acts as an output stream for emitting the RSS feeds. An instance of the XmlWriter is constructed by using the Create() method of the XmlWriter class. The stream passed to the constructor is supplied to the Create() method so that the newly created instance of XmlWriter writes to that stream.

435

Coding Stream-Related Operations

The stream needs to be closed and flushed to ensure that the emitted data is saved correctly. The two overridden methods—Close() and Flush()—do just that. Listing A-8 shows these methods.

Listing A-8. The Close() and Flush() Methods

```
public override void Close()
{
  objStream.Close();
  writer.Close();
}
public override void Flush()
{
  writer.Flush();
}
```

The Close() method calls the Close() method of the underlying stream as well as that of the XmlWriter. Similarly, the Flush() method calls the Flush() method of the XmlWriter so that data is flushed to the stream.

Defining Enumerations for RSS-Specific Tags

It would be nice to readily provide RSS tag and attribute names so that you need not remember them. This is achieved by creating two enumerations: RssElements and RssAttributes. The enumerations are shown in Listing A-9.

Listing A-9. Enumerations for Representing RSS Tags and Attributes

```
public enum RssElements
{
  Rss,Channel,Title,Description,Link,Copyright,Generator,Item,PubDate
}

public enum RssAttributes
{
  Version
}
```

The RssElements enumeration contains values for representing RSS elements. The RssAttributes enumeration contains just one value—Version—which represents the version attribute of the <rss> element.

Writing Elements

To emit the RSS feed, you need to write elements such as <rss> and <item> onto the output stream. We will create three methods for this purpose: WriteElement(), WriteElementString(), and WriteEndElement(). The complete code of these methods is shown in Listing A-10.

Listing A-10. Writing Elements

```
public void WriteStartElement(RssElements element)
{
  string elementName = "";
  switch (element)
  {
    case RssElements.Channel:
      elementName = "channel";
      break;
    case RssElements.Copyright:
      elementName = "copyright";
      break;
    case RssElements.Description:
      elementName = "description";
      break;
    case RssElements.Generator:
      elementName = "generator";
      break;
    case RssElements.Item:
      elementName = "item";
      break;
    case RssElements.Link:
      elementName = "link";
      break;
    case RssElements.PubDate:
      elementName = "pubDate";
      break;
    case RssElements.Rss:
      elementName = "rss";
      break;
    case RssElements.Title:
      elementName = "title";
      break;
    }
    writer.WriteStartElement(elementName);
}

public void WriteElementString(RssElements element, string value)
{
  string elementName = "";
  switch (element)
  {
    case RssElements.Channel:
      elementName = "channel";
      break;
    case RssElements.Copyright:
      elementName = "copyright";
      break;
    case RssElements.Description:
      elementName = "description";
      break;
```

```
        case RssElements.Generator:
          elementName = "generator";
          break;
        case RssElements.Item:
          elementName = "item";
          break;
        case RssElements.Link:
          elementName = "link";
          break;
        case RssElements.PubDate:
          elementName = "pubDate";
          break;
        case RssElements.Rss:
          elementName = "rss";
          break;
        case RssElements.Title:
          elementName = "title";
          break;
    }
    writer.WriteElementString(elementName, value);
}

public override void WriteEndElement()
{
    writer.WriteEndElement();
}
```

The WriteStartElement() method accepts a parameter of type RssElements that indicates the element name to be written. It contains a switch statement that checks the supplied element name against various values from the RssElements enumeration. The name of the element is stored in a string variable. Finally, the WriteStartElement() method of XmlWriter is called by supplying the element name stored in the variable.

The WriteElementString() method accepts two parameters: RssElements and the value of the element. It contains a similar switch statement as in the previous method and stores the element name in a variable. The WriteElementString() method of the XmlWriter class is called by passing the element name and its value. Note that WriteStartElement() and WriteElementString() are new methods—that is, they are not defined by the XmlWriter base class.

The WriteEndElement() method simply calls the WriteEndElement() method of the XmlWriter instance so that the end tag of the nearest element is emitted.

Writing Attributes

Just as we added methods for writing elements, we also need to add methods for emitting attributes. Three methods—WriteStartAttribute(), WriteAttributeString(), and WriteEndAttribute()—will do that job. Listing A-11 shows these methods.

Listing A-11. Writing Attributes

```
public void WriteStartAttribute(RssAttributes attb)
{
  if (attb == RssAttributes.Version)
  {
    writer.WriteStartAttribute("version");
  }
}

public void WriteAttributeString(RssAttributes attb, string value)
{
  if (attb == RssAttributes.Version)
  {
    writer.WriteAttributeString("version",value);
  }
}

public override void WriteEndAttribute()
{
  writer.WriteEndAttribute();
}
```

The WriteStartAttribute() method accepts a parameter of type RssAttributes. Inside it checks whether the attribute to be emitted is Version, and if so, calls the WriteStartAttribute() method of the XmlWriter instance to write the attribute.

The WriteAttributeString() method accepts two parameters: RssAttributes and the value of the attribute. It then calls the WriteAttributeString() method of the XmlWriter instance by passing the supplied value and version as the attribute name.

The WriteEndAttribute() method simply calls the WriteEndAttribute() method of the XmlWriter instance.

Writing Data

Although the methods that we created for writing elements will take care of most of the RSS feed generation, you may need additional methods to emit comments, character data, whitespaces, and so on. To accomplish this task, we will write a set of methods, as shown in Listing A-12.

Listing A-12. Methods for Writing Data

```
public override void WriteCData(string text)
{
  writer.WriteCData(text);
}

public override void WriteChars(char[] buffer, int index, int count)
{
  writer.WriteChars(buffer, index, count);
}
```

```
public override void WriteComment(string text)
{
  writer.WriteComment(text);
}

public override void WriteWhitespace(string ws)
{
  writer.WriteWhitespace(ws);
}

public override void WriteString(string text)
{
  writer.WriteString(text);
}
```

These methods do not contain much code. They simply call the corresponding method on the XmlWriter instance. For example, the WriteCData() method accepts a string and calls the WriteCData() method of the XmlWriter by passing the string. The WriteChars(), WriteComment(), WriteWhitespace(), and WriteString() methods also call the respective methods of the XmlWriter instance.

Writing an XML Declaration

An RSS feed is an XML document and from that point of view should contain an XML declaration. The methods WriteStartDocument() and WriteEndDocument() emit an XML declaration with a version of 1.0. These methods are shown in Listing A-13.

Listing A-13. Writing an XML Declaration

```
public override void WriteStartDocument()
{
  writer.WriteStartDocument();
}
public override void WriteStartDocument(bool standalone)
{
  writer.WriteStartDocument(standalone);
}
public override void WriteEndDocument()
{
  writer.WriteEndDocument();
}
```

The WriteStartDocument() method has two overloads. The one with a Boolean parameter emits a stand-alone attribute. Both the methods call respective overloads of the WriteStartDocument() method on the XmlWriter instance. The WriteEndDocument() method simply calls the WriteEndDocument() method of the XmlWriter instance.

That's it: the RssWriter class is now ready. Compile the class library to get its output assembly.

Using the RssWriter Class

To consume the RssWriter class we just created, you will need to create a new web site in Visual Studio. Add a reference to the assembly in which RssWriter resides. Open the default web form in the IDE and write the code shown in Listing A-14 in its Page_Load event handler.

Listing A-14. Using the RssWriter Class

```
protected void Page_Load(object sender, EventArgs e)
{
    Response.ContentEncoding = System.Text.Encoding.UTF8;
    Response.ContentType = "text/xml";
    RssWriter writer = new RssWriter(Response.OutputStream);
    writer.WriteStartElement(RssElements.Rss);
    writer.WriteAttributeString(RssAttributes.Version, "2.0");
    writer.WriteStartElement(RssElements.Channel);
    writer.WriteElementString(RssElements.Title, "My Web Site");
    writer.WriteElementString(RssElements.Link, "http://localhost/mywebsite");
    writer.WriteElementString(RssElements.Description, "Latest Articles from My Web Site");
    writer.WriteElementString(RssElements.Copyright, "Copyright (C) My Web Site. All rights
    reserved.");
    writer.WriteElementString(RssElements.Generator, "My XML RSS Generator");
    writer.WriteStartElement(RssElements.Item);
    writer.WriteElementString(RssElements.Title, " Create and consume RSS Feeds");
    writer.WriteElementString(RssElements.Link, "http://localhost/mywebsite/Articles/
    displayarticle.aspx?id=242");
    writer.WriteElementString(RssElements.Description, "This article explains how to create
    and consume RSS feeds.");
    writer.WriteElementString(RssElements.PubDate, "Mon, 04 Sep 2017 12:00:00 AM GMT");
    writer.WriteEndElement();
    writer.WriteEndElement();
    writer.WriteEndElement();
    writer.Close();
    Response.End();
}
```

The code sets the ContentEncoding property of the Response object to UTF-8 (that is, ASCII). It also sets the ContentType property to text/xml. This way, the browser knows that the response is XML data rather than HTML. A new instance of the RssWriter class is then created. The OutputStream of the Response object is passed as a parameter to the constructor of the RssWriter class. This way, the XML data will be written directly on the response stream.

Then, one by one, RSS tags are emitted so as to output an RSS feed, as shown in Listing A-5 earlier. Notice how the RssElements enumeration has made our job easy. Various methods, such as WriteElementString() and WriteStartElement(), make extensive use of the RssElements enumeration. After the feed has been written, the RssWriter instance is closed. Finally, the End() method of the Response object is called so that the response stream is flushed off to the client.

■ **Note**   For the sake of simplicity, the code emits hard-coded values. In most real-world cases, you will retrieve data such as the title, URL, and publication date from a database table.

441

If you run the web form after writing the code, it should look similar to Figure A-3.

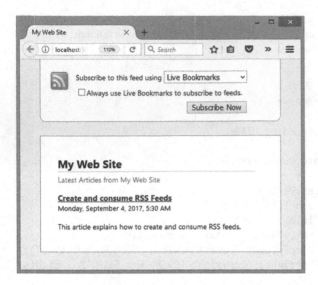

Figure A-3. *RSS feed displayed in the browser*

As you can see, Firefox has identified the response as a valid RSS feed and displayed in a special way for easy reading. If you view the Page Source of the page, you will see the raw XML markup, as shown in Figure A-4.

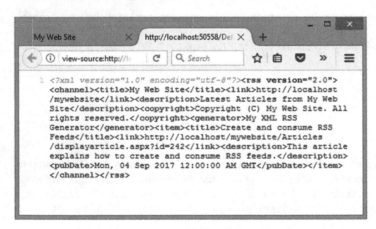

Figure A-4. *Raw XML of the RSS feed*

This is the same RSS feed markup you emitted from the web form code-behind.

Summary

In this appendix, you learned to create custom implementations of the XmlReader and XmlWriter classes. The XmlReader and XmlWriter classes are abstract classes. To create custom readers and writers, you need to inherit from them and override various properties and methods. This way, you can easily extend the out-of-the-box functionality exposed by these classes for specific scenarios.

APPENDIX B

Resources

The following resources will help you learn more about XML, .NET Framework, and allied technologies.

W3C Web Site for XML Specifications

http://www.w3.org/XML

W3C Web Site for XML Schema Specifications

http://www.w3.org/XML/Schema

W3C Web Site for XPath-Related Information

http://www.w3.org/TR/xpath

W3C Web Site for XSL-Related Information

http://www.w3.org/Style/XSL

W3C Web Site for SOAP Specifications

https://www.w3.org/TR/soap

System.Xml Reference

https://msdn.microsoft.com/library/system.xml.aspx

© Bipin Joshi 2017
B. Joshi, *Beginning XML with C# 7*, https://doi.org/10.1007/978-1-4842-3105-0

.NET/ASP.NET/WCF/Web API

https://www.microsoft.com/net
https://www.asp.net
https://docs.microsoft.com/en-us/dotnet/framework/wcf
https://docs.microsoft.com/en-us/aspnet/web-api

Wikipedia—XML Section

http://en.wikipedia.org/wiki/XML

Author's Web Site on .NET and Web Development

http://www.binaryintellect.net

XML Notepad—XML Editor

https://github.com/microsoft/xmlnotepad

Sandcastle Help File Builder

https://github.com/EWSoftware/SHFB

SQLXML Programming

https://docs.microsoft.com/en-us/sql/relational-databases/sqlxml/sqlxml-4-0-programming-concepts

Index

A

Address class, 218
ADO.NET
    assembly, 178
    connected data access, 175–176
        ExecuteXmlReader() method, 180–182
    DataAdapter class, SqlDataAdapter and
        OleDbDataAdapter, 179
    DataRow insertion, 205–206
    DataSet object, 180
    disconnected data access (*see* Disconnected
        data access)
    namespaces, 178
    OLEDB data provider, 177
    Oracle data provider, 178
    SqlCommand and OleDbCommand, 179
    SqlConnection and OleDbConnection, 178
    SqlDataReader and OleDbDataReader, 179
    SqlParameter and OleDbParameter, 179
    SQL Server data provider, 177
    typed DataSet
        application, 208
        DataTable, 206, 208
        declaration, 209
        EmployeeID column, 207–208
        Employees table, 207
        Fill() method, 209
        insertion, updation, and deletion, 209–210
        Solution Explorer, 208
        toolbox, 208
        xsd.exe tool, 210
    untyped DataSet, 204
AppendChild() method, 49, 106–107
ASP.NET
    Click event handler, 348
    configuration system
        application configuration files, 365–366
        machine configuration files, 365–366
        web.config file (*see* Web.config file)
    _Default class, 348
    Default.aspx, 350
    definition, 342
    DocumentSource property, 365
    Employees.xml, 363–364
    execution, 351
    MailMessage, 349
    sending e-mails, 349
    server controls
        definition, 342
        web site creation, 343–344
    site map
        attributes, 361
        SiteMapDataSource control, 362
        SiteMapPath control, 361–362
        structure, 359
        Visual Studio, 359
        Web.sitemap file, 360
    SmtpClient class, 349
    validation error, 350
    Web Form designing, 344–348
    XML comments
        class library (*see* Class library)
        SHFB, 383–385
    XML data source control
        Menu control, 357–358
        Navigation.xml file, 351
        transformations, 354–356
        TreeView control, 352–353
        TreeView DataBindings Editor, 352
        XPath expression, 356–357
Attributes() method, 402
Author's web site, 444
Auto option, 199

B

Breadcrumbs, 361
Business-to-business (B2B) applications, 9
button1_Click() method, 340

© Bipin Joshi 2017
B. Joshi, *Beginning XML with C# 7*, https://doi.org/10.1007/978-1-4842-3105-0

■ C

Child nodes, 35
Class library
    Calculator class, 378–379
    <list>, <item>, and <listheader>, 381–382
    paragraphs, 379–380
    parameters, 380
    return values, 380
    scope and permissions, 380
    < (see > and <seealso> tags, 381)
    summary and remarks, 379
    XML documentation, 382–383
Comma-separated values (CSV) files, 2
Connected data access, 176
Connection classes, 178
Content Model View, 118
CreateAttribute() method, 49
CreateText() method, 317
Custom XmlReader
    advancing reader, 430
    attributes navigation, 429
    class-level variables, 427
    Close() method, 428
    MoveToAttribute() method, 429
    MoveToElement() method, 429
    MoveToFirstAttribute() method, 429
    OleDbDataReader class, 430
    properties and methods, 422–424
    reading attributes, 428
    reading values, 430
    retrieve total number of attributes, 428
    returning values, 431
    TableReader class, 423–426, 431–433
Custom XmlWriter
    Close() and Flush() methods, 436
    enumerations for, 436
    properties and methods, 434–435
    RSS feed display, 442
    RSS feed markup, 442
    RSS markup, 433–434
    RssWriter class, 435, 441
    RssWriter, constructor of, 435
    WriteAttributeString() method, 439
    writing attributes, 439
    writing data, 439–440
    writing elements, 437–438
    XML declaration, 440

■ D

DataAdapter class, 179
DataBind() method, 370
DataBindings property, 357
DataContext property, 342

DataContractSerializer class, 212
    deserialization, 227
        Click event handler, 228
        Employee class, 228
        ReadObject() method, 229–230
        XML document, 229
    serialization, 227
        Click event handler, 228
        customization, 230–231
        Employee class, 228
        ReadObject() method, 229–230
        XML document, 229
DataGrid control, 341–342
Data Modification Language (DML), 332
DataReader class, 179
DataTable class, 184
Delete() web method, 252
DeleteSelf() method, 108
Descendants() method, 399–400
DiffGram option, 199
Disconnected data access, 176–177
    adding menu items, 201–202
    DataAdapter class, 184
        accessing, 187–188
        architecture, 184–185
        Command objects, 185
        DataRow, 188
        DataRowState, 189–190
        Delete() method, 189
        Fill() method, 186–187
        Save button, 190–192
        Select() method, 188–189
    DataSet class
        accessing, 187–188
        architecture, 183
        collections, 183
        DataRow, 188
        DataRowState, 189–190
        DataTable, 184
        Delete() method, 189
        DiffGram format, 195, 196
        Fill() method, 186–187
        functionality, 186
        GetXml() method, 197
        GetXmlSchema() method, 197
        ReadXml() method, 197–200
        Save button, 190–192
        Select() method, 188–189
        WriteXml() method, 192, 193
        WriteXmlSchema() method, 196–197
        XML with schema information, 195
        XML without schema
          information, 194, 196
        XmlWriteMode enumeration, 194, 196

InferXmlSchema() method, 203–204
ReadXmlSchema() method, 203
Document Object Model (DOM)
    access types, 31
    handling events, XmlDocument Class, 57–58
    memory footprint, 31
    namespaces, 54–55
    opening, existing XML document, 33–34
    read/write access, 31
    sample XML document, 32
    specific elements and nodes
        GetElementById() method, 38–41
        GetElementsByTagName() method, 37–38
        SelectNodes() method, 41–42
        SelectSingleNode() method, 43
    tree representation, XML document, 30
    whitespace
        definition, 50
        loading document, 51
        PreserveWhitespace property, 50–53
        XmlWhiteSpace vs.
            XmlSignificantWhiteSpace Classes, 53
XmlDocument class, 56
XML document navigation, 35–36
XML document, parts of, 29–30
XML documents modification
    adding new content, 48–49
    CurrentNodeIndex variable, 46
    deleting existing content, 47–48
    Employees.xml file, 44
    existing content, 46–47
    filling controls, 45
    Helper methods, 50
    navigation buttons, 45
    System.Xml classes, 44
XML DOM classes, 31
XmlNodeChangedEventArgs class, 56
Document type definition (DTD), 112
DOM-based parsers, 8

■ E

Elements() method, 397
Emails, 218
The EmployeeType enumeration, 218
Event-based parsers, 8
ExecuteStream() method, 317
ExecuteXmlReader() method, 180–182
Extensible Application Markup
        Language (XAML), 21, 335
Extensible Markup Language (XML)
    benefits of, 2–3
    classic architecture, 4
    definition, 1

documents parsing, 8–9
DTDs and XML schemas, 7
grammar, rules of, 5–7
LINQ, 9
simple document, 1
web-based application, 3
XML-driven architecture, 5
XPath, 10–11
XSLT, 9–10
Extensible Style Sheet Language Transformations
        (XSLT)
    applying templates, 153–154
    compiled style sheets, 171–173
    definition, 149
    embedded function, 169
    enabling scripting, 169
    extension objects, 171
    GetBirthDate() function, 170
    HTML table, XML document converted, 151–152
    <xsl:choose> and <xsl:when> branching, 156–158
    <xsl:if> branching, 154–156
    output after passing, 166
    passing parameters, 164
    sample XML document, 150
    script blocks, 166–168
    style sheet, 152, 162–163
    Transforming Employees.xml, 158–160
    XslCompiledTransform class, 161–162
    XsltArgumentList class, 165
Extensible Style Sheet Language (XSL), 21
External DTDs, 136
External schemas, 137

■ F

FillControls() helper method, 403, 406
FillControls() method, 50, 403
FillEmployees() method, 187, 190
FirstChild, 35
Functional construction, 394

■ G

GetBytes() method, 62
GetElementById() method, 38, 41, 114
GetElementsByTagName() method, 38
GetEmployees() method, 390
GetObjectData() method, 234
GetValue() method, 235
Graph View, 118

■ H

Hypertext Markup Language (HTML), 1

■ I, J, K

InferSchema option, 200
InferXmlSchema() method, 203–204
Inline DTD, 136
Inline schema, 137
Insert() web method, 251

■ L

Language Integrated Query (LINQ)
    architecture, 387–388
    attribute values, 400–402
    data selection, 393
    Descendants() method, 399–400
    Employee class, 389–390
    filtering data, 392–393
    GetEmployees() method, 390
    grouping data, 390–391
    namespace handling, 394
    namespaces, 412–413
    sorting operation, 392
    standard query operators, 388
    static methods, 394
    Validate() method
        creation, 413
        Employees.xsd, 414
        error message, 415
        XSD Schema file, 414
    visual construction, 394
    W3C standards, 394
    white spaces, 394
        LoadOptions and SaveOptions
          enumerations, 409
        LoadOptions.None, 410
        LoadOptions.Preserve
          Whitespace, 410
    XML class hierarchy, 395
    XML data modification
        employee's details, 406
        Employees.xml file, 402
        FillControls() helper method, 403
        loading, 403
        new employee element, 404
        Remove() method, 405
        Save() method, 406
        SetElementValue() method, 405
        XElement class, 404, 407–408
    XmlDocument class
        TreeView control, 397–398
        XElement class, 395–397
    XML fragments, 393
    XML nodes, renaming, 394
    XML transformation, 394
    XML tree transformation
        projection, 418–419
        scenarios, 415
        shape, 416–417
LastChild, 35
Location path, 86

■ M

Manager class, 221, 223
Menu control, 357–358
Menu DataBindings Editor, 357
MoveToAttribute() method, 69
MoveToElement() method, 69
MoveToFirstAttribute() method, 69
MoveToNextAttribute() method, 69
MyHandler() method, 415

■ N

Name table, 65
.NET Core, 12
.NET Framework
    Base Class Library, 12
    definition, 11
    vs. .NET Core, 12
    Stack of, 11
    XML
        ADO.NET, 17
        ASP.NET Web Forms, 17–18
        assemblies and namespaces, 13–14
        classic XML parsing model, 14
        configuration files, 15–17
        documentation, 19–21
        LINQ-based parsing model, 14
        serialization, 18
        SQL Server, 21
        XAML markup, 21
NewEmployeesRow() method, 210
NewRow() method, 188
NextSibling, 35
Nodes() method, 397
Node tests, 86
Nonvalidating parsers, 9

■ O

Object Linking and Embedding
        Database (OLEDB), 177
OnDeserializing() method, 236
Open Database Connectivity (ODBC), 177
OpenRead() method, 62
OPENXML function, 313–315
OutputResults() helper method, 391

■ P, Q

Parameter class, 179
ParentNode, 35
Predicates, 87
PreviousSibling, 35

■ R

ReadAttributeValue() method, 430
ReadElementContentAsBase64() method, 84
ReadOuterXml() method, 70
ReadSchema option, 200
ReadString() method, 70
ReadToDescendant() method, 67
ReadToFollowing() method, 67
ReadToNextSibling() method, 68
ReadXml() method, 197–200
ReadXmlSchema() method, 203
Really simple syndication (RSS), 433
Relational database management
        system (RDBMS), 177
RemoveChild() method, 48
ReplaceChild() method, 47
REpresentational State Transfer (REST)
    characteristics, 289
    HTTP, 290
    WCF
        changes, 290
        client application, 294
        configuration, 293–294
        Delete() method, 293, 298
        EmployeeManager class, 291–293
        GetAsync() method, 296
        IEmployeeManager interface, 290
        Insert() method, 293, 297–298
        Load event handler, 295
        properties, 291
        SelectByID() Method, 296
        StringContent object, 298
        Update() Method, 298
        XML markup, 296
    Web API
        client application, 302–303
        creation, 299
        CRUD operations, 300
        DataContractSerializer, 304
        SelectAll() and Post(), 301–302
returning the table/column name, 431
Role-based security, 371
RowState property, 190

■ S

Sandcastle help file builder(SHFB), 383–385, 444
SelectByID() web method, 251

SelectNodes() method, 41–43
SelectSingleNode() method, 43, 47
SELECT statements
    AUTO mode, 306–307
    EXPLICIT mode, 309–312
    PATH mode, 309
    Query window, 306
    RAW mode, 307–308
    ROOT clause, 313
    XMLSCHEMA clause, 308–309
Serialization
    deep serialization, 212
    shallow serialization, 212
SetElementValue() method, 405
SignOut() method, 374
Simple Object Access Protocol (SOAP), 3, 211
SiteMapDataSource control, 362
SiteMapPath control, 361
Skip() method, 68
SmtpClient class, 349
SoapFormatter class, 212, 231
    deserialization
        Click event handler, 232
        customization, 235–236
    serialization
        Click event handler, 232
        customization, 234–235, 237
        Employee class, 231
Split() method, 219
SqlCommand object, 182
SqlDataAdapter class, 192
SQL Server
    FOR XML clause (see SELECT statements)
    OPENXML function, 313–315
    SQLXML
        classes, 315
        DataSet objects, 319–320
        DiffGram, 326–328
        SELECT queries, 316–319
        SqlXmlAdapter class, 320–322
        XML templates, 325–326
        XSLT templates, 322–324
    XML data type
        CONVERT function, 330
        DML, 332
        exist() method, 331
        inserting and updating, 329
        query() method, 331
        table creation, 329
        Transact-SQL, 329
        value() method, 331
        XQuery, 333
SQLXML programming, 444
Standards, 240
Start View, 118

■ T

TransformFile property, 354–356
Tree-based parsers, 8
TreeView control, 352–353, 398
TreeView DataBindings Editor, 356

■ U

UNION ALL clause, 311
UpdateLabel() method, 50
Update() web method, 252

■ V

Validating parsers, 9
Valid documents, 7
Visual Studio
    class libraries creations, 26–28
    Designer, 337
    MessageBox class, 25
    sample run of, 25
    Visual Studio 2017, 21
    Windows application, Visual Studio IDE, 23
    Windows form, Button control, 23
    Windows forms application, 22

■ W

W3C Web Site, 443
Web.config file
    custom error pages
        administrative pages, 376
        Click event handler, 376
        Default.aspx, 376
        HttpException, 377
        mode attribute, 377
        specification, 377
        statusCode attribute, 377
        statusCode attribute, 378
        web forms arrangement, 376
    employee listing, 370–371
    Form authentication
        Authenticate event handler, 372–373
        <authentication>, 372
        Click event handler, 373
        Default.aspx and Login.aspx, 372, 373
        defaultUrl attribute, 372
        login page, 374
        loginUrl attribute, 372
        Page_Load event handler, 373
        role-based security, 371
        SignOut() method, 374
        users attribute, 372

inheritance behavior, 367
retrieving database connection strings, 370
retrieving values, 368
session state, 374–375
storing database connection strings, 369–370
storing values, 368
structure, 367
Web services
    ASMX, 242
    call web methods
        Delete() web method, 259
        dropdown list, 257
        Insert() web method, 258
        SelectAll() method, 258
        SelectByID() web method, 258
        Update() web method, 259
    component, 239
    CRUD functionality
        code-first approach, 249
        database connection string
            information, 249
        Delete() web method, 252
        Employee Entity class, 250
        Employees table, 250
        Entity Framework, 247–248
        Insert() web method, 251
        Northwind context class, 250
        SelectAll() web method, 251
        SelectByID() web method, 251, 253
        Update() web method, 252
    Description property, 247
    EmployeeManager.asmx.cs file, 242
    Empty project template, 241
    HelloWorld() method, 246
    help page, 243
    Invoke button, 245
    Namespace property, 243
    proxy, 240, 254–256
    SOAP
        headers, 260–263
        request, 245, 259
        response, 246
        XML serialization, 264–265
    string parameter, 247
    in Visual Studio, 241
    @WebService directive, 242
    WSDL, 244
        binding, 267
        elements, 266
        EmployeeManager web service, 265–266
        port types, 267
        request and response model, 266
        type definitions, 266
    WS-I organization, 243

Web Services Description
  Language (WSDL), 240, 270
Web Services Interoperability (WSI)
  specification, 243
Wikipedia, 444
Windows Communication Foundation (WCF), 227
  ADO.NET Entity Data Model, 274
  code-first approach, 274
  DataContractSerializer, 288
  definition, 269
  EmployeeDataContract class, 273
  EmployeeService class, 275–276
  EmployeeWCFService, 271
  hosting
    App.config file, 277
    behavior, 277
    employee details, 281
    Employees list, 280
    EmployeeWCFServiceClient, 279
    EmployeeWCFServiceHost, 276
    HTTP-based communication, 278
    IIS, 285–287
    Main() method, 278
    modifications, 281
    ServiceHost class, 278
    service reference, 280
    Solution Explorer, 280
    testing, 283–284
  IEmployeeManager Interface, 272
  SelectByID() method, 276
  software, 271
  Update() method, 276
  WCF test client, 288
  WSDL, 270
Windows Presentation Foundation (WPF)
  applications
  backing types, 339
  button1_Click() method, 340
  Class attribute, 339
  Click event handler, 339, 340
  elements, 339
  namespaces, 339
  toolbox, 337–338
  Visual Studio, 335
    Employees.xml file, 336
    MainWindow.xaml file, 336–337
  XAML markup, 335
  XAML markup responsible, 338–339
  XML data, 340–342
Wireless Application Protocol (WAP), 3
Wireless Markup Language (WML), 3
World Wide Web Consortium (W3C), 1
WriteAttributeString() method, 75, 439
WriteBase64() method, 82

WriteStartAttribute() method, 439
WriteStartDocument() method, 74
WriteStartElement() method, 74–75, 438
WriteXml() method, 192, 196
WriteXmlSchema() method, 196–197

■ X, Y, Z

XAttribute class, 398
XElement class, 398
XmlDataProvider object, 341
XML data reduced (XDR) schema, 112
XmlDocument, 29
XML documents validation
  attaches schema, 146
  DTDs, 112
  node explicitly, 143
  OnValidationError function, 144
  SOM
    Add() method, 134
    complex type, 128, 132–133
    core SOM classes, 126
    creating schema, 129–130
    DTD and XML schemas, 136–142
    name, simple type for, 128, 131
    notes, simple type for, 128, 132
    object hierarchy, 127
    phone numbers, simple type
      for, 128, 131–132
    root element, 134
    top-level complex type, 133
    Windows application, 128
    Write() method, 135
    XmlQualifiedName class, 131
    XmlSchemaAnnotated class, 127
    XmlSchema class, 127
    XmlSchemaComplexType classes, 127
    XmlSchemaParticle class, 127
    XmlSchemaSet class, 134
    XmlSchemaSimpleType class, 127, 131
  structure creation
    Content Model View, 118, 121
    DTD, Employees.xml, 113
    Employee class, 125
    Employees.xml file, 112
    EmployeeType, 119
    Graph View, 118, 121
    NameSimpleType, 120
    Start View, 118, 122
    Visual Studio IDE, 122–123
    XML Editor, 118
    XML Schema Definition tool, 123
    XML Schema Explorer, 118, 120
    XSD data types, 115

XML documents validation (*cont.*)
 xsd.exe Tool, 124
 XSD Schema, Employees.xml, 118–119
 XSD Schemas, 115
 XDR Schema, 112
 XmlDocument class, 142–143
 XPathNavigator, 145
XML Editor, 118
XmlNode, 31
XmlNodeReader class, 60
XML Schema, 111
XML schema definition (XSD)
 schema, 112
XML Schema Explorer, 118
XmlSerializer class, 212
 deserialization
  Click event handler, 214
  complex types, 220–221
  EmpCode attribute, 217
  Employee class, 213
  events, 216–217
  Manager class, 223–224
  modification, 217
 serialization
  application, 212–213
  array element names, 227
  changing array, 227
  complex types, 218–221
  customization, 224–226
  element names, 226
  Employee class, 213
  Employee object, 215
  enumeration identifiers, 227
  inheritance, 221–223
  null objects, 227
  public members, 226
  XML format, 213
  XML root element, 226
XmlSignificantWhitespace, 53
XmlTextReader
 definition, 59
 loading tree, 63–64
 loading XML document, 62
 MoveToAttribute() method, 69
 MoveToFirstAttribute() method, 69
 MoveToNextAttribute() method, 69
 moving between attributes, 69
 namespaces, 66
 name table, 65
 read attributes, elements, and text, 63
 ReadElementString() method, 65
 reading XML documents, 61
 ReadOuterXml() method, 70
 ReadString() method, 70

ReadSubTree() method, 66–67
ReadToDescendant() method, 67
ReadToFollowing() method, 67
ReadToNextSibling() method, 68
Skip() method, 68
XmlNodeReader class, 60
XmlTextReader class, 60
XmlValidatingReader class, 60
XmlTextWriter
 definition, 59
 encoding class, 75
 exporting columns, 73–75
 exporting data, 72–73
 formatting XML document, 76–78
 namespace support, 78–80
 nontextual data
  Base64 format, 83
  reading Base64 Data, 83–84
  writing Base64 data, 82
 output format, 76
 SqlConnection class, 73
 Windows Forms application, 71
 WriteStartDocument() method, 74
 WriteStartElement() method, 74
XmlValidatingReader class, 60
XmlWhiteSpace, 53
XNode abstract class, 395
XPath property, 356
XPath data model
 axes, 86
 functions
  return Boolean values, 88
  set of nodes, 88
  work on numbers, 88
  work on strings, 88
 inner and outer XML, 97
 InnerXml and OuterXml properties, 97–99
 location path, 86
 node tests, 86
 predicates, 87
 SelectAncestors() method, 96
 SelectChildren() method, 96
 Select() Method, 92–94
 SelectSingleNode() method, 94–95
 XPath expression, 96
 XPathNavigator
  appending new nodes, 106–107
  CreateNavigator() method, 91
  creation, 89–90, 105
  declaring XmlDocument, 105
  deleting nodes, 108–109
  DisplayDetails() helper
   function, 101–102
  GetAttribute() method, 92

HasChildren property, 92
modifying nodes, 107–108
modifying XML document, 104–105
MoveToParent() method, 92
MoveToRoot() method, 91
ReadSubtree() Method, 100–101
resultant file, 103
resultant XML document, 104
retrieving Details, 105–106
Save() method, 109

TreeView, 90
Windows Forms application, 90
WriteSubtree() method, 102–104
XmlReader, 100
XmlWriter, 102
XPath expressions, 94, 356–357
XPath property, 356
XQuery expressions, 333
XSD data types, 115
XslCompiledTransform class, 363

Get the eBook for only $5!

Why limit yourself?

With most of our titles available in both PDF and ePUB format, you can access your content wherever and however you wish—on your PC, phone, tablet, or reader.

Since you've purchased this print book, we are happy to offer you the eBook for just $5.

To learn more, go to http://www.apress.com/companion or contact support@apress.com.

Apress®

Printed in the United States
By Bookmasters